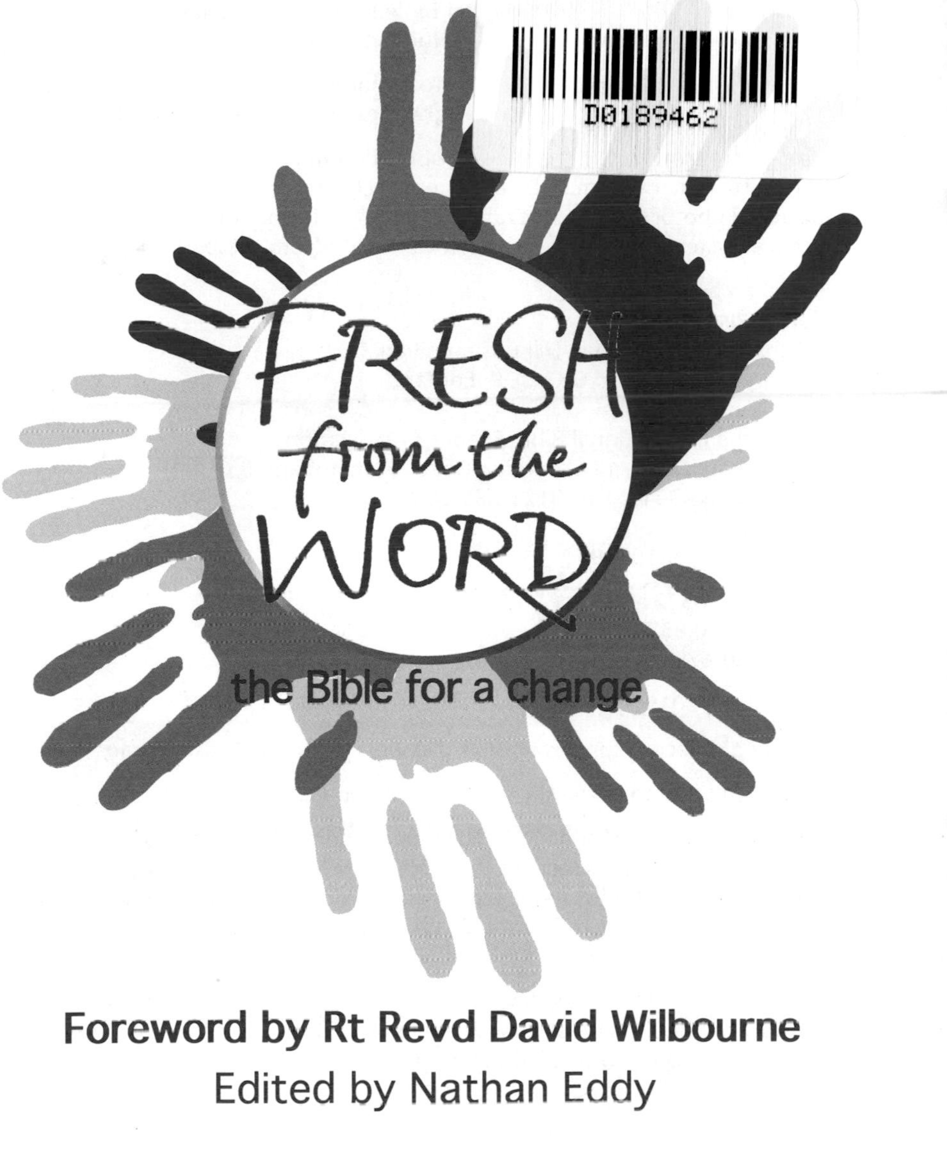
FRESH
from the
WORD
the Bible for a change

Foreword by Rt Revd David Wilbourne

Edited by Nathan Eddy

IBRA
International Bible Reading Association

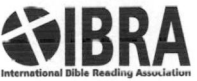

MONARCH
BOOKS

Published by
Lion Hudson Limited
Wilkinson House, Jordan Hill Business Park,
Banbury Road, Oxford OX2 8DR, England
www.lionhudson.com
and by the International Bible Reading Association
5–6 Imperial Court, 12 Sovereign Road, Birmingham, B30 3FH
Tel: 0121 458 3313; Fax: 0121 285 1816
www.ibraglobal.org
Charity number 1086990

ISBN 978 0 85721 959 6
e-ISBN 978 0 85721 939 8
ISSN 2050-6791

First edition 2019

A catalogue record for this book is available from the British Library

Printed and bound in the UK, July 2019, LH26

Fresh From the Word aims to build understanding and respect for different Christian perspectives through the provision of a range of biblical interpretations. Views expressed by contributors should not, therefore, be taken to reflect the views or policies of the Editor or the International Bible Reading Association.

The International Bible Reading Association's scheme of readings is listed monthly on the IBRA website at www.ibraglobal.org and the full scheme for 2020 may be downloaded in English, Spanish and French.

Contents

Foreword

In 1881, just one year before the International Bible Reading Association was founded, Christopher Wordsworth, Bishop of Lincoln, published *The Four Gospels*. A signed copy of his ancient leather-bound commentary fell into my hands when I was a teenager, and has been my constant companion ever since, offering insight and inspiration behind every Gospel verse. It is a conservative work, immune to the fads and fashions of radical scholarship that were yet to dawn. Its strength is a meticulous knowledge of the original Greek in which the Gospels were written, combined with an equally deep knowledge of Christian history and the faith born afresh in successive generations. Whenever I scratch my head about what to preach or teach, I have only to turn to this book for Christ's light to dawn. For instance, did you know that most weddings at the time of Jesus took place on the third day, because that was the only day in the Genesis schemata of creation when God performed a double creation? 'On the third day a wedding took place ...' in John 2:1, besides alluding to the ultimate Third Day, accurately catches a contemporary custom, proving John's historical veracity.

A more modern favourite is Jonathan Magonet's *Bible Lives*, written by a rabbi who, though mindful of critical scholarship, is keen to give colour to the scriptural text itself and promote the message. For instance, noting the similarity of two Hebrew words, he argues that David didn't sling his stone at Goliath's forehead (Hebrew: *meitzach*). Instead he targeted his knee (Hebrew: *mitzchat*), where there would have been a necessary chink in his armour to allow movement. Goliath then fell forward and, paralysed by the heavy armour, David was able to finish him off. Magonet's interpretation gives additional sense and force to the story.

Christians are sometimes called the 'people of the book', along with Jews and Muslims, but truly the Bible is the 'book of the people', charting the right turnings and the wrong turnings, the soul-searching highs and the soul-denying lows of the people of God. We need to enter into their story imaginatively to make it our story, to learn from their successes and failures to chart our journey, and so feel our hearts burning within us as Christ travels along our own road. People like Wordsworth and Magonet have so helped bring the Bible alive for me, and I am confident that the excellent range of writers of Fresh from the Word will do the same for you.

Rt Revd David Wilbourne

How to use *Fresh From the Word*

How do you approach the idea of regular Bible reading? It may help to see daily Bible reading as spiritual exploration. Here is a suggestion of a pattern to follow that may help you develop the discipline but free up your mind and heart to respond.

- Before you read, take a few moments – the time it takes to say the Lord's Prayer – to imagine God looking at you with love. Feel yourself enfolded in that gaze. Come to scripture with your feet firmly planted.

- Read the passage slowly before you turn to the notes. Be curious. The Bible was written over a period of nearly 1,000 years, over 2,000 years ago. There is always something to learn. Read and reread.

- If you have access to a study Bible, pay attention to any echoes of the passage you are reading in other parts of the biblical book. A word might be used in different ways by different biblical authors. Where in the story of the book are you reading? What will happen next?

- 'Read' yourself as you read the story. Be attentive to your reactions – even trivial ones. What is drawing you into the story? What is repelling you? Observe yourself 'sidelong' as you read as if you were watching a wild animal in the forest; be still, observant and expectant.

- What in scripture or in the notes is drawing you forward in hope? What is closing you down? Notice where the Spirit of Life is present, and where negative spirits are too. Follow where life is leading. God always leads into life, even if the way feels risky.

- Lift up the world and aspects of your life to God. What would you like to share with God? What is God seeking to share with you?

- Finally, the † symbol is an invitation to pray a prayer that has been written for the day's reading. You are invited to say these words aloud or in silence with thousands of other readers around the world who will be reading these notes on the same day in dozens of languages.

Introduction from the editor

The election of Donald Trump as US president four years ago, the recent Brexit debate in the UK, and popular movements in Europe and the Middle East all underscore the changing times we live in. It truly feels as though the tectonic plates that balance world power are shifting beneath us. In this book of IBRA devotions, we don't consider these political issues head on. Publishing as far in advance as we do, we aren't able to, even if that were our aim. Instead, we take a step back and consider the times we live in from a wider theological perspective.

Our Lenten theme this year approaches the changes in the world in this way. The theme of 'The responsibilities we share' looks at our role as people of faith and committed citizens, regardless of where we live. And the theme 'The Bible on the world stage' coincides with the US election in 2020, inviting us to think through leadership from a Christian perspective with figures such as Martin Luther King, Jr, Mother Theresa, and Desmond Tutu. In a week entitled 'Fake news and the Good News' we consider the Bible alongside social media and the wider media scene.

Beyond these themes, *Fresh From The Word 2020* offers a diverse feast of creative and close readings of the Bible. Themes include coping with disappointment, 'On the road', the image of fire in the Bible, the Bible at the Olympics to coincide with the Tokyo games in July, approaching 'the holy' in Advent, and even an exploration of cosmic themes to mark NASA's Mars rover mission, which is scheduled to blast off in July. We look at the theme of light in Epiphany and 20:20 vision in the year 2020. And we feature continuous readings of the Gospel of Matthew, the Song of Solomon, Romans 9–16, Jeremiah, 1 and 2 Thessalonians, and 1 and 2 Peter.

As in previous years, we feature creative and faithful writers from around the world. This year we have entries from South Africa, India, Argentina, Brazil, Nigeria, Samoa, the US, the Caribbean and elsewhere, as well representing a spread of regions and churches within the UK.

However, the primary work of IBRA is not in publishing, writing or editing, but rather in the daily reading of scripture. This has been our aim and organising principle since our founding more than 135 years ago. Each day we commit to reading the same scripture together wherever we live. We do this in good times and uncertain ones, praying that God will work through our resolve and commitment. May God work through us in the year ahead as well.

Yours in Christ,

Nathan

Acknowledgements and abbreviations

The use of the letters a or b in a text reference, such as Luke 9:37–43a, indicates that the day's text starts or finishes midway through a verse, usually at a break such as the end of a sentence. Not all Bible versions will indicate such divisions.

We are grateful to the copyright holders for permission to use scriptural quotations from the following Bible versions:

MSG   Scripture quotations marked MSG taken from The Message. Copyright © 1993, 1994, 1995, 1996, 2000, 2001, 2002. Used by permission of NavPress Publishing Group.

NIV   Scripture quotations marked NIV are taken from the Holy Bible, New International Version®, NIV®. Copyright © 1973, 1978, 1984, 2011 by Biblica, Inc.™ Used by permission of Zondervan. All rights reserved worldwide. www.zondervan.com. The "NIV" and "New International Version" are trademarks registered in the United States Patent and Trademark Office by Biblica, Inc.™

NIVUK   Scripture quotations marked NIVUK are taken from the Holy Bible, New International Version Anglicised. Copyright © 1979, 1984, 2011 Biblica, formerly International Bible Society. Used by permission of Hodder & Stoughton Ltd, an Hachette UK company. All rights reserved. 'NIV' is a registered trademark of Biblica. UK trademark number 1448790.

NRSV   Scripture quotations marked NSRV are taken from the New Revised Standard Version Bible, copyright © 1989 National Council of the Churches of Christ in the United States of America. Used by permission. All rights reserved worldwide.

NRSVA   Scripture quotations marked NRSVA are taken from the New Revised Standard Version Bible: Anglicised Edition, copyright © 1989, 1995 the Division of Christian Education of the National Council of the Churches of Christ in the United States of America. Used by permission. All rights reserved.

NRSVCE   Scripture quotations marked NRSVCE are taken from the New Revised Standard Version Bible: Catholic Edition, copyright © 1989, 1993 National Council of the Churches of Christ in the United States of America. Used by permission. All rights reserved worldwide.

Against the grain: looking again at familiar stories

Notes by **Jane Gonzalez**

Jane is a Roman Catholic laywoman. She is finishing a doctorate in Pastoral Theology, looking at new approaches to adult faith formation. She occasionally reviews the Sunday papers from a Christian perspective. She and her husband have a share in a narrowboat and spend four weeks of the year enjoying the quiet pleasures of life on the canals of England. Other leisure activities include gardening, golf and reading. Jane has used the NRSVCE for these notes.

Wednesday 1 January
Going the extra mile ...

Read Luke 10:25–37

Just then a lawyer stood up to test Jesus. 'Teacher,' he said, 'What must I do to inherit eternal life?' He said to him, 'What is written in the law? What do you read there?'

(verses 25–26)

I wonder if the disciples of Jesus ever got frustrated with his seeming reluctance to respond to a query with a straightforward answer? Often he replies to a question with a question of his own or tells a story in response. He seems to be asking us to work things out for ourselves. It is up to us as enquirer or reader to come up with and act upon the answer.

As we begin a new year of reflecting on and praying with scripture, maybe it is time for us to ponder the lawyer's question, 'What do you read there?' We all have our favourite passages and verses in the Bible and our preferred interpretations – shaped by our culture, creed and upbringing – of familiar texts. The enduring challenge of the gospel is to resist the complacency of the familiar and to look afresh and deeply at texts we think we know well. The parables are an invitation to revisit what may have become comfy and cosy. The Samaritan of the parable goes further than he needs in his compassionate response to another's distress. Is it time for us to go the extra mile in the way we read his story?

† Father, give me the courage to read your Word with fresh eyes and to listen to your teaching with attention and openness.

1

Thursday 2 January
The path of life

Read Psalm 23

Even though I walk through the darkest valley, I fear no evil;
For you are with me; your rod and your staff – they comfort me.

(verse 4)

We spend our summers in Spain, where we are privileged to own a house in the country. It's a very different environment from home … we live near a small town where agriculture is the main source of employment. Our friends are more likely to commute to work by tractor than by train. Cecilio is one such friend. He is a shepherd who brings his flock across our fields to graze for a while before moving with them to other places of pasture. In a landscape that, in the summer, resembles a 'dry and weary land where there is no water' (Psalm 63:1), there are no lush meadows nor is there much in the way of grass. Sheep are not left to their own devices but led and guided to their food.

Cecilio knows his flock intimately – the unique character of each of them – the laggard, the adventurous, the shy … And his flock trusts him to care for them. There may not be wolves around but there are roads and traffic to negotiate as together they criss-cross the terrain in search of grazing. Cecilio's attentive and watchful presence ensures the safety of his flock, as well as satisfying their hunger. We live in a world where shepherds have mobile phones rather than crooks. It is also a world where the 'ideals' of self-sufficiency and self-determination sometimes lead us to an over-reliance on our own resources. Is it time to reflect more deeply on how the Lord, our shepherd, knows and understands us better than any human being and to recommit ourselves to accepting more fully his loving care and concern?

† Father, give me the grace to follow you always in humility and trust and to accept the guidance you offer.

For further thought

Reflect on the many meanings of the word *humility*. Where do I need to be more grounded and more aware of my dependence on God's providence? And where do I resist his grace?

Friday 3 January
Party time ...

Read Luke 15:11–32

'... You are always with me, and all that is mine is yours. But we had to celebrate and rejoice, because this brother of yours was dead and has come to life; he was lost and has been found.'

(verses 31b–32)

Franco Zefirelli's film, *Jesus of Nazareth*, remains, for me, a classic retelling of the life of Jesus. I remember being entranced by it even though, at the time, I was not a practising Christian. There was a freshness about it and an imaginative approach that I found very appealing. Zefirelli did not take too many liberties with the text but brought an artist's eye to the familiar scenes and characters. One of the most striking was his use of the parable of the Prodigal Son. He imagines Jesus going to a party at Matthew's house (where the guests are as disreputable as Matthew) and Peter's attempts to stop him. As Jesus tells the story of the reconciliation of the errant son to his father and the reaction of the older brother, we see Peter being drawn into the story and into the courtyard of the house. As Jesus utters the words of our verse, Matthew and Peter draw closer into an embrace of forgiveness and acceptance. Brother forgives and accepts brother.

Jesus finishes the story with the older brother still outside, refusing to come in and nursing his grievance. Zefirelli gives us a conclusion, a glimpse into a 'what-comes-next scenario', a happy ending. There are other possible, less palatable outcomes that we could posit – no reconciliation, a poisoning of relationships in the household, bitterness and hate. Which would we wish upon our family and ourselves? Or like the older son in the story, are we too concerned with perceived fairness or unfairness rather than the healing that forgiveness brings to both bestower and recipient?

† Father, help me to forgive those who hurt me. Give me the courage to offer the embrace of reconciliation instead of nurturing hurt and anger.

For further thought

Take some time to reflect on the Lord's Prayer. Where do I need to offer and receive forgiveness? Can I be the one to take the first step?

3

Saturday 4 January
The answer lies in the soil

Read Mark 4:1–20

'And these are the ones sown on the good soil: they hear the word and accept it and bear fruit, thirty and sixty and a hundredfold.'

(verse 20)

My father's pride and joy was his garden. My mother was the one adept at changing plugs and basic plumbing! His endeavours, in rain or shine, provided us with abundant vegetables and flowers throughout the year. It was hard work, however, and he often commented that the ground grew stones better than anything else. As children, he paid us a penny a bucket to shift the stones so that digging was a little easier for him. He knew that the earth had to be properly prepared if we were to have a decent return on the investment in time and effort – and pennies – when harvest time came around.

In our spiritual lives we also need to prepare the ground so that the Word can root itself in us and grow and flourish. The mulch of prayer and sacrifice, the dressing of silence and stillness – these are necessary if we are to bear fruit and produce a harvest. The spiritual equivalents of weeds, pests and bad weather – sin and apathy and life in general – may impede growth. The stones of hardship and sorrow tempt us to give up. The Lord is kind, however, and does not make demands on us that we cannot fulfil. He asks for fruitfulness but understands that not every harvest is abundant or one hundredfold; that in spite of our efforts what we produce might not be as plentiful as we wish; that there may be fallow times. He is content that we produce something; that we are diligent and attentive in our preparation and work. He will do the rest.

† Father, your grace is at work in my life. Accept the fruits of my labours and help me to be more fruitful.

For further thought

What prevents a good return in my spiritual life? What can I learn from the fallow periods or when growth is hard to discern?

Epiphany: light to the nations – 1 Stars and the blues

Notes by **Jane Gonzalez**

For Jane's biography, see p. 1. Jane has used the NRSVCE for these notes.

Sunday 5 January
The best things come in small parcels

> **Read Micah 5:2–4**
> *But you, O Bethlehem of Ephrathah,*
> *who are one of the little clans of Judah,*
> *from you shall come forth for me*
> *one who is to rule in Israel.*

(verse 2a)

Each year the Christmas season seems to start earlier – the summer holidays are scarcely over and the shops are full of Santas and snowmen. The first of December sees many people putting up their tree and bedecking their houses with lights. Then, come Boxing Day, the fairy-lights disappear and darkness returns to our streets. The traditional Twelve Days of Christmas which culminated in the great feast of Epiphany are subsumed in the New Year's preoccupation with a 'dry' January and diets and gym membership, by Christians and non-Christians alike.

As we move into January, maybe it is time 'recapture' Epiphany and to delve a little deeper into its meanings and how it complements Christmas. The word actually means 'manifestation' – God revealing himself to humankind. January is a dark month, in many respects, but Epiphany encourages us to look for the light wherever it shows itself, often in the smallest and unlikeliest of places. The light of the world comes to be born in an obscure town in a small occupied country; God blazes in the darkness of human life, in the most unexpected of places and people, if only we have the eyes and the will to perceive him.

† Father, let me not be made despondent by dark days or the darkness of hardship. Help me to seek and find your light.

Monday 6 January
Follow your star

Read Matthew 2:1–12

When they had heard the king, they set out; and there, ahead of them, went the star that they had seen at its rising, until it stopped over the place where the child was.

(verse 9)

One of the joys of spending our summers in rural Spain is the opportunity to sit out under the stars at night. There is relatively little light pollution and it is possible to see the Milky Way most nights and the blaze of shooting stars in August with the naked eye. Our home in the United Kingdom is in a large town and there are few stars visible, even on a clear night, and certainly no Milky Way. The artificial light in which we all live obscures the sky and the heavenly bodies that exist there. We rely not on our own observation of the stars, but on radio telescopes and astronomers to bring news of dwarf planets, new galaxies, new stars rising. Often we stop looking up and concentrate on what's down, on ourselves and our preoccupations and wants.

Looking up, however, even at dimly reflected stars, is important for us spiritually. The psalmist – looking at God's work, the moon, the stars, the heavens – asks, 'What are human beings that you are mindful of them?' (Psalm 8:4). He reminds us of our position in the cosmos and our rightful relationship with the Creator. We are privileged and blessed, but creatures nonetheless. How often do we forget this in our relentless drive to exert our individuality and autonomy! We stray from the path laid down for us and resist following our star, the one that leads to God. Can we begin again to emulate the wise men – confident in the rightness of the journey and trusting in the truth of the destination?

† Father, help me to be mindful of the glories of your creation and to endeavour to protect and preserve it.

For further thought

How can I be a wise and obedient steward of creation? Can I make a genuine effort to reuse, repair and recycle and to encourage my parish or church community to greater concern?

Tuesday 7 January
Don't curse the dark

Read Isaiah 42:1–9

... a bruised reed he will not break,
and a dimly burning wick he will not quench;
he will faithfully bring forth justice.

(verse 3)

My goddaughter stayed overnight with us recently and we were able to help her with a little bit of homework. Fortunately, it was English language, not maths! I was reminded of my own grounding in grammar many years ago – an exercise about exclamation marks. I have always remembered one phrase in particular, 'How far that little candle throws his beams! So shines a good deed in a naughty world' (*The Merchant of Venice*, Act 5, Scene 1). I was more interested in the grammatical exercise than in the meaning of the phrase at the time but it occurs to me now as particularly apt for today's reading. A little candle, a tiny rushlight, a small oil-lamp in a world where electricity was unknown; these would have been welcome points of illumination, however small.

Sometimes in spite of all our efforts, our attempts to lead good and honest lives as people of faith, we are conscious only of inadequacy. Our good intentions seem to come to nothing. Maybe, in these early days of the year, our resolutions falter and fail. Isaiah speaks words of comfort to us. Let us not forget that the dimly burning wick, like the little candle, emits light. An unquenched light has the potential to flare into brilliance; the small act of kindness may have repercussions in the lives of others unbeknownst to us.

When faith seems faint and failing, we should remember that the Lord guards the flame, tends and protects it. In time, that flame could blaze into a beacon ... In the meantime, doing something is better than doing nothing.

† Father, increase my faith and trust in you. Let me never doubt your active presence in my life.

For further thought

Today, dwell not on your shortcomings but praise God for the good that you have done.

Wednesday 8 January
Like moths to a flame

Read Isaiah 49:1–7

*'I will give you as a light to the nations,
that my salvation may reach to the end of the earth.'*

(verse 6b)

I have to confess to being a fair-weather gardener. I'm not keen on labouring in my plot when it is wet or freezing, so I try to get as much done as possible on good days. The splendid autumnal weather at present has enabled me to do a lot of clearing and cutting back and to appreciate the truth of the sentiment that we are nearer God's heart in a garden than anywhere else (as evoked by Dorothy Frances Gurney in her poem 'God's Garden'). I am careful, in my enthusiasm, to watch out for the creatures with whom I share the garden – I don't want to trample on any of the beetles, worms and bugs who do a lot of worthwhile and unsung work there on my behalf! It's one of the reasons that we build and maintain bug boxes throughout the winter – to protect the insects and creepy-crawlies that are our co-workers.

It is easy to overlook the quiet and less showy inhabitants of the garden: to prefer bees to beetles, butterflies to moths. In the same way, we can overlook the quiet, unobtrusive work done by those who labour alongside us in God's vineyard. Perhaps we look on ourselves in this light and envy the gifts and charisms of others? Our role, as missionary disciples, is to draw people to the Lord, attract and encourage them. Some of us will be blazing beacons, but for most of us, the quiet, steady work of evangelisation will be a case of lighting small votive lamps to guide those we meet and with whom we live, along the path to salvation.

† Father, you have blessed me with many gifts. May I always be thankful and use them, however humble, in your service.

For further thought

Who are the unsung heroes and heroines in our community? Encourage those who lead your faith community to celebrate their work and witness in some way.

Thursday 9 January
Sleeping like a baby

Read Isaiah 52:7–10

Listen! Your sentinels lift up their voices,
*   together they sing for joy;*
for in plain sight they see
*   the return of the Lord to Zion.*

(verse 8)

We live in a digital age and it affects all aspects of our lives. One of these that has been the subject of much recent research is how sleep patterns are disrupted by the lights from appliances in the bedroom and by our incessant examining of mobile devices at all hours of the day or night. It is recognised that we all need to sleep more, and better, in order to function properly. How refreshing it is to get our 'eight hours' or 'a good night's sleep'! Most of us, though, with or without electronic devices, have experienced sleeplessness or awoken in the small hours, prey to anxiety and fear, both of which seem worse in the dark.

When I find myself unable to sleep, I try to concentrate on and count my blessings (rather than sheep!). I am not bereft or benighted; I have a warm bed, a roof over my head, people who care for me. I give thanks for the countless people who are awake when I sleep – those who keep me safe like the emergency and security services, those in the health service who keep vigil with the sick, those who wait with the dying: all those who are modern-day sentinels and watchmen. Like the watchmen of the psalm, they neither sleep nor slumber (Psalm 121:4).

As Christians we can be certain that we are watched over. John tells us that we will have trials and troubles but will not be overcome (16:33). There is no place, even in that darkest hour before dawn, where God is not with us.

† Father, when I am anxious and fearful, help me to remember that you are always near me.

For further thought

Consider offering your services, in some way, to those organisations, local or national, who work with the vulnerable, especially those for whom the night brings little rest or respite.

Friday 10 January
Darkness my companion

Read Isaiah 60:1–9

For darkness shall cover the earth,
and thick darkness the peoples;
but the Lord will arise upon you,
and his glory will appear over you.

(verse 2)

January is often called the longest month. It seems to start just after Boxing Day! The days are short and dark. The weather can be depressing. There seems little to look forward to. It is no wonder that many people find themselves afflicted by SAD (Seasonal Affective Disorder) or what is called winter depression. Lack of light, particularly sunshine, is a major contributory factor and those affected experience persistent low spirits and lethargy. Living can seem like a dark place with no way out. And even if we do not suffer the extreme effects of SAD, many of us will find surviving the dark days of January a slog. Imposing restrictions on the things that give us pleasure – sometimes necessary after the excesses of the festive season – can add to the gloom.

Maybe one approach to the January blues might be for us to endeavour to turn them to our advantage; to use the darkness; to embrace a form of 'hibernation' wherein we take time to ponder, even if it is just a few moments each day. Isaiah talks of the treasure of darkness and 'riches hidden in secret places' (45:3). What might these be and where do we find them? Hardship, sorrow, suffering – none of these are to be desired but our faith demands that we mine all our experiences in order to grow in wisdom. Darkness need not be our enemy but a companion on a journey to new insights and to growth. Without darkness, how would we ever be able to appreciate the light?

† Father, give me the wisdom to see your hand at work in my life. Help me to find the light even in the darkest places.

For further thought

Kindness is a much-overlooked virtue in our world and often it is ourselves we are hardest on. This January, be kind to yourself as well as to others.

Saturday 11 January
Clock watching

Read Luke 2:25–38

'... for my eyes have seen your salvation,
which you have prepared in the presence of all peoples,
a light for revelation to the Gentiles
and for glory to your people Israel.'

(verses 30–32)

Our daughter stayed with us recently, on her way to a hen party, and discussion turned to the way things have changed since we ourselves got married. I never had a hen 'do' and my husband simply went out for an evening with his friends ... Many couples have set up home before they marry and need for nothing except a donation to the holiday (rather than honeymoon) of a lifetime. I remarked particularly on the gift we had from my aunt – it was a clock which graces our mantelpiece to this day. Young people today simply do not have clocks. In this 24/7 society all you need is a mobile phone – as clock, alarm, diary ...

How different from the world of previous generations, including my own! Life was more structured, with rhythms and seasons and hours for particular activities and functions. A world where the clock was watched in the best sense of the word.

Monastic communities still watch the clock – their days remain shaped by the traditional hours of prayer alongside the hours of work, food, recreation and silence. My own tradition encourages us to pray the prayer of the Church, in the morning, at midday, in the afternoon, evening and at night, as part of our unceasing prayer (1 Thessalonians 5:17). Simeon's canticle, from which our verse is taken, is used at Compline, the office that completes the day. Simeon has 'watched the clock', in the daily, weekly and yearly rituals of prayer in the temple, and his patience, trust and diligence are rewarded. The Word is revealed to him.

† Father, help me to be diligent in prayer. Let my days be punctuated with thanksgiving and praise and my nights illumined by your rest and peace.

For further thought
Do I structure my day around prayer or do I simply fit in prayer when I can? Learn 'The Canticle of Simeon' off by heart and use it as your prayer before sleep.

Epiphany: light to the nations – 2 The mystery revealed

Notes by **Revd Sham P. Thomas**

Sham is a priest in the Mar Thoma Syrian Church, presently serving the Enathu Mar Thoma Church in Kerala. Formerly he was a professor at The United Theological College, Bangalore and James S. Stewart scholar at the University of Edinburgh. He continues to lead retreats and conferences. Sham has used the NRSV for these notes.

Sunday 12 January
Jesus' baptism

Read Matthew 3:13–17

And when Jesus had been baptized, just as he came up from the water, suddenly the heavens were opened to him and he saw the Spirit of God descending like a dove and alighting on him. And a voice from heaven said, 'This is my Son, the Beloved, with whom I am well pleased.'

(verses 16–17)

In recent times, there has been an array of big-budget films in my native state of India, launching the sons of established film stars in the lead role. Their effort is to endorse their own progeny and seek the allegiance of fans. One may wonder whether they have taken a cue from the baptism of Jesus.

The baptism of Jesus was a curtain raiser on the mystery of God in two ways. First, it revealed Jesus to the wider public as God's beloved Son and agent. His appearance from nowhere before John the Baptist was dramatic and his request for baptism was mysterious. It was a puzzle for John that the sinless Jesus, the star of salvation, chose to be baptised by him and stand on par with the sinful people. This action revealed the mystery of Jesus to the world.

Second, besides bringing him to the public domain, the baptism had turned out to be a revealing moment for Jesus himself. The heavenly voice pronouncing him as the beloved Son was the first public revelation Jesus received from God. With that endorsement Jesus was assured of God standing shoulder to shoulder with him. The implications of such a revelation are the focus of our reflections this week.

† Revealing God, enable us to be sensitised to that revealing moment in our life which will shape our lives, perspectives and practices. Amen

Monday 13 January
Mystery hidden for ages

Read Ephesians 3:7–21

...this grace was given to me to bring to the Gentiles the news of the boundless riches of Christ, and to make everyone see what is the plan of the mystery hidden for ages in God who created all things.

(verses 8b–9)

In recent times, when the hidden chamber of a temple in India was opened following a court order, a mind-blowing collection of treasures worth one trillion dollars was discovered. This may only be a tiny fraction of the hidden treasures as the inner chamber is still under lock and seal following the same judicial order. Hitting on such a hidden treasure can be a jackpot!

Paul testifies to Jesus as the hidden treasure of God's mystery. In him, the mystery hidden for ages was revealed for the first time in human history in concurrence with the great plan of God and at the appointed time. Since Jesus is the only source and route to reaching God and knowing God's plan, Paul discards the possibility of any other means as a detour to God's mystery. The old saying 'all roads lead to Rome' will not hold true for all time!

Those who recognise Jesus as God's revelation have the responsibility to display it as it is the golden opportunity privileged for our ages. Paul is grateful for his access to this treasure irrespective of his inadequacies. He is all the more grateful for the privilege given to him to reveal this news to the Gentiles who were denied this opportunity before. In response to these great privileges, he expresses his willingness to go to any extent or to bear any sufferings to fulfil this responsibility of witnessing. Paul has no doubt that the only cause for the Church is to continue inviting all humans to the presence of God through the only mediator, Jesus Christ.

† We, as the treasure chests, thank you God, for keeping your treasure in us too, for the sake of your son Jesus Christ, our Lord. Amen

For further thought

In certain inter-religious dialogues there is a tendency to suggest that Jesus is one of the ways to God, if not the only way. How would you react to this?

Tuesday 14 January
Knowledge of God's mystery

Read Colossians 2:1–15

I want their hearts to be encouraged and united in love, so that they may have all the riches of assured understanding and have the knowledge of God's mystery, that is, Christ himself, in whom are hidden all the treasures of wisdom and knowledge.

(verses 2–3)

A mechanic repaired a minor complaint of a car in no time and charged 100 Indian rupees for the same. The car owner was annoyed and asked whether it was fair to demand such an amount for just tightening a screw or two. The response of the mechanic was crisp: 'Sir, for tightening the screw you may pay only two rupees, the rest is for knowing which screws are to be tightened.'

Knowledge is the key to unravelling mysteries and to taking informed actions. We reflected yesterday about Jesus being the sole medium to the mystery of God. In today's reading Jesus is acclaimed as the knowledge of God's mystery, rather than just a means to it. Jesus being the knowledge is distinct, as it is a person rather than a system of philosophy, logical arguments or a set of principles. It is a relationship-oriented knowledge rather than systematically developed rational arguments.

As knowledge stems from our relationship with Jesus, it has an origin and its growth depends on consolidating and deepening of that relationship. This multidimensional and all-encompassing relationship with Jesus provides the manure for the roots of faith to grow and yield fruits of faith. It also is the norm for us to understand and relate with all other philosophies and received wisdom like traditions which are competing for our adherence. They are to be judged on their efficacy in helping us to move with Christ. Nothing that moves us away from Christ can be considered knowledge, however glorified that could be.

† All-knowing God, help us to be knowledgeable in knowing you. Amen

For further thought

Jesus being the knowledge of God for us, how do we understand astrology and the use of the lunar calendar?

Wednesday 15 January
Jesus manifests his glory

Read John 2:1–11

Jesus and his disciples had also been invited to the wedding. When the wine gave out, the mother of Jesus said to him, 'They have no wine.' ... Jesus did this, the first of his signs, in Cana of Galilee, and revealed his glory; and his disciples believed in him.

(verses 2–3, 11)

Jesus inaugurated his public ministry at Cana by transforming water into wine. He went out of his way to do this so that a couple would start their marital life on a joyful note rather than in shame. It was indeed glorious!

Many factors contributed to this manifestation of glory at Cana. First, Jesus was invited to the wedding. The family wanted him to be part of their joy and celebration. In today's world, celebrating life with Jesus can be reckoned as outdated. Some others, however, beckon him when things go awfully wrong in life. It is, however, encouraging that, when we share our joys with him, he will share our sorrows as well.

Secondly, he was informed of the crisis in the family. Even though Jesus had not performed any miracles to date, his mother informed him of the problem and believed that he would do something to solve the crisis. Her initiation paved the way for a miraculous sign. Jesus can be approached to share our problems and needs, not necessarily as just an 'ambulance' that is to be called in an emergency.

Thirdly, his instructions were followed. A group of unnamed labourers filled the jars with water to the brim when he ordered them to fill water and unquestioningly carried the same to the master of ceremonies. Had it been for them to debate the purpose for which they had been instructed or to haphazardly fill the jars, they would not have become participants in the first sign of the Messiah in the world. By accepting his instructions without question or hesitation, we can also become part of manifesting his glory in the world.

† Glorious God, help us to be instruments to make lives around us pleasant and beautiful. Amen

For further thought

Think of situations where people are forced to live in shame and humiliation. What is your response?

Thursday 16 January
Deliverance to the needy

Read Psalm 72:1–14

For he delivers the needy when they call, the poor and those who have no helper. He has pity on the weak and the needy. From oppression and violence he redeems their life; and precious is their blood in his sight.

(verses 12–13a, 14)

Mahatma Gandhi, the father of the Indian nation, is credited with the statement that if God should appear before the poor, it should be in the form of bread! In the same vein, he exhorted that the parliament, while making laws, should place the poorest of the poor in focus and make sure that the laws enacted would benefit them the most.

Of course, what Gandhi has suggested is echoed already in the Bible, as in today's psalm. It declares a manifesto for rulers on the use of power and authority. If followed, this would nullify the common saying, 'Power tends to corrupt, and absolute power corrupts absolutely.' Power gets corrupted when it is arrogated and accumulated. When power is made to serve the ruler, he ends up as the greatest beneficiary of the rule and he conquers others only to rule over them. The psalm upholds an alternative vision of power being used to empower the weak and the vulnerable.

A just ruler, like God, whom any earthly ruler should emulate, cannot be neutral or impartial. In a world of unequal status and discrimination, justice necessitates being positively partial to the victims. This is both a protest and protection. It is a protest against all who defy God's will and plan of mutually dependent and complementing persons living together. It begs to differ with exploitation and unaccountable use of power resulting in dehumanisation. Protection is the corollary to the protest as it is a way of preservation and hope for the silenced and victimised people. God takes sides not because God wants to be partial but because God cares for those who are in dire need of him.

† Liberating God, may we make a compelling impact through our decisions and acts that builds our sensitivity towards the vulnerable people around. Give us your courage to be positively inclined to the disadvantaged. Amen

For further thought

Identify the most important factor that makes large sections of people vulnerable in your context, like the caste system in India. What would you propose to tide over the same?

Friday 17 January
Disciples' commission

Read Matthew 28:16–20

When they saw him, they worshipped him; but some doubted. And Jesus came and said to them, 'All authority in heaven and on earth has been given to me. Go therefore and make disciples of all nations ... And remember I am with you always, to the end of the age.'

(verses 17–18, 19a, 20b)

There is a saying that the 'first impression is the best impression'! Some may counter it by saying that the 'last impression is the lasting impression'. With Jesus there is nothing much to choose between these two sayings. In fact, his first and last public expressions are distinctly similar; both were about mission and commissioning.

As we have seen earlier this week, at his baptism, Jesus was endorsed and commissioned for mission in the world. In the last scene of earthly Jesus, which constitutes today's reading, he endorses and commissions the disciples to continue his mission. He also empowered them. The power Jesus shares for mission is gained through his cross at Golgotha rather than the imperial power offered to him by Satan soon after his baptism. The power for mission is the power and authority of the crucified and risen Lord and not of a crusading emperor.

Empowered with this power, the disciples were commissioned to be transforming witnesses in the world. Obviously, they were not to impose themselves or conquer others. Rather, they were to be a persuasive presence following the model of Jesus, who offered to be present (Emmanuel) in their mission journey. The purpose of this presence is the formation of a new global and inclusive community in the name of the divine community called the Triune God.

It is almost a mystery that Jesus entrusted this enormous task to a small band of disciples, who showed their inadequacies even in their last meeting with the earthly Jesus. The spread of the gospel reveals the result of this mystery and we are also invited to be part of this mission, which again is a glorious mystery!

† Commissioning God, enhance our mission in the spirit of your crucified Son, rather than diminishing us with the spirit of a crusader. Amen

For further thought

What are the deterrents against Christian mission in your context?

Saturday 18 January
Gift of the Holy Spirit

Read Acts 10:34–48

While Peter was still speaking, the Holy Spirit fell upon all who heard the word. The circumcised believers who had come with Peter were astounded that the gift of the Holy Spirit had been poured out even on the Gentiles, for they heard them speaking in tongues and extolling God.

(verses 44–46a)

While writing this note, my native state is embroiled in a controversy and resultant unrest following a court order permitting women in their reproductive age to visit a famous temple where the worshipped idol is a celibate! The custom to prohibit women in this age range was on their perceived inability to be pure for 41 consecutive days, which would prepare them to visit the deity. Their biological cycle is perceived to be polluting!

Codes of purity and pollution have contaminated culture and creed in many countries in one way or another. A cursory look at the book of Leviticus substantiates this with regard to the biblical tradition. Jesus lived above all such taboos and stigmas and as in today's reading the advent of the Holy Spirit coincided with a colossal breaking of the purity–pollution cycle.

In the story of Peter and Cornelius, the Holy Spirit is depicted to have broken the customs and practices reared on purity–pollution mainly in two ways. First, the Holy Spirit initiated the conversion of a conservative like Simon Peter to understand that there is no hierarchy of purity between people of different origins before God and that each one has to be accepted as of equal worth. Secondly, the Holy Spirit confirmed the acceptance of a 'gentile' like Cornelius, breaking all protocols – including baptism – as preconditions for such anointing. The Holy Spirit was mysteriously and majestically outpoured in a Gentile home, which eventually paved the way for the church to open her doors to people of all origins without any discrimination. The Kingdom era is ushered in by the overwhelming Holy Spirit!

† O Lord, soak us in your spirit of discernment where we are condemning others. Pour on us your Spirit to confirm our worth when we are condemned. Amen

For further thought

How do we make the declaration of Paul that there is no distinction in Christ (Galatians 3:28) a norm in our everyday life?

The Gospel of Matthew (1) – 1 Salt of the earth

Notes by **Revd Norman Francis**

Norman pastors Meadowbrook United and St Paul's (Maverly) United Churches, congregations of the United Church in Jamaica and the Cayman Islands in Kingston. He has also pastored congregations in Zambia, England and Scotland. On the rare occasion when he's not engaged in ministry-related activities, he spends his time in the great outdoors with camera in hand. He is married to Karen and has two adult sons, Norman and Kareem. Norman has used the NRSV for these notes.

Sunday 19 January
Blessed are the peacemakers

Read Matthew 5:1–12

'Blessed are the peacemakers, for they will be called children of God.'

(verse 9)

In April 2010, five-year-old Christina was murdered by gunmen who shot at the car she was travelling in with her father Christopher, who was also injured, as he drove through Montego Bay, Jamaica. Amid this senseless bloodshed, we see clues pointing to the Beatitudes in Matthew 5:1–12.

The first clue is Christina's name, which means 'follower of Christ'. Next, is her father's name, 'Christopher', which means 'carrier of Christ'. Finally, there's the place where Christina was killed – Felicity Road – the word 'felicity' meaning 'beatitude'; a meaning that points to Jesus' counter-cultural manifesto known by the same name. Christopher, in the face of violence, demonstrates what it means to be a peacemaker – those described in the Beatitudes as 'children of God'. 'Blessed are the peacemakers,' Jesus says (verse 9). Are you willing, like Christopher, to live as one who carries Christ, the Prince of Peace?

This week we will consider Jesus' Sermon on the Mount: his words about how we are to live, following his teaching. What can Jesus' words mean for us today?

† God of peace, give us grace to bear the cost of being peacemakers in a world broken by conflict and desperately in need of healing.

Monday 20 January
Courageous connections

Read Matthew 5:13–16
'You are the salt of the earth … You are the light of the world.'

(verses 13a and 14a)

In today's text, Jesus presents his counter-cultural manifesto of human society transformed by God's kingdom values.

He introduces two metaphors using everyday items essential to life – salt and light. Apart from its universal use in preserving meat when there was no refrigeration, salt was used to ratify agreements and signify loyalty. It was used to make purchases and there were even times when wages were paid in salt. So when Jesus says we are the 'salt of the earth', he is speaking of many important functions.

Jesus also speaks of our role as 'light', with its one intrinsic role – to banish darkness. Florence Nightingale, pioneer of modern nursing, earned the name 'the Lady with the Lamp' because on her own at night she walked among the beds with a small lamp in hand, checking the wounded. An impossible task without a lamp.

Friends, we cannot fulfil our purpose as Christians without connecting with people. Think about it – salt must be rubbed in, sprinkled or ingested, and light must shine in the darkness before either one can be effective.

Jesus now calls us to do what he did to be effective – connect with people. He did not discriminate. He socialised with undesirables, outcasts and the friendless. Consequently, he was ridiculed as 'a glutton and a drunkard' and called a 'friend of sinners' (Matthew 11:19). Will you connect with people and risk being ridiculed and misunderstood, as you become an agent of change?

† Lord, grant me the desire and the courage to become more like Jesus, by doing whatever is necessary to be more effective as 'salt' and 'light', beginning in my community. Amen

For further thought

Who are the disadvantaged in your community? What could you do to be salt and light for them?

Tuesday 21 January
'Spirit' vs 'letter'

Read Matthew 5:17–20

'Do not think that I have come to abolish the law or the prophets; I have come not to abolish but to fulfil.'

(verse 17)

As you're driving home, you approach an intersection with a stop sign. You reduce your speed but, since there are no approaching vehicles, instead of coming to a complete stop you accelerate through the intersection. A police officer stops you, stating that you disobeyed the traffic sign by not coming to a complete stop. Despite protesting that there was no danger of an accident since there were no oncoming vehicles, you get ticketed. This story brings out the difference between following the 'letter of the law', i.e. doing exactly what the law states, and obeying the 'spirit of the law', i.e. doing what the law was *intended* to accomplish. Today's reading focuses on this oftentimes controversial issue of 'letter' vs 'spirit'.

In making his point, Jesus refers to the Pharisees, a Jewish sect of men who had consecrated themselves to strictly keeping the law, which was a combination of scripture and oral traditions. So intent were the Pharisees on following the 'letter of the law', they missed the whole point of the law, in Jesus' view (see, e.g., Matthew 23:23–24). In contrast, Jesus brought new understanding that went beyond the 'letter of the law' and consequently was accused of coming 'to abolish the law'. This was a grave misunderstanding, for Jesus' only purpose was to reveal God's true intent towards human relationships.

There are many Christians who, like the Pharisees, have a legalistic approach towards matters of faith, and have lost sight of God's love and grace. This is evident in acts of obedience devoid of love rather than those which reveal God's heart of love towards everyone.

† God of grace, help me to be obedient to more than just the letter of the law, but to strive to live by the values that ultimately matter – loving you and loving my neighbour. Amen

For further thought

If you tend to live according to the letter of the law in practising your faith, what can you do to live out God's greater purpose?

Wednesday 22 January
'If looks could kill'

Read Matthew 5:21–26

'You have heard that it was said to those of ancient times, "You shall not murder"; and "whoever murders shall be liable to judgement." But I say to you that if you are angry with a brother or sister, you will be liable to judgement.'

(verses 21–22a)

We're all familiar with the expression, 'If looks could kill …', used of someone who looks at another with great anger and contempt. The use of this phrase implicitly acknowledges the connection between anger and murder, in which the simplest provocation sometimes does lead to bloodshed. Because of uncontrolled anger, people have been murdered over the simplest things, such as a boxed lunch worth less than US$3; over mobile phones; and even over a phone charger!

It is evident that a popular belief and teaching among the Pharisees in Jesus' day was that it is certainly wrong to shed innocent blood, as the sixth commandment clearly states (Exodus 20:13). Nevertheless, by interpreting this prohibition against murder in the narrowest way possible, the Pharisees believed that it didn't matter how angry one becomes, as long as it doesn't provoke one to literally take another's life. They missed the wider and deeper intention behind the law – that an intense, malicious anger and seething animosity are tantamount to murder.

We all tend to think of murder only as an outward act, but Jesus now invites us to take one step back to the very source of it all – the heart. God's ideal for human relationships, then, is more than just not committing murder in a literal sense; it is to get rid of all bitterness from our hearts. The moral of the story is that sin lies not only in one's wayward actions, but in the ill-feelings that prompt such actions. Starting today, what will you do to ensure your heart is a home of kindness towards others?

† God of peace, may I rise above the destructive effects of uncontrolled anger. Help me to channel all instances of provocation into constructive responses towards those who aggravate me. Amen

For further thought

If you struggle with a bad temper, why not seek the help of someone who is able to offer you some practical guidance and encouragement?

Thursday 23 January
The wandering eye

Read Matthew 5:27–30

'You have heard that it was said, "You shall not commit adultery." But I say to you that everyone who looks at a woman with lust has already committed adultery with her in his heart.'

(verses 27–28)

A few years ago, a church-owned hospital in Kingston, Jamaica, issued a strongly-worded warning to its employees, to much public outrage, that all hospital staff could face severe disciplinary action or even dismissal for fornication or adultery. According to the hospital, this drastic measure was part of its attempt to maintain 'high moral and ethical standards[1]'. In response, attorneys protested and questioned the legality of firing someone for 'adultery' or 'fornication'.

In a more extreme move, the ancient Israelites tried to legislate against adultery by imposing the death penalty (see, e.g., Leviticus 20:10), but they failed to understand that while it is certainly possible to legislate against undesirable actions, a much more difficult thing is to legislate against undesirable attitudes. We see this in Jesus' encounter with the woman who was about to be stoned to death, having been caught in the act of adultery (John 8:1–11), even though, presumably, she knew that death awaited her if she were caught. The fact that the offence was committed, even when there were laws against it, shows the limitations of legislation! The point Jesus is making here is that one's outward action, such as adultery, is only an outworking of what is already in one's heart. Adulterous actions stem from lustful thoughts. The heart of the matter is the matter of the heart. That's where we must begin.

† Merciful God, reveal to me the areas in my thought life that need to come under the transforming gaze of your all-seeing eyes, so that my conduct will always be upright towards others. Amen

For further thought

Spend some time in self-examination. Is your thought-life pure? Are your thoughts able to withstand God's scrutiny? How do you think God would answer?

---

1 Virtue, E. (2016), 'Sex Police - Seventh-Day Adventist-Operated Hospital Threatens To Dismiss Staff Guilty Of Fornication Or Adultery', *The Gleaner* (www.bit.ly/2IFFBjo, last accessed 16 May 2019).

Friday 24 January
Marriage: till death us do part?

Read Matthew 5:31–32

'It was also said, "Whoever divorces his wife, let him give her a certificate of divorce." But I say to you that anyone who divorces his wife, except on the ground of unchastity, causes her to commit adultery; and whoever marries a divorced woman commits adultery.'

(verses 31–32)

When Jesus uttered these words, divorce was a thorny issue … just like today. At the time, two conflicting schools of thought regarding divorce contended with each other: one, a liberal view; the other, extremely conservative. In today's text, Jesus seems to take the conservative road, laying down an absolute prohibition against divorce, allowable only in the case of adultery. The biblical understanding of divorce was certainly not what it is today, and so we should not be hasty in drawing conclusions on the matter. The word translated in our English Bibles as 'divorce' meant to 'send away' or 'set free' – a right which belonged only to the husband. In this context, adultery was seen as a breach of the husband's absolute right over his wife … never the other way around! The wife was open to all manner of abuse at the whim of the husband. Could this be what lies behind Jesus' strict interpretation of the divorce laws of his day? Was he protecting married women from abuse?

In today's world, it is no longer up to the husband to dissolve his marriage; divorces are awarded by the courts, where a judge makes a ruling based on the case presented by either or both marriage partners. Thus, modern divorce laws in most countries offer the kind of protection which women lacked in antiquity. So, what do we do with Jesus' words against divorce? If Jesus were to address the issue of divorce today, he probably would insist that instead of focusing on a legalistic understanding of a marriage covenant, we should focus on building life-affirming marriages.

† Faithful God, you have called us into covenant with you, which irrevocably binds us to you in a loving relationship. Enable me to demonstrate your faithfulness in all my relationships, especially with significant others. Amen

For further thought

In the light of today's divorce laws, how would you justify, or otherwise, the prevalence of a view which says 'No' to divorce?

Saturday 25 January
'Cross my heart ...'

Read Matthew 5:33–37

'Again, you have heard that it was said to those of ancient times, "You shall not swear falsely, but carry out the vows you have made to the Lord." But I say to you, Do not swear at all ...'

(verses 33–34a)

An oath is an assertion that one has spoken, or is about to speak, truthfully, or that one will faithfully carry out an intended act. The solemnity of such an assertion is guaranteed by invoking God as witness. In the midst of the apparent prevalence of oath-taking in the ancient world, Jesus says, 'Do not swear at all, either by heaven, for it is the throne of God, or by the earth, for it is his footstool, or by Jerusalem, for it is the city of the great King. And do not swear by your head, for you cannot make one hair white or black' (verses 34–36). Jesus said all this because the Pharisees had developed intricate rules to circumvent the law about using the name of God to swear: if one made an oath using God's name to guarantee one's word, that word had to be honoured. But if one swore by something else, such as heaven or earth, Jerusalem, or even one's own head, one could go back on one's word without any undue penalty. Through the clever choice of words when making an oath, an individual could mask any intention to deceive ... and get away with it!

Jesus argues that it doesn't matter if an oath contains God's name or not, for anything you use as the basis of your oath is still somehow connected to God: heaven is 'the throne of God'; earth is God's 'footstool'; Jerusalem is 'the city of the great king'; and even one's very head is under God's control; we can't even change the colour of our own hair.

† God of truth and faithfulness, may I be known as a trustworthy person, having no need to swear. May my 'Yes' always simply be 'Yes' and my 'No' always simply be 'No'. Amen

For further thought

Should we practise taking oaths in formal settings, e.g. in marriage vows, in the light of Jesus' pronouncements against taking oaths? Why, or why not?

The Gospel of Matthew (1) – 2 Praying and fasting

Notes by **Simei Monteiro**

Simei is a Brazilian poet and composer. She has worked as worship consultant at the World Council of Churches in Geneva, Switzerland. Interested in worship and the arts, her book *The Song of Life* (ASTE/IEPG 1991) explores the relationship between hymns and theology. A retired missionary from the United Methodist Church, USA, she lives in Curitiba, Brazil, with her husband Revd Jairo Monteiro. They have two daughters and three grandchildren. Simei has used the NRSVA for these notes.

Sunday 26 January
Turning the other cheek

Read Matthew 5:38–42

'But if anyone strikes you on the right cheek, turn the other also ... and if anyone forces you to go one mile, go also the second mile. Give to everyone who begs from you, and do not refuse anyone who wants to borrow from you.'

(verses 39b, 41–42)

The passages for this week call us to a life in which faith and action are interconnected. What might this mean in everyday life?

If anyone strikes you, the most important thing is to discover what moved this person to do it and avoid responding with the same hatred. Revenge is not an act of courage, patience or resilience. Turning the other cheek is to give the offender a chance to understand the roots of the hatred. Also, we know that it is hard to go the second mile or to give freely something we have: part of our time or energy or money. If we are to do this it must be the love of God acting in us, not because we just want to be a good Christian or receive applause.

Studying in Buenos Aires, during the military regime in the years 1972–74, sometimes I and my little family were in deep need without the means to live. Several friends and members of the church we attended gave support to us, even knowing I would never be able to pay them back. They helped me without expecting any return.

What have they received back? My eternal gratitude!

† Dear God, help us to be calm when facing a danger and give us a merciful heart towards those in need!

Monday 27 January
Who is my enemy?

Read Matthew 5:43–48

'But I say to you, "Love your enemies and pray for those who persecute you, so that you may be children of your Father in heaven; for he makes his sun rise on the evil and on the good, and sends rain on the righteous and on the unrighteous."'

(verses 44–45)

After many years of proclaiming that Jesus is the Prince of Peace, we still live in a world where hatred and discrimination are rife! Because of the political, economic and social chaos in Venezuela, we are getting more and more refugees in Brazil. According to the Brazilian Constitution, no one can be denied refuge. Each day we are receiving approximately 500 refugees coming through our borders, including indigenous people.

In August 2018, a group of Brazilians set fire to one of the refugees' shelters. Why such hate? It is true that we are facing a great economic defeat in Brazil and that we have approximately 13 million unemployed people. For some of us, the refugees are deprivers of our own rights, jobs and healthcare. Are we jealous of the treatment the refugees are receiving? It seems we are considering all the immigrants as enemies! In fact, 90 per cent of Brazilians are considered as Christians and the majority of our population is descended from immigrants.

We need to remember that Jesus went to Egypt as a refugee. Perhaps we need to recall that we are to pray for those who persecute us, not exclude them. Perhaps we need to remember God's commandment: 'When an alien resides with you in your land, you shall not oppress the alien. The alien who resides with you shall be to you as the citizen among you; you shall love the alien as yourself, for you were aliens in the land of Egypt: I am the Lord your God' (Leviticus 19:33–34).

Perhaps we need to open our borders and hearts to the refugees.

† God, our friend, help us to pray for human beings in a friendly way. Give us the wisdom to be tender-hearted towards our neighbours and express your love for all humanity.

For further thought

If you have refugees in your country, try to visit them in their own place, bringing some goods and praying with them.

History of IBRA

The International Bible Reading Association (IBRA) was founded by the Sunday School Union (SSU) committee in 1882 under Charles Waters, a bank manager in King's Cross. A devout young man and Sunday school teacher, Waters had arrived in London in 1859 to further his career, and there encountered the inspirational teaching of Charles Spurgeon. He threw himself, heart and soul, into working with Spurgeon and the SSU who wrote to all members in Britain and overseas inviting them to join the newly formed IBRA, circulating lists of daily Bible readings supported by brief commentary notes.

The response was amazing. By 1910 the readership had exceeded a million people and was touching the lives of soldiers fighting wars, sailors on long voyages to Australia, colliers in the coal mines of Wales, schools in Canada, Jamaica and Belfast and prisoners in Chicago. People all over the world, alone and in groups, felt comforted and encouraged by the idea of joining other Christians throughout the world in reading the same Bible passages. And they still do!

We often receive endorsements from people whose lives are transformed through IBRA. Below are extracts from two letters; one from 2015 and the other from 1907. Can you tell which was written when?

66 *I can truly say the Daily Bible reading is a great help and blessing to me. It seems to bring me daily nearer Christ and higher up in the sunshine of God's love.* 99
A. Roberts, Buryas Bridge

66 *People are really excited ... In a country where the daily income is low, some are unable to buy [a] printed guide of daily Bible readings. They are expressing a deepest gratitude for free available IBRA material.* 99
Baptist Community of the Congo River, Democratic Republic of the Congo

Today, over 135 years later, this rich history lives on, touching the lives of hundreds of thousands of people across the world. God is the same yesterday, today and forever – therefore our original mission continues today and will do into the future!

Tuesday 28 January
The invisible piety

Read Matthew 6:1–6

'Beware of practising your piety before others in order to be seen by them ... your alms may be done in secret; ... go into your room and shut the door and pray to your Father who is in secret; and your Father who sees in secret will reward you.'

(verses 1a, 4a and 6b)

If we do something good in public, it is almost normal to take pleasure thinking about it and feeling proud of ourselves. There is nothing wrong with this. But this self-satisfaction, this caress of our ego, can also bring us to tell others about our success and so to expect acclaim.

Even when performing at charity shows, artists always seek the applause of the audience and a social recognition. Some of them become ill and depressed when they are no longer in the limelight. Others get an image through media which does not match with their real profiles.

If you are a musician, a performer, if you have good ideas and inventions, remember that what you produce or do should be able to be used to the glory of God and not for your self-seeking glory.

Our actions do not necessarily need to be recognised. We don't need constant applause. Sometimes, a good action or a helpful idea caught and shared in a video or photo is good to promote identical actions or solve problems. This is the case of the inventions and discoveries now recognised, copied and used all around the world.

But it is also true that our good deeds – done in secret in our neighbourhood, done in a small village in West Africa or Brazil, actions that will never be noticed in the mass media – will perhaps never have public recognition. But their fruits will be forever.

This is God's reward!

† Dear Creator, give me a humble heart and a humble mind. Make it that all I think or do can be only to your glory!

For further thought

Try to express your love and interest towards your family members or friends without words or with secret gestures like a card or small gifts.

Wednesday 29 January
Daily bread and daily pardon

Read Matthew 6:7–18

'... for your Father knows what you need before you ask him. Pray then in this way: Our Father in heaven, hallowed be your name. Your kingdom come. Your will be done, on earth as it is in heaven. Give us this day our daily bread. And forgive us our debts, as we also have forgiven our debtors.'

(verses 8b–12)

There are some interesting differences between lifestyles among countries and cultures. For some cultures, it is very important to plan for the future or work. In other cultures, where we do not know what will be happening the next day or if we will have food or money to buy something we need, we just try to survive each day. The majority of Latin American families do not make plans for the future; they are used to saying: life drives me.

While planning a morning prayer service for an international and ecumenical gathering, I asked a Christian girl from Palestine to sing the Lord's Prayer in Arabic and then lead us in the English version. She said the English version was mistranslated and explained that the expression 'thanks for the bread we always have' was not the same as 'give us this day our daily bread'. Sometimes all we have is bread for today, and we need to strive for it every day. For most of us, living in wealthy countries, this mistranslation seemed not so important, but for her this phrase was disturbing.

Normally we are used to storing our food and we do not strive for food each day. Also, we do not strive for a daily life without sin. We love packages, combos, and perhaps we are just saying 'God, forgive the multitude of our sins.'

In the Lord's Prayer: 'give us this day our daily bread' cannot be isolated from '... and forgive our debts, as we also have forgiven our debtors.' This daily prayer reminds us that God cares for us as a father and will provide all we need for this day including being forgiven and also forgiving our neighbours.

† Dear God, from whom all blessings flow; help me to place my all dependence on you and in your loving care for this day. Amen

For further thought

Write in your own words a Lord's Prayer; ask or give thanks for each of your daily activities in which you will be involved.

Thursday 30 January
Where is my treasure?

Greed is very present in our world. Sometimes it takes the names of property, goods, heritage, wealth, greatness, etc.; most of these values are managed by the market. The market can become an idol tempting us with commodities and placating our anxieties. If we do not take care of our lives and souls we can even become ill.

Once I heard someone say that private property is a gift from God. I am not sure about this, as I received different wisdom from my ancestors. Some indigenous communities believe that all the goods they have belong to the entire clan. So if you bring a gift to them you cannot just deliver it to an individual; you must bring it to the chief who will share it or keep it as a common good. This rule is accepted and practised without any discussion. Also, nature is considered a common good and it is natural to preserve the ground, the seeds and the environment.

On the other hand, in most Western cultures, the sense of property is totally dominated by individualism and private property well protected by marketing laws.

Obsession with personal wealth ruins our relationship with God and with our neighbours. It also makes us completely indifferent towards the pain and suffering of others. When we love our neighbour as we love ourselves; when we are able to share what we possess in favour of others; when we discover the goods of salvation and God's spiritual gifts, then we will be storing our treasure in heaven.

† Giver of life, give me wisdom to evaluate and keep only things that are essential to my daily life. Enrich me with spiritual gifts and protect me from greed and usury.

For further thought

'The lover of money will not be satisfied with money; nor the lover of wealth, with gain. This also is vanity' (Ecclesiastes 5:10).

Friday 31 January
Striving for the Kingdom of God

Read Matthew 6:25–34

'Therefore I tell you, do not worry about your life, what you will eat or what you will drink … your heavenly Father knows that you need all these things. But strive first for the kingdom of God and his righteousness, and all these things will be given to you as well.'

(verses 25a, 32b–33)

In the Lord's Prayer, we pray: 'Your kingdom come. Your will be done, on earth as it is in heaven'. If we pay attention to all the previous Bible passages, it is very clear that Jesus is referring to a way of living here and now and not only in heaven. 'All these things will be given to you' is about things and blessings we are receiving during our lifetime.

Striving for the Kingdom of God means that we are trying very hard to align our actions with Jesus' vision, even if it costs us or presents us with great difficulties.

As a Christian composer I believe that salvation is the song of life itself; a life that desires to reach the dimension of Christ, the perfect human being!

If God and humanity act together a better world will be possible. This is not just a dream of the Christian imagination; we can already start a new life in our family and neighbourhood. Salvation includes the responsibility to build a better world where justice and peace may prevail. Jesus himself said, 'For, in fact, the kingdom of God is among you' (Luke 17:21b).

If we are convinced that we are striving for the kingdom of God right now, we cannot just wait for an eschatological reality at the end of time. We must make the kingdom of God our horizon. We must strive to see its signs and enact it in our daily life, in our society and in our world.

† Heavenly king, help us to discover and promote the signs of your realm in our daily life while searching for a simple life.

For further thought

What signs of the kingdom do you see around you today?

Saturday 1 February
The pointing of the finger

Read Matthew 7:1–6

'Do not judge, so that you may not be judged. For with the judgement you make you will be judged, and the measure you give will be the measure you get. Why do you see the speck in your neighbour's eye, but do not notice the log in your own eye?'

(verses 1–3)

A pointing finger is a complex sign. One of its powerful and sometimes misused meanings denotes judgement.

The easy judgement expressed in malicious language is a new phenomenon in social networks. We see so many lazy judgements and misinterpretations posted on Facebook, Twitter and YouTube. It seems people do it without any previous reflection!

Hence, we must be careful and suspicious when we receive information like this in our pages: fake news on blogs and websites without any information on its sources.

The most popular interpretation of these words of Jesus sounds like a warning: do not judge, so that you may not be judged. We are afraid of being judged and we then feel compelled to avoid any judgement.

But, what if you see something completely wrong and you point it out? Does it mean you are wrong to do so? What if it is about a loved person or group?

If we read on in the text we will see that there is a strong admonishment about hypocrisy. It speaks about perception and a clear vision of reality. It means that perceiving first that you also have a log in your own eye, you will be able not only to take it out, but to see clearly enough to take the splinter out of your brother's eye.

So if we correct or, at least, ask forgiveness for our own behaviour – if we try to live properly – then, and only then, we can exercise a fair judgement and help others to do the same.

† Dear just and righteous God, search me and know my inner being; point out anything in me that offends you; help me to see my wrong judgements; protect my soul against the speaking of evil!

For further thought

Practise pointing your finger. What do you think when moving it in different directions? It may include God!

Dealing with disappointment

Notes by **Edna Hutchings**

Edna lives in the beautiful county of Dorset, England, and is a retired accounts assistant. She is a member of a United Church (Methodist and United Reformed) and is facilitator for one of the church homegroups. Her voluntary work includes assisting with bookkeeping at a local Christian bookshop. She enjoys writing short stories and poetry, reading, knitting, walking and messing about with paints. Edna has used the NIV for these notes.

Sunday 2 February
Meditate on God's word

Read Joshua 1:1–11

'Keep this Book of the Law always on your lips; meditate on it day and night, so that you may be careful to do everything written in it. Then you will be prosperous and successful.'

(verse 8)

There must have been great disappointment when Moses died. Were there murmurings of discontent among the people? Apathy? But God is constant. He expects Joshua to take his place in leading the Israelites into Canaan. Imagine Joshua's fears of inadequacy. Did God really think he could take the place of the great Moses? He must have felt overwhelmed with the magnitude of getting the Israelites motivated again. Where should he start? He started by listening to God.

Three times God tells Joshua to be strong and courageous. But, as well, he must constantly meditate on the Book of Law, the first chapters of the Old Testament, and obey the rules there. God is prepared to give as much attention to Joshua as he did to the great Moses – and as he does to you and me.

This week's readings tell us that we should not give up hope in times when everything seems hopeless. The first and most important thing that we should do in any difficult situation is meditate on God's word. Just as Joshua does here.

How were Joshua and the whole people to cope with the disappointment of losing their leader and then how could Joshua bear being given the responsibility himself? By meditating on God's word. By prayer.

† Father God, thank you that you are always there for us even when our problems seem unsolvable to us.

Monday 3 February
Persistence in prayer

> **Read 1 Samuel 1:1–20**
>
> *'I have been praying here out of my great anguish and grief.' Eli answered, 'Go in peace, and may the God of Israel grant you what you have asked of him.' … Then she went her way and ate something, and her face was no longer downcast.*
>
> (verses 16b–17, 18b)

Elkanah's second wife bore him many children. But Hannah wanted to bear her husband a son herself, especially as Peninnah, a mother of several, took delight in looking down on Hannah for her childlessness. This was a problem that neither Hannah nor anyone else could solve. And it seemed to Hannah that God was not listening to her prayers. Every month she would have held her breath in anticipation. Perhaps this time? Only to be disappointed yet again.

There seem to be two problems for Hannah here. She was unable to conceive, but she also struggled with depression. Why was God not answering her prayers? But she persisted and her silent articulation from the heart came to the attention of Eli. Eli's calm assurance and further prayer gave her hope and lifted her depression. And eventually God answered her prayer by providing the son she so wished for.

Sometimes we need the help of a church leader or friend to give us courage to carry on. I turned to my church minister at a time when a relationship ended badly. There were complications and emotional upsets that I thought would continue forever. Life ahead seemed hopeless. He suggested I read the Bible passage where Jesus tells the story of the persistent widow (Luke 18:1–8) which helped me to continue praying with patience. That difficult period is now a distant memory and I have found living alone very rewarding. Never give up praying. God will answer. At the same time it can help, as it did for me, and as it did for Hannah, to share the problem.

† Lord, we know you always hear our prayers. Give us patience to wait for your answer in your time, not ours.

For further thought

You may like to read what Jesus had to say about persistence in prayer: Luke 18:1–8.

Tuesday 4 February
In times of despair

Read Nehemiah 1:1–11

'Lord, let your ear be attentive to the prayer of this your servant and to the prayer of your servants who delight in revering your name. Give your servant success today by granting him favour in the presence of this man.' I was cupbearer to the king.

(verse 11)

Nehemiah is in despair when he hears the news about the boundaries of Jerusalem. Not only boundaries but morals have broken down and apathy has taken its place. A town without strong boundaries was considered unsafe and the people live in fear. He wants to do something about it but he is hundreds of miles away from the problem.

So he prays. First, he acknowledges the problem. Then he confesses and asks God's forgiveness on behalf of others as well as himself. Nehemiah does not expect God to intervene in some miraculous way, but pleads for God to help and guide him into action. 'Give your servant success today' (verse 11). He has faith that, with God's help, what seems impossible becomes possible. His task is the rebuilding of the walls of Jerusalem and rebuilding a strong community. As cupbearer, he has influence. We know he returned to Jerusalem and inspired the people there to rebuild the walls. He also introduced social reforms for the good of the people. Prayer leads to action.

I don't drive and with no railway station in my town it is difficult to visit elderly relatives in other parts of the country. Like Nehemiah, I pray, and send postcards and letters, or organise visits. As well, I often despair at the state of wicked things happening that we see on our television screens. Even though we are not personally responsible and can do nothing about them, we can ask God's forgiveness and know that he hears our prayers – and be moved to action, in our own way.

† Lord, forgive us when we fail to live up to your expectations. And when we do not know which way to go, please show us the way forward.

For further thought
Is there any action you should be taking as a result of your prayers?

Wednesday 5 February
Living in hope

Read Isaiah 40:27–31

But those who hope in the Lord will renew their strength. They will soar on wings like eagles; they will run and not grow weary, they will walk and not be faint.

(verse 31)

This beautiful passage from Isaiah tells us that however hopeless our situation appears and however faraway God seems to be, he is always close by. In times of disappointment and stress, it is 'hope in the Lord', believing in God's constancy and promise, that can keep us from falling into despair.

'Even youths grow tired and weary' (verse 30). We know that stressful situations happen at any age. Today's young people have to cope with exams and worries about the future, and often on top of that they suffer from relationship difficulties. Then family and finance problems can afflict us in later life. And when we are elderly, we grow tired more quickly but seem to have added duties thrust upon us; we are disappointed that retirement is not quite the life of leisure we had anticipated. I said 'no' recently when more responsibility was asked of me – so difficult to say – but a team was formed to do the job that was too much for one. God found a solution to the problem.

God promises that with hope in him we will get through the difficult patches. The eagle uses the flow of air under his wings to keep him soaring and hovering. We can use our hope in the Lord to keep us 'riding high' too.

I memorised verse 31 many years ago and would say it to myself when there wasn't an opportunity to take time out to pray. Just thinking this message of hope and trust in God's promises would lift me up.

† Lord, you are always near to us even when we cannot sense your presence. Never let us lose hope in you.

For further thought

Is there a text you have found helpful in times of weariness to remind you of God's constancy? If not, try memorising verse 31 and using it throughout the day.

Thursday 6 February
Overcoming doubt

Read John 20:24–29

Then he said to Thomas, 'Put your finger here; see my hands. Reach out your hand and put it into my side. Stop doubting and believe.' … Then Jesus told him, 'Because you have seen me, you have believed; blessed are those who have not seen and yet have believed.'

(verses 27 and 29)

Thomas is one of my favourite biblical characters. I can understand his disappointment at what he thought was the end of Jesus' ministry. We can identify with him and his doubts. Thomas was able to have proof but Jesus knew that most of us would have to rely on faith alone. We rely on trust.

I bought a poor-looking plant from a charity shop. Just a few spindly leaves, but I was assured that it would flower. Months went by and several times I thought I would throw it on the compost heap. It wasn't doing anything. There were leaves, but no sign of a flower bud. But I kept watering it and one day a bud showed itself and, as I write, that spindly plant is in full bloom, a magnificent vermillion red. I don't have 'green fingers' and am not even sure of its name; it might be some kind of amaryllis. But I'm so glad I kept faith with it, kept it watered and gave it light. My Christian faith is a bit like that. Sometimes God seems far away. I need to keep it 'watered' and give it light, pray regularly, read the Bible, attend church, even when I'm not 'in the mood', and glimpses of God always appear.

In Mark's Gospel we have the story of Jesus healing the boy whose father exclaims, 'I do believe; help me overcome my unbelief!' (Mark 9:17–27). The man's sincerity and his faith were enough for Jesus.

† Father God, so often, like Thomas, we have doubts. Help us to overcome those doubts, to keep praying to you. Thank you for always being there even when we cannot feel your presence.

For further thought

Today, try looking for things around you that remind you of God's wonder, and give thanks.

Friday 7 February
Open to change

Read Luke 18:18–27

Those who heard this asked, 'Who then can be saved?'
Jesus replied, 'What is impossible with man is possible with God.'

(verses 26–27)

I used to worry over this passage. Was Jesus saying I should sell my humble home and belongings and give it all away? I don't think so. He is, however, telling me to put God first. In the rich ruler's situation his priority was his wealth, obtaining it and keeping it above all else. The ruler was rich – it was his stumbling block.

What are my stumbling blocks to being a good Christian? I sometimes think I spend too much time just being busy – making 'to do' lists and ticking them off. Nothing wrong with being organised but I need to drift away from it sometimes. This morning clearing out my wardrobe was on my list. The window in my bedroom looks out onto the pavement. Glancing up I saw a neighbour who uses a mobility scooter looking at me over the garden wall. She loves to chat. This morning I wanted to get through my chores so I just waved and carried on sorting the disarray on my bed. Then, like the rich man, I was sad, and looked up again, intending to go out to her for a quick chat. The wardrobe could wait. But too late – she had carried on home. I had put my slavery to domestic lists before kindness to a neighbour.

But Jesus gives hope to all of us who struggle with putting God first. 'What is impossible with man is possible with God' (verse 27). He is always there to guide us and forgive.

† Father God, please help us to put your will above our own. Seek out any changes we need to make, knowing that you are always there to guide us.

For further thought

Are there any small changes you could make to your life, in order to place God first?

Saturday 8 February
Joy out of suffering

Read John 16:16–24

'Now is your time of grief, but I will see you again and you will rejoice, and no one will take away your joy … Until now you have not asked for anything in my name. Ask and you will receive, and your joy will be complete.'

(verses 22 and 24)

In today's reading, Jesus is warning his disciples of the sorrows to come and that without the sadness, joy will not be possible; without the crucifixion there could not be the resurrection followed by the coming of the Holy Spirit. Sorrow will turn into joy.

Many of us have had experience of medical surgery. Yes, you have to go through pain and discomfort in order to get better. I became gradually deaf throughout life until ten years ago I was profoundly deaf and gave up going to meetings and doing the communal things I enjoyed. I made adjustments and coped. But when the opportunity came along to have a cochlear implant I jumped at it. It meant an operation to the head which is not pleasant at the time; it was sore and I was advised not to wash my hair for two weeks. It also meant losing any natural hearing left in the implanted ear so I was totally deaf for a month while the wound healed. But what joy when the processor was attached and I could hear again – much better than I expected. It took a while to get used to it: 'a little while' which varies from person to person. I had to go through some discomfort and pain but now I feel as if I have my life back again. I thank God for this gift I've received.

As Jesus promised, so I experienced: that sorrow can, and will, turn into joy, if we persist and make the effort.

† Father God, help us when we are sad and grieving, and give us faith that things will get better in time.

For further thought

Don't wait for Easter, but turn today to Luke chapter 24 and be reminded of the joy of the resurrection.

Song of Solomon

Notes by **Anthony Loke**

 Anthony was formerly an ordained Methodist minister and Old Testament lecturer in the Seminari Theoloji Malaysia for many years. He is now a layman with an itinerant teaching, preaching and writing ministry. He serves as an adjunct lecturer in two AG Bible Colleges. His wife is an English teacher in a private international school. They have two adult children, Charis and Markus. Anthony has written eleven books and is currently writing on the book of Daniel. His latest book is *Song of Songs Made Simple* (Pustaka Sufes 2018). Anthony has used the NRSVA for these notes.

Sunday 9 February
Kiss me with the kisses of your lips

Read Song of Solomon 1

For your love is better than wine, your anointing oils are fragrant.

(verses 2b–3a)

It is strange to find a book of love songs in the Bible. Equally strange is that the opening words in verse 2 are a 'beginning without a beginning'. Out of the blue the book opens with explosive words where the maiden desires to be kissed by her beloved! There is no formal introduction to the key characters of the book. A female voice speaks and will dominate the rest of the eight chapters. In the book, we are brought into an idyllic world where a maiden loves a man and finds her love reciprocated. The couple sing love songs and tease each other with playful images. He likens her to a 'mare of Pharaoh' which may be insulting to a modern woman!

The pastoral images in chapter 1 evoke a picture of Eden restored. In the original Eden, the man and woman love each other without hindrances. The fall marred the image of God in them and defiled eros. In the Song, eros is restored to its highest and purest state. The chapter ends with the couple locked in passionate embrace on their verdant couch which is a 'bed' of grass. Nature is the playground for the couple.

† Lord, you made each of us different and unique. Help us to accept ourselves just as we are. Amen

Monday 10 February
A rose by any name

Read Song of Solomon 2

Do not stir up or awaken love until it is ready!

(verse 7c)

The maiden calls herself a simple flower of the field but in the man's eyes, she stands out from among the brambles. Likewise, in the maiden's eyes, the man is like an apple tree standing out from the other trees in the dark wood. Call it by any other name, a rose is still a rose, for beauty lies in the eyes of the beholder!

When one falls in love, it is the most wonderful feeling. One no longer walks but floats in heaven! The maiden is sick with love but she asks for sweet stuff that only intensifies her feelings. One cannot cure lovesickness with things made of love. When it is the time for love, let it bloom. But when it is not the time, do not stir up or awaken love 'until it is ready' (verse 7). Like the pop song, 'You Can't Hurry Love', originally recorded by The Supremes in 1966, love cannot be hastened, for it takes time to grow and to mature love.

Catch the little foxes that can ruin the vineyard. There may be little obstacles and stumbling blocks in a relationship that need to be nipped in the bud. If not dealt with, they may cause havoc later. For a relationship to grow well, a couple needs to continually work on it. Give it TLC (tender loving care), and let it bloom when it is ready!

† Lord, may we grow each day more into your perfect likeness, mirroring your love in our relationships. Amen

For further thought

If you are in a committed relationship, where in that relationship do you need to give love time to grow at the moment?

Tuesday 11 February
Night fantasy

Read Song of Solomon 3

'I will seek him whom my soul loves.'

(verse 2c)

We do not know whether the maiden is dreaming or having a night fantasy in verses 1–4. Propelled by her deep desire to possess the man, she dreams of pursuing him in the dark streets of the city although aware of the dangers of the night. When she finally finds him, she clutches him tight and will not let him go. Her goal is to take the man into the bedchamber of her conception – which is an intimate place for lovemaking. Sometimes when a person is in love, we do not think or care about the dangers involved. Love compels us to seek out our beloved, for love is a powerful driving force.

The wedding of Solomon is described in the second half of the chapter. A royal wedding, full of opulence and grandeur, is a dream wedding for many couples – like the wedding of Prince Harry and Meghan Markle in 2018! In a Malay wedding called a *Bersanding*, the couple is feted like a king and queen. They are affectionately called *raja sehari* ('king for a day'). In the Song, the maiden wishes that her wedding will be as grand as Solomon's royal wedding. A wedding is the public ceremony by which two persons vow to spend their lives together in marriage. Love, and subsequently marriage, is never a private affair. There is a public dimension to it, for it brings and unites together families and friends.

† Lord, we know that marriages on earth are not made in heaven but that a couple must earnestly seek to work at it. Amen

For further thought

'Therefore a man leaves his father and his mother and clings to his wife, and they become one flesh' (Genesis 2:24).

Wednesday 12 February
Anatomy of love

Read Song of Solomon 4

A garden locked is my sister, my bride, a garden locked, a fountain sealed.

(verse 12)

In a relationship, a couple often teases and heaps praises on each other. Despite the fact that the majority of couples are ordinary people and do not belong to the 'rich and famous', in each other's eyes, the other has no comparison. A tantalising wink, a flick of a lock of hair, or a coy smile can raise one's blood pressure or cause a skipped heartbeat.

The man describes the maiden with superlatives (verses 1–7): she is indeed without blemish (verse 7). He invites her to come down from her lofty heights (verse 8). Her mesmerising beauty ravishes his heart and 'drives him crazy'. Yet her inaccessibility is for their good (verse 12). She is not a fountain that is opened to any passer-by but only for her partner at the eventual time. She may be a locked fountain but its waters of love still flow freely (verse 15). Abstinence from sex before marriage may not sound like a fashionable thing today for many couples, especially when modern society openly flaunts sex appeal and sexuality. Yet, to save the best for each other, and that includes each other's body, is to acknowledge that the human body is a gift from God. It must be well regarded in order to be well received. We save it to be a once-for-all gift to our beloved.

† Lord, thank you for the gift of sexuality and all that it entails and may we save it to give to the one that we love the most. Amen

For further thought

Shakespeare once wrote in *Othello* that 'our bodies are our gardens, to which our wills are gardeners' (Act I, Scene 3).

Thursday 13 February
Absence and presence

Read Song of Solomon 5

This is my beloved and this is my friend, O daughters of Jerusalem.

(verse 16b)

In the second dream account, the maiden speaks of her deepest fear: losing her man. She is slow to respond to her beloved's request to open the bedroom door. When she finally opens the door, he has already left. Frantically she searches for the man in the city but this time she fails to find him. Instead, the city sentinels or watchmen find her. Being less than sympathetic to a single girl running around unescorted at night and mistaking her to be a prostitute, they beat her up. She then requests the female chorus, the daughters of Jerusalem, to help her look for her man. In reply to their question why they should help her, the maiden describes the man with what is technically called a *wasf*, or a descriptive song. This time, it is the maiden's turn to describe the man with superlatives (verses 10–16). In short, he is godlike and stands out one in 'ten thousand' (verse 10).

Sometimes in a relationship, there are elements of conflict. When the man is ready, the maiden is not; when she is ready, he is no longer present. Every relationship goes through its rhythms of frustrations and delight, with absence and presence. But absence can make the heart grow fonder. At the end of the day, she calls him her beloved and friend (verse 16). Relationship and eventually marriage are for lifelong companionship and comradeship.

| Lord, help every couple to be able to go through the ups-and-downs in a relationship and may they grow stronger through the occasional absence. Amen

For further thought

To the maiden, the man is most desirable and beautiful because he is also most loved (verse 16).

Friday 14 February
Poetry in motion

Read Song of Solomon 6:1–7:7
I am my beloved's, and his desire is for me.

(chapter 7, verse 10)

The man describes the maiden in his second descriptive song and here he uses military images; the maiden is 'terrible as an army with banners' (6:4 and 10). While we today may think that it is not appropriate to use such images to describe love, the ancients have no qualms about it. The Ancient Near-Eastern goddess of love, Ishtar, was also the goddess of war. In using a military image, the man highlights the maiden's beauty which arouses desire but, at the same time, instils a sense of awe and fear. In verse 10, her earthly beauty is so awe-inspiring that it even surpasses the majestic heavenly hosts.

In chapter 7, the man continues to describe the maiden. Starting from her feet, he is mesmerised by her dainty feet in sandals which enhance their erotic beauty. He ends with her long flowing tresses which can entrap even kings (verse 5). She is, in every sense of the word, 'queenly' (verse 1). She is poetry in motion.

There is nothing wrong in praising physical beauty. Beauty and sexuality are not taboo in God's eyes. It is we humans who make things taboo. Humans are not mere souls encased in a physical body. We are total human beings with feelings – a sense of touch, a nose for scents, an eye for beauty, an ear for praises and a heart of emotions. We are beings capable of love and being loved in return.

† Lord, help us not to frown upon human sexuality but to learn to embrace and experience it with joy and thanksgiving as God's gift to humans. Amen

For further thought

'God saw everything that he had made, and indeed, it was very good' (Genesis 1:31).

Saturday 15 February
Strong as death

Read Song of Solomon 8

Set me as a seal upon your heart; as a seal upon your arm; for love is strong as death, passion fierce as the grave.

(verse 6)

The last chapter of the book contains some of the most sublime verses on love. Many wedding sermons have been preached based on verses 6–7. The maiden desires to be set as a seal upon the man's heart as a sign of possession. Just like death, which is an irresistible force, love is equally strong and passionately fierce as the grave. Love can consume and burn if not controlled. It is a most powerful flame where many waters cannot quench it. Unlike normal fire, the flames of love cannot be easily extinguished. If it can be easily put out, then it is really not love. In the movie *Indecent Proposal,* the billionaire John Gage, played by Robert Redford, offers a bankrupt couple a million dollars to spend one-night with the wife. Can one put a price tag on love? Is a one-night stand worth a million dollars? Money may be able to buy many things but it cannot buy love, for love is priceless.

In Song of Solomon chapter 8, the brothers act like chaperones on the maiden's behalf. They become over-protective of her budding sexuality by insisting that she remains chaste. The maiden affirms that she has the right to choose whom she loves. Her vineyard, or her body, is her very own. Verses 11–12 serve as a rebuke to any 'Solomon' who thinks they can take by force and impose love upon others. The woman's body is hers to keep and hers to give alone. If we love someone, then 'true love waits'.

† Lord, help us to truly understand more of love so that we can love more and more fully. In Jesus' name, Amen.

For further thought
True love is possessive in not letting go of the other, persevering in that it does not die out easily, and priceless in that it can never be bought and sold.

1 and 2 Peter – 1 Strangers in the world

Notes by **Catrin Harland-Davies**

Catrin is Methodist co-director of the Centre for Continuing Development in Ministry, at the Queen's Foundation in Birmingham, where she works with those in training for, or newly embarked on, ordained ministry, as well as ministers who want to develop their professional expertise. She was previously Methodist chaplain at the University of Sheffield. She is a New Testament scholar, with a particular interest in the life and leadership of the early Church. Catrin has used the NRSVA for these notes.

Sunday 16 February
When the world turns against you

Read 1 Peter 1:1–16

In this you rejoice, even if now for a little while you have had to suffer various trials, so that the genuineness of your faith – being more precious than gold that, though perishable, is tested by fire – may be found to result in praise and glory and honour when Jesus Christ is revealed.

(verses 6–7)

'I'm sorry that you're suffering, but take comfort in the knowledge that it's all part of God's plan.' Words like these too often cause real pain, when spoken to someone who is grieving, dealing with serious illness or finding life unbearably difficult. They risk belittling their suffering, or presenting it as somehow imposed by God. On the other hand, many do find it a comforting idea that, in some way they can't currently understand, God is still in control and all will ultimately turn out for good.

The book of 1 Peter is written to various Christian communities in Asia Minor, who really knew the meaning of suffering, never sure when popular hatred or official persecution might erupt.

The letter encourages them to be glad of their suffering, because it tests, proves and refines their faith. I wonder how I would have reacted to such encouragement; would it be a profound reminder that I didn't suffer in vain, or an insult added to injury? Persecution isn't purely a historical thing. Still today, around the world, people lose life, freedom or property because of who they are or what they believe. Our response, in supporting victims sensitively, and challenging injustice robustly, really matters!

† Pray for all who suffer, especially those who suffer persecution because of who they are or what they believe. Pray for justice, compassion and grace.

Monday 17 February
God's people abroad

Read 1 Peter 1:22–2:10

But you are a chosen race, a royal priesthood, a holy nation, God's own people, in order that you may proclaim the mighty acts of him who called you out of darkness into his marvellous light. Once you were not a people, but now you are God's people.

(verses 9–10a)

Yorkshire Tea, Marmite, Cadbury's chocolate and streaky bacon. If you visit a British friend living abroad, these are the foodstuffs you are most likely to be asked to bring. There are even websites that cater for these very British cravings. During my years working with international students in Sheffield, it was noticeable that there was a real appetite for food, clothes, traditions and language that reminded them of home. It's not just nostalgia or homesickness, but something fundamental about identity. Of course, we want to adjust to a new culture when we move, but we don't want to lose our sense of who we really are.

If this is a normal human need, perhaps it's even more true for a community that is suffering, and that feels as though it doesn't belong within wider society. It becomes even more important for a persecuted group to have pride in its identity.

From the very opening of this letter, the Christians it is written to are referred to as foreigners. This isn't literally true, but they are religious outsiders as Christians in a hostile environment, and as gentiles in a faith emerging from Judaism. They are, in a sense, citizens of heaven living as expats on earth.

As gentiles, they were not part of God's chosen nation. But although they have set themselves outside the religious culture of their communities, they have the most glorious identity of all as God's people, to come before him in priestly worship, serving as his ambassadors in the world!

† Loving God, your Son was the stone the builders rejected; make us into living stones. With Christ as our cornerstone, build us into a temple, inviting all the world to join us in worshipping you.

For further thought

How does being a citizen of heaven shape your relationship with the world? Are you set apart and separated, or more closely committed and involved?

Tuesday 18 February
The law of the land, the Law of God

Society functions because we agree a set of laws, and live by them. That's one understanding of the basis of community life. And it's usually accepted that this applies equally to those who move into a society; they agree to live by the norms and rules of their adoptive home. They will, however, also bring with them some different perspectives and cultural assumptions, which can enrich and broaden the life of the host community.

All of that is true for the Christian communities in Asia Minor who received this letter. They are called 'foreigners', living away from their heavenly homeland, and that identity is empowering and sustaining. But they are not to detach themselves from the society in which they live. Nor are they to consider themselves above the law. They are to honour the emperor and governors, and to seek to live good, law-abiding lives.

But this raises some complicated ethical questions. Presumably, their obedience to the law only goes so far. What if their very identity as Christians – their worship of God and their denial of the gods of Greek and Roman religion – is deemed illegal? And what are we to do with the call to slaves and wives to submit? We might argue that this is simply practical advice to those who are in positions of powerlessness. If you can't overturn the structures of society, how do you still find a way to witness? But we might also feel uncomfortable about the lack of challenge. When does obedience to the law of the land become disobedience to the Law of God?

† Pray for your elected leaders, local and national; for those charged with upholding the law; for all who are in positions of powerlessness in your society, especially those who don't have political power or franchise.

For further thought

What would drive you to disobey the law? How can you challenge unjust systems legally, and when would that make you complicit in the injustice?

Wednesday 19 February
(Not) getting thrown to the lions: a survival guide

Read 1 Peter 3:8–22

Always be ready to make your defence to anyone who demands from you an account of the hope that is in you; yet do it with gentleness and reverence.

(verses 15–16a)

A popular challenge, associated with roadside church signs, asks, 'If you were charged with being a Christian, would there be enough evidence to convict you?' This hypothetical scenario requires some clarification: is it Christian belief or practice that is supposed to be illegal? What would demonstrate genuine Christian faith? But for the communities addressed by 1 Peter, this was no rhetorical question.

The letter offers them some advice. It suggests that they can make life easier by refraining from behaviour which is inherently deserving of punishment. If they are to suffer, let it be righteously, following in Jesus' footsteps. Why give their accusers greater ammunition? It must presumably be harder to convict someone whose faith clearly leads them to do good, not evil. And besides, if people like you, they're less likely to bring charges against you!

But there's more to it than this. The call to righteousness is not primarily about reducing persecution and saving their own skins, but about showing a different quality of life, which will make people notice and wonder, and ask, 'What makes you different? How can you be so loving in the face of such hatred?'

Most of us know people who seem so filled with the love and joy of God that it radiates from them, or who work tirelessly and selflessly for the kingdom, often in unglamorous ways, receiving very little reward. Such people would find it almost impossible to deny their faith; against them, the evidence would be overwhelming. From the hope that is in them, maybe, we have most to learn?

† Loving God, fill me with faith in your love, confidence in your grace and joy in your salvation. Give me the courage of my conviction, that I may be your faithful witness.

For further thought

If someone wanted an account of the hope that is in you – if they wanted to know why you believe – how would you answer?

Thursday 20 February
Covering a multitude of sins

Read 1 Peter 4:1–11

Whoever speaks must do so as one speaking the very words of God; whoever serves must do so with the strength that God supplies, so that God may be glorified in all things through Jesus Christ. To him belong the glory and the power for ever and ever. Amen.

(verse 11)

When I was a university chaplain, I used occasionally to meet students who were exploring Christianity and who wanted answers to their questions. Among the regular queries, one stood out: what constitutes sin, and what are the consequences of sinning? What am I allowed to do?

Defining sin, and identifying sinful acts, has been an ongoing struggle for the church. Perhaps the first readers of this letter, relatively new to this emerging religion, wondered this, too. They knew that certain kinds of behaviour would be wrong, including those associated with the festivals of their former 'gods'. But what should they be aiming for?

It is very tempting to produce lists of good and bad behaviours. We like clarity and precision in our codes of conduct. It feels unfair to be held to account if we don't know exactly what's expected of us. The mark of an unreasonable legal system is one in which no one knows what the laws require or what the penalty might be.

But this passage doesn't deal in the specifics. Some broad guidelines are summarised, in verse 7 onwards, by the call to be serious and disciplined in prayer, to love and care for one another and to use their gifts for the glory of God. This may be disconcertingly imprecise. But it is also, surely, very liberating! We are not judged against an ethical tick-list, but called to respond to God's love by loving God and our neighbour.

If we can build that kind of love, the details will fall into place, because 'love covers a multitude of sins' (verse 8).

† Loving God, you call us to love. Help us to be more concerned with love of you and of others than with our own salvation, in faith that, in your love, our salvation is secure.

For further thought

Think about the teachings of Jesus. Does he provide any helpful lists of behaviour, or general principles, to teach us how to live?

Friday 21 February
When duty calls, or danger ...

Read 1 Peter 4:12–19

Beloved, do not be surprised at the fiery ordeal that is taking place among you to test you, as though something strange were happening to you. But rejoice in so far as you are sharing Christ's sufferings, so that you may also be glad and shout for joy when his glory is revealed.

(verses 12–13)

'Costly grace ... is costly because it costs a man his life, and it is grace because it gives a man the only true life. It is costly because it condemns sin, and grace because it justifies the sinner. Above all, it is costly because it cost God the life of his Son: "ye were bought at a price," and what has cost God much cannot be cheap for us. Above all, it is grace because God did not reckon his Son too dear a price to pay for our life, but delivered him up for us. Costly grace is the Incarnation of God.'

(Bonhoeffer, *The Cost of Discipleship*)

Dietrich Bonhoeffer was executed in Germany, in 1945, for his opposition to the Nazi regime. He was painfully aware that grace, which he saw being offered cheaply, was in fact immensely costly, because it cost Christ and demands a cost of us, too.

Today's passage speaks of a profound and shocking anguish, arising in reaction to the churches' faith. History is littered with people whose commitment to Christ, love, justice and peace has led them into suffering. Standing against oppressive regimes, joining our voices to those that have been marginalised, speaking out against environmental irresponsibility and speaking difficult truths to power are all potentially dangerous activities. At times, they can cause us to be disliked or ridiculed. In extremes, they can lead to imprisonment, humiliation or death.

And yet, in this 'fiery ordeal' (verse 12) stands Christ, who knew all too well the cost, but whose love for us carried him, and carries us, safely home to God.

† Christ, unjustly tortured and killed, strengthen and bless all who suffer and die because of their commitment to justice, peace and love, and their faithfulness to your name.

For further thought
How might you support those who are persecuted for their faith, political beliefs or identity? Amnesty International may provide ideas and ways of getting involved.

Saturday 22 February
Belonging to the communion of saints

Read 1 Peter 5:1–13

[Be] steadfast in your faith, for you know that your brothers and sisters throughout the world are undergoing the same kinds of suffering.

Through Silvanus, whom I consider a faithful brother, I have written this short letter to encourage you, and to testify that this is the true grace of God.

(verses 9, 12)

1 Peter opens by addressing the recipients as 'the chosen ones, exiles of the diaspora' (1:1, my translation). 'Diaspora' is a powerful concept, asserting a shared identity for a scattered people. I grew up as part of a Welsh diaspora, taught to be proud of my inherited language and culture, belonging to a place where I'd never lived. Similarly, I have friends who describe themselves as part of an African, Jewish or Sheffield diaspora. It speaks of a profound unity, even among those whose lives, culture or mother tongue may be very different.

If, then, Christians should see themselves as part of a heavenly diaspora, it is no surprise that a theme of the closing chapter is solidarity, even among worshippers who have never met and who have little but their faith in common. They have a shared experience of belonging to Christ, and all too often of suffering for that belonging. The writer speaks to the elders, or leaders, of the churches, pointing out that he too is an elder, sharing in the Christlike work of shepherding the flock. He closes by passing on the greetings of the church in 'Babylon' (probably code for Rome) and of Mark, presumably known to them. And he describes his relationship with both Silvanus and Mark in family terms – 'a faithful brother' (verse 12) and 'my son' (verse 13).

All of this reflects a profound sense of interconnectedness and relatedness. In the struggles and joys of our faith, our brothers and sisters in Christ – at home, around the world and throughout history – may be one of God's greatest gifts to us.

† Pray for the Church around the world, and give thanks for the richness brought by each tradition, culture and language. Give thanks, too, for the riches of faith inherited from those who have gone before.

For further thought

Perhaps you could choose a part of the world that you don't know well, and try to learn something about the Christian church there?

1 and 2 Peter – 2 God's provision

Notes by **Catrin Harland-Davies**

 For Catrin's bio, see p. 48. Catrin has used the NRSVA for these notes.

Sunday 23 February
Living memory for a living faith

> **Read 2 Peter 1**
>
> *I think it right, as long as I am in this body, to refresh your memory, since I know that my death will come soon … And I will make every effort so that after my departure you may be able at any time to recall these things.*
>
> (verses 13–14a, 15)

Like many people, I have become interested in delving a little into my family history. I have not taken the trouble to trawl archives and cemeteries, nor have I joined the growing number of people receiving a home DNA testing kit for Christmas. But I have spent some time browsing census returns and birth records, trying to piece together my ancestors' lives. I've found some facts that sound tantalisingly as though they represent an interesting story – there are emigrants to Pennsylvania; a foremother whose third husband was only two years older than her son; the warden of a military prison …

But without memories, these remain simply dates, names and places. My parents can flesh out the stories of some more recent forebears, but it is hard to bring to life those who have faded from living family memory.

Today's passage places a high value on eyewitness testimony and the memory of a generation, which was fast dying out at the time the letter was written. It encourages the readers in their faith, and reminds them that this faith is based not on fancy or fiction, but on shared memory, lived experience, and stories passed from one generation to another.

I may never really know about the lives and personalities of my great-great-great-grandparents. But I can know Jesus, not as a series of dates and facts, but as one brought to life in the testimony of scripture, especially the Gospels.

† Thank you for those who have gone before us and shared with us their knowledge of Christ, so that we, too, may know him.

Monday 24 February
A warning from history

Read 2 Peter 2

But false prophets also arose among the people, just as there will be false teachers among you, who will secretly bring in destructive opinions. They will even deny the Master who bought them – bringing swift destruction on themselves.

(verse 1)

'Those who cannot remember the past are condemned to repeat it.' This was declared by George Santayana in *The Life of Reason.* And perhaps the writer of this letter would agree, as he tells stories of false prophets and disobedient angels, to remind his readers of the certainty of judgement. But in amongst these stories are reminders of God's grace and faithfulness towards Lot and Noah. Just as God's justice is sure, so is God's mercy.

None of this is history for history's sake. The readers are supposed to take warning. False teachers, they are told, are present now as much as then. And the same message is true for us. The truth is a fragile thing and needs to be constantly defended. But the truth is also not always easy to determine. How do we know who speaks prophetic truth and who speaks falsehood? How do we test the truth of what is spoken?

Of course, this matters. It matters because we need to base our faith and our lives on truth and not on lies. It matters, too, because part of the prophetic task of the church, surely, is to speak truth in a world in which 'fake news' feels so prevalent. And it matters because we need to speak difficult truths to power.

But the fact that it matters still does not mean that we can always be sure. So we need confidence in the truth, coupled with humility to recognise that occasionally we, too, may be the false teachers. This is a difficult, but important, balance to hold!

† God of truth, give us wisdom to discern truth from falsehood, courage to challenge the falsehood, grace to celebrate the truth, and humility to know when we've got it wrong.

For further thought

Discerning together what is true, and where we may have got it wrong, is a vital task for the church. How do we go about it?

Tuesday 25 February
Judgement, justice, mercy and grace

Read 2 Peter 3

With the Lord one day is like a thousand years, and a thousand years are like one day. The Lord is not slow about his promise, as some think of slowness, but is patient with you, not wanting any to perish, but all to come to repentance.

(verses 8b–9)

Having been reflecting on the past, the writer of 2 Peter now turns his attention to the future. There are warnings and promises about judgement and the end of time.

Judgement is a difficult topic for many Christians, as it sounds threatening and unfriendly. We prefer to think about mercy and grace. But judgement is fundamentally about the bringing about of justice. For those, like much of the early church, who are persecuted for their faith, judgement is about vindication. If we want to bring about justice for those who have suffered abuse or pain at the hands of others, that implies judgement. If God is a God of justice, then God is also a God of judgement.

And without judgement there can be no mercy or grace. Grace is not about turning a blind eye, but about acknowledging the full reality of human brokenness and yet still loving us enough to die for us. Judgement, and the grace which follows, is the means by which damaged relationships can be restored, with God and with one another. The promise of judgement is a promise that all can be put right.

Perhaps, though, the difficult part is the lack of control. We are promised a judgement which will be on God's terms and in God's time. That should be a relief, but can be hard. That we can allow God, whose justice and mercy are perfect, to take control of our future is an act of faith, but it is faith in God's infinite love, and what could be surer than that?

† Pray for those who long for justice and are the victims of unjust systems. Pray for those who cannot forgive – especially those who cannot forgive themselves. And pray for grace to forgive and be forgiven.

For further thought
What does the idea of 'judgement' mean to you? What will the 'day of judgement' (verse 7) actually mean, do you think?

The responsibilities we share – 1 Fresh start

Notes by **Lynne Frith**

Lynne loves playing with words – whether writing poems and prayers or playing Scrabble. She is looking forward to retirement in 2020 from ministry as a Methodist Presbyter in Auckland, Aotearoa (New Zealand), where she is privileged to serve with an inclusive, welcoming congregation. Lynne has used the NRSVA for these notes.

Wednesday 26 February (Ash Wednesday)
Power's allure

Read Matthew 4:1–11

Then the devil left him, and suddenly angels came and waited on him.

(verse 11)

During my first ministry appointment, I attended a national churchwomen's gathering. The keynote speaker was a woman minister from another country. What she had to say about power and status, at a time when women in many denominations were struggling to have their gifts recognised, has guided me throughout my ministry. She had been asked to accept nomination for a significant leadership position in her denomination. In her process of discernment, she became aware of how the knowledge, power and status that the position would confer were very seductive, and that there were insufficient other reasons for accepting nomination. Her challenge was to always examine ourselves for the level of attraction to the power and knowledge in a particular role, and not allow that to be our reason for accepting leadership. Rather, she encouraged us to be driven by the avenues of service that a role might offer.

Most human beings are subject to the temptations of knowledge, power and status. Today, Ash Wednesday, I invite you to reflect on the temptations associated with the roles you hold in your church.

† Pray for the self-awareness to discern when the power and status of a role you hold have become more important than the role itself, and for the strength to take the appropriate action.

Thursday 27 February
A clean heart

> **Read Psalm 51:1–12**
>
> *Create in me a clean heart, O God, and put a new and right spirit within me.*
>
> (verse 10)

I imagine that a cardiologist might say that a clean heart is one in which the muscle works strongly and rhythmically, there is no build-up of deposits in the blood vessels, and valves open and close efficiently.

There is plenty of advice available to us about how to maintain a healthy heart – much to do with diet, exercise and attitude. Equally, there is a great deal of advice about both how to recognise the signs of a heart in trouble and how to render assistance to a person having a heart attack.

We might be less aware of when our emotional or spiritual 'heart' is in trouble and have even less knowledge about how to remedy the situation.

On the other hand, like the psalmist, we might be aware that something needs to change, and plead for God's mercy. When we acknowledge that we need help, we are taking the first steps towards transformation.

In this twenty-first-century world, it is all too easy to be ensnared by the relentless cycles of busyness, to feel unable to take a holiday or even a short break.

Lent is a good time to refocus on or take the opportunity to acquire new spiritual practices such as meditation or contemplative prayer. In the southern hemisphere, where the Lenten season coincides with autumn, it is a time to reflect on what needs to fall to the ground to make room for new growth. In the northern hemisphere, where spring is making an appearance, the reflection may be on what buds are breaking open with a burst of new life.

† Pray for retreat leaders, spiritual directors and others who provide guidance for those seeking a clean heart.

For further thought

Find out about the retreats available in your community and, if possible, attend one that uses different meditation or spiritual practices from those you would usually use.

Friday 28 February
Turn to the Lord

Read Hosea 6:1–6

For I desire steadfast love and not sacrifice, the knowledge of God rather than burnt-offerings.

(verse 6)

It sounds so easy. If we return to God, then God will do the rest. Nothing is more certain than that God will heal, revive and refresh us. Or so say the voices in verses 1–3. There's no acknowledgement of what has gone before, what paths the people had taken, what other gods they had followed, nor any indication of what change has motivated the return.

But God responds with despair, reflecting that the love of the people of Ephraim and Judah is transitory, like the morning dew. What God longs for is not mere fulfilment of the rituals, but a change of heart, mind and way of living that is trustworthy and reliable, whatever the circumstances.

I have lost count of how many church meetings I have attended at which people are searching for remedies for what they perceive as the problem of being a small congregation. If we sing different songs, paint the doors a bright colour, install more technology, use social media to promote ourselves, or … the list goes on.

Less attractive, and more challenging, is the encouragement to be steadfast, to be thankful for the committed people who are there and to get on with the work of justice, compassion, peace and loving that is so desperately needed in our communities and our world. Our church buildings, our choirs, our liturgies and our institutional regulations are not an end in themselves, but rather the means by which God's steadfast people are nurtured and strengthened, have their lives transformed, in order to be fully present in the world.

† Pray for those who are seeking to renew their relationship with God.

For further thought

What does steadfast love look like, and whom do you know who exemplifies it in your community? How might you encourage and strengthen each other?

Saturday 29 February
Choose life

Read Deuteronomy 30:15–20

See, I have set before you today life and prosperity, death and adversity.

(verse 15)

In my childhood, we were each encouraged to make a sacrifice, to give up something, for Lent. Most often, it was by putting a portion of our weekly pocket money into the Lenten Appeal for the Leprosy Mission or something similar.

Our healthy diets did not leave much room for giving up a food item, although I do recall my father giving up sugar in his tea.

The reasons for this 'giving up something for Lent' were loosely described as helping us understand what it was like for Jesus in the wilderness. I do not remember any teaching about spiritual disciplines.

In my adult years, I have applied a variety of spiritual practices in Lent in addition to the traditional disciplines of contemplation and almsgiving.

Sometimes, rather than giving up chocolate, or social media, or going to the movies, I have added something in – something that is life giving and renewing, either for myself or for others.

It may be putting aside one item each day in a box for a local charity shop.

It may be going for a walk in a park or green space each day.

It may be listening to a piece of beautiful music each evening.

It includes setting aside a grocery item every day in Lent for our church's food pantry collection.

It is all about choosing life, whatever our personal circumstances. It is not quite as simple as always looking on the bright side of life, but rather about making choices that are life giving, for ourselves, for our family, for our community.

† Give thanks for all that is life-giving for you.

For further thought

Consider what might be life giving for yourself or others, and resolve to carry out one such practice or discipline daily throughout Lent.

The responsibilities we share – 2 Living planet

Notes by **Terry Lester**

Terry has been an Anglican priest in the Diocese of Cape Town, South Africa, for more than three decades. Widowed after more than thirty years of marriage, he has three adult children and a granddaughter. He ministers in Constantia, and is involved in a Heritage and Education community project, which seeks to preserve the stories of those removed from their former homes along the foot of Table Mountain and were settled in the flat plains of the Cape Peninsula. Terry has used the NRSVA for these notes.

Sunday 1 March
Look at the heavens!

Read Psalm 8

What are human beings that you are mindful of them, mortals that you care for them? You have made them a little lower than God, and crowned them with glory and honour.

(verses 4–5)

The psalmist announces with such conviction and without any ambivalence that the place humans occupy in relation to God their creator is that they are 'a little less than' or, put differently, slightly behind. Our place is less than a half-step behind God! Why then do we spend so much energy jostling to get a nose ahead of each other? Is it not pointless to consider yourself more than another?

This putting down of others happened in my country when we were divided on race. It was the case too when the world was divided between communist East and capitalist West and when Christians were pitted against socialist and atheistic state religion.

I once heard Archbishop Desmond Tutu tell a story that cut across the rhetoric people tended to use to put each other down. At a conference on religion and the state, the archbishop intoned, a brilliant Soviet professor spoke with great erudition and eloquence, setting out all the reasons why he did not believe in God. To which an old priest gently but firmly replied to the learned professor, 'That's OK. Because God believes in you!'

We have no reason to consider anyone or ourselves insignificant or inconsequential for we are created 'a little less' than God!

† Holy, Creator God, what a wonderful comfort knowing that you see us even with just the slightest glance over your shoulder for we are that close behind you! Thank you! Amen

Monday 2 March
Rejoicing in the world

Read Proverbs 8:22–31

The Lord created me at the beginning of his work, the first of his acts long ago. Ages ago I was set up, at the first, before the beginning of the earth.

(verses 22–23)

The book of Proverbs is considered part of Wisdom literature and, in an earlier chapter (3:19), speaks of Yahweh as founding the earth by wisdom. Chapter 8 goes further by personifying wisdom as an entity created before the world and then assisting in God's creative work. Like Adam in Genesis, who gave names to what God created, so Wisdom played a role in putting the world together – not as initiator, but vital for the created order as we know it. The one (God) existed before the other (wisdom or Adam) and created the other but together, as a collaboration and partnership, they are responsible for everything!

Visitors to Cape Town, the city of my birth, are usually bowled over by the sheer natural beauty which frames this city. To the north, the Atlantic Ocean is like a huge basin with Robben Island squatting in the middle of it, and to the south, overlooking the city bowl, Table Mountain, flanked by Devil's Peak and Lion's Head, broods over the city like a gigantic mother hen. On certain days though, a 'tablecloth' of low cloud comes in off the ocean and obscures the mountain, like a magician, disappearing it! For that brief duration Capetonians imagine the city without the mountain … but not for long because, in truth, the one without the other is unimaginable.

† Lord our Creator, we praise you for the beauty of the earth and the wonder of inviting us to be collaborators in its care and preservation. Amen

For further thought
Find one thing you can do and do it so that, in this way, you are working alongside God as carer and preserver of your environment.

Tuesday 3 March
Where were we?

Read Job 38:1–9

Then the Lord answered Job out of the whirlwind: 'Who is this that darkens counsel by words without knowledge?'

(verses 1–2)

After everyone had spoken and after a very long silence, God speaks! Various friends had tried to make sense of the madness and mindlessness of the losses and suffering Job and his family had to endure, but none of it fully satisfactorily. Wisdom writing begins and ends with God, like bookends which hold everything together. It invites the reader to embrace God's action in our lives from beginning to end even in seeming silence – God is present.

In the book *One Flew Over the Cuckoo's Nest*, Chief Bromden, a patient in a psychiatric institution, at first is a mere silent observer despite being the narrator! Late in the movie, when Randle McMurphy offers him chewing gum, he speaks. The chief then says: 'I been silent so long now it's gonna roar out of me like floodwaters and you think the guy telling this is ranting and raving my *God*, you think this is too horrible to have really happened, this is too awful to be the truth!'[2]

This chapter in Job is like God letting the floodgates open for God has stood by for too long. Satan has contended that people serve God only out of fear or for what they can gain. Job has shown that people worship God because God is God. They may not have seen God working from the beginning, nor always understood, nor known why things happen the way they happen, but God does and nothing happens without God knowing.

† Speak Lord, your servant is listening, whether in the long silence or in the noisy and bustling world, help me hear you. Amen

For further thought

Silence is a language with God; being silent with oneself or silent communally is a wonderful way of learning to hear God speak. Try it!

---

2 Kesey, K. (1962), *One Flew Over the Cuckoo's Nest* (New York: Viking Press/Signet Books).

Wednesday 4 March
The Word and the world

Read John 1:1–5

He was in the beginning with God.

(verse 2)

This passage forms part of the Christmas Day gospel and speaks of the light and life force of God breaking into our human story and into our world which God loves, not only shattering the darkness forever, but also exposing our preferences. 'Heaven wedded to earth' is how it has been described. God spoke the Word in the beginning and brought all things into being. This is John's version of the birth narratives. Whereas Matthew and Luke speak of a small happening in an insignificant town which grows inch by inch, reshaping the landscape into God's kingdom – like a mustard seed – in John, God crashes into the world and re-begins it. The result is a complete re-creation and reforming of the created order. There is a suggestion in the passage that we should not so much be looking up for guidance and direction, but rather, we are invited to look around us, at human beings in whom the Word becomes flesh and re-begins us and those around us. Human net worth is not determined by what they own or possess, but rather, humanity's intrinsic net worth is predicated on the fact that God has taken on flesh in Christ, thereby raising humanity's value and worth once and for all and forever.

† Loving God and Father, help me to recognise you in those around me and enable me to receive your Son, Jesus, as God's love and life coming to your own people. Amen

For further thought

Note how often we recoil when reading or hearing about a dastardly or cruel deed committed by humans on humans and then remind yourself that God embraces our humanity in all our weakness and sinfulness.

The responsibilities we share – 2 Living planet

March

Thursday 5 March
God's care for the world

Read Luke 12:22–31

Consider the ravens: they neither sow nor reap, they have neither storehouse nor barn, and yet God feeds them.

(verse 24a)

We have many water masses around the flat Cape Peninsula where weaverbirds proliferate. Watching weaverbirds build their nests is both fascinating and hilarious. The male prepares the nest with meticulous industriousness, carrying grasses often from some distance, flapping up and down while weaving the grasses with his beak into an impressive home. The rounded nest, woven tightly onto an overhanging willow branch with an inlet pointing down to the water, bounces rhythmically as he tugs and pulls. Once done, a neat chamber holds the eggs secure and is safe enough when the chicks hatch so that they don't accidentally fall out of the nest and into the water!

But no matter how hard he has worked or how secure and neat it all looks to the untrained eye of an admiring human, if the female is not satisfied, she rejects the nest and he is forced to start all over again on another branch! Perfecting the art of the weave for which the female serves as the quality controller is no doubt the reason the weaverbird has not joined the long list of the extinct. This passage is not an invitation to sit on one's laurels and let God do the work, rather it is an invitation to use our God-given agency to build a perfect world for God.

† Teach me, O Lord, to find the energy and grace You provide, for me to be and do the best I can be and do. Amen

For further thought

Our passage is not about glorifying how little we need to do but rather how wonderfully God has equipped creation to provide for its needs. List ways that you use what you have been equipped with to assist others.

Friday 6 March
Our care for the world

Read Genesis 1:26–31

Then God said, 'Let us make humankind in our image, according to our likeness'

(verse 26a)

The flood plains of the Tigris and the Euphrates are fertile, rich in nutrients and served as the food basket for the Babylonian Empire. The Israelites were settled here after the destruction of Jerusalem. These plains were a far cry from the harsh desert environment of Judah but even here there were challenges. It served as a daily reminder to the Israelites of how they had lost their land because of their forebears' hardness of heart. Each passing day made them ask themselves if they would ever again regain their favoured place with God. In exile, their life as a nation had become like a 'formless void', and with the periodic flooding of the plains and 'darkness covering the face of the deep', it was also a constant struggle for meaning. How would they reorient their life again and reconnect with God and with each other?

These questions about meaning are dressed up as the 'creation story' in Genesis which builds to a climax with God making humans in God's image and then resting after, seeing that it was 'very good'. Rediscovering humanity's place in God's heart and in relation to the created order begins with hearing afresh the special care God put into making humanity. The call to rest in the goodness of it all is to live in right relationship with all.

† Lord God our Creator, may we know the unique place we occupy in creation and help us overcome the stifling darkness and chaos which often make us forget. Amen

For further thought
The lives of so many people are characterised by constant chaos to the point where it has become the new normal. Find an organisation or family where this is the case and offer them friendship and support.

Saturday 7 March
What a wonderful world!

Read Psalm 104:1–13

You make springs gush forth in the valleys; they flow between the hills, giving drink to every wild animal; the wild asses quench their thirst.

(verses 10–11)

The Creator's deeds of provision and care are described with poetic and rhythmic eloquence. God the Creator is not only at work in the natural order that surrounds us but God is also at home in creation, like a king in a palace! The wonderful world in which we are privileged to live and move and have our being is holy ground, we share it with the Creator and our response to it ought to be not only one of reverence and awe but also of fascination and wonder. Living where I do at the foot of the Constantiaberg Mountain, it is a common sight seeing streams gushing down after a heavy winter downpour and cascading into the ravines which are carved into the Table Mountain sandstone. As the streams meet in the deep crevasses, they swell and strengthen till they form life-giving rivers and water masses which sustain a variety of flora and fauna on the sandy plains of the peninsula. During a recent drought, people have been known to queue for hours at the various freshwater springs which are dotted along the mountain. Were it not for these life-giving streams, our situation could have turned dire and nasty as people jostled for this precious and naturally occurring resource. It has taken a crippling drought to make us realise some truths about our wonderful world here at the tip of Africa.

† Lord God, Your word describes justice as an ever-flowing stream. Quench the thirst many have for justice that it may refresh the hope and peace which many long to taste – in our lifetime. Amen

For further thought

Water justice is receiving more and more attention as an area of great disparity and injustice in our world. How does it impact you and how are you contributing to this?

The responsibilities we share – 3 Building a community

Notes by the **Rt Revd Dr Peter Langerman**

Peter is a pastor in a Presbyterian Church in Durbanville, Cape Town and he is the Moderator of the General Assembly of the Uniting Presbyterian Church of South Africa. He is married to Sally and they have four daughters. Peter is passionate about the dynamic rule and reign of God. He believes that God invites all to be part of God's transformative mission through love, and that the most potent and powerful agent for the transformation of local communities is the local church living out faithfulness to God. Peter has used the NIVUK for these notes.

Sunday 8 March
Love your enemies

Read Exodus 23:1–11

'For six years you are to sow your fields and harvest the crops, but during the seventh year let the land lie unploughed and unused. Then the poor among your people may get food from it, and the wild animals may eat what is left. Do the same with your vineyard and your olive grove.'

(verses 10–11)

The people of Israel did not have a fixed identity when they came out of Egypt. God knew that it would take some specific laws to shape them into a community. Central to many of the laws that God gave them was the reminder that they were once slaves and dependent upon others and that, therefore, they should always bear in mind those who were dependent upon them. Hence whenever they would plant and harvest, they should always think not only of themselves, but also of the poor and destitute among them.

In our dog-eat-dog world, where profit maximisation and exploitation of the poor are part of our lives, one wonders how modern people might respond to the implementation of such a law today. It would, I imagine, be met with derision and disbelief, and be ignored or circumvented wherever and whenever possible. As people of faith, how might we show compassion for those who are poor among us without being patronising and without enabling those with addiction issues? Such are the questions we face, and there are no easy answers.

† In the course of this week, ask God to make you aware and conscious of those around you whom you might be able to help in practical ways without being patronising or enabling.

Monday 9 March
Be open-handed and generous

Read Deuteronomy 15:1–11
However, there need be no poor people among you, for in the land the Lord your God is giving you to possess as your inheritance, he will richly bless you ... There will always be poor people in the land.

(verses 4 and 11)

God's desire that there should be an end to poverty is to be balanced with the reality that the poor will always be with us. The solution to poverty is both obvious and complex: those who have more than they need should share with those who have less. If we lived this way, then there would be no more poverty.

Recently I spent almost three weeks visiting churches and communities in and around Johannesburg. The contrasts were stark and shocking. In some areas people live in informal housing, made from corrugated iron, wood and plastic, squashed together with barely a gap between the houses, at the mercy of the elements. In other areas, not far away from these, single families live in palatial houses with lavish gardens and swimming pools. The differences between abject poverty and opulent wealth seem obvious. What is hidden is that in some of those informal areas, people are careful with what little money they have and share easily what they have with their neighbours. On the other hand, in some of the richer neighbourhoods, people are estranged from the neighbours and so indebted they can hardly breathe.

God's desire is that people should have enough for what they need, and God is against both rampant greed and debilitating poverty. The solution lies in the text – cancelling debt and generous sharing will ensure that there is space for everyone to survive. As people of faith, this is a great challenge to us all as we seek to live out our faith faithfully and responsibly.

† As you move around today, be aware of the differences between the haves and have-nots. Pray about what it means for you to share what you have.

For further thought
If you have debt in your life, consider reducing your debt and share the saving with others.

Don't exploit others

Read Deuteronomy 24:10–18

Pay them their wages each day before sunset, because they are poor and are counting on it. Otherwise they may cry to the Lord against you, and you will be guilty of sin.

(verse 15)

Many of us have the privilege of employing others. Some of us have people who work for small or medium entities that we own or manage, or we are in management at a multinational company that employs large numbers of people. Some of us are fortunate enough to be able to have people who assist us, either part-time or full-time in our homes: people who clean our homes or look after our children or keep our gardens looking beautiful.

Whether we employ someone in our home, or we are responsible for the employment of people at work, such a relationship places upon us a responsibility. We have the responsibility to make sure that we pay people a fair and just wage for the work they do. But this passage places upon us a further obligation to ensure that people are paid on time and in full.

The relationship between employer and employee is often a complicated legal entanglement, but what we fail to recognise is that it is a relationship in which both parties owe one another something. This passage emphasises the responsibility of the employer not to take the worker for granted and not to deprive him/her of the wages that are owed. There is also the injunction to prevent workers from incurring excessive debt – a healthy corrective in this society where unscrupulous lenders tie heavy burdens around the necks of the poor.

† Pray for the people who earn very little. Are they paid what is due to them on time? Bring them in prayer before God and ask what you might do to help them.

For further thought

How might you be instrumental in helping to ensure that people are paid what is fair, just and equitable?

March

The responsibilities we share – 3 Building a community

Wednesday 11 March
Don't take interest on loans

Read Nehemiah 5:1–13

So, I continued, 'What you are doing is not right. … But let us stop charging interest!'

(verses 9a and 10b)

I was in the bank this week negotiating a student loan for one of my daughters and was looking at the interest being charged by this particular bank for the loans they made to their clients. I wondered how the manager might react if I told her that, in line with this scripture, I was not going to pay what they charged me in interest on the loan I was seeking.

As much as the laws and commandments we have looked at so far this week enable the building of community, through having regard to strangers and not exploiting fellow members of the faith community, the word from this text is rather shocking. In a world where we base so many decisions upon the prevailing rates (the repo rate, prime lending rate, inflation rate), this scripture shockingly tells us not to charge interest to fellow believers. How would our banking system and our entire economic order survive if we were to implement such a law in a sophisticated twenty-first-century economic environment? What if Christians operated banks that didn't exploit other Christians by charging rates well below prime? Would such an entity survive, would it make a profit, and would the shareholders be satisfied when the profit margins were so much narrower than they would be had the entity charged what other banks were charging? Do we just write this off as wishful thinking, or is there something in here that we should take to heart if we are to build community?

† If you, or someone you know, is in financial difficulty, bring the matter before God and ask him to intervene.

For further thought

What does the injunction against charging interest practically mean for us, and how can we live out this injunction in our relationships?

A word of warning!

> **Read Amos 8:1–9**
>
> *'In that day,' declares the Sovereign Lord, 'the songs in the temple will turn to wailing. Many, many bodies – flung everywhere! Silence!' Hear this, you who trample the needy and do away with the poor of the land.*
>
> (verses 3–4)

The word of the Lord through the prophet Amos is particularly chilling: the people are ripe for judgement because they have exploited the poor for their own gain. They have leveraged their positions of power and influence to tip the scales and boost prices. Their goal is to trample on the needy and to ignore the cries of the poor.

I was driving around our community last week quite late, on my way home from a meeting. On street corners, in bus shelters, on park benches and often huddled together, were homeless people, desperately trying to keep warm and dry. How often do we not notice poverty any longer, or get so overwhelmed by the enormity of the problem that we assume that there is nothing that we can do to help those with whom we so frequently come in contact? How often do we sing worship songs inside the church when, on our doorstep, there are those who are desperate for some small help?

In our neighbourhood we have a 'Give Responsibly' campaign where members of the community are encouraged not to give money but vouchers that can be redeemed for a meal and contact with a social worker at our community kitchen. Aware as we are of our responsibility to provide food for the hungry, we also want to make sure that those in our community who need help will be able to find the help they need when they need it.

† What are some of the needs of the poor in your community? Begin to pray that God might give you some wisdom, insight and discernment in knowing what you might do to help.

For further thought

Walk the streets of your neighbourhood and become conscious of the needs of your community. What would it take to respond to people with compassion and empathy?

Friday 13 March
Act justly

Read Micah 6:6–8

*He has shown you, O mortal, what is good. And what does
the Lord require of you?
To act justly and to love mercy and to walk humbly with your God.*

(verse 8)

Every day we are confronted with images of corrupt economic practices that destroy community and family life. People are filled with terror, despair, hopelessness and mourning. Leaders who should help others devour them instead; prophets sell God's word for a profit and we all feel vulnerable. People's faith lies shipwrecked and battered. Maintaining hope seems impossible for those living under oppression and experiencing terror-filled injustice. In this deadly predicament we join those who, in faith and despair, cry out: 'How long, O Lord?' God's simple message spoken through the prophet Micah echoes through the ages for those who long for God to act.

In order to work together with God, we are required to:

• Act justly: We all long for justice. But when we have been wronged our longing so easily becomes a hope for revenge. God's way of justice is not about just us. As followers of Jesus, acting justly happens when we choose not to repay evil with evil, but to replace evil with good.

• Love mercy: Justice and mercy together form God's response to human injustice. Justice and mercy work together for good. We who have received mercy should be abundantly merciful.

• Walk humbly with your God: Humility is demonstrated in all our relationships. In humility we adjust our route to follow Jesus. We adjust our pace to keep in step with God and to include others. In humility we discover that we can never walk alone.

Through God's grace, together we can do what God requires. When we obey, we will experience the power of good over evil. When we do what God requires we will see and will witness to God's saving grace in the world.

† Ask God to help you act justly instead of wanting revenge; to help you to be eager for mercy to prevail; and to walk in humility before God and others.

For further thought

What changes do you need to make to your everyday life to enact justice, love mercy and walk humbly with God and others?

Breaking chains of injustice

> **Read Isaiah 58:6–11**
>
> *'Is not this the kind of fasting I have chosen: to loose the chains of injustice and untie the cords of the yoke, to set the oppressed free and break every yoke?'*
>
> (verse 6)

In a world that is besotted with eating, where fast-food chains are on every street corner and in which we are told that unless you eat three substantial meals every day, something is wrong, fasting is a forgotten discipline. For those who do fast, whether during Lent or at some other times, there is a right way and a wrong way to fast:

- True fasting involves setting free those who are bound by the chains of injustice: fasting should open our eyes to the injustices around us and make us conscious of those who cry out for justice.
- True fasting gives you an opportunity to share what you have with others: fasting is an opportunity to share what we have with others. If you fast, then you can take what you have saved by not spending it on food or something else and do something useful for another person in need. Fasting always goes together with prayer and caring for others.
- True fasting helps you to practically love God and other people: fasting shows our devotion and love for God, but also our love and compassion for people who are made in the image of God.

Fasting entails giving up something to be able to focus on things that are important to God. Whether you fast from food or from TV or from social media, the experience should enable us to use that time to become aware of the needs of others.

† Ask God to help you to undertake a fast in the near future.

For further thought
What could you give up on a regular basis to be made aware of the needs of people around you?

The responsibilities we share – 4 Life in community

Notes by **Wayne Hawkins**

Wayne works for the Council for World Mission as acting Deputy General Secretary, Programme. He is responsible for leading his team in delivering CWM programmatic work. Prior to this he was minister of two local Congregational churches in Southam, Warwickshire and Scunthorpe. He is passionate about equipping the church for mission in its local community. Wayne lives in Warwickshire with his wife and two children. He has used the NIVUK for these notes.

Sunday 15 March
Do not cheat

Read Mark 10:17–27

He went away sad, because he had great wealth.

(verse 22b)

The readings for the week focus on New Testament attitudes to wealth and riches in the context of what it means to be a community of people who – like it or not – have to live together on this one planet called Earth. How do we live in a world where there is enough for everyone but, because of inequality, many have to go without?

Today's reading is often called the story of the 'rich young ruler' who comes to Jesus looking for an answer to his question about eternal life. Jesus tells the young man to keep the commandments and focuses on the six ethical commands, but read closely and see that Jesus replaced 'do not desire another man's house …' with 'do not cheat', or more accurately 'defraud', showing that Jesus is more concerned with where this rich young man's wealth comes from than his claims to be good.

In Jesus' day, land was frequently accumulated by the wealthy through smallholder farmers defaulting on their debts. Jesus does not invite the young man to use his wealth more compassionately or try harder to be good. The way for him to become a disciple is by giving up his wealth.

And 'he went away sad, because he had great wealth' (verse 22).

† Jesus, give me the strength to give away all that stops me being your disciple and following you today.

Monday 16 March
One in mind and heart

Read Acts 4:32–37

All the believers were one in heart and mind. No one claimed that any of their possessions was their own, but they shared everything they had.

(verse 32)

Today's reading speaks of a Christian community that is alive with new growth and vitality, a community of believers that is flourishing and winsome. Having received the gift of the Spirit at Pentecost, we now read of how the Spirit enabled this new community to live together as they were 'one in heart and mind' (verse 32).

In Acts 4:31, immediately before today's verses, we read that the community was at prayer and the Spirit came with such power that 'the place where they were meeting was shaken'. The disciples who were once hiding behind locked doors and filled with fear are now overflowing with boldness and confidence. And as a consequence of this newfound Spirit-filled boldness they are 'one in heart and mind'. Their unity of purpose and action is played out in their willingness to share all that they had with one another. That the believers shared and practised care for the vulnerable is a witness 'to the resurrection of the Lord Jesus …' (verse 33). These two things are closely connected – being 'one in heart and mind' is a powerful witness to the amazing news of Christ's resurrection.

It is in service to the weak and vulnerable, the pushed out and excluded that service to God is proved. Service to God without action is lip service, and service to others without God is timid and devoid of hope. A community of faith –'one in heart and mind'– is focused on loving God through serving others and so witnessing with great power to the resurrection of Jesus Christ.

† In word and action; in silence and stillness; in one heart and mind may I witness to the transforming power of Christ's resurrection and new life.

For further thought

Today how can I work to be of 'one heart and mind' with others? In what ways do I need to change and to be a change-maker?

77

Tuesday 17 March
'Hospitality – you are welcome'

Read Acts 6:1–6

'Brothers and sisters, choose seven men from among you who are known to be full of the Spirit and wisdom'

(verse 3a)

Almost immediately after the morning service I was asked to talk to a lady who had arrived part way through the service. She was clearly in distress and would only talk to the minister, which meant no one else could offer her any help. She had recently left an abusive relationship and was consequently homeless. She was unwilling to go to a women's shelter and, for a host of other reasons, couldn't access other services. It fell to the church to find some immediate accommodation, food and, the following day, some legal advice. I was very grateful that members of the congregation had strong networks of support and contacts they could call on.

We live in a world of insiders and outsiders, where some are welcome and others are permanently pushed out. As humans we are expert at exclusion because we prefer the familiar and comfortable over the 'stranger' whose presence is a challenge. The same desire for the safe and familiar is seen in our churches. We may not consciously build divisions, but they are definitely present. In a world that is increasingly harsh and divided, we are called to imitate Jesus by being sacraments of God's hospitality in the world.

This reading in Acts and the selection of church leaders dedicated to a ministry of hospitality reminds us that welcoming others and showing hospitality is the most important calling for the church today. Not an occasional gesture but a way of life. Not an interruption to our lives but a habit and culture we nurture that characterises us as followers of Jesus.

† Jesus who comes as friend and stranger, may we discover you in the care and hospitality we offer those in need.

For further thought

As I am reminded of the welcome shown to me by others and by God, what actions can I take to welcome others?

Wednesday 18 March
The gift of generosity

Read 2 Corinthians 8:10–15

'The one who gathered much did not have too much, and the one who gathered little did not have too little.'

(verse 15)

Earlier this week we read in Acts 4 of the Jerusalem church that had 'one heart and mind' and shared all they had with one another as an expression of the gift of generosity. In today's reading, Paul is writing about the same gift of generosity to the Corinthian church. He is encouraging the gentile church in Corinth to support a collection for the Jewish church in Jerusalem, challenging them to give from the resources and riches that they already have.

We are reminded that grace is given to us from God despite our failing and sin and generates action from us as we become companions and partners in sharing God's grace. The invitation to be generous is not to buy divine favour or pay God back but to share with God in loving the world. Paul is bringing together the gentile church in Corinth and the Jewish church in Jerusalem through this collection. The economics are quite straightforward and based on the story of the people of Israel in the wilderness when they were collecting manna (Exodus 16) – you can share with those in need out of the plenty you enjoy. There is also the challenge to only 'collect' enough food for the day.

The collection for the needy in Jerusalem is an opportunity for Paul to remind the church that, despite theological differences and many diversities of worship or practice, the people of God are one community of people who are called to show the gift of generosity as God is generous.

† Loving God, giver of every perfect gift, make me generous with the gifts you have given that we might partner with you in sharing your abundant life with the world.

For further thought

In what ways is demonstrating generosity to imagine and work for a fairer and more equal world?

Thursday 19 March
Love that sets us free

> **Read 1 Corinthians 8**
>
> *Be careful, however, that the exercise of your rights does not become a stumbling-block to the weak.*
>
> (verse 9)

Today's reading with Paul's instructions about eating or not eating meat can seem very distant and removed from the questions we might ask about our Christian faith. However, the important message Paul shares with the church at Corinth is of vital importance for our discipleship and shared church life.

The apostle Paul tells the church at Corinth that it is acceptable to eat meat offered to idols because idols do not exist. Whether the god is Zeus or Poseidon they are imaginary and that meat offered in their honour remains meat, so enjoy your dinner! However, if eating such causes harm to relationships with others then we must stop.

Knowledge of Christ sets us free, but that freedom is to be understood in the context of responsibility and especially of love. Knowledge and insight are always relational and people are always in focus. Whatever the behaviour or action, Paul would have us ask, 'what does this mean for those around me, my relationship with them and with God?' Correctness – whether in law, worship practice or doctrine – must be considered in the setting of multidirectional love. When getting it right is the most important thing, relationship will often be wrong.

Knowledge that sets us free is not about being right but about enjoying right relationships. Our relationship with God in Christ is at the core of our 'knowledge' and the context in which we are 'known'. In a Jesus-shaped faith, it is love which matters most and is the basis of our identity. It is love that sets us free.

† Love that comes to us in Christ, set us free to have right relationships founded on love and acceptance of each other.

For further thought

Take time to think about the broken relationships in our lives and reflect on what you need to do to put things right.

Friday 20 March
Making the link

Read James 2:1–9

Listen, my dear brothers and sisters: has not God chosen those who are poor in the eyes of the world to be rich in faith and to inherit the kingdom he promised those who love him?

(verse 5)

For James there is a link between the faith we confess and our daily lives. If faith is to be more than a religion making a difference to our lives then there are links to be made between faith and living. How can the followers of Jesus discriminate against others? James gives the example of showing more attention, time and honour to a person based on their appearance and their wealth.

If we are content that we don't discriminate against people because of their wealth, maybe we do discriminate or treat people differently on the basis of their gender, ethnicity or sexual orientation. There is a link between the faith we confess and how we engage with others, especially those who express themselves differently to us.

I am currently in Georgetown, Guyana, where later today some of our group will visit community projects in Plastic City, a squatter settlement in West Demerara. Churches and community groups are busy supporting the community to improve health and education for the community. Plastic City residents are equally loved and precious to God as you and I are, yet their experience of life is very different.

Purity codes in the Bible are concerned with cleanliness and justify people's inclusion or exclusion from the community. But Jesus turns these codes and expectations upside down as he includes women and children, foreigner and outcast. Jesus discriminates in favour of the pushed-out or abused victim. Making the link between the faith we confess and the life we lead brings abundance and fullness of life to the world.

† God of the poor, embrace the homeless and hungry today. May our lives show your compassion and acceptance, bringing transformation to your world.

For further thought

While we show God's love for the poor and needy, how might we, for good, change the systems that keep people poor?

Saturday 21 March
Money, money, money

Read James 5:1–6

Your wealth has rotted, and moths have eaten your clothes. Your gold and silver are corroded. Their corrosion will testify against you …

(verses 2–3a)

We live in an increasingly divided world where one per cent of the world's population own fifty per cent of the world's resources. Nations measure wealth as gross domestic product whereas the poorest measure wealth in terms of whether they can feed themselves or their children. What does James say about wealth? Three things from today's reading:

Firstly, wealth entraps us. James warns us that we all too easily become emotionally attached to our wealth and a desire to accumulate more consumes us. The rich young ruler (Mark 10) whom we read of earlier this week is just one example of Jesus' teaching about wealth. He sought to lay down layer after layer of money, amassing and hoarding it, owning it and yet finding that his wealth owned him. And James addresses the way in which we can fall into the trap of judging others by their appearance and wealth as we read yesterday.

Secondly, wealth deceives us. Money and wealth will convince us that we have arrived and are successful, but as God's people we know that this is not the path to greatness or success. We must recognise that our wealth is found in an ever-deeper relationship with God and others, that true riches are to be discovered in giving ourselves away in service to others rather than hoarding whatever we do own.

Finally, wealth cheats others. James reminds us that whilst the rich hoard away, the poorest go without and so they are cheated out of even the little that they have or earn.

† Generous God, help me to be grateful for the riches that fill my life and to remember all we have comes from you.

For further thought

How might we live more simply so that we can be more generous and lessen our grip on the things we own?

The responsibilities we share – 5 Bearing the burden

Notes by **Noel Irwin**

 Noel is a Belfast boy and a Methodist minister. In 2000, he moved to Sheffield: firstly working for the Church of England as a community outreach worker, then as superintendent of the Methodist Mission in the city centre. After working as Director of the Urban Theology Unit in Sheffield, he is now tutor in Public Theology at Northern College Manchester and trains community workers for the United Reformed Church. In his spare time, he enjoys running in the hills and Brazilian Jiu Jitsu. Noel has used the NRSVA for these notes.

Sunday 22 March
Wise generosity

Read Psalm 112

It is well with those who deal generously and lend, who conduct their affairs with justice.

(verse 5)

When I started to commute from Sheffield to Manchester, the first time I walked out of Piccadilly Station, I was shocked by the number of people begging. In our psalm, which is a song outlining the features of a righteous life, the writer sees characteristics of a person who fears the Lord being how they 'deal generously and lend' (verse 5) and 'They have distributed freely, they have given to the poor' (verse 9a).

We see similar teaching in the Book of Tobit, which is included in Roman Catholic and Orthodox Bibles: 'Give alms from your possessions, and do not let your eye begrudge the gift when you make it. Do not turn your face away from anyone who is poor, and the face of God will not be turned away from you' (Tobit 4:7). There is a debate as to whether we should give to those who beg. I try to give, make sure I speak to the person, introduce myself and ask their name. It is little enough. In Luke's Gospel, almsgiving is seen as being about the redistribution of wealth, it is a constant duty with no reward for the giver and it could involve considerable amounts of money, as with Zacchaeus (Luke 19:8).

† Today, take a moment to pray for all those who are begging on the streets.

Monday 23 March
Equal responsibility

Read Exodus 30:11–16

The rich shall not give more, and the poor shall not give less, than the half-shekel, when you bring this offering to the Lord to make atonement for your lives.

(verse 15)

Who would have thought counting people and taxation could be so interesting? Once you unpack this message there are lots of fascinating details and questions. The first oddity is that though it seems to be God who has ordered the census, they still need to watch out and pay out in case a plague attacks them for getting themselves registered. Who would have sent the plague? Well, it is very clear in the Book of Exodus it would have to come from God. Very puzzling. Though if you read in the Hebrew scriptures about other attempts to have a census of the people of Israel, you will see (2 Samuel 24, 1 Chronicles 21) they are also fraught with difficulty.

There is no doubt this is a regressive tax. Both rich and poor pay the same. However, with the amount being equal to two days' wages for a labourer, it is clear the poor were hit much harder than the wealthy. The fact the tax is the same for all adult men means they are seen as equal in the eyes of God. Did equal payment actually equate to equal status and respect? This token equality in Exodus finds its fulfilment for all, not just adult males, not through taxation but through baptism! Galatians 3:27–28: 'As many of you as were baptized into Christ have clothed yourselves with Christ. There is no longer Jew or Greek, there is no longer slave or free, there is no longer male and female; for all of you are one in Christ Jesus.'

† God of all, help us take up our share of responsibility, and fight for the equal standing of all in your sight. Amen

For further thought

In reality, what does equality in the eyes of God actually mean?

Tuesday 24 March
Community contribution

Read Numbers 18:21–32

To the Levites I have given every tithe in Israel for a possession in return for the service that they perform, the service in the tent of meeting.

(verse 21)

The first part of Numbers 18 outlines the privileges and duties of both the priests and the Levites. In a society where wealth and status were largely measured by land, they were not to own land – God was to be their share and their possession (verse 20). Our passage focuses on the Levites (who assisted the priests at the outer structures of the tent of meeting) and how they received a tithe (a tenth), then they had to give a tithe of that to the priests, but not only that, it had to be the best part they gave to them (verse 29). As to the rest of it they could eat and drink it, though not 'profane the holy gifts' (verse 32) – perhaps by not treating them with due reverence?

In 1 Corinthians 9:13–14, Paul harks back to our passage today and then adds in verse 14: 'In the same way, the Lord commanded that those who proclaim the gospel should get their living by the gospel.' Over the centuries, the idea of supporting Christian ministers has generally been taken for granted by most denominations, though what that support has actually involved has varied hugely depending on time and place. Some ministers have struggled to make ends meet, while others have achieved wealth far above and beyond those they are supposed to serve. When Jesus sent out the seventy(ish!) in Luke 10:7 he said, 'the labourer deserves to be paid' not 'the labourer deserves to be paid equivalent to the salary of the chief executive of a large company'!

† Pray for your ministers and leaders. Think about their duties and privileges. Are they receiving sufficient support both material and spiritual?

For further thought

The salaries and 'golden handshakes' given to chief executives have been a point of controversy in the UK in recent years. Do you think there should be a salary cap for CEOs?

March

The responsibilities we share – 5 Bearing the burden

Wednesday 25 March
Don't exploit

Read 2 Kings 23:31–37

Jehoiakim gave the silver and the gold to Pharaoh, but he taxed the land in order to meet Pharaoh's demand for money. He exacted the silver and the gold from the people of the land, from all according to their assessment, to give it to Pharaoh Neco.

(verse 35)

As a student, I remember struggling to remember the names of the last three kings of Judah before it was captured by the Babylonians. Our Professor suggested 'HAZ KIM A CHIN' to help us; Jehoahaz, Jehoiakim and Jehoiachin! Our text today deals with two of them; neither of them, according to the author of Kings, made much of a fist of being king, at least according to the standard assessment of verses 32 and 37. According to 2 Kings, each of them 'did what was evil in the sight of the Lord, just as all his ancestors had done'.

We see here taxes being inflicted punitively firstly by the Egyptian Pharaoh Neco, then by the new king Jehoiakim, who tax the land heavily to pay the original fee demanded by Egypt. There is no doubt taxation has been used as a tool by dictators through the centuries to inflict punishment, misery and hardship. But when it is fair, equitable and accountable (remember the slogan that started the American revolution in the eighteenth century: 'No taxation without representation') it funds vital public services, provides education and healthcare for all, and offers a safety net for the needy and vulnerable in society. This is true not just for individuals but also for corporations and companies. All depend on a government to do its job in maintaining a healthy economy, sustaining the infrastructure of a country and upholding the rule of law while providing security for its citizens. If everyone is benefiting from these things then it is only right all should pay their fair share to keep them.

† Gracious God, help us to give joyfully to our communities and work for the rights of all, for the good of all. Amen

For further thought

Church Action for Tax Justice stands for a fairer and more effective tax system, where democratic governments set taxes to reflect the common good, and individuals and corporations pay their share. Visit www.catj.org.uk to find out more.

Thursday 26 March
Fundraising for the temple

Read 2 Chronicles 24:4–14

So those who were engaged in the work laboured, and the repairs went forward at their hands, and they restored the house of God to its proper condition and strengthened it.

(verse 13)

It is a bit of a feature in Chronicles for a king to start out well and then for it all to go wrong. Not so much a game of two halves, but a reign in two halves! Our passage is about the first half of Joash's reign and how he was helped in the restoration of the temple by the priest Jehoiada. On Monday we looked at Exodus 30:11–16; the order of Joash in verse 8 re-establishes this tax, not for a tent but for what we would call 'bricks and mortar'. By the time of Jesus, this is a yearly payment, a temple tax. In Matthew 17:24–27, Jesus questions the practice, connecting it to foreign kings and maybe even Rome in verse 25.

According to verse 10, the people and the leaders were more than happy to pay the tax. Of course the paying of religious taxes through the centuries has not always been quite so popular! From my own background in Ireland, the majority population was forced to pay tithes to support the established Church of Ireland, which even led to a 'tithe war' in the 1830s.

Having been in charge of a large city-centre church, I am well aware of the difficulties and sometimes the ethical dilemmas involved in the upkeep of buildings. More and more of my ministry seemed to be sucked into questions related to the building – yet with the gentrification and the closing down of social spaces in the city centre, our church became a much-needed home for many organisations, and thus for people seeking help. Blessing or curse, I constantly asked myself?

† Loving God, help us to put our buildings in the correct place – in every sense! Give us your perspective that our church buildings might be assets, not liabilities, for kingdom and community.

For further thought
Money is not our only gift to give the church, but it is an important one. How much do you give financially to support your own church community?

Friday 27 March
Pay your tax!

Read Mark 12:13–17

Jesus said to them, 'Give to the emperor the things that are the emperor's, and to God the things that are God's.' And they were utterly amazed at him.

(verse 17)

There are many texts in the Gospels which are abused and verse 17 (above) is right up at the top of the list. When it is taken out of context, as an abstract principle, it is used to justify a proper separation of the concerns of the church (spiritual) and the state (political). Yet, when we put the story in context it is clear it means something very different from the interpretation mostly given in our churches.

Yes, it is an attempt at the entrapment of Jesus, putting him into a 'no-win' situation where he either outs himself as a political rebel or as a collaborator and yes, Jesus is very clever in his answer. Taxation was a central element in all the Jewish rebellions against the Romans, so he turns the political challenge back at his opponents: whose side are they on? Why should he commit himself while they will not? No Jew would have accepted that the debt they owed to God had any connection at all with any other human claim. Jesus' teaching is crystal clear: by the time you have paid 'Abba' all you owe there is absolutely nothing left for anyone else and certainly not for someone like the Roman Emperor, who styles themselves as 'Lord'. Jesus provides an option which is neither collaboration or violent revolt; it is the way of the cross, standing in judgement over all the claims of state or religion.

† God of the cross, help us walk your way and value your rule above all else; and help us find joyful fulfilment in doing so.

For further thought

'The earth is the Lord's and all that is in it, the world, and those who live in it' (Psalm 24:1). In terms of politics and economics, what does this mean for us and our churches?

Saturday 28 March
Obey and pay!

Read Romans 13:1–7

Therefore whoever resists authority resists what God has appointed, and those who resist will incur judgement.

(verse 2)

While Mark 12:17 is an abused text, Romans 13:1–7 is in a league of its own in terms of texts used to justify oppression and persecution. Historically it has been used to buttress unjust kings and emperors, while more recently it has been wheeled out in support of Nazi Germany and Apartheid South Africa. Indeed, the South African Kairos document written in 1985 devotes a whole section to countering the view that Romans 13:1–7 means Christians must support the white Nationalist government.

The difficulty with Romans 13:1–7 is not the view that the state is divinely willed, existing for the common good, but that this can be absolutised into the view that all governments, no matter who they are and what they do, must be owed unqualified obedience. The central problem of the passage is that there is no analysis of the problem of political force. Very few Christians, if any, want to give a theological justification for unrestrained power. In relation to the state, much of the struggle of the church has been, and should be, the holding together of the words of Acts 5:29 ('We must obey God rather than any human authority') with Romans 13:1 ('Let every person be subject to the governing authorities; for there is no authority except from God, and those authorities that exist have been instituted by God'). If we do not hold these two texts together and in tension, we end up with the rather odd position of retrospectively condemning Moses and the children of Israel for securing their liberation from Pharaoh and the Egyptians!

† God of our liberation, give us the wisdom to support our societies where they need supporting, and challenge them where they need challenging. In the name of Jesus, the Prince of Peace. Amen.

For further thought

Which situations in our country and around the world do we connect to Acts 5:29, and which to Romans 13:1?

The responsibilities we share – 5 Bearing the burden

The Passion with Matthew – 1 Stories and questions

Notes by **Bruce Jenneker**

Bruce is director of liturgy at Trinity Church Wall Street in New York City. He was formerly senior priest of the Diocese of Saldanha Bay and Rector of All Saints Church in Durbanville, a suburb of Cape Town. Worship and liturgy have been his lifelong passions. He served as precentor at Trinity Church on Copley Square, Boston, Massachusetts, and canon precentor of Washington National Cathedral and of St George's Cathedral in Cape Town. Bruce has used the NRSVA for these notes.

Sunday 29 March
A new beginning: become like children

Read Matthew 18:1–10

Jesus called a child, whom he put among them, and said, 'Truly I tell you, unless you change and become like children, you will never enter the kingdom of heaven. Whoever becomes humble like this child is the greatest in the kingdom of heaven.'

(verses 2–4)

Matthew was an early Christian teacher – he could be called a 'scribe' of the gospel. 'Jesus said to them, "Therefore every scribe who has been trained for the kingdom of heaven is like the master of a household who brings out of his treasure what is new and what is old"' (Matthew 13:52). This definition aptly describes the evangelist and his methods.

Matthew highlights the discontinuities and continuities with the past that Jesus represents: inaugurating the New Covenant at the same time that he fulfils the Old. Matthew affirms both in a radical comprehensive unity. For the First Gospel, there is no either/or, only both/and. Those who follow Jesus as disciples are called to be innovative and traditional, revolutionary and conservative. In Jesus' definition of discipleship there is a 'preferential option' for the new, not over against the old, but in interdependent unity with it.

Matthew's paradigm is about change. It demands courageous risk and brave commitment. For this reason, Matthew's Gospel begins as it ends with the consoling exhortation: 'Do not be afraid.' The consolation occurs seven times in Matthew, in an arc from the angel's appearance to Joseph (1:20) to Jesus' parting words to his friends (28:10).

† O God our help in ages past, break into our present to make it anew, and keep us rooted in your enduring faithfulness.

Monday 30 March
Values overturned: a contrary economy

Read Matthew 18:12–14

'And if the shepherd finds the lost sheep, truly I tell you, he rejoices over it more than over the ninety-nine that never went astray. So it is not the will of your Father in heaven that one of these little ones should be lost.'

(verses 13–14)

Obviously, Matthew is not really speaking about livestock here. The focus is precisely on how we in the church treat our sisters and brothers who 'go astray', and the role of the 'shepherd' in seeking and finding them. The eleven verses preceding the parable of the Lost Sheep address the unacceptable power-grabbing that often characterises our church communities. Matthew denounces those who cause their weaker sisters and brothers to 'stumble', as well as those who are so arrogant and judgemental that they refuse to forgive those who repent and be reconciled with them. By implication the parable denounces imperious and self-serving leaders who are willing, cavalierly, to abandon those who repent and cherish only those who remain in the fold.

Not so in the reign of overturned values that Jesus inaugurates. Every single one of God's flock has intrinsic worth and unassailable value, and must never be sacrificed. Overbearing leaders are placed over against the repentant sinner and it is the leaders who are found wanting.

Children were generally held of little or no account in the ancient world. Slaves, women and children only had value in so far as they 'belonged' to a male. The warmth that Jesus always displayed towards children and the way in which he made becoming 'childlike' and being born again absolute tenets of his gospel are, therefore, all the more remarkable. A spirit of healthy childlike dependency and innocent trust are hallmarks of those who say 'Yes' to Jesus.

† You embrace us as a loving parent: give us the childlike faith that believes all things are possible and the innocent trust that allows us to surrender to you and your will.

For further thought

Become mindful of the times you override the childlike, less jaded impulses that rise up in you spontaneously. Could you listen to these impulses more?

Tuesday 31 March
A counter-cultural paradigm: a community of forgiveness

Read Matthew 18:15–20

'Truly I tell you, if two of you agree on earth about anything you ask, it will be done for you by my Father in heaven. For where two or three are gathered in my name, I am there among them.'

(verses 19–20)

In six short verses, Jesus offers guidelines for living in community that resonate in our times. We are ruggedly individualistic, aggressively self-absorbed, fiercely competitive, keeping scores and planning to settle them vengefully, and in all things looking out for number one. Against these cultural predispositions, Jesus counsels encountering, listening to and engaging with others. First, he calls the church to motivate those in contention to foster genuine and honest encounter, with the accuser and defendant investigating the matter privately in the hope of restoring unity.

The word 'church' appears only in Matthew's Gospel: thrice here in chapter 18 and in the passage in which Jesus calls Peter the rock on which he builds his church (16:18). Then, Jesus the Incarnate Word, listening to a speaking world, invites his followers to be listeners first and last: attentive, self-abasing, eager listeners. Four times in just 150 words Jesus refers to listening, making it an imperative, a vocation and a ministry for those who choose to follow him.

Ours is a culture of demanding to be heard, ready to react even before we have heard what has been said by others. Jesus advocates turning our predisposition upside-down and choosing the counter-cultural way.

It is here that Jesus gives the assurance of his 'real presence' with his followers who gather in his name. Not in the context of the accounts of the Eucharist do we find this promise and guarantee, but in the context of conflict and disagreement when it is transformed by attentive listening and embracing the other in community – there, where love prevails Christ is ever found.

† Fount of mercy and forgiveness: make us gentle, and when discord arises make us eager to be forgiving because it is in our loving that we find you really present with us.

For further thought

What is most difficult about life in community? What is it in you that responds negatively? Examine how your motives determine your actions.

Wednesday 1 April

A gospel economy: the extravagant excess of salvation

Read Matthew 18:21–35

'Then his lord summoned him and said to him, "You wicked slave! I forgave you all that debt because you pleaded with me. Should you not have had mercy on your fellow-slave, as I had mercy on you?"'

(verse 32–33)

This passage concerns the enormity of our sin and the extravagant excess of the gospel. Peter asks whether forgiveness should extend to the holy number of seven times, considering that an appropriately excessive number of times. Jesus responds that it should extend to the immeasurable seventy-seven times.

The debt owed by the unmerciful servant is unimaginably enormous. However the value of the gold is reckoned, 10,000 bags or talents of gold (verse 24) would represent a figure many, many times the average salary. The point Jesus is making with these vast numbers is to put sin and forgiveness in relation to each other. The enormity of our sin is overmatched by the unimaginable lavish outpouring of forgiveness.

Hannah Arendt, the German Jewish philosopher, wrote that Jesus 'was the discoverer of the role of forgiveness in human affairs'.[3] Forgiveness and related words occur some forty times in the Gospels and form the central petition of the Lord's Prayer. If Christianity is the counter-cultural world of Christ's gospel, then over the gate to it is proclaimed, 'All who enter here forgive and are forgiven.' Forgiveness is the dynamic in which our true identity is discovered, renewed and restored.

† No matter how far we stray or how thoroughly we tarnish your image in us, you always seek and find us, forgive and restore us: make us forgive as you forgive, love as you love.

For further thought

Have you ever sought forgiveness and been forgiven? How did being forgiven affect you? Have you ever forgiven someone? What did forgiveness cost you?

April

The Passion with Matthew – 1 Stories and questions

3 Arendt, H (1998), *The Human Condition* (Chicago, Il: Chicago University Press, 2nd edition), p. 238.

Thursday 2 April
A gospel economy: costing no less than everything

Read Matthew 19:16–30

Jesus said to him, 'If you wish to be perfect, go, sell your possessions, and give the money to the poor, and you will have treasure in heaven; then come, follow me.' When the young man heard this word, he went away grieving, for he had many possessions.

(verses 21–22)

Our culture measures worth and assigns respect based on credentials, money and possessions ranking highest among them. Brand names – in big things like automobiles and in smaller things like designer clothes and packaged food – matter so much that we will pay significantly more for a preferred name brand. People matter more when they have more. Whether we live in a cosmopolitan mega-metropolis, a big city or a small rural town, we are consumers in a consumer culture, lured by clever advertising to embark on reckless retail therapy. Possessions delight us, announce our worth and undergird our sense of security. Possessions make us self-sufficient; the more we have, the less we depend on anyone or anything else.

When the young man learns that to have eternal life – to enter the kingdom of heaven here and now – he must give up and give away everything that he has, the cost is too high. His enthusiasm for his high goal dissipates and, heartbroken, he abandons his quest.

Ultimately this exchange is about surrender. It is about choosing Jesus above all things, recognising that I need Jesus more than anything else, acknowledging that Jesus is the foundation and horizon of my reality.

Everything else is ballast that makes me so thick and broad that, like a camel attempting to go through the eye of a needle, I cannot enter the narrow gate into the kingdom of heaven.

The meaning of the good life, eternal life, is surrender to and alignment with Jesus Christ, more than to anything else, above whatever other loyalties may have claims on us.

† Jesus Christ, Lord of my life and desire of my heart: draw me ever closer to you that I will find in you my all-in-all and offer myself to you without reserve.

For further thought

Does supreme surrender deny personal worth and freedom? How can I become what I am called to be and still surrender all that I am?

A gospel economy: the disruptive values of the kingdom

Read Matthew 20:1–16

'"I choose to give to this last the same as I give to you. Am I not allowed to do what I choose with what belongs to me? Or are you envious because I am generous?" So the last will be first, and the first will be last.'

(verses 14b–16)

Paul Green describes Matthew's parables as those of the Disruptive Kingdom.[4] This is an interpretation of the concept 'Disruptive Innovation' used in commercial marketing strategy. A 'Disruptive Innovation' is a modern advance or novelty that creates a new market and value network that eventually disrupts an existing market and value network.

Jesus used parables to provide glimpses of the 'Disruptive Kingdom' he proclaimed. He employed familiar themes from everyday life, turning them inside out and upside down to present fresh, counter-cultural concepts that were unexpected and even foreign to the customs, norms, values and worldviews of his contemporaries. He inaugurated the strategic process which began with the familiar but inserted something radical within it to change worldviews, attitudes and behaviours.[5]

Jesus radically transforms the notion of expectation of just remuneration for hours of work to illustrate the 'Disruptive Innovation' that is a hallmark of the reign Jesus proclaims and inaugurates: that the last will be first, and the first will be last (verse 16).

This norm or 'law' of Christ's reign is based on God's extravagant generosity and not on the merits of any person. The focus is not on the number of hours that the workers put in, but on the unearned and undeserved, lavish and beyond-expectation generosity of God.

† Open our hearts to your generosity: you keep no score of wrongs or tally of good deeds, but pour out your blessings upon us, in good measure, pressed down, shaken together, running over.

For further thought

Do we follow the 'counsel of perfection' – 'be perfect ... as your heavenly Father is perfect' (Matthew 5:48) – in our dealings with the people in our lives?

4 Green, P. (2013), 'Kingdom of God Parables in Matthew 13', *Clarion Journal of Spirituality and Justice*, March 2013.

5 Christensen, C., Dyer, J. and Gergersen, H. (2011), *The Innovator's DNA: Mastering the Five Skills of Disruptive Innovators* (Boston, MA: Harvard Business Press).

April

The Passion with Matthew – 1 Stories and questions

Saturday 4 April
A gospel economy: an invitation to life

Read Matthew 20:17–23

Jesus said to them, 'You will indeed drink my cup, but to sit at my right hand and at my left, this is not mine to grant, but it is for those for whom it has been prepared by my Father.'

(verse 23)

Jesus is on the way to his betrayal, condemnation and execution in Jerusalem. During the events recorded in the verses we have been reading this week, this reality looms in Jesus' awareness. Three times he predicts his death (Matthew 16:21; 17:22–23; 20:17–19). This time, Jesus has hardly uttered this ominous prediction when the mother of James and John comes to request the highest places of honour in the kingdom for her sons.

This request ignores everything that Jesus has been teaching in these chapters. The reign of Christ is about life in the all-embracing love and mercy of God from which no one is excluded, or forgotten or left behind. There is no hierarchy of salvation, only the rich and free promise of it. Christ's reign demands the surrender that costs no less than everything and it is the promise of abundant life, full and free, extravagantly available to all who follow Christ faithfully, serving, loving and sacrificing self in imitation of him.

This week we have followed Jesus' teaching about living in his reign here and now. It is an invitation to a life full of the promise of all the goodness of God lavished upon us – unearned, unmerited, undeserved but unconditional, unlimited, without reserve. This grand offer invites a response of total surrender – the surrender that costs no less than everything. In it, the fullness of the Creator meets and accepts the fullness of the creature: boundless divinity in amazing grace embracing human persons in the fullness of their identity, their humanity and frailty, their potential and wonder.

† Liberate me from all pride and self-serving; open my eyes to your redeeming work and make me an instrument of your saving love.

For further thought

Can I drink the cup that Jesus has to drink? What extent of sacrifice am I willing to make? What makes sacrifice difficult?

The Passion with Matthew – 2 The holy city

Notes by **Kat Brealey**

After studying theology at university, Kat went on to spend a formative year working with Coventry Cathedral's reconciliation ministry team. More recently her work has focused on interfaith engagement, and she is particularly interested in understanding the way religion can contribute to peace. Kat enjoys cycling and singing in a gospel choir. Kat has used the NRSVA for these notes.

Sunday 5 April
Asking afresh, 'Who is this?'

Read Matthew 21:1–11

The crowds that went ahead of him and that followed were shouting, 'Hosanna to the Son of David! Blessed is the one who comes in the name of the Lord! Hosanna in the highest heaven!' When he entered Jerusalem, the whole city was in turmoil, asking, 'Who is this?'

(verses 9–10)

Matthew spends almost a third of his Gospel detailing the events of Holy Week and the account is familiar to many of us. So in search of a fresh perspective, this week we'll focus on the 'supporting cast'. Each day our reading will include someone who is with Jesus in the last week of his life, talking either about him or to him. What might these encounters reveal? On Palm Sunday, Jesus' ministry reaches a crescendo as he enters Jerusalem. The city is in turmoil (as indeed it was at the time of Jesus' birth in Matthew 2:3), because stories of his healing and teaching had spread. While some are ready to recognise him as their king, others are unsure. Rumours swirl around. Many different labels and expectations are being pinned on Jesus – which in the week ahead will be both fulfilled and subverted. We may more naturally identify with the voices crying 'hosanna' is this?' and make that our question today. As we enter Holy Week, what are our hopes and dreams about who Jesus might be to us and what he might do for us?

† Gracious God, help us to grow in knowledge and love of you as we journey with Jesus through the week ahead.

Monday 6 April
Out of the mouths of babes …

Read Matthew 21:12–17

The blind and the lame came to him in the temple, and he cured them. But when the chief priests and the scribes saw the amazing things that he did, and heard the children crying out in the temple, 'Hosanna to the Son of David', they became angry …

(verses 14–15)

As many parents will have experienced, often to their embarrassment, children have a knack for picking up words and phrases and repeating them loudly in public. In today's passage we discover this is not a recent phenomenon! Some children at the temple are heard echoing or mimicking the cry of the crowds as Jesus entered Jerusalem, perhaps re-enacting the events as they play. Yet while they are obviously talking about Jesus, it's not clear that they are specifically speaking to him. Do these little ones understand what they are saying? Are they making a conscious declaration of faith? It's tempting to say yes, creating a dichotomy between the children who recognise Jesus, and the chief priests and scribes who reject him. However, I'm not convinced these children grasp the implications of their words – but the fact they are declaring truth unconsciously doesn't lessen its value. A parallel might be Psalm 19's statement that the heavens declare the glory of the Lord – which is not an informed decision on their part!

As all this was going on, Jesus was healing people. As such, the children's words act as the soundtrack to people being made whole – a narration of how this is possible. Words and actions come from different sources, but attest to the same reality of Jesus' identity and the nature of his kingdom. We too are surrounded by things which point us to Jesus, some deliberately but many unconsciously. Do we notice them? Are we looking?

† Loving God, open our eyes and ears to recognise those things in the world around us which proclaim your truth and point to your glory.

For further thought

Think about how you might cultivate habits which help you to pay attention to God and curb those which distract you from God.

Actions speak louder than words

Read Matthew 26:1–16

Now while Jesus was at Bethany in the house of Simon the leper, a woman came to him with an alabaster jar of very costly ointment, and she poured it on his head as he sat at the table.

(verses 6–7)

One spring day, my boyfriend suggested we go for a walk. Turning a corner, we came upon a picnic laid out among the trees – and then he pulled a ring out of his pocket. He must have said, 'Will you marry me?' but I don't remember the words, just his actions. The same is true in today's passage. Although it seems unlikely that the whole episode was conducted in silence, Jesus notes that specifically 'what she has done' means she will be remembered. It is this which is recorded, but as we aren't given Mary's rationale for her action, this leaves us to do some interpretation of what it might be saying about Jesus. There are at least three potential strands. The first is gratitude; it was Jesus who had raised her brother Lazarus from the dead. The second is anointing, which was a sign of kingship, indicating Mary at least partially recognises who Jesus is. But there is a third strand which is likely beyond her conception and it is this one which Jesus explains to those present. She has prepared him for burial and this makes her action a prophetic one. Prophetic actions are found throughout the Bible, particularly in the Old Testament. Prophets like Jeremiah and Ezekiel go beyond words to communicate their message, using objects like clay pots, yokes and even their own bodies to represent what God is going to bring to pass. Unlike them, Mary wasn't aware of her prophetic function, but much like the children in the temple, she contributes to the telling of a larger story.

† In your prayers today, express gratitude to Jesus, recognise him as your king and prepare yourself for what is still to come this Holy Week.

For further thought

Reflect on whether and how your actions might help to tell Jesus' story.

April

The Passion with Matthew – 2 The holy city

Wednesday 8 April
Definitely maybe

> ### Read Matthew 26:17–30
> *When it was evening, he took his place with the twelve; and while they were eating, he said, 'Truly I tell you, one of you will betray me.' And they became greatly distressed and began to say to him one after another, 'Surely not I, Lord?'*
>
> (verses 20–22)

Today Jesus is celebrating Passover with his closest friends, but things take a darker turn when he predicts that one of them will betray him. They clearly want to deny it, yet their hesitant tone suggests they sense Jesus knows what is going to happen despite their best intentions. And at this point there is an important lesson we can learn from the disciples. Though we often malign and ridicule them, when Jesus reveals that one of those around the table will betray him, they immediately question themselves rather than accusing one another. Perhaps they were jumping to clear their own names, but it's striking that each disciple was more focused on their own place at Jesus' table, than on whether others belonged there.

While most of the disciples call Jesus 'Lord', Judas opts for 'Rabbi'. This is only a tiny detail but it can make it seem clear to us that Judas is the guilty party. We must remember we have the benefit of hindsight! The disciples, on the other hand, seem not to notice and each speaks directly to Jesus, as opposed to discussing with one another who might be at fault. Jesus doesn't cause a scene and expose Judas; instead his response is ambiguous and he simply reflects Judas' words back to him.

In the context of a church which is so often divided, all this is humbling to see. The opportunity to publicly hold someone to account can be hard to resist. Equally, self-examination is not often our first response to an accusation, wherever this comes from.

† Reflect on a particular situation of accusation and blame in your context, seeking God's grace and peace for all involved.

For further thought

What would change if we examined ourselves before pointing fingers, whether in interpersonal disputes or in issues affecting our communities?

Thursday 9 April
All good things come to an end?

Read Matthew 26:36–56

Now the betrayer had given them a sign, saying, 'The one I will kiss is the man; arrest him.' At once he came up to Jesus and said, 'Greetings, Rabbi!' and kissed him. Jesus said to him, 'Friend, do what you are here to do.'

(verses 48–50a)

We'd had a lovely holiday in France and now my friend was driving us back to the UK. On the last leg of the long journey I was meant to be staying awake, keeping her company, but I nodded off. Similarly, today Jesus is alone, surrounded by sleeping friends, despite his recent stories about the need to stay alert. When they are awake, while only one of Jesus' friends actively betrays him, the rest don't do much better. Indeed the only words spoken to or about Jesus in these verses are those which betray him. In response, Jesus still calls Judas 'friend', but the Greek word is *hetairos*, used to describe a person who has abused a privileged relationship. This is fitting because although we often focus on this moment as a beginning, setting in motion Jesus' arrest, trial and ultimately his death, it is also an ending as Jesus and Judas' friendship comes to a close.

Whether it's a marriage ending or saying goodbye to an elderly relative, how the final moments of a relationship play out can determine whether we dwell on it continuously or are able to move on in peace. Jesus will die the following day and Judas not long afterwards. Maybe Jesus knows all this, and that is why he calls Judas *hetairos*. It's bittersweet, but he could be harsher. Yet in this ending, Jesus is still full of grace, even for those who abandon and betray him in his hour of need. Tonight, the disciples fail to watch with him; tomorrow, the soldiers will watch over him.

† Seek God's healing for an ending in your life which feels unresolved, whether recent or historic.

For further thought

In some churches, the Maundy Thursday service today will finish with the altar being stripped of decoration and people leaving in silence. How does this ending prepare us for Good Friday?

Friday 10 April
Sticks and stones

Read Matthew 27:32–50

Those who passed by derided him, shaking their heads and saying, 'You who would destroy the temple and build it in three days, save yourself! If you are the Son of God, come down from the cross.'

(verses 39–40)

We tend to focus a lot on the physical violence of the crucifixion, but in this passage what people say to and about Jesus reminds us of the verbal violence and abuse he also suffered. In these verses, the whole gamut of society add their own judgement to that rendered by the Romans: from the religious leaders, to the everyday passers-by, to the criminals. The specific things they say indicate that they were familiar with Jesus' words. The insults were not generic, but tailored to things Jesus had said about himself during his ministry. People had remembered these and now, as he approaches death, they use them against him.

For those of us who cannot relate to the physical violence of the crucifixion, this aspect of Jesus' treatment may be more familiar. The old saying goes, 'Sticks and stones may break my bones, but words will never hurt me.' However, I think we know that this is often not the reality, especially in the age of social media. Cruel words can be incredibly damaging, especially for younger people, and may have tragic consequences. Perhaps you have had your words taken and used against you, or seen this happen to people you know, or to those in the public eye? Or maybe you've done it to others. This aspect of the crucifixion narrative reminds us that Jesus knew the pain words cause. His death on the cross is a sign of his full humanity and demonstrates his understanding of our human condition, including all the forms of violence this entails.

† Write down any words which have been used to hurt you. As you scrunch up the paper, ask God to transform any pain which remains.

For further thought

Where do you see words being used cruelly? How can you challenge this or model something different?

Saturday 11 April
A calculated risk

Read Matthew 27:57–66

When it was evening, there came a rich man from Arimathea, named Joseph, who was also a disciple of Jesus. He went to Pilate and asked for the body of Jesus; then Pilate ordered it to be given to him.

(verses 57–58)

This is the only place Joseph of Arimathea appears in the Gospels – but it's certainly an important one. All four Gospels agree on what Joseph did, but the extra details in each account allow us to piece together an interesting picture. We're told that Joseph was a follower of Jesus, but kept this a secret. He was taking a risk in coming to Pilate, given that news of his request might well spread. However, in fact, Joseph hadn't kept his feelings about Jesus entirely under wraps up to this point. Luke reports that Joseph, 'though a member of the council, had not agreed to their plan and action' (23:50–51), making this at least the second time that Joseph had taken risks in what he said about Jesus. We don't know what that earlier exchange looked like and how he expressed his opposition, but it seems likely he used his position tactically. He spoke up for his convictions, but in a way that leveraged his position as a respected member of the council, rather than undermined it.

Watching children diving off a harbour wall into the sea recently, I reflected on my tendency to play it safe. While my husband would have loved to join them, I was perfectly happy on dry land; because where he saw exhilaration, I saw danger. Yet the risks Joseph takes are calculated, not rash. His example is helpful. Sometimes we may feel our only option is to defend Jesus vigorously regardless of the consequence, which means in practice we often stay silent. What can we learn from Joseph's more nuanced approach?

† Are there situations where you feel it is risky to speak about Jesus? Ask God for wisdom and courage.

For further thought
Consider where you might be respected or be held in high regard and how you might utilise this to seek good.

April

The Passion with Matthew – 2 The holy city

Easter: with the rising of the sun – 1 Break of day

Notes by **Joshua Taylor**

Joshua is vicar of St John's Anglican Church in Timaru, New Zealand. He, his wife Jo and their daughters Phoebe and Esther have been exploring what it means to be a family on mission. Josh recently completed his master's thesis on consumerism and its impact on how we 'do' church. In his spare time he writes a blog (longstoryshort.nz) summarising theology books. He loves to spend his days off being mocked by fish while holding a fishing rod. Joshua has used the NRSVA for these notes.

Sunday 12 April
Dawn on the First Day

Read Matthew 28:1–10

'Do not be afraid; go and tell my brothers to go to Galilee; there they will see me.'

(verse 10b)

On Easter Sunday, we celebrate the resurrection of Jesus. It is the decisive moment of the Christian story.

Millions of followers of Jesus have claimed this story as their own and lived lives of faith, hope and love because of it. Countless people have experienced transformation – forgiveness of sin, healing of hurts, a peace that surpasses all understanding. The proof is in the pudding, and Jesus' resurrection was the beginning of something new for humanity. This resurrection moment was the first dawn of a new creation, and ever since God's resurrection power has brought the fresh light to countless lives.

The women meet the risen Jesus himself in verse 10 and he says, 'Go and tell my brothers to go to Galilee; there they will see me.' 'Go' is the repeated phrase throughout the passage.

When the explorer Captain Cook and his crew anchored near the shores of New Zealand in October 1769, they described the dawn chorus of native birds as 'deafening'. There is something wired into the birds to announce the dawn with joy and with song. The wonderful news of the resurrection is that a new dawn is here. Like the birds welcoming the dawn with their chorus, we too are called to share the news with joy.

† Lord, through your resurrection you make all things new. May I know the power of your resurrection in my life today. Amen

Monday 13 April
Coming to the tomb early

Read John 20:1–10

Early on the first day of the week, while it was still dark, Mary Magdalene came to the tomb and saw that the stone had been removed from the tomb.

(verse 1)

For those of us who have seen one or two Easter productions, the element of surprise in the story has somewhat faded. Sadly, this story can be all too predictable. This is because we work backwards from the good news of resurrection.

Today's passage opens with Mary going to the tomb. It's important for us to remember that she isn't wandering to the tomb with hope to find Jesus raised from the dead. Mary is going to grieve and mourn the loss of Jesus. She is shocked and interrupted by an unexpected sight: the stone had been removed from the tomb.

Mary, devoted as she was, hadn't got there in time, but God was at work well before she arrived. Mary is up early, leaving home while it is still dark to go to see Jesus, yet she is not early enough. I love the shock and surprise of this passage. The rest of the passage is breathless. Mary runs to Peter and John who run to the tomb, discover the surprise too and then presumably run to tell the others. God is at work and everyone else in this story is running to catch up. I find this is often the case in my own life; God is at work ahead of me and I have to try to keep up.

† Lord, thank you that you surprise us with the hope you bring through your resurrection. Help us to follow where you lead this day. Amen

For further thought

Where have you seen God at work ahead of you, preparing the way or surprising you with his goodness and grace?

Easter: with the rising of the sun – 1 Break of day

April

A new gardener

Read John 20:11–18

Supposing him to be the gardener, she said to him, 'Sir, if you have carried him away, tell me where you have laid him, and I will take him away.'

(verse 15b)

Mary, weeping, confused and racked with anguish, wonders what on earth has happened to Jesus. The tomb is empty and it seems someone has robbed the grave, as if things weren't bad enough! Mary turns to see a man in the garden and John tells us that she supposes he is the gardener. This little assumption contains a lot of theological weight. Whilst Mary hasn't yet recognised the resurrected Jesus, her assumption points to a profound truth. The story of scripture begins in a garden. In the first garden in Genesis we encounter the wonder of creation and humanity living in harmony with God and one another. We also encounter the first story of human brokenness and pain. Sin enters the world through the disobedience of Adam and Eve. The garden is spoiled.

John 20 is set in another garden and we meet a gardener, Jesus. He is the one who is bringing forth the new creation. Jesus is the one who wipes away Mary's tears and he is the one who will wipe away every tear from our eyes, too (Revelation 21:4).

As we read this passage we might think of our own lives and of our communities as a garden. Where is God bringing new life and growing new things? Where is the resurrection power of Jesus bringing fresh growth?

† Lord Jesus, thank you that you are the good gardener who causes fruit to grow in our lives. Please tend to me and bring new growth this day. Amen

For further thought

If you were to view your life/community as a garden, where is Jesus at work growing new things? What is being pruned and trimmed back?

106

Dawn catch

> **Read John 21:1–8**
>
> *Jesus said to them, 'Children, you have no fish, have you?' They answered him, 'No.' He said to them, 'Cast the net to the right side of the boat, and you will find some.'*
>
> (verses 5–6a)

I love fishing. I am so into it that the night before going fishing I often wake up early with anticipation, like a child on Christmas morning early. During fishing season, I even dream about trout (I am not joking).

Fishing is a rather technical pursuit and it requires that you have some idea what you are doing. I discovered this after several bird nests, lost hooks and fruitless hours on the lake. The thing about fishing is that it's best done early, often at the break of day. It's also best to fish in a spot where fish are actually present.

In today's passage, Jesus gives some seasoned fishermen a fishing lesson.

The lesson for me in this reading is that they don't quibble with Jesus, suggesting that they know best. After all, they had been fishing long before he called them to follow him. Rather, the disciples trust Jesus and simply follow his instructions. Upon doing so, they haul in more fish than they can carry.

The fruitfulness of the early church mission largely depended on this kind of obedience to Jesus, and the fruitfulness of any of our mission endeavours still does. This fishing story reminds us of the need to change plans and be obedient when Jesus calls us to do something, even if we think we may have a better idea.

† Lord, help me to trust you when you call me to do something for you, even if I think I know better than you. Amen

For further thought

Do you find it easy to trust Jesus when you feel that he is calling you to do something? Do you have the humility of the disciples to simply listen and drop the net on the other side?

April

Easter: with the rising of the sun – 1 Break of day

Thursday 16 April
Wrestling until break of day

Read Genesis 32:22–32

Then the man said, 'You shall no longer be called Jacob, but Israel, for you have striven with God and with humans, and have prevailed.'

(verse 28)

In the Bible, names matter. We too have names we are born with, and also the many nicknames we have been called throughout our life. And we also name ourselves. We might seek to name ourselves through our success at work, through our relationships or by acquiring things that make us look important.

Central to being human is a longing for a name, a longing for meaning and identity. In Genesis we encounter Jacob. Here is a story of a man who desperately attempts to make his own name, only for God to interrupt his plans.

Jacob began his life wrestling. He was a twin and even in the womb he struggled with his brother Esau. At birth, Jacob came out grasping his brother's heel, which is how he got the name Jacob, meaning 'holder of the heel' or 'supplanter'.

In Genesis 32, the night before a fraught reunion between the twins, a man came and wrestled Jacob until dawn. The identity of this man is obscure at first but later in the story Jacob calls the wrestler *Elohim*, a word used for God in the Hebrew Bible. The one who wrestled with his brother now wrestles with God. The turning point of the story happens as this stranger reveals who he is, blessing Jacob and giving him a new name.

In some Christian communities, when people are baptised, they are given a new name. The spiritual reality is that when we are baptised, we, like Jacob, are given a new name. God, by his grace, gives us a new name through faith in Jesus Christ. In the end this name is the only name that matters.

† Lord, may I know that I am made in your image, that my identity is found in you and that I am loved.

For further thought
What names have you been called? What has formed your identity?

Friday 17 April
Rescue at the break of day

Read Daniel 6:16–24

Then, at break of day, the king got up and hurried to the den of lions. When he came near the den where Daniel was, he cried out anxiously to Daniel, 'O Daniel, servant of the living God, has your God whom you faithfully serve been able to deliver you from the lions?'

(verses 19–20)

'Daniel and the Lions' Den' was one of the first Bible stories that captured my imagination as a child. The imagery of fierce lions waiting to devour Daniel was scary and the hope that God would save him was thrilling. The flannelgraphs and colourful children's books don't quite capture the terror, though.

Imagine for a moment being Daniel in this situation. You have had trumped-up charges made against you and been sent to your death because of it; even the king is powerless to stop the laws leading to your execution. A stone is laid over the mouth of the den and it is just you and the lions.

The thought is horrifying. Daniel ends up in the den because of his religious beliefs. He was caught in the act of prayer and the political players of his day make moves to use this against him for their own purposes. Even today for many Christians across the world this reality is not unfamiliar. Christians across the globe still face much persecution, particularly in countries where religion and politics are closely intertwined. As I reflect on the book of Daniel, I am aware that many of my brothers and sisters in Christ face the situation that Daniel faces. My hope for them too is that, like Daniel, they may experience the break of day, a moment when God steps in to rescue them from danger. For those who don't experience God's rescue in this life, my prayer is that they may know the hope of resurrection, a new day for eternity.

† Lord Jesus, lion of Judah, rescue those persecuted like Daniel that they may know the hope of the new day. Amen

For further thought

What do you know about the persecuted church across the world? Do some research and pray for those facing opposition like Daniel.

Easter: with the rising of the sun – 1 Break of day

Awake, my soul

> **Read Psalm 108**
>
> *Awake, O harp and lyre! I will awake the dawn. I will give thanks to you, O Lord, among the peoples, and I will sing praises to you among the nations.*
>
> (verses 2–3)

When I was a child, I was famous for sleepwalking. Sleepwalking is a relatively common phenomenon. In fact, it is more common than we might think and it doesn't necessarily just occur when we are in our pyjamas. It seems a common enough human phenomenon to find ourselves sleepwalking through life.

It's a bit like when you have been driving for a while and you catch yourself arriving at a destination: 'Where am I?' 'Oh, that's right, I'm at the supermarket, how did I get here?' You don't remember the trip because you have been driving for long enough that you do it almost unconsciously. Many of us can so easily find ourselves sleepwalking through life. There are various kinds of sleepwalking:

- Busyness. We get busy with life. Work and family and routine mean we feel like we are on the treadmill and everything is just happening fast as can be.
- Conformity to others. We can lose touch with our own soul, our unique identity as the person God has made us, and we can spend our lives worrying about what others think, conforming to an image of whom others want us to be.
- Denial of reality. Life can be tough. Sometimes it gets so tough that we check out of it. Physically we can still be present, but internally we can become numb to what is really going on. We may use alcohol, TV or other distractions to check out from the issues facing us.

Today's psalm is a welcome interruption, an invitation to wake up! Awake, my soul! We are invited to find our life in connection to the God who made us and loves us.

† Lord, awake me from sleep. Rouse me that I may live my life to the full. Amen

For further thought

In what way do you sleepwalk through life? How might God be waking you up?

Easter: with the rising of the sun – 2 Rising early

Notes by **Carla A. Grosch-Miller**

 Carla is a practical theologian, educator and poet based in Northumberland. Her research areas are sexual–spiritual integration and congregational trauma. Author of *Psalms Redux: Poems and Prayers* (Canterbury Press 2014), she has also published articles in the *Journal for Adult Theological Education* and in *Theology and Sexuality*. She is an avid swimmer, regularly joining a group that swims in the North Sea, and lives with her husband David. Carla has used the NRSVA for these notes.

Sunday 19 April
My brain at 3 a.m.

Read Genesis 19:15–28

When morning dawned, the angels urged Lot, saying, 'Get up, take your wife and your two daughters who are here, or else you will be consumed in the punishment of the city.'

(verse 15)

Ordinarily, I am a very sound sleeper. But in my preaching years I would regularly awaken at around 3 a.m. on a Sunday morning with new thoughts about my sermon. I became convinced that 3 a.m. was the Spirit's hour. I would feel around my bedside table for sermon notes and pen, snap on the light and begin scribbling to capture the ideas that couldn't wait until dawn.

Three a.m. may indeed be the Spirit's hour. Our brains are highly active while we sleep, transforming memories from short- to long-term and conducting repair and restoration activities. Creative activity is highest during and immediately after sleep; lowered inhibitions enable free association of ideas. We wake at 3 a.m. able to hear angels' whispers, be they alarming or illuminating.

There is a lot of alarm in this week's texts, some tossing and turning and a call to prayer. We will meet Abraham, Lot, Job and Jesus early in the morning, some anguished but all resolute and ready for the day. Today we read of Lot's wake-up call which is an act of mercy, saving him from the fate of Sodom and Gomorrah, allowing him to shelter in insignificance (in the tiny town of Zoar).

What mercy seeks you out at 3 a.m.?

† Guardian God, sing me to sleep and wake me to watchfulness, working in my depths through the night and preparing me for the day ahead.

Monday 20 April
God Who Sees

Read Genesis 21:8–20

But God said to Abraham, 'Do not be distressed … I will make a nation of Ishmael also, because he is your offspring.' God was with the boy, and he grew up.

(verses 12a, 13b and 20a)

It would not surprise me if God came to the distressed Abraham at 3 a.m. on the morning he sent Hagar and Ishmael away. By daybreak, Abraham was ready. It was an act of trust.

Things can look bleak at 3 a.m. There is a 'my brain at 3 a.m.' meme which includes sayings like, 'I can see you are trying to sleep, so I would like to offer you a selection of every memory, unresolved issue, or things you should have said or done today or in the past forty years!' Our brains can beaver away unproductively and make molehills into mountains in the wee hours. But we also sometimes wrestle difficult dilemmas in those hours, looking for a way where there appears to be none.

Hagar thought that death would be the only way out of her impossible situation. No parent can read this story without a gasp of horror at the child Ishmael cast away under the bushes to die. Hagar had not heard God's promise to Abraham. She was, however, on a first-name basis with the Holy. In Genesis 16:13 she became the only person in the Bible, female or male, to name God (as '*El-roi*', God Who Sees). And now God opens her eyes to a well of water that means survival for the two.

Terrible things happen. People may cast us away for reasons unknown to us. But we are never cast away from God Who Sees. It is darkest before the dawn, but dawn will come. We choose to trust the promise: God is with us.

† God Who Sees, in the darkest hour when I do not know where to turn, turn my gaze to you and let me find there the well that delivers living water. Amen

For further thought

What may God see here and now? What does that move you to think, do or pray?

Tuesday 21 April
You want me to do what?!

Read Genesis 22:1–14

After these things God tested Abraham ... He said, 'Take your son, your only son Isaac, whom you love, and go to the land of Moriah, and offer him there as a burnt-offering on one of the mountains that I shall show you.'

(verses 1a and 2)

The binding of Isaac (*akedah*) is my least favourite story in the Bible. God says (probably at 3 a.m.), 'Take your son ...' and Abraham does it! There is no way that Sarah knew about this; she would have thrown herself in front of the cart or taken the knife and sacrificed Abraham on the spot. Here's why I don't like this story:

- It portrays God as testing human beings. (Life tests us, not God.)
- It portrays God and Abraham as potential child abusers.
- It even valorises militarism, ennobling national calls for the sacrifice of young men and women for sometimes spurious reasons.

But as distasteful and terrifying as this story is, it remains foundational for the People of the Book. In Judaism, the sacrificial mountain becomes the site of the Holy of Holies in the Jerusalem Temple; the story is told every New Year (Rosh Hoshanah). In Islam, it is called *al-adhabih*, the 'intended sacrificial offering'. The son, who is not named, is told of the plan and assents to it. By ninth-century CE consensus in Islam, Ishmael became the identified victim. And in Christianity, Jesus becomes the sacrificial lamb, whose passion is celebrated in the days leading to Easter. The binding of Isaac is read at the Great Easter Vigil.

Why is this story so powerful? Has its credibility been eclipsed in the modern age by 'enlightened' sensibilities? Or does it convey the deep truth that following God can be costly and we'd best get on with it whether we like it or not?

† God of costly grace, sharpen my hearing and steel my will so that I may prayerfully discern and faithfully fulfil the tasks that you have for me. Amen

For further thought

God promises Abraham that both of his sons will become great nations, both blessed, both potentially a blessing. What may this mean for interfaith relations?

Wednesday 22 April
Lamentable

Read Job 7:4–19

'... my eye will never again see good ... Therefore I will not restrain my mouth; I will speak in the anguish of my spirit; I will complain in the bitterness of my soul.'

(verses 7b and 11)

When things go very wrong, the only response can be lamentation. Job, tossing and turning through the night, cannot make sense of how his life has come to this: his entire family dead, his herds carried off, his servants killed. His friend Eliphaz says no one is guiltless: take the punishment and move on. But Job knows better.

To complain bitterly is to lament, a lost art in our cheerful churches, but one known well to the psalmists. There are more psalms of lament than of any other genre in the Psalms. To lament is to take our pain to the heart of God and insist God answer. It is a noble and necessary act. It enables our hearts and minds to process the pain.

When my daughter was young, I discovered that a man had approached her in a way I felt was inappropriate. In fact, I was livid. That night I spent half an hour with Job in my hand, standing in my living room and shouting at God (expletives included). When I finally lay down exhausted, I heard, 'Did you think you would be immune from the world?' Apparently I had. I went to work the next day and calmly confronted the problem head-on.

There are three types of songs that are universal in human cultures: lullabies, wedding songs and laments. The earliest written text with a named author that we have is a lament written by Enheduanna, Sumerian poet and priestess, 4,300 years ago.[6] From ancient times until now, God has been more than willing and able to hear our pain.

† God of every time and place, hear the cries of the earth and her peoples. Hear and respond. Amen

For further thought

John Swinton, in *Raging with Compassion* (Eerdmans 2007, p. 128), recommends writing a lamentation. Use this form: address God, complain in detail, ask for what you need, vow your trust.

6 Lee, N.C. (2010), *Lyrics of Lament: From Tragedy to Transformation* (Minneapolis, MN: Fortress Press), pp. 7, 27.

Thursday 23 April
The Spirit's hour

Read Psalm 119:145–152

I rise before dawn and cry for help … you are near, O Lord.

(verses 147a and 151a)

Three a.m. – the Spirit's hour. So far we've contemplated moments of illumination and moments of agony that arise in the wee hours. The psalmist reminds us: it is also a time for prayer.

Although I usually sleep through the night, when life is difficult the pattern is interrupted and my brain at 3 a.m. revs up, perseverates and rambles. In one of those periods I researched insomnia and tried warm milk, melatonin tablets, getting up and reading, counting backwards, body relaxation and acupressure aids, with little success. Wordy prayers didn't help much; my mind kept spinning. Now I wonder, why didn't I turn to the Psalms? I would have found good company there, though, depending on the problem I was wrestling and my capacity to dwell with the Word of God, I may just have argued with what I was reading.

Better, I think, to use the kind of calming breath prayer known to contemplatives and mystics: breathing in God's peace and presence, breathing out trust. You can choose a mantra to go with the breath, like 'You are near' (in breath); 'I am Yours' (out breath).

When the scribes copied out the Psalms, they identified the middle word and letter to check their accuracy. The middle letter of the Psalms is ע, *ayin*. *Ayin* is also a word meaning 'eye'. The psalmists offered their prayers under the eye of God.

In the Spirit's hour, tossing and turning, we can remember the nearness of God, under whose loving gaze we live, and surrender confusion and conundrum into the breath of God.

† God of the Spirit hour, in my tossing and my turning, bring me to breathe in your peace.

For further thought
Create a breath prayer and practise it daily for one minute and then for longer periods. It will come more easily in the Spirit hour.

Easter: with the rising of the sun – 2 Rising early

April

Friday 24 April
Dream on

Read Genesis 40:5–19

And Joseph said to them, 'Do not interpretations belong to God? Please tell them to me.'

(verse 8b)

It was dreaming that landed Joseph in Egypt. Sharing his own megalomaniac dreams with his brothers, they connived to deprive him of the opportunity. 'Here comes the dreamer,' they exclaimed, and they dumped him in a pit before selling him to traders, who sold him to Potiphar in Egypt. There he rose to become overseer of Potiphar's house, until he refused Potiphar's wife and she accused him of assault.

Imprisoned, Joseph interprets the dreams of his cellmates. Never one to miss an opportunity, he asks them to put in a word with Pharaoh. Two years later Pharaoh's dreams perplex and the Hebrew lad languishing in jail is remembered. Joseph is hauled out and interprets the dreams as warning of famine to come. Pharaoh elevates Joseph, making him overseer of the whole land. The story ends years later when Joseph saves his brothers and father when they are in a time of need.

I've had three God dreams over the past 30 years, all in a time of transition, all revealing the Divine in some numinous way. Each time I was stunned and grateful. Each time the images and feelings lingered. I do not doubt that the Spirit reaches into our dreams.

Some West African traditions hold that there is a dream that is dreaming us.[7] Yes. God's vision of a world at peace, where steadfast love and faithfulness meet and justice rolls down like mighty waters, has captivated the imaginations of religious folk everywhere. Permeating our consciousness, the dream has had the power to shape lives and fuel courageous acts.

† Dream on, dear God, dream on. Infect me with the daring of Your dreams and inspire me to offer my life to their fulfilment.

For further thought

What dream fuels your passion and enables you to take risks for its fulfilment? Whose dream is it?

---

7 Ida Postma, 'A Dreaming of Us', from *Sunrise magazine* (Theosophical University Press, November, 1976) (www.theosophy-nw.org/theosnw/world/africa/my-ida4.htm, last accessed 3 October 2018).

Saturday 25 April
Early in the morning

Read Mark 1:35–39

In the morning, while it was still very dark, he got up and went out to a deserted place, and there he prayed.

(verse 35)

There is something about early morning, before the sun has peeked over the horizon. The stillness sharpens the senses.

From time to time the group I swim with in the North Sea organises a dawn swim. Driving to the beach in the half-light of pre-dawn, I've startled owls, jerked to a halt for scrambling bunnies and narrowly missed a fox slinking across the road. Such is the only life I usually see until I pull up in the car park. Once in the water, we stroke and glide, one eye set to the east to see the fiery ball that will emerge if the clouds permit. When it does and its fire makes a path over the sea, my heart explodes with joy. There is nothing like it. And, as one of my swimming buddies always says, 'It's completely free.'

I imagine Jesus seeing first light and seeing it as the gift and wonder that it is. Those moments communing with his Abba and witnessing the start of a new day gave him what he needed to do what he needed to do. A number of times the Gospels report that he stole away early in the morning to be with God.

Often I think I'm too busy for that kind of communion. Whom am I kidding? Martin Luther is reported to have said that when he had much to do, he would spend the first three hours of the day in prayer. The busier he got, the more he needed the peace, power and presence of God to prepare him for the day.

† Creator of sun, sea and stars, call me into communion with You and all that You have made, that I may live and love as You desire.

For further thought

What enables you to commune with the Holy? How often do you do it? What's stopping you?

1 and 2 Thessalonians –
1 The labour of love

Notes by **John Proctor**

John works in London as General Secretary of the United Reformed Church, supporting local church life and witness around Britain. He previously taught New Testament studies in Cambridge and prior to that was a parish minister in Glasgow. John has written commentaries on Matthew (BRF 2001) and the Corinthian letters (WJK 2015) and Grove booklets on the Gospels and Acts. He is married to Elaine and they live near Cambridge. John has used the NRSVA for these notes.

Sunday 26 April
Looking back, looking forward

Read 1 Thessalonians 1

We always give thanks to God for all of you and mention you in our prayers, constantly remembering before our God and Father your work of faith and labour of love and steadfastness of hope in our Lord Jesus Christ.

(verses 2–3)

This is a letter of memory. Paul remembered his friends in Thessalonica. Their Christian life had begun abruptly and harshly. After making a fresh and full-hearted commitment to the gospel, they met angry and painful opposition in their local community. So Paul looked back with sadness and pride at the pressures these new Christians had faced and the courage they had shown. He remembered them in prayer too, thanking God for the signs he had seen of the Holy Spirit's work among them.

So this is also a letter of hope. What God begins, God sustains. Part of the gospel Paul brought was a word about waiting (verse 10). The church waits for God's great act of triumph and mercy, when the earth shall be changed and the risen Jesus shall reign. We look forward. Hope of this kind brings 'steadfastness' (verse 3). It gives Christians spine and strength. There are countries and settings today where this message sounds a deep echo, where liberty and even life are under threat because people believe in Jesus. Let us remember these people and places, with thanks, in prayer and with sorrow and pride.

† May the Christ of the cross and of Easter give steadfast hope and courage to all who suffer for their faith in him.

Monday 27 April
Teaching and trust

Read 1 Thessalonians 2:1–12

So deeply do we care for you that we are determined to share with you not only the gospel of God but also our own selves, because you have become very dear to us.

(verse 8)

People are more likely to take our faith seriously if they find they can trust us. It was the same in New Testament times. The reputation of the Christian good news depended on the people who spoke and shared it. Conduct commends. Integrity gives credibility. Good character is itself an advocate for the gospel.

These verses were not, however, written to commend the faith to outsiders. They were a reminder to new Christians, whose faith was under test and threat, of the qualities of the people who had brought them the message. The aim was to strengthen and encourage, to refresh the bond between preachers and people, to give the Thessalonians a model for their own conduct and to show that the Christian faith could hold its head up as a worthy and honest way of life.

Some of the language here was also used by Greek philosophers. Integrity, courage and candour were virtues to which many teachers in that era aspired, and Paul was willing for his ministry too to be assessed by these standards. But there may still be something a little distinctive about the way Christians spoke. They looked on one another as family: 'brothers and sisters' (verse 1); 'a father with his children' (verse 11); deep care and sharing (verse 8). They were animated by strong and tender love and a steady sense of belonging and mutual support. That's still a pattern to follow, a resource to draw upon and a reason for giving ourselves generously and gladly to one another.

† God of love, please refresh my love for the people around me. Help me to be generous, caring and honest, as Jesus was. Amen

For further thought
Who are the people who have helped your Christian life? What was it about them that made an impact on you?

Tuesday 28 April
Blessing and bruises

Read 1 Thessalonians 2:13–16

We also constantly give thanks to God for this, that when you received the word of God that you heard from us, you accepted it not as a human word but as what it really is, God's word, which is also at work in you believers.

(verse 13)

Many a letter in the ancient world began with thanksgiving. This one does (1:2), and the note of thanks reappears at 2:13, as it will again at 3:9. Paul is intensely grateful for the commitment his friends in Thessalonica have shown to their faith, in a stressful and unsettling situation, and this gratitude overflows into his writing. He is sure that their courage and strength come from God and from the power and truth of 'the gospel of God' (2:2, 8, 9), the good news about Jesus.

Then as Paul recalls his friends' steadiness under pressure, he starts to think about similar struggles that had afflicted the church in the Holy Land. He remembers their tussles with religious leaders in Israel and the way these tensions had spilled over into the gentile world (verses 14–16). In many towns, synagogue Judaism and messianic Judaism (what we now call Christianity) found themselves at odds and in competition. Certainly this had been the case in Thessalonica (Acts 17:1–9), where the people of Jesus had taken some hard knocks.

Those clashes and pains are background to the harsh language of these verses. Some of Paul's bruises come out in his writing. Yet Christians are surely called to a different style of speech today, when we talk with and about Jewish people. Anti-semitism is an ugly and growing reality in many parts of the world. The church ought to stand firmly against that trend and to build bridges of respect and peace with our Jewish neighbours.

† Pray for the good news of Jesus to be a powerful force in your life, giving you courage, confidence and wisdom, whatever pressures you face.

For further thought

Pause to reflect on any tensions in your local or national community, and consider what you might do to build bridges across the divisions.

Wednesday 29 April
Distance and desire

Read 1 Thessalonians 2:17 – 3:5

For what is our hope or joy or crown of boasting before our Lord Jesus at his coming? Is it not you? Yes, you are our glory and joy!

(verses 19–20)

Paul had left Thessalonica hastily (Acts 17:10) and had travelled onwards through Greece. Before very long he reached Athens (3:1), a calmer and quieter place, about 200 miles to the south. But it hurt him to be so far away. He wanted to see his friends in Thessalonica and to know how they were faring. He felt that they were in a spiritual battle, and the same malicious power that might be leading them astray (3:5) was making it difficult for him to get back and offer support (2:18).

So eventually, he sent Timothy, a young helper, back to Thessalonica (3:2). Timothy was a gentler character than Paul, rather less likely to attract attention and controversy. He could give the church some discreet encouragement without stirring up opposition in the town. He would help them to hold the faith and stay the course, and then he could report back to Paul.

So these verses describe a practical step that Paul took. But they are full of intense emotion too: 'made orphans by being separated from you' (2:17); 'we could bear it no longer' (3:1, 5). This is a pastor who really loved his people. The churches of the New Testament had strong networks of contact and care which spanned the miles and lasted through the years. Part of their motivation was hope. Christians looked forward to the final coming of Christ, when all they had shared on earth would be rich joy in heaven.

† Remember people far away for whom you care deeply. Pray for them and remember especially any difficulties that may be troubling them at the moment.

For further thought
Where have you known bonds of Christian fellowship that remained strong across the miles and the years? What can you do to strengthen these now?

Thursday 30 April
Good news of great joy

Read 1 Thessalonians 3:6–13

Now may our God and Father himself and our Lord Jesus direct our way to you. And may the Lord make you increase and abound in love for one another and for all, just as we abound in love for you.

(verses 11–12)

Timothy had returned from his follow-up visit to Thessalonica. By now it seems that Paul was in Corinth, a little further on than Athens (Acts 18:5). Timothy's report was good. These new Christians were keeping the faith and living in love, and they longed to see Paul as keenly as he remembered them. This news brought Paul encouragement, gladness and a fresh energy in his prayers (verses 7–10). It made him feel alive and hopeful. His work had stood the test and borne fruit. His people were standing firm.

The last short paragraph of chapter 3 is a so-called 'wish prayer'. 'I hope and pray that God will …' is the meaning. There are a few of these wish-prayers in the two Thessalonian letters, although this form of words is rather unusual elsewhere in the New Testament. The others are at 1 Thessalonians 5:23 and 2 Thessalonians 2:16–17, 3:5 and 3:16. Their concern is always positive and practical – that the Thessalonians be sustained by God, to follow a faithful and wholesome pattern of life.

This first wish-prayer gives a condensed preview of themes in the chapters just ahead. 'May God direct our path to your door,' it asks. 'May God cause you to grow in love, and strengthen you to live holy lives' (verses 11–13). Holy living will then be the concern of 4:1–8, love will be the topic in 4:9–12, and 'the coming of our Lord Jesus with all his saints' (verse 13) will be the thread that runs from 4:13 to 5:11. Hope, lifestyle and relationships are the stuff of which discipleship is made.

† Remember a piece of good news that lifted your heart, and thank God once again for all that it meant to you.

For further thought

What do you pray for when you pray for Christian friends? Can today's wish-prayer suggest concerns you could take up with God on their behalf?

Friday 1 May
Living for God and neighbour

Read 1 Thessalonians 4:1–12

Finally, brothers and sisters, we ask and urge you in the Lord Jesus that, as you learned from us how you ought to live and to please God (as, in fact, you are doing), you should do so more and more.

(verse 1)

The news that Timothy brought must have been somewhat mixed. By and large, it seems, members of the Thessalonian church were committed to the Christian way and took its values and demands seriously. But with such a group of new believers, there were bound to be a few issues to straighten out. Life is testing, and the heady blessings of new faith evidently had to be supplemented by some sober teaching about everyday relationships.

Sex can lead to many a misjudgement. In the Greek and Roman worlds, married men were sometimes casual rather than careful about their relationships. But Paul saw marital loyalty as a mark of a person's loyalty to God. Faithfulness and self-control were matters of honour, of self-respect, of duty to promises and to partner. Words that mean 'holy' or 'holiness' come up four times in quick succession (verses 3, 4, 7, 8). Our most intimate relationships should reflect our relationship with Christ.

What we may, and must, share freely is the duty of practical love. At times this will involve giving to sisters and brothers in need. But that is not the point here. It appears that some Christians in Thessalonica were too ready to receive, to draw on the generosity of fellow-believers. 'Don't live like that,' is the message of verses 9–12, 'if you can help it.' Supporting ourselves, as fully as we reasonably can, is a sign of our love for people around us. It's a way of giving them space and resource for the living of their own days and years.

† In a world that is often needy and sometimes careless, let us ask Jesus Christ to give us open and generous hearts and careful and watchful lives.

For further thought

What warnings and corrections do you think would help your Christian living to stay on track?

Saturday 2 May
Grieving in hope

Read 1 Thessalonians 4:13–18

But we do not want you to be uninformed, brothers and sisters, about those who have died, so that you may not grieve as others do who have no hope. For since ... Jesus died and rose again, even so, through Jesus, God will bring with him those who have died.

(verses 13–14)

Here we see another of the pains that the new Christians in Thessalonica had to bear: bereavement. What had faith to say when loved ones were taken and the world felt cold and hollow? Where had these friends gone when they died? What hope did they have of resurrection? Where would they be when Jesus came in victory and power? This hope, that his glory would be seen and his kingdom spread across the earth, would be sadly dimmed if departed friends could have no share in it.

To this sorrow and uncertainty, Paul's letter gives no shallow advice about not grieving, or about bereavement not mattering much. The wounds of loss go deep and swift and careless words will not mend them. But Christians can speak of hope. We grieve but we do not despair. Look forward without fear. The cross and risen life of Jesus have the strength and reach to raise his people to new life. When he comes in victory and power, those who have died will rise to meet him. Jesus' 'cry of command' that called Lazarus from the tomb (John 11:43) will sound again, calling his sleeping people to rise (verse 16).

Some church people are very much helped by Paul's language of trumpet and clouds. Others instinctively think in less graphic ways. But whichever group you are in, do read these verses as words of promise. The Lord whose life reached beyond death can reach into our bereavements and our frailty too, to turn grief into hope and dying into resurrection.

† Remember anyone you know who has been recently bereaved and pray that they will know the company and care of Jesus on their journey through grief.

For further thought

What do you believe that will help you to die without fear? How can you renew your grip on this part of your faith?

1 and 2 Thessalonians –
2 Do not be shaken

Notes by **John Proctor**

For John's biography, see p. 118. John has used the NRSVA for these notes.

Sunday 3 May
Disciples of the dawn

> **Read 1 Thessalonians 5:1–11**
>
> *When they say, 'There is peace and security', then sudden destruction will come upon them, as labour pains come upon a pregnant woman, and there will be no escape! But you, beloved, are not in darkness, for that day to surprise you like a thief …*
>
> (verses 3–4)

Yesterday's reading spoke with warmth and assurance about the Lord's coming. Today's verses are more measured. Christians can look forward to 'that day' without distress or alarm, yet we must be watchful. Confidence and calm are not at all the same as carelessness and complacency. Vigilance matters: not for tracking the details of a cosmic timetable, but as steady care for our own discipleship. Faith need not be surprised by God's dawn. We can respond even now to the promise of its light.

In New Testament times, 'peace and security' (verse 3) was a political manifesto. Propaganda of this kind was beloved by Roman emperors. It proclaimed and publicised the benefits of their reign. To their citizens, around the colonies and even among conquered peoples, these words said, 'You're alright with us. The empire keeps you safe.' So when Paul uses them, he may be hinting that even the most potent and permanent of earthly powers will be overtaken by the judgement of God. A new world is coming to life, and its birth will stretch and strain the regimes of our small day.

So beside 'Be vigilant' come two further commands: 'Be sober.' Sobriety is not just about alcohol. It means not letting our sense and stability be swept away by the heady potions of time, by the myths of celebrity, slogan, prosperity or power. And 'Be armed.' Not literally. Carry the defences of faith, hope and love. Let these be the outward face of your character and conduct, and you will not be overcome.

† May Christ give his people vigilance of heart and life, clarity of mind and will, strength of character and spirit. So may we who wait for the day be glad to welcome its coming.

Pastors in practice

Read 1 Thessalonians 5:12–28

… respect those who labour among you, and have charge of you in the Lord and admonish you … Be at peace among yourselves. And we urge you, beloved, to admonish the idlers, encourage the faint-hearted, help the weak, be patient with all of them.

(verses 12b and 13b–14)

This last half-chapter of the letter moves forward to an affectionate farewell and confident blessing. On the way it gives several pieces of shrewd advice. People, prayer, patience, praise, gifts, service and teamwork all come under the spotlight for a few seconds. This is the ordinary, active, beautiful, holy and messy tapestry of being Christians together. The first topic is loving your leaders.

We do not know who led the Thessalonian church. Those who had been Christians longest, or had houses big enough to meet in, or wealth to share with the poor, or gifts of public speaking? Or none of the above? The credibility of a leader, according to these verses, comes chiefly from service, from hard work, commitment and consistency, from 'labour among you' (verse 12). That deserves respect. People who work hard earn the right to be taken seriously. Part of the church's response to good leadership is to work at our own Christian relationships, to be at peace with one another.

What leaders owe the church in return is to see people as individuals, to treat us all according to need and to care for each one personally. That may mean different styles of caring, for people with varied circumstances and temperaments. But there will be one absolute constant: be patient with everyone. Pastoring takes time. Whether Christians are growing, learning or healing, going deep with God or opening out to neighbour, we generally do it slowly. Blessed is the church whose pastor can support God's work, patiently and gradually, in the lives of God's ordinary, beautiful, untidy, fallible, Christian people.

† Pray for church leaders that you know – especially for any who are running out of energy or love or patience – and ask God to refresh them.

For further thought

Name the Christians with whom you are most deeply and firmly linked. In what ways do you depend on their patience, and they on yours?

Struggle and stamina

Read 2 Thessalonians 1:1–5

Therefore we ourselves boast of you among the churches of God for your steadfastness and faith during all your persecutions ... This is evidence of the righteous judgement of God, and is intended to make you worthy of the kingdom of God, for which you are also suffering.

(verses 4–5)

Several important themes from the first letter to the Thessalonians surface again in Second Thessalonians. The writing style is similar too, but the tone and mood are a little edgier and more anxious. There is more tension in the writing and surely in the background situation also. Fresh news may have come from Thessalonica, and Paul is concerned about how the Christians there are faring. Amid opposition and resentment in their local community, suffering and struggle have become quite persistent factors in their church life.

Paul is clearly proud of this church's courage and steadiness. Yet he is keen to help them too. So he reminds them that their suffering is not in vain. It is already making a difference both to their lives and to other people's well-being. For as Paul visits and writes to other churches, he has told of the believers in Thessalonica and of their resilience and commitment. This has proved an example, an encouragement and a challenge. Good news like this can strengthen nerve and spine, and inspire other Christians to hold firm when they are tested.

Not only this, but suffering has actually helped the Thessalonians. Their steadfastness confirms that they are on track in their Christian journey. It shows that they are kingdom people, citizens of heaven as well as residents on earth. Despite the pressures they have faced, their faith and love are growing (verse 3). Their pilgrimage may be a rough and uphill struggle, but they are making progress and heading towards the destination.

† Remember someone you know who is under pressure or in pain at the moment. Ask God to give them the perspective and patience they will need to get through another day.

For further thought

Has it been true for you, as it is for some Christians, that times of great difficulty have also been seasons of gain and growth?

May

1 and 2 Thessalonians – 2 Do not be shaken

Wednesday 6 May
Uncomfortable words

Read 2 Thessalonians 1:6–12

For it is indeed just of God to repay with affliction those who afflict you, and to give relief to the afflicted as well as to us, when the Lord Jesus is revealed from heaven with his mighty angels in flaming fire, inflicting vengeance on those who do not know God …

(verses 6–8a)

Christians do not usually find judgement a comfortable topic to explore. We prefer to focus on the gentle and generous side of God's nature. Yet the Bible often affirms that the final reckoning of things is in God's hands, and scripture can be surprisingly positive at the thought of God coming to judge. For that will be a moment of truth, which is generally a good thing in itself. It will be a time for creation to laugh rather than weep. On that day, wrongs will be put right, oppressed people will breathe freely again, and damaged hearts and spirits will know that God is on their side. For God judges 'with righteousness'. See for example Psalm 96 or 98.

This is the frame of thinking that makes best sense of today's severe verses. Some of the readers have suffered badly at the hands of neighbours and persecutors, and Paul reminds them that this order of things will not go on for ever. Relief will come. The balance will be corrected. Jesus is Lord, and one day his lordship will reshape history and humanity.

Then, says Paul, people who have deliberately put energy and effort into mocking and undermining this new and fragile church will discover that it was Jesus whom they were persecuting. Even that need not mean that Jesus' mercy could not reach them – as Paul himself knew – but if they persist in despising that mercy, there may be no other safety net available. That, I think, is what these unusually direct and severe verses are getting at.

† God of justice, we pray for places where people are treated brutally, carelessly or unfairly. Teach your world that you weigh and test our living and that your ways and values matter.

For further thought

Remember people you know who have to judge others: in law, in exams, in interviews. Ask God to keep them clear, careful and fair.

Thursday 7 May
Concern and confidence

Read 2 Thessalonians 2:1–12

... we beg you, brothers and sisters, not to be quickly shaken in mind ... to the effect that the day of the Lord is already here ... for that day will not come unless the rebellion comes first and the lawless one is revealed, the one destined for destruction.

(verses 1b–3)

Although parts of this chapter defy explanation, the opening couple of verses are reasonably clear. Something has given the Thessalonian church the idea that the 'day of the Lord' has already arrived. Perhaps they took so seriously Paul's words about Jesus' sudden and unpredictable coming (1 Thessalonians 5:1–11) that they now fear this event might have been invisible too. Perhaps Jesus has come in glory and they never noticed. So Paul tries to allay their alarm.

He describes the 'coming of our Lord Jesus' (verse 1) as part of an era of struggle and crisis, as one of a series of events that will convulse history. First there will be a great stirring of evil in the activity of a 'lawless one' (verses 3–8), who will thumb his nose at God and assert his power as if he were God. Only when this evil has succeeded in savaging and souring human life will Jesus come in power, to reclaim the territory for God and restore wholeness and hope to the world. That certainly will not happen, says Paul to the Thessalonians, without your noticing it.

Meanwhile, 'you know', Paul tells them, 'what is now restraining' that lawlessness (verse 6). What he meant, we do not now know. Yet the picture is much clearer when Jesus is in view: the word 'coming' (verse 8) also means 'presence'. The Christian hope is that Jesus will one day be present in the world, visibly, powerfully and fully. Then evil will end and goodness will have its long and lasting day.

† Lord Jesus, we ask for wisdom and courage to live in hope. Keep us from despair, from anxiety, from impatience and from false fears. We trust you. Help us to know how to trust you.

For further thought

Do you find it helpful to answer 'I don't know what the world's coming to' with 'I do know who's coming to the world'?

May

1 and 2 Thessalonians – 2 Do not be shaken

Life forces

Read 2 Thessalonians 2:13 – 3:5

... God chose you as the first fruits for salvation through sanctification by the Spirit and through belief in the truth. For this purpose he called you through our proclamation of the good news, so that you may obtain the glory of our Lord Jesus Christ. So then, brothers and sisters, stand firm ...

(verses 13b–15a)

Yesterday's reading assured the Thessalonians about God's large-scale purposes: what was happening to the world? Today's reading has a more personal slant: what was happening in their lives? Paul talks of three personal and positive forces that have shaped these people's faith. What he says reaches much further than this one church. It speaks of the lively and loving relationships that are regularly at work in Christian experience.

God has been the prime mover. 'God chose you' (verse 13), yet not as if people were pawns on a chessboard. God reached out in loving relationship to mould lives from within. When the Spirit stirs within us, then 'sanctification' gets under way. We become more holy, more Christlike. That's what God intends, desires and makes possible.

Other people contribute too. The 'proclamation of the good news' (verse 14) can be like a beam of light shining into our hearts. This does not often happen in isolation. It depends on someone else making the effort to tell us. Christian life is not generally solitary, and it usually starts as a shared experience, a personal response to a message that others have brought to us.

Finally, Christian living asks for deliberate and sustained commitment from each believer. 'Stand firm and hold fast,' says Paul (verse 15). The fact that God is at work in us is not an excuse to freewheel. It's a reason to be serious and determined about our life with Christ, a motivation to go forward with steady consistency in the strength that God gives.

† Think back to the people who helped you believe the Christian message. Thank God for them and remember in your prayers any challenges they may be facing now.

For further thought

How do you react to the thought that God chose you? Does it ring true to your experience? What responsibilities might it give you?

Personal touch

Read 2 Thessalonians 3:6–18

For you yourselves know how you ought to imitate us … when we were with you … we worked night and day, so that we might not burden any of you … I, Paul, write this greeting with my own hand.

(verses 7–8 and 17a)

Today's portion returns, quite emphatically, to a theme from 1 Thessalonians (4:9–12). Some in the church were too willing to live by the generosity of others and Paul urges these people to look for a job and work hard at it. He also warns the church not to bail out members who are content to drift and doze through life. He recalls that he had not asked local people to resource his ministry in Thessalonica. Later, he did accept their gifts, to support his mission in other places (2 Corinthians 11:7–11). For he aimed to make the gospel free at the point of delivery. On the basis of this example, he urges the Thessalonians to support themselves as well as they can.

That situation is, of course, not the same as that of the person who is prevented from working by health or family needs or lack of opportunity. In those circumstances we should try to help. Yet in a society like Thessalonica, where patronage – little pyramids of personal dependence – was quite common, Paul's message was surely a salutary reminder. In Christian fellowship, our only real patron is Jesus. Doing what we can for ourselves is a mark of our trust in him.

Finally Paul takes over from the friend who has scribed the letter, and signs it off himself. Again he is hands-on. This personal touch with pen and ink helps to make vivid the memory of his manual labour. When he speaks of peace and grace (verses 16, 18), it is as if he is handing these gifts directly to the people he loves.

† 'Now may the Lord of peace himself give you peace at all times in all ways' (verse 16). For whom would you wish this today? Pray for that person.

For further thought

Have you ever challenged somebody, or been challenged yourself, to 'stand on your own feet'? Was that a difficult conversation? What did it teach you?

May

1 and 2 Thessalonians – 2 Do not be shaken

On the road – 1 First steps

Notes by **Jan Sutch Pickard**

Jan, a poet, preacher and storyteller, lives on the Isle of Mull, having worked and raised a family in Nigeria, Notting Hill and New Mills. Working as an editor for various Methodist publications, she joined the ecumenical Iona Community. After six years on Iona, becoming warden of the Abbey, she served with the Ecumenical Accompaniment Programme in Palestine and Israel. Jan has used the NRSVA for these notes.

Sunday 10 May
Walking in the garden

Read Genesis 3:1–13

They heard the sound of the Lord God walking in the garden at the time of the evening breeze, and the man and his wife hid themselves from the presence of the Lord God among the trees of the garden.

(verse 8)

Here's a God with feet on the ground. Storytellers long ago didn't imagine a remote figure of authority, but a Being relishing the evening breeze, enjoying a fruitful garden: a God who created living, growing things, including human beings.

I remembered this story when helping to harvest damsons in a friend's orchard one damp September day. As we shook the branches, laughing, ripe fruit pattered down on every side. I remembered, too, joining Palestinians in the olive harvest: a different climate but the same celebration of God's bounty, amid laughter of people working together. But here God walks into a scene where those created to enjoy the garden have run for cover, hiding their guilt. Where on earth do we go from here?

This week we'll be hearing from poets and chroniclers of an ancient world, about a walk with God that's not always straightforward: uncertain first steps, moments of confusion in a journey of exploration. The blaming can begin as soon as things go wrong. No one wants to accept responsibility. Instead, hostility and fear can mean that nations build walls and block the way for others. But God can show wanderers in the wilderness that there is another, better way.

† Show us that way, God, to enjoy your creation, without exploiting or wasting it, to share its goodness with others, without guilt or blame. Amen

Monday 11 May
Prayer walking

Read Genesis 24:1–21

… There was Rebekah … coming out with her water jar on her shoulder … she went down to the spring, filled her jar, and came up. Then the servant ran to meet her and said, 'Please let me sip a little water from your jar.' 'Drink, my lord,' she said …

(verses 15–18a)

In the cool of the evening a woman walks to the well. With other women, carrying water-pots, she comes from the city to this outlying spring, where local shepherds bring their flocks and travellers wait their turn to water their camels. One has come many miles, on an errand from his master Abraham: searching for a bride to continue the nomadic family's line. The servant's prayer is that he will find the right woman among those coming to draw water. He is a man with a mission, hoping God will guide him with a sign.

While Rebekah, going gracefully about her daily task, is not looking for a husband, what does she hope for, what is her prayer? Perhaps it's beyond words. She puts one foot in front of another on stones still warm from the sun. She balances the water-pot on her shoulder, feeling its smooth curve, expecting the weight of the water; she pauses, sees a stranger, hears his voice, understands his human need for a drink. Today we might call this 'mindfulness': wholly present in the moment, being the person God created her to be. This woman embodies her prayer, as she is open to what God may do in her life.

Spoken prayers may express wonder, regret, gratitude or yearning, maybe about our needs or those of the world. But prayer can also be wordless, a state of being, present in God's world using all of our senses. Whether on pilgrimage to new places or moving around our familiar community, a prayer walk can bring us closer to God.

† Pour a glass of water, and thank God as you drink. With eyes closed, let the sounds of the world, near and far, prompt prayers.

For further thought

Take a walk through your community, pausing by places like the library, shop, bus stop, health centre, school. Pray for those who need and use them.

Tuesday 12 May
Road closed/no way!

Read Numbers 20:14–21

But Edom said to him, 'You shall not pass through, or we will come out with the sword against you.' The Israelites said to him, 'We will stay on the highway; and if we drink of your water ... we will pay for it ... just let us pass through on foot.' But he said, 'You shall not pass through.'

(verses 18, 19 and 20a)

Picture a great crowd of people on the road, not heading for a football match or a carnival, but seeking a place of safety, a new home. Five years ago, thousands of migrants – mostly refugees – made their way on foot across Europe, along motorways, across fields. Many individuals and families still try to make the journey from places of conflict in Africa and the Middle East. But in 2015, there was a mass movement of desperate people on the move. Sometimes local people, motivated by Christianity or common humanity, displayed signs saying 'Refugees welcome' and put that welcome into practical action. In other places, the doors were shut and governments closed the borders: even to those who simply wanted to pass through.

I am writing midway between such remembered scenes from newspapers and television (which you may even have witnessed in person) and your reading this. The closing of borders goes on, and the building of walls. Is there still a wall/fence between the US and Mexico, a separation barrier between Israelis and Palestinians?

Read the whole of this passage describing the Hebrews, a migrant people at this stage in their history, in transit along the edge of Edomite territory. The chronicler tells how they tried to show that they would not pose a threat, would not deplete the land's resources, or would pay for what met their basic needs, taking nothing, leaving only a footprint. But the answer from the ruler of the Edomites was, 'You shall not pass through' (verse 20). 'No way' is the message of those who fear and reject difference.

† God, we are all people on the move, all our lives long; help us to be open to the needs and the journeys of others, for in your presence all are welcome. Amen

For further thought

How do we as nations, communities and individuals react to those we see 'invading our space'?

Wednesday May 13
'This is not the way'

Read 2 Kings 6:8–23

Elisha said to them, 'This is not the way, and this is not the city; follow me.' … When the king of Israel saw them he said to Elisha, 'Father, shall I kill them? Shall I kill them?' He answered 'No!' … So he prepared for them a great feast; after they ate and drank and he sent them on their way.

(verses 19a, 21–22a, 23a)

Hostile nations and warring tribes, disputing territory, imposing the will of rulers by force. Is this the Middle East 800 years before Christ, or our own times and other parts of the world? It could be both.

This begins like a spy story: 'Once when the king of Aram was at war with Israel …' (verse 8). Elisha, the man of God, an undercover agent, was able to keep the king of Israel informed of the plans and movements of the Arameans. With his cover blown, Elisha was hunted down by the angry king of Aram, who surrounded his hideout in Dothan (a city between present-day Jordan and Egypt) with a great army. His servant's consternation was met with calm assurance by Elisha, disclosing that the place was protected by another army, with chariots of fire.

The story goes on that God, who'd provided this supernatural bodyguard, enabled Elisha to strike his opponents blind. So far this sounds like a violent version of what it means to have God on one's side. But we shouldn't jump to conclusions. Elisha tells his pursuers, now helpless, 'This is not the way …' (verse 19). He leads them as far as Samaria and restores their sight. The king of Israel is eager to destroy enemies delivered into his hands. But Elisha says, 'No.' Again, this is not the way. Instead, the prophet says, 'Set food and water before them so that they may eat and drink; and let them go to their master' (verse 22). In place of the bloody denouement of a spy thriller, there is feasting, forgiveness, homecoming, a promise of peace.

† Loving God, remind us that we are safe in your hands and that, because you are a merciful God, our well-being doesn't depend on outwitting or outdoing others; that there is another way.

For further thought

Can you think of a time when you have needed to be reminded of this? How did you respond?

Thursday May 14
Walking by the river

> **Read Exodus 2:5–9**
>
> *The daughter of Pharaoh came down to bathe at the river, while her attendants walked beside the river. She saw the basket among the reeds and sent her maid to bring it. When she opened it, she saw the child. He was crying, and she took pity on him.*
>
> (verses 5–6b)

The great River Nile flows through fertile land, irrigated so that crops flourish green and gold to the horizon. A princess has come to bathe in the cool water. Her attendants walk along the bank as she floats with the current. They are keeping watch: women always need to be watchful. But this is a peaceful scene. Compare this story with yesterday's, set amid the conflicts of powerful men.

There is a different kind of threat here. Crouching among the reeds, a small child is also keeping watch. She's one of the enslaved Hebrew people, whose numbers have grown so great that Pharaoh has decreed a cull: all male babies should be killed. One woman has hidden her boy-child in a basket bobbing among the reeds. Now his sister sees with horror the family's enemies find the basket, hears the baby crying (imagine the atrocities of genocide, in Rwanda, in Myanmar). But the princess is moved to pity, and the little sister inspired to offer her mother as a wet-nurse.

And so, in a dangerous world, not only is this child's life saved, but he's restored to his mother's breast, then adopted by royalty and brought up in a royal palace. An earlier part of this story names Shiphrah and Puah, subversive midwives who cheated soldiers to save the children. The women here – mother and daughter, servants and princess – are nameless, but the baby, we know, has a name: Moses, drawn out of the water. He becomes a man who will save his people by taking them on a long walk through the wilderness to freedom.

† Imagine a child crying. Think of some of the dangers small children face, from natural disasters and hunger, to the cruelty of other human beings. In your imagination, put those children into God's loving hands.

For further thought

Find a charity focusing on the needs of children. Read about its work. In what small way (it might not be money) could you help?

Friday May 15
'Go to the springs'

Read 1 Kings 18:1–16

The word of the Lord came to Elijah, in the third year of the drought, saying, 'Go, present yourself to Ahab; I will send rain on the earth.' ... Ahab said to Obadiah, 'Go through the land to all the springs of water ... perhaps we may find grass to keep the horses and mules alive ...'

(verses 1 and 5)

The land's dying because of the drought. Men make their way across burning hillsides and empty wadis. Ahab here seems desperate for the welfare of animals and people. He and Obadiah go in different directions, searching for water and any chance of grazing. Meanwhile Elijah searches for Ahab: God has challenged him to speak face to face with this cruel and capricious man, before the drought can be lifted. Obadiah's caught in the middle; a compassionate and God-fearing man, he's already defied Ahab secretly, saving the lives of prophets threatened with death. Now here's Elijah, with a price on his head, asking Obadiah to take a message to Ahab. Why should Obadiah get involved? He suspects that God will save Elijah at the last minute, while Ahab, finding no prophet, will kill the messenger. Obadiah is sure it will all end in tears.

Reading Obadiah's dramatic (almost comic) protests, it's possible to forget the drought. But Elijah doesn't, and he persists with the task God has given him. Obadiah at last agrees to go and find Ahab, and survives! The prophet and the king meet. The drought ends with the miracle of rain.

There's also meaning in the springs of water. In limestone hills there may be little surface water but deep below the ground aquifers flow, which can be tapped by deep wells; sometimes surprising springs appear. Both Elijah and Obadiah, with all his fears, tap into springs of courage. Even Ahab cares for his people and their animals. Today, in places where suffering people thirst for justice, such springs can still be found.

† May God, who offers us living water, refresh our spirit like the rain, and lead us to drink from deep springs of encouragement.

For further thought

What do you know about the water that comes from your tap: its source, how it's purified? Where did your community get water 150 years ago?

May

On the road – 1 First steps

137

Mind your step/being led astray

Read Proverbs 7:6–18

I observed ... a young man without sense, passing along the street ... taking the road to her house in the twilight, in the evening ... Then a woman comes towards him, decked out like a prostitute ... her feet do not stay at home.

(verses 7–11)

What an interesting way to end a week of inspiring and challenging human stories. Here's a foolish young man being led astray by a woman of ill-repute: a lively caricature, containing folk-wisdom like much of the Book of Proverbs. But not the whole picture!

Here's a warning of how easily we can be led astray. The young man wandering aimlessly, follows a prostitute, is invited into her house. Underlying this image is fear of female sexuality, which has caused centuries of religious rejection and social oppression. But when we start blaming, we're back with Eve, caught between the serpent and Adam! We have to share responsibility for what goes wrong in the world. And each of us needs to 'mind our step', or maybe 'mind the gap', between common sense and human impulses, lusts and delusions.

There's something else to notice about the 'loud and wayward' woman: 'her feet do not stay at home' (verse 11). In popular wisdom, a woman's place is in the home. But what would have happened if Elijah had stayed at home, or Elisha or Obadiah, or Abraham's servant, or Moses? Can only men follow God's call?

Read more of the Book of Proverbs to find the bigger, more positive, picture – 'call wisdom your sister' – she's not about temptation and blame, but all that connects human understanding and God's justice. Here are riches from the ancient world's Wisdom literature. In chapter 8, Wisdom, God's beloved first creation, is seen as a woman calling all to follow in God's way, a companion on that journey.

† God, our Guardian and our Guide, we are easily distracted from your way. But there is delight, too, in this journey. May Wisdom be our companion, every step of the way. Amen

For further thought

How would you put the way of Wisdom into your own words and describe it to a friend who has not read the Bible?

May

On the road – 1 First steps

On the road – 2 Walking with Jesus

Notes by **Barbara Easton**

Barbara is Director of Education for the Methodist Church in Britain. She started her working life as a secondary school RE teacher and wound her way to headship, taking in a number of challenges on the way. A local preacher in the Methodist tradition, her personal and professional life has given her the opportunity to follow interests in world religions, mysticism and worship, while sometimes detracting from her desire to finish more quilts. Barbara has used the NRSVA for these notes.

Sunday 17 May
A pilgrimage

Read Luke 2:41–52

Jesus said to them, 'Why were you searching for me? Did you not know that I must be in my Father's house?' But they did not understand what he said to them.

(verses 49–50)

When I learned this story as a self-righteous teenager, I was very judgemental about the carelessness of Mary and Joseph. Entrusted with the world's most precious child, they only go and lose him amongst the crowds returning north from the pilgrimage. Motherhood brought me a different perspective: life seemed to give me particularly adventurous children. I still laugh at some of those memories and go cold thinking of others.

The teenage me also felt pretty smug when considering the response of the religious leaders here. Fancy calling themselves 'learned' and yet not recognising the Truth when it's standing right in front of them. Tut! Life, of course, has graced me with deeper wisdom. As a teacher, I have been shaped by encounters with many children and, in life, by the unexpected insight of complete strangers – if only I am prepared to listen.

It is noteworthy that all the characters in this story are busy trying to do religion 'right', whether travelling on pilgrimage or remaining every day in the temple. We could even say that it is precisely their absorption in dutiful religion that causes them to miss Jesus ... the one whom all this religion is supposed to be about ...

† God whom I seek, seek me; God whom I long to know, know me; God whom I miss, catch me.

Monday 18 May
Hill walking

Read Mark 3:13–19

Jesus went up the mountain and called to him those whom he wanted, and they came to him. And he appointed twelve, whom he also named apostles, to be with him, and to be sent out to proclaim the message, and to have authority to cast out demons.

(verses 13–15)

This is a passage which is deceptively familiar. My picture of Jesus with his first disciples is coloured by the sunny lakeside scene in my children's Bible and I've frequently skimmed this passage to check the names of the twelve. I confess I have rather glossed over the opening words, which remind us that Jesus' call to discipleship is to join him on the mountain: for me, a more challenging place altogether.

I have friends who take mountain walking, quite literally, in their stride; it goes with all their natural inclinations. That is less the case with me. On a good day, my love for the hills resonates with Jesus' call: it enables me to see the workaday world in better perspective; my spirit is lifted by beauty and a rare purity; I discover something about myself – maybe, that I can do things I never thought possible. But that is the ideal! Often, a trip to the mountains involves pushing against my natural inclinations: allowing the challenges to outweigh the joys; struggling with too heavy a burden, sometimes of things that are not mine to carry; much yearning, and huffing and puffing. That echoes my discipleship too.

In the Bible, mountains are often the settings for a special experience of God. They are places of holiness and transfiguration. Discipleship is a call to journey with Jesus on the mountain in which we are transformed through knowing God more deeply. Sometimes, the walk seems like an uphill struggle. But we walk in great company and in the safe hands of outstanding mountain leadership!

† Lord, you call us to your easy yoke and your light burden. Take from me the weights which tie me to earthly things. Lift my eyes to the hills.

For further thought

God promises us 'a crown of beauty instead of ashes' (Isaiah 61:3, NIVUK). What do these words mean to you as a disciple at the moment?

Walking with Jesus

> **Luke 9:57–62**
>
> *Jesus said to him, 'No one who puts a hand to the plough and looks back is fit for the kingdom of God.'*
>
> (verse 62)

A friend of mine used to say that the world is like a shop window where someone has broken in overnight and swapped all the price labels around. Society gives inflated value to things which are really not so important, while things of real worth are often disregarded. At a simple level, we can look around and see that that is very true. But that is not the case with this passage, which cuts much deeper.

Here Jesus challenges those who would be his followers to set aside even legitimate human needs and responsibilities in his service. This would have been particularly shocking to his contemporary listeners, for whom the Law specifically recognised circumstances in which the demands of real life could be permitted to take precedence over religious observance. Family, home and social duties come high up the list. Although we live in a much more secular age, our modern world also has its values, often not much different, which don't mind a bit of religion so long as it's kept in its place. Tribal loyalties to family and nation, being sensible about money and employment, acting ethically but not to the point of inconvenience – these are often the challenges of being 'in the world'. The incarnate Christ knows this: he wanted his friends with him in Gethsemane, he made sure his mum was taken care of while he was dying. But here he speaks at a time of urgency. When the discipleship rubber hits the road, how do friends of Jesus live in the world, but not of the world?

† Incarnate Son of God, you knew a life like mine. Teach me to seek a life like yours.

For further thought

Where are the price labels in the 'shop window' of your life? Can you make a counter-cultural act today which tells others more about God's 'shop window'?

Wednesday 20 May
A beggar by the road

Read Mark 10:46–52

When Bartimaeus heard that it was Jesus of Nazareth, he began to shout out and say, 'Jesus, Son of David, have mercy on me!'

(verse 47)

In the early days of Christianity, people on the journey of faith often called it simply 'The Way'. This is a story about walking with Jesus featuring a blind man who, at the beginning, is 'beside the way' and ends the story as a follower 'on the way'. His journey is, oddly, impeded by other people who are already with Jesus – who quite literally are 'in the way'. How are we to understand this story? At the simplest level, it is just another miracle. However, scholars helpfully point out that, with the similar 'blind man' story in chapter 8, it bookends the important passage in between. Here we have the tipping point of the gospel, in which people gain both understanding about who Jesus is and confusion about what that might mean. These 'blind man' stories together become more like acted parables picturing how our discipleship might grow as we walk with Jesus. Our understanding may become steadily clearer, but is not always 20:20 vision.

Digging even deeper, the story has some interesting and puzzling features. Perhaps they are simply the colourful details of eyewitness memory. But maybe they are also mini-parables in themselves. What can we learn, for example, by contrasting the healing Bartimeaus receives from Jesus with the hindering he receives from those who already walk in The Way? There's a whole sermon here about exclusivism in the church! And why does Jesus push Bartimaeus to declare what he needs? Surely Jesus can see that he is blind? But walking in The Way sometimes requires a decision; disciples who are walking cannot also be sitting on the fence.

† Lord of light, let me be on the way and not in the way. Illumine my path so that, like Bartimaeus, I can see that what I most need is to be found in you.

For further thought

Blind people often challenge our use of blindness as a metaphor for dimness. Look up the books by John Hull, for example. How can we work around this?

Thursday 21 May
Companions on the road

Read Luke 8:1–3

The twelve were with Jesus, as well as some women who had been cured of evil spirits and infirmities: Mary ... Joanna ... Chuza, and Susanna, and many others, who provided for them out of their resources.

(verses 1b–3)

I had been a Christian for a long time before the detail of this passage really struck me. I don't remember ever noticing it read in church but that's understandable. It is only a few verses – an interlude in the real 'meat' of the gospel. However, many commentators would see, in the sidelining of this story, a darker truth about the sidelining of women in the church throughout the centuries. Women have generally moved on the stage of Christian history as an army of shadows. When pushed into the limelight it has generally been as saints, virgins and martyrs. Such women make worthy heroes, but fairly impossible role models. The pictures in my children's Bible rather overlooked the prominence of women in the ministry of Jesus too. Yet this story tells us that there were many women, and what a mixed company they were. It's interesting to speculate about them. Male theologians seem often to have enjoyed speculating about the backstory to Mary Magdalene, maybe a little too enthusiastically. But what about the story of Joanna? Admittedly defined by her husband's job, we can nevertheless imagine someone who moved in senior court circles, a woman with a position in the world. The Bible has so few practical details about the earthly life of Jesus that Luke must have thought this important information to include. If it only tells us about the role of women, it is enough. But maybe it speaks about all disciples – that the role of some walkers with Jesus is to use what they have to enable other walkers to make the journey.

† Just as I am, I come to you, Lord. I bring to you my story, who I am and what I do. I offer you myself. Let my story become part of your story.

For further thought

Look at some pictures or sculptures of Jesus surrounded by his disciples. Do they resonate with the gospel picture? Is it only women who are missing?

A roadside carnival

Read John 12:12–19

'Hosanna! Blessed is the one who comes in the name of the Lord – the King of Israel!'

(verse 13b)

Every April, the Sikhs in my home city of Wolverhampton organise a huge procession through the streets to celebrate all things Sikh. Pretty well every Sikh for miles around comes, with buses laid on for those too elderly to walk. It is colourful, loud and exuberant. There's martial arts and drumming and food stalls press free snacks on everyone en route. One year my nephew was visiting. I found him in the crowds, his pockets (and his mouth!) stuffed with samosas. 'What religion's this?' he asked, in genuine admiration. We had just come out of Sunday service – I could hear the contrast in his voice!

As the numbers of Christians decline in the West and our society becomes increasingly secularised, we sometimes spend more time talking about how to keep the church walls up than how to break through them to share the joy. Today's reading is usually heard on Palm Sunday in a chilly church, stripped for the barren season of Lent. The note of celebration is tinged with bitterness and the atmosphere sombre. It's sometimes easy to forget that, for most of Jesus' three-year ministry, people walking with Jesus were having a blast! It must have been a bit like being one of Doctor Who's companions or helpers – not entirely understanding what was going on but proud as punch to be part of it, even if it sometimes got a little bit scary and sometimes downright odd. Here, as the public ministry reaches its climax, the joy of being part of the Jesus story cannot be contained. Even the stones themselves would burst out singing (Luke 19:40).

† 'Let everything that breathes praise the Lord!' (Psalm 150:6). Today, Lord, I step aside from my workaday world and sing with all creation of your glory. I delight in your goodness. I am held in your light.

For further thought

Today, you may not feel much like rejoicing. Find the German theologian Dietrich Bonhoeffer's poem, 'Men go to God when they are sore bestead' as an alternative.

Saturday 23 May
A true follower

Read John 21:20–25

When Peter saw the disciple whom Jesus loved, he said to Jesus, 'Lord, what about him?' Jesus said to him, 'If it is my will that he remain until I come, what is that to you? Follow me!'

(verses 21–22)

As a teacher, I have supervised many generations of young people in the exam hall. There's always the one who needs to be given several sheets of additional paper or the one who finishes with a flourish a good half-hour before the end of the exam. We probably remember, from our own youth, how unnerving this can be. Am I writing enough or too little? Why has he finished if I haven't? Am I clever enough for this? However single-minded we are, watching others can put us off our stride and knock our confidence.

Several years ago I heard an Olympic champion being interviewed on TV after a race that a casual observer might have feared she would not win. As I recall it, the conversation went like this: 'Weren't you bothered that everyone seemed to be going past you?' asked the commentator.

'Not really,' replied the athlete. 'My coach has trained me to concentrate on my own race and not to worry about the people around me. I knew I would be all right if I just did what he said.'

It's a bit of a truism to say 'Jesus is our coach', but the athlete's single-mindedness draws out some helpful parallels with this passage. Jesus calls us each to our own Christian walk, not to try to walk the way of another. We must each understand, and believe for ourselves. But, as we each commit to discerning our own way, our paths will cross with those of many fellow pilgrims, all called to their own journeys. Maybe we will wonder at our difference, but this too is part of our calling.

† Just as I am, you call me to you. 'You have set my feet in a broad place' (Psalm 31:8); set me on a path which is mine to follow. Walk with me, Lord.

For further thought
If Jesus calls us all to focus on our own individual path, does the church lay too much emphasis on orthodoxy and unity?

On the road – 3 The journey of faith

Notes by **Karen Francis**

Karen is the Council for World Mission's Mission Secretary for the Caribbean and co-ordinator of CWM's Partners in Mission. A commissioned minister in the United Church in Jamaica and the Cayman Islands, Karen served in various roles including Director of Communication. She has degree in mass communication and a master's in theology. In her local congregation she is a worship planner, co-ordinator and trainer. Karen has used the NRSVA for these notes.

Sunday 24 May
What do you see?

May

Read Acts 3:1–10

When [the lame man] *saw Peter and John about to go into the temple, he asked them for alms. Peter looked intently at him, as did John, and said, 'Look at us.'*

(verses 3–4)

In Jamaica, churchgoing is an activity which is taken seriously. In Kingston, where I live, it is not unusual to see persons dressed in their 'Sunday best' travelling by car, bus or on foot up a hill, through residential communities or public thoroughfares.

Consider what churchgoers pass by on the way to church. Whom do they bump into or step over? What do they see? On their way to the temple Peter and John saw a person living with a physical disability placed strategically at the gate of the temple by 'helpful' churchgoers so he would be in the way of the faithful. I wonder how many were busy with 'church business' as they passed.

Peter and John saw the man. They did not overlook, ignore or explain him away. They saw him. They invited him to see them. He expected to receive from their resource of money, but they gave from their resource of faith.

On our way to church, whom do we see? Whom do we see in need of nourishment, warmth, companionship or assurance? Are we so focused on where we are going – to church – that we forget we are the church, bearers of the good news of Christ in word and deed?

† Lord, may our efforts to feed our faith by gathering for worship never prevent us from exercising that faith on the way.

What do others see?

> **Read Acts 5:12–16**
>
> *... so that they even carried out the sick into the streets, and laid them on cots and mats, in order that Peter's shadow might fall on some of them as he came by.*
>
> (verse 15)

In the rough and tumble of life we cross paths with many people. I particularly enjoy encounters in supermarkets, in stores and on public transportation. The animated expressions by aggrieved or excited Jamaicans reveal their heart and spirit in unbridled and eye-opening ways. I see them, but what do they see in me? Do they know that I love and serve Christ? Do they know that I have chosen a life of faith in God?

In our text, Peter and the other apostles were not only seen by the people, they were also known by people. The people gave them a place of honour. People in the streets came to faith because of what they saw: signs and wonders; and what they experienced: transformation through salvation. The power of God was evident in the lives of the apostles. They were so well known for what they spoke, stood for and their miraculous works that the people craved even Peter's shadow which they believed would bring healing to the sick.

In the city streets – where we rub shoulders with the rich, poor, politically active or indifferent, male, female, adults and youth – what do people see in us who believe? How would they know what we believe? Is it evident in our speech: a word of hope instead of joining in the litany of 'what is wrong with the world'; or in the matters we give attention, where we offer a ready hand of help? Is the power of God evident in our lives and does our presence make a difference in the city streets?

† In your interactions with people in public spaces today, how could the good news and power of God be communicated?

For further thought

On the journey of faith we should be alert to the possibilities for positive impact on those we encounter.

Tuesday 26 May
A call to discomfort

Read Acts 8:26–40

Then an angel of the Lord said to Philip, 'Get up and go towards the south to the road that goes down from Jerusalem to Gaza.' (This is a wilderness road.) So he got up and went.

(verses 26–27a)

I don't do very well with instructions which are counter-intuitive. How can it make sense to go to a place without the creature comforts to which I am accustomed? Why would I be willing to go into a situation of discomfort likely to cause me hardship? Ministers in Jamaica, much like other parts of the world, are confronted with those questions when contemplating a call to ministry in contexts considered 'undesirable'. Whether it is the prospect of greater needs than resources, or mammoth problems which seem unsolvable, the flight instinct is great.

Philip chose the path to a desert place, presumably because of what was possible rather than because of what was promised. His response to the instructions of the angel of the Lord is likely to have come out of trust in God. That trust was demonstrated through obedience. It is reasonable to consider that he anticipated that he would be useful to God in that desert place.

Philip acted in faith and found someone searching for faith, in need of illumination. He then spoke of whom he knew, Jesus, and what he had experienced with him and was able to help the Ethiopian officer to understand the words of Isaiah about this same Jesus.

Are you among those who need to be assured that the conditions of service and specifics of environment are pleasant, manageable and known before you sign on the dotted line? Do you contemplate how this seemingly undesirable situation or place could actually be a place of possibility for service to God?

† Twice in this text Philip followed divine instructions. Have you heard the voice of God beckoning you to service? How will you respond?

For further thought

Consider the desert roads in your current journey of faith. Why have you defined them as such and how might your journey to such a place be a point of growth for you and blessing for others?

Wednesday 27 May
A call to radical living

Read Acts 9:1–19

'Brother Saul, the Lord Jesus, who appeared to you on your way here, has sent me so that you may regain your sight and be filled with the Holy Spirit.' And immediately something like scales fell from his eyes, and his sight was restored.

(verses 17b–18a)

It is one thing to go to a place which is likely to be uncomfortable. It is quite another to be sent to a place of known danger. Two ministers in the United Church in Jamaica and the Cayman Islands lead congregations in downtown Kingston. This business district is troubled by high levels of crime perpetrated by rival gangs. These ministers knew that ministry to the whole community often meant encountering criminals. They tell stories of such encounters which were intended to help the criminals, who could cause harm, to see a new way.

Ananias was given the mission to help Saul, a known persecutor of believers in Christ. Who would want that mission? The *Mission Impossible* TV and film series begins with classic scenes in which the protagonist Ethan Hunt receives his instructions, which he is given the clear choice to accept or reject. Well, Ananias did not want to accept this mission. Following his protest, the rationale behind this risky encounter was explained to Ananias: Saul (soon to become Paul) would become God's instrument of blessing to the Gentiles.

It occurred to me that Ananias could have taken advantage of that moment. Someone who caused harm to others was now vulnerable before him. Do I hear the opening of a door of opportunity for revenge? Ananias' choice was to embrace God's vision for Saul. At the point of encounter, Ananias himself had made quite a journey; he addressed Saul as 'Brother'.

Ananias presents a challenge to us on our journey of faith to be willing to face the enemy when mission requires it.

† Lord, give me courage to respond in faith to your beckoning even if I am fearful of what it may cost me.

For further thought

In your times of personal prayer, remember those whose work puts them in danger.

Thursday 28 May
When God does the impossible

Read Acts 12:6–19

They said to her, 'You are out of your mind!' But she insisted that it was so. They said, 'It is his angel.' Meanwhile, Peter continued knocking; and when they opened the gate, they saw him and were amazed.

(verses 15–16)

Many believers in Christ raise passionate petitions through prayer when faced with impossible situations. Calls for national days of prayer, all-night prayer meetings, and prayer marathons on Christian radio are common in Jamaica at the initiative of churches and Christian organisations. Usually this is in response to national crises.

Peter's incarceration may not have been considered a national crisis but for the followers of Christ it constituted a crisis for the early church. That they gathered at the home of Mary to pray may not have been an unusual act for believers in Christ. The first chapter in Acts indicates that the early church 'were constantly devoting themselves to prayer' (Acts 1:14). James speaks of gathering the elders to pray for the sick (James 5:14) and Paul advocates a lifestyle of calling for prayer in the event of illness and in times of necessity for intercession and petition (1 Timothy 2:1).

However there is more to this story. Peter's miraculous deliverance from prison (and subsequent appearance at the all-night prayer meeting) was a dramatic outcome of the petitions to God. Remember, it was the reason they gathered – to pray: 'While Peter was kept in prison, the church prayed fervently to God for him' (Acts 12:5). So if the gathering was intentionally praying about Peter's imprisonment, why was Rhoda, the maid who heard Peter's voice at the gate, not believed when she told the intercessors that Peter was there? Why were they amazed when they saw Peter for themselves? Could it be that they did not believe God would answer their prayers for Peter's release?

† What are your expectations when you pray? Do you always pray in faith believing God will act?

For further thought

Reflect on times when God's answer to prayer has surprised you. Consider the reasons you were surprised.

Friday 29 May
Is that you, God?

Read Acts 16:6–15

... they attempted to go into Bithynia, but the Spirit of Jesus did not allow them; so, passing by Mysia, they went down to Troas. During the night Paul had a vision: there stood a man of Macedonia pleading with him and saying, 'Come over to Macedonia and help us.'

(verses 7b–9)

In the walk of faith, how do you understand hindrances? As the impetus to be persistent, showing resilience and determination? Or as the timely divine work of God to prevent us from doing something we shouldn't?

Perhaps your car wouldn't start and this delayed your departure. You later learned of an accident on the way you would have taken. You may have failed in a chosen area of work which led you to another career path. This alternative path provided far greater fulfilment and compatibility with your gifts. How did you interpret those 'hindrances' at the time you experienced them?

Paul's mission was to share the good news of Christ and build the church. He went from town to town. Why would he be prevented from going to a specific place? What was wrong with Bithynia? Perhaps nothing, but Paul was needed in Macedonia at that time.

We should not interpret every hindrance as divine intervention to prevent disaster or bad decisions. However, neither should we believe that God is unconcerned about our lives.

How do you distinguish between impressions and the supernatural leading of the Spirit? Sometimes they are one and the same. In my experience it is through constant communication with God. Keep speaking and listening to God for God's voice. Don't make broad assumptions, ask God to help you to understand. I don't believe there is a magic formula to knowing God's will. I believe we must draw on the intimacy of our relationship with God to discern God's guidance in decision-making. And like Paul, when we are convinced, we must be obedient.

† Reflect on your history of relationship with God. How have you been sure of God's guidance in the past?

For further thought

At times, our impression is that God is leading us to a place we don't want to go. Reflect on how Jonah and Jesus responded.

On the road – 3 The journey of faith

May

151

Saturday 30 May
What's on your 'to-do' list?

Read 1 Corinthians 16:5–12

But I will stay in Ephesus until Pentecost, for a wide door for effective work has opened to me, and there are many adversaries.

(verses 8–9)

This week we have explored our responsiveness to those we encounter as we pursue our relationship with God, contemplated how others see us as we interact with them, reckoned our willingness to venture into uncomfortable and risky places for God, opened ourselves to God's supernatural moves and tried to understand how to discern the leading of God's Spirit. How does Paul challenge us as we conclude this week together?

In our reading, Paul's note to the Corinthians is like the calendar of a CEO. Notice that Paul sets out his 'to-do' list when he visits and also outlines the work he will be doing before he visits. Not a sloth, is he? Sounds like a man on a mission.

The Christian's core mission is to share the good news so others will accept God's love and begin to walk in faith. It is an urgent and unrelenting task. God's disciples should be busy for God, open to and seizing opportunities to competently engage people as we encounter them.

Paul recognised opportunities to share the good news of Christ. However, we sometimes feel there is very little opportunity to share the good news because people are unwilling to receive it and so we don't try. Eventually we become unaware of the doors of opportunity opening around us.

Friends, there will always be the work of ministry to be done and while the result of that work is not in our hands, we must be faithfully discerning, embracing and doing for Christ. It is our calling and a part of our journey of faith.

† Lord, help me to be alert and responsive to the opportunities you place before me to share the good news with others.

For further thought

Think about your home, work and social environments. How can you be faithful to Christ in sharing the good news in word and deed?

Fire in the Bible – 1 God and fire

Notes by **Vinod Shemron**

Vinod is a theology graduate from the United Theological College, Bangalore. He works with the Student Christian Movement of India in Bangalore as Associate Executive Secretary of the Mission and Scholarship Desk and pastorally assists at the Church of South India Memorial Church. His interests are music, theatre, poetry and creative writing. He blogs at: vinodsreflections.blogspot.com. Vinod has used the NRSVA for these notes.

Sunday 31 May (Pentecost)
Tongues of fire

Read Acts 2:1–13

... tongues, as of fire, appeared among them, and a tongue rested on each of them.

(verse 3)

God and Fire will be the theme for this week. We shall reflect over the next seven days on how we discern this fire that comes from God as recorded in the biblical texts. Fire is one of the five natural elements – *Prithvi* (Earth), *Jal* (Water), *Vayu* (Air), *Agni* (Fire) and *Akash* (Sky) – that comprise our universe according to Indian philosophy. Fire holds two significant characteristics. Fire is seen as a purifying agent and, on the other hand, as an agent of destruction.

The passage today speaks of the fire that came from above, enabling people to talk in the native languages of others, overcoming the tongues of confusion that dispersed people when the tower of Babel was built (Genesis 11:1–9). Whereas the tower of Babel was built with the greedy intention of reaching the heavens, the people gathered here to celebrate a holy festival, the feast of weeks. Every day we, too, create our own worlds based on the way we use our tongues. Do we use our tongues to make life better for us and for the people around us, or are we using the tongue just to make ourselves comfortable? This is the question that this passage asks. Our answers live in our daily deeds.

† God of grace, lead us into using our tongues compassionately so that people who hear us will not be disturbed but be comforted. Amen

Monday 1 June
Burning, yet not

Read Exodus 3:1–10

There the angel of the Lord appeared to him in a flame of fire out of a bush; he looked, and the bush was blazing, yet it was not consumed.

(verse 2)

We have all come across instances of injustice. How do we react? Perhaps we immediately open our smartphone or take out our laptops, log into social media, update our status or post pictures. And wait for people to 'like', 'react' and 'comment'. We then gain a sense of satisfaction that we have raised our voice against the injustice that we have witnessed. How passive and naïve our protest against injustice has become!

The passage from Exodus for today too has imagery of this sort. The bush 'was' burning but it 'wasn't'. Moses saw the bush blazing but the fire did not consume it. Many a time we too behave like this bush. We are burning, but we aren't. We feel the need to react and speak out, but we tend to do it passively rather than actively and resort to easier and more comfortable means. Moses is somewhat passive as well, at least at first. In the conversation between him and God, Moses at first wants to avoid responsibility. But God's voice persuades him to go out there and stand up for justice, though his mind was wracked with fear and uncertainty.

God is talking to us every day through a fire blazing around us and even within us. Will we allow ourselves to be persuaded by God's voice to stand up and work for justice, as Moses did, or will we remain wracked with doubts? The choice is ours. Let us summon the courage to say 'yes' to stand against the injustice around us.

† Dear God, grant us the courage to stand up against the evils of society like Moses did, so that we may be agents of justice through the fire blazing within us. Amen

For further thought

How can you more forcefully protest against the injustice around you?

Tuesday 2 June
A pillar of fire

Read Exodus 13:17–22

The Lord went in front of them in a pillar of cloud by day, to lead them along the way, and in a pillar of fire by night, to give them light, so that they might travel by day and by night.

(verse 21)

Let us just try to imagine how we would feel if a pillar of fire were going ahead of us. Would we even follow it? If this traditional imagery happened in reality, all of us would run away from such a fire, not follow it! But the imagery of the 'pillar of fire' and the 'cloud by night' need not necessarily be understood as we understand it today. I wonder, in simple terms, if the pillars meant the 'sun' and the 'night sky'. The sun by day was fiery in its blazing brightness, and the night sky in its coolness could offer these migrants the sense of God's presence, guidance and assured security.

God journeys with us even to this day, as God did with the Israelites. The day and night could be seen as signs of God's presence with us. As then, the heat in the day and the coolness of the night bring us to a sure knowledge that God protects. The brightness and the darkness reveal God's guidance through all phases of our lives, whether bright or dark. God of the pillar of fire and the cloud by night poses challenges to each of us, each passing day.

Let us reflect on how we are receiving these blessings from God. God is present with us, God guides and protects us, but are we translating and mirroring these attributes of God in our lives?

† Ever-present and ever-guiding God, lead us through your grace to mirror your lessons of life to our neighbours and your creation around us. Amen

For further thought

What blessings and divine protection or sustaining have you received today?

Burnt thank offerings

Read 2 Chronicles 7:1–11

When Solomon had ended his prayer, fire came down from heaven and consumed the burnt-offering and the sacrifices; and the glory of the Lord filled the temple.

(verse 1)

King Solomon in the passage for today consecrated a place for burnt-offerings, offered burnt-offerings and sent the people away to their homes, joyful and in good spirits for the goodness that the Lord had shown to David, Solomon and the people of Israel. The fire from God was a symbol that Solomon's offering was accepted.

Thanksgiving is a beautiful word that ignites a sense of gratitude for anything received. Thanksgiving is celebrated worldwide in different festivals. In India, Pongal and Shankranti are celebrated as thanksgiving festivals of the agrarian communities. They are often misunderstood to be Hindu festivals. Both these prominent festivals of South India signify God's grace on the community through land, rains and harvest. Their purpose was to give thanks to God not only for creating but also for preserving and the continued sustenance of agriculture, as expressed by the communities dependent on agriculture. The festivals are still celebrated, but are slowly dying.

Today we have forgotten how the rice gets to our plates every meal. We do not know who was involved in its preparing and making. We have ended up thanking the multitude of companies that crowd out traditional farming, and have let down the agricultural communities. With the increase in new scientific research into pesticides and genetically modified crops, rural communities have suffered in India and agriculture has declined. If this continues, the future can only bring a human race that will depend on lab-made products. It is time to give thanks for what God made by investing in, propagating and developing communities that depend on agriculture. Only such an offering of the whole community will be acceptable to God.

† God of field and forest, thank you for your creation and all the goodness we receive. Lead us, that we thankfully remember communities dependent on agriculture.

For further thought

What are your local traditions of thanksgiving?

Thursday 4 June
Transforming fire

Read Luke 3:15–18

'His winnowing-fork is in his hand, to clear his threshing-floor and to gather the wheat into his granary; but the chaff he will burn with unquenchable fire.'

(verse 17)

The Student Christian Movement of India (SCMI), where I presently work, is a faith-based students' movement that translates faith into action. In the recent past, atrocities against struggling communities have rapidly increased. If we are silent even now, we too will be a part of the greatest sin humanity is committing. It is in such a context that SCMI, whose student-members play the role of the winnowing-fork, seeks to work for justice whenever and wherever it is denied. It takes interest in realising a fuller humanity, and in motivating the student community to develop leadership skills for transformative action in society. SCMI understands transformation of lives as the mission of God. Transformation of lives does not necessarily mean economic improvement, but the holistic development of students who develop their own communities.

In today's passage, we read about the wheat that needs to be separated from the chaff to become edible. A winnowing-fork is what separates the wheat from the chaff. Wheat in the passage can possibly signify everything we need, while the chaff could portray everything unnecessary. As this imagery denotes, we too are called to be a winnowing-fork in the hand of God. We are to separate justice from injustice and love from hatred so that the world becomes a better place to live. Are we ready to take up this challenge to clear the threshing-floor (our country), gather the wheat (justice) and burn the chaff (injustice) with unquenchable fire?

† Harvester God, we are willing to become winnowing-forks in your hand. Use us to separate wheat from chaff in our society, so that our children may see a better world. Amen

For further thought

What are the wheat and chaff in our society that we need to gather or do away with?

Friday 5 June
An offering by fire

Read Leviticus 6:14–17
I have given it as their portion of my offerings by fire; it is most holy.

(verse 17b)

Today's passage describes the ritual of the grain offering presented by the Israelites to God as a thanksgiving for the harvest. In the ancient Israelites' culture it was offered to God by the priests before the altar where the fire kept burning on it without being extinguished. It was the fire that played the role of a mediator for the grain offering between the priest who offered and God. The significance of this fire was that it was never blown out throughout the process of ritual which was considered holy. In the Indian context, especially the Hindu tradition, the presence of fire is considered auspicious. The *Puja* (worship) is clearly visible on special occasions like festivals, marriage, birth, death and so on.

People considered fire as a symbol of divine presence. Thus, fire is regarded as a holy element. In India's Parsi culture as well, fire has been held in the highest regard. An eternal fire keeps on burning in the temple which is the sacred place of worship for the Parsi community. This fire keeps on burning on a silver urn and only the priest is allowed to enter the room where the fire burns. Only the priest offers prayers on behalf of the worshippers. Perhaps we could also say that justice sanctifies our social living like fire sanctifies sacrifices offered. If we keep the fire of justice burning within us, we make ourselves more acceptable to God as living sacrifices. Are we ready to burn with the fire of justice?

† God of fire, we pray that you set our life, family, society and nation on your fire so that everything that we contribute for your reign's sake would be acceptable by you. Amen

For further thought

What does fire mean to you? What does it symbolise in your culture?

The agony of fire

Read Luke 16:19–31

'He called out, "Father Abraham, have mercy on me, and send Lazarus to dip the tip of his finger in water and cool my tongue; for I am in agony in these flames."'

(verse 24)

We have all made mistakes in life. My little brother was the naughtier of the two of us. All his pranks were well known. Now he is married and has a son. Seeing the way his two-year-old speaks and does things, my brother began to apologise to my parents for the naughty pranks he played when he was a kid, in fear that his son will be repeating the same naughty pranks he played.

The passage for today also speaks of the rich man regretting living a lavish life and not feeding the hungry outside his gate. Life does have many ups and downs. On many occasions, we too have lavished money on our lifestyle like the rich man, and fed our personal greed rather than being content with what we have and sharing with the needy. Feeding the hungry is an imperative of every Christian. There will be a time in life where we have everything, and suddenly it will topple down to nothing. It is in our nothingness that we realise that we could have done better when we were well-off. The gospel of Christ urges us to share with those who are hungry. Does the rich man's voice from Hades ring a bell in our minds to feed the poor? Let the image not frighten us; instead let it create in us a sense of sharing the things we have in excess.

† O God, grant us the heart to serve and share. Bind the spirit of greed, and release us from the bondage of accumulation. Amen

For further thought

Feed the hungry when you have food in your hand, so you may never think it would have been better to share your food than to waste it.

June

Fire in the Bible – 1 God and fire

Fire in the Bible – 2 The power of fire

Notes by **Shirlyn Toppin**

Shirlyn is a presbyter in the Methodist Church in Ealing, London. She passionately believes in the preaching of God's word without compromise or fear, and exercising a pastoral ministry of grace. Her favourite pastime is shopping, especially for shoes. Shirlyn has used the NRSVA for these notes.

Sunday 7 June

A mountain ablaze

Read Deuteronomy 4:9–14

You approached and stood at the foot of the mountain while the mountain was blazing up to the very heavens, shrouded in dark clouds. Then the Lord spoke to you out of the fire. You heard the sound of words but saw no form; there was only a voice.

(verses 11–12)

The whole mountain ablaze: the event in Deuteronomy 4 was a momentous occasion for Moses, where God's awesome presence and voice were revealed in the mountain on fire. Yet this is not Moses' first encounter with God at Horeb. In Exodus 3, God appears in a burning bush instead of a mountain ablaze. There is something assuring about this continuity; God's nature is consistent, and his revelation of himself can be similar, yet unique.

Mount Horeb represents the presence of God and the changing of lives. God met with Moses so he could effectively communicate his message to the people again, enabling them to live according to his commandments. Moses went from being a reclusive shepherd to a leader of a great nation, whose covenant relationship with God was for the transmuting of other nations. Encounters with God are life transforming! Encounters are a twofold process, because you are transformed to transformed others.

A mountain ablaze may not be the norm by which God seeks to meet with people today. However, there are Horebs in each of our lives, and we too must not remain unchanged. Where will you meet God in the fire this week and how might you be transformed – to transform others?

† Lord, help me to discern the Mount Horebs in my life, so I may continually be transformed for your glory. Amen

Monday 8 June
Thrown in the fire

Read Daniel 3:19–30

'Was it not three men that we threw bound into the fire?' They answered the king, 'True, O king.' He replied, 'But I see four men unbound, walking in the middle of the fire, and they are not hurt; and the fourth has the appearance of a god.'

(verses 24b–25)

The saying 'seeing is believing' aptly fits with Nebuchadnezzar's response to what he saw in the burning furnace. Surely his eyes tricked him! Not only were the three men walking around unbound and unharmed, they were accompanied by a fourth person, whom the king later described in verse 28 as an angel. Nebuchadnezzar's astonishment is understandable, but not surprising given God's promise in Isaiah 43:2.

What is proven in this incident is that God does not always prevent us from being thrown into the fire, but he comes in with us. God's presence in the midst of a crisis is a reassurance even when things seem bleak and hopeless, which Meshach, Shadrach and Abednego experienced as they valiantly held onto their faith in God. Conversing with one of my members made this point more succinct as we spoke of her ongoing treatment for cancer and her unwavering faith in God, echoed in her words, 'He is carrying me.' God did not prevent her from being diagnosed with cancer, but she testified of his presence in her furnace of fire.

An easy-going, pain-free discipleship was never promised. Many people often forget this, and when life's challenges become too much, they feel abandoned by God and feel they have been left in the furnace of fire alone. In contrast, there are many who do not view their suffering as God departing, but as God appearing. These people testify of encountering God more deeply in spite of their adversity.

† Gracious God, may those facing persecution and suffering experience your comforting and strengthening presence. Amen

For further thought
Suffering is not always preventable, but it can be transformable.

Tuesday 9 June
The fire of the Lord

Read 1 Kings 18:30–39

Then the fire of the Lord fell and consumed the burnt-offering, the wood, the stones, and the dust, and even licked up the water that was in the trench.

(verse 38)

Today's reading illustrates again how God's presence in fire is transformative. However, before transformation could take place, preparation was needed. It may seem odd that Elijah summoned the people to watch him rebuild an altar to offer sacrifice to God. And yet, his bizarre behaviour is an illustration of the centrality of God amidst his people. The altar had perhaps been desecrated by Jezebel, 'thrown down' as said in verse 30; the necessary groundwork was needed to establish that which honours God. However, the ritualistic act of erecting the altar was just a prelude of what was to come, confirmation that the God of Abraham, Jacob, Isaac and the people of Israel was indeed 'I am who I am'.

Elijah prayed, fire came down, God showed up! Present in the fire that consumed not only the sacrifice but everything: all that was used in constructing the altar, even the dirt and water. It was a powerful demonstration that left the people falling in reverence and fear. This, too, has been an experience familiar to many; but, for others, God's non-appearance has resulted in spiritual pessimism.

Did God answer Elijah's bidding to prove his sovereign power over other gods or because Elijah's prayer allowed the glory to be unto God and not himself? It's easy to believe that God is not listening; not interested; not desiring to respond with fire and consume everything that's causing you to feel downcast, thrown down. As with Elijah, maybe the answer lies in first erecting God's place in your life.

† Lord, may your holy renewing fire restore my rightful place with you. Amen

For further thought

Are there any areas in your life in which you need God's cleansing fire?

Wednesday 10 June
The warmth of a fire

Read Mark 14:66–72

When she saw Peter warming himself, she stared at him and said, 'You also were with Jesus, the man from Nazareth.'

(verse 67)

'Even though all become deserters, I will not' (verse 29). A bold statement from Peter declaring resolute loyalty to Jesus. He managed to fulfil his promise to Jesus in a minimal sort of way by going to the high priest's courtyard, but he still denied knowing him. His cowardly act resulted in him seeking comfort by warming himself by the fire. Did he hope that the warmth from the fire would somehow make the coldness of his disloyalty bearable? Or that the fire would become a distraction from his being in the right fellowship? Maybe he was hoping against hope that the fire would cleanse his guilt-ridden thoughts.

It may seem easier to seek comfort rather than confront situations that make us feel uncomfortable, and all the more so when dealing with convictions of guilt. Burying one's head in the sand like an ostrich was Peter's option: to blend in unnoticed by the campfire, hopeful that his status as a follower of the accused would not be detected. But by seeking consolation from the warmth of a fire, he was exposed. Fire can be both transforming and revealing, given Peter's reaction when he felt his back was against the wall. Sin of denial and doubt superseded his professed confidence, rendering him helpless, overcome with tears – miles away from his typical behaviour as a fearless disciple.

Yet the warmth of a fire, though a place of absolute denial, was also instrumental in absolute restoration. In John 21:9–14, around a charcoal fire like the fire in the high priest's courtyard, fellowship was renewed and forgiveness was offered and received.

† Lord, have mercy upon us; when our flesh fails us, cleanse and restore us in a right relationship with you. Amen

For further thought
No one is beyond God's restorative mercies.

Thursday 11 June
The tongue is a fire

Read James 3:1–6

How great a forest is set ablaze by a small fire! And the tongue is a fire. The tongue is placed among our members as a world of iniquity; it stains the whole body, sets on fire the cycle of nature, and is itself set on fire by hell.

(verses 5b–6)

An uncontrolled blaze set alight by accident or on purpose can cause devastation when it burns unnoticed. Lives and places are irrevocably changed. A fire starts off small then becomes a great force of destruction; and the tongue, too, we are told by James, is a fire. The tongue is only a small member of the human body, but it has life-transforming impact. Proverbs 18:21 describes the tongue as having a similar power: 'death and life are in the power of the tongue.' The dual nature of the tongue is like day and night, love and hate, and good and evil. Though the tongue can effectively communicate words of support, hope and praise to God, equally it can be condemning and disparaging.

Therefore, words spoken insensitively or compassionately are powerful and the consequences can be affirming or discouraging. Words shape our thought process in how we perceive ourselves and others. Negativity, criticism and bullying have far-reaching implications at home, at work, in school or on social media. Additionally, gossip, slander and lies are symptomatic of an uncontrollable tongue resulting in immense hurt and irreparable relationships. As such, the tongue has the power to build up, tear down, strengthen, heal, destroy and restore.

Like the other aspects of fire seen this week, the tongue can be compared positively to fire; it can be a tool for transformation when used to spread the gospel, communicate God's love and mercies, and denounce lies. Do you use your tongue to bless, or to curse?

† Gracious God, like the psalmist may you 'set a guard over my mouth' and 'keep watch over the door of my lips' (Psalm 141:3). Amen

For further thought

Have you spoken words recently that will affirm, or cause harm?

Friday 12 June
A welcoming fire

Read Acts 28:1–10

The natives showed us unusual kindness. Since it had begun to rain and was cold, they kindled a fire and welcomed all of us round it.

(verse 2)

Warmth on a cold day is bliss! Wrapped up snuggly on a wintry day is delightful! To enter a cold church vestry on a chilly morning and be greeted with warmth says welcome. To be shipwrecked on an unknown island would not be on anyone's bucket list and yet, for the survivors from today's reading, their situation surely beat the other possible outcomes. Battered, exhausted and shivering, they came ashore on an island to a potentially hostile crowd, surrounded with people speaking an unfamiliar language. Was this a better prospect than what they had endured? Was their life further endangered? In spite of the barriers of language and religious belief, welcome was extended through a fire.

A welcoming fire became the channel for transformation! What was done as an act of kindness had a great impact on all, even those with prejudiced beliefs. Consider how lives were changed: hospitality enabled temporary refuge; strangers became honoured guests and friends; healing ministry was established; and generosity was given as the emptied left filled.

The Ealing Churches Winter Night Shelter programme is an analogy of the welcome seen in Acts. Varied churches offer temporary places of warmth nightly (food and bed) to a recommended number of homeless men and women for three months. Denominational differences, political beliefs and preconceived notions are insignificant as the destitute are welcomed, referred to and honoured as guests. The welcoming fire for the shipwrecked in Malta and the warm buildings for the homeless in Ealing are a mediation of God's grace.

† Loving Father, enable us to be beacons of the warmth of your grace, generosity and hospitality. Amen

For further thought

Examine yourself to see whether you are an agent of warm welcome.

June

Fire in the Bible – 2 The power of fire

Saturday 13 June
A refining fire

Read Isaiah 48:9–11

See, I have refined you, but not like silver; I have tested you in the furnace of adversity.

(verse 10)

Refining fire cleanses! Refining fire reveals what is worthy! Refining fire transforms! Refining is a severe and thorough process: the metal is placed in the middle of the fire, the hottest part of the furnace, to burn away all its impurities and reveal the best of the metal. Refining fire changes what may be perceived as a useless piece of object into something of beauty and value. The television show *Forged in Fire* exemplifies this procedure as the contestants are asked to make a knife from scrapped metals, which seems impossible to the unskilled. They work tirelessly, melting and shaping the metal in the furnace; gradually the crafted item becomes visible from a long and gruelling process. What is quite clear is that transformation is a process, not always instantaneous but worthwhile.

A refining fire would not be the chosen medium for transformation for most people, even Christians. Many would prefer a less arduous method. And yet, without the burning, cleansing and purging away of our impurities only possible through the Refiner's fire, believers are unable to reflect new life in Christ. Refining conforms us to Christ, purifying our hearts and our character as stated by Paul: 'So if anyone is in Christ, there is a new creation: everything old has passed away; see, everything has become new!' (2 Corinthians 5:17). Without refining fire, holiness and purity remain unattainable. What is most precious would not be unveiled and our lives would not be transformed into God's image and likeness.

† Refining God, continue to burn away the impurities in us, so we may reflect the character of Christ. Amen

For further thought

What areas in your life need to go through the Refiner's fire?

The Gospel of Matthew (2) – 1 Ask, seek, knock

Notes by **Michael Jagessar**

Michael is a writer and researcher 'at large'. More on Michael's biography and writings can be found at www.caribleaper.co.uk. Michael has used the NRSVA for these notes.

Sunday 14 June
A door opens

June

Read Matthew 7:7–12

'Ask, and it will be given to you; search, and you will find; knock, and the door will be opened for you.'

(verse 7)

We stand in the middle of two worlds: kingdom world and empire world. Given the fact that the journey towards justice is a long one, we are invited to persist in a different economy and style. Ask, seek and knock are suggested imperatives of how we may navigate the economy of the world and that of God in Christ: by thoughtful interaction and bold persistence. Here, 'asking' is a communal seeking after what is just. People of the Jesus way will do well in reframing their questions from the perspective of generosity and heightened awareness. 'Seeking' underscores an intentional presence shaped by generosity. It is easier to ask than to be present. And 'knocking' implies an invitation: 'May I? Can you invite me in?' Here are suggested reversals of empire's world of imposition, arrogance and force. God's economy in Christ is shaped by grace, graciousness and love that inverts economic logic by its illogic. Here it is: God is present; God is good; God loves; God gives away. This is what our asking, seeking and knocking are motivated by.

† God who offers full life for all, help us to ask better questions, seek out the most vulnerable with intentional presence and cross over walls and barriers – living out and walking the way and example of Jesus.

The Gospel of Matthew (2) – 1 Ask, seek, knock

Monday 15 June
Which way?

Read Matthew 7:13–14

'For the gate is narrow and the road is hard that leads to life, and there are few who find it.'

(verse 14)

It has been suggested that the word 'narrow' carries a layered history. Among the various meanings in its evolving story is that of 'to groan' (I suppose under pressure). If we can avoid restricted spaces, groaning under pressure, limited movement, or a long queue through a narrow entrance we would do so at all costs. This may especially be the case if another way is offered that would give one priority and an assurance that life would be less stressed out. The easy way, that is the one that would demand less of us, would be the one we would most likely opt for.

It is no wonder that Jesus lost so many followers along the way. His call to a different way, one less taken, proved too challenging for many. In spite of the assurances that this 'path of groans' offers a lasting kind of freedom at the end, our instinct is for that which is considered safer, logical and sensible to take. Let's stick to the wide way as that of 'empire' with all its allure and firm hold on us. The Jesus way, that of a different set of values, is a risky undertaking demanding too great a 'turnaround', going against the flow of the dominant traffic, reshaping our understanding of neighbour, enemies, money, those on the margins and much more. This way of Jesus is in plain sight – yet only a few can change course and throw themselves after him.

Are you able to risk the adventure of flourishing life?

† Source of all goodness, shape us with your open-ended will and grant us the confidence and peace of your unbounded Spirit so that your deepest desires and dreams become ours.

For further thought

Reflect on the current need in your community to change course. Consider your part in that 'turning' and those whom you would wish to partner with.

Tuesday 16 June
Character

Read Matthew 7:15–20

'You will know them by their fruits.'

(verse 16a)

My now-deceased grandmother's mantra was, 'Forget looks or charm: character matters.' It never failed her. An illiterate Hindu woman, she was an astute judge of people and the habits that shaped them. In retrospect, I can now see why she was able to sort numerous disputes and conflicts in our village. With her soft and confident look, she was able to see what many others could not see: the heart or character inside. It is not that there were always evident 'fruits' by which she could have made her evaluation. I think it had more to do with her ability to go for something deeper than looks and station.

Speaking words about the Divine and evaluating what is of God and not of God are more complex than what this brief portion of scripture intends to convey. Words about God or those offered up on behalf of the Divine's way from those called prophets would always run the risk of misrepresenting the Divine. Hence, it is imperative for all who preach, teach and write about God's way in Christ to do so provisionally and with humility. Even some of what has come down to us as 'deposits of faith' have been misleading signposts.

For me, the way of Jesus is about walking a life, modelling a way, living out of costly grace, as Jesus did. The nicely polished, near-perfect and waxed fruits of empire do not exemplify the Jesus way. His way of full life for all is about embodying habits of love, joy, patience, peace, goodness and faithfulness among others.

† God-of-life, take our words and release them to speak of you; take our minds and broaden them; take our hearts and set them alight. In the name of the one full of love, Jesus Christ.

For further thought
Reflect on the 'fruits' that you embody (what you think you see; what others see/know and experience) and the role of these in your discipleship.

June

The Gospel of Matthew (2) – 1 Ask, seek, knock

Missing the boat

> **Read Matthew 7:21–23**
>
> *'Then I will declare to them, "I never knew you; go away from me, you evildoers."'*
>
> (verse 23)

I love how The Message Bible translation (Eugene Peterson) puts verse 23: 'And do you know what I am going to say? "You missed the boat. All you did was use me to make yourselves important. You don't impress me one bit. You're out of here."' We miss the boat or the mark when our focus is on right beliefs or doctrines rather than living out righteousness. Or, differently stated: people of faith should be less obsessed with carving out truth as if we can fully comprehend the mind of the Divine and invest more in 'truthing truth'. We all can confess and believe: the bottom line is how we live our faith out. It is about faithfulness.

Among the gems of Kierkegaard is the following (attributed to him): 'Jesus wants followers – not admirers.'[8] Discipleship is ultimately about the compassionate heart of the Jesus way that overflows and gives away life and love all the time. The unnerving and old-fashioned way of stating it is: 'surrendering all to the Jesus way'. This, I suggest, is not about writing tomes or belting out hymn lines on Jesus as Lord to tickle ears and soothe consciences: it is about simply living lives of deep compassion for the sake of people who need it the most. Currently, our world is in desperate need of Christian practices and habits that will not use the name of Jesus for selfish purposes!

† May the whole of our lives be embodied testimonies of the way of God, the Divine Lover in Christ – the way of love given for the whole world.

For further thought

Where in my Christian practices am I betraying the way of Jesus? What of this way energises and challenges me the most?

8 Kierkegaard, S. (1944), *Training in Christianity*, trans. Walter Lowrie (Princeton, NJ: Princeton University Press), p. 231.

Thursday 18 June
Building well

Read Matthew 7:24–29

'Everyone then who hears these words of mine and acts on them will be like a wise man who built his house on rock.'

(verse 24)

The theme continues. I suppose that in surveying his own religious landscape Jesus must have been troubled over the gap between what was professed, preached or taught and the behaviour and action of people of faith. Forget dependence on religiosity, words, performance and random acts of charity: living out our faith is at the heart of the matter.

The offer of grace has an ethical demand: love for/devotion to God in Christ has to be seen in a life that honours God. Walkers of the way of Jesus must live lives that reflect values and beliefs that promote an economy of full and flourishing life for all. We are invited to an encounter with God and to a different way of living life. An alternative set of values, a set of values distinct from that of the economy of world-empire, must be our building blocks. This is a solid foundation.

Would it be reasonable to suggest that Matthew's emphasis on discipleship may be characterised by 'doing'? It would seem that 'right acts' or 'righteous actions' are given greater agency than 'right confession'. While trusting what God is doing, followers of Jesus' way are reminded to be mindful of their actions to be the kind of people God intends us to be. Perhaps the image of building on rock captures this. I understand this to suggest a certain quality of faith and faithfulness that runs deep and enables resilience despite the raging storms around.

† Generous God, help us respond to your invitation to share in 'fullness of life' that we might extend your blessing throughout our community. Remind us that the places where we find you become altars in our world.

For further thought

Consider what may be a current proposal, programme or scheme you or your community are embarking upon: what needs to be excavated and replaced? What do we need to give up or shed for God to reshape us for God's purpose?

Friday 19 June
Messy faith – transgressing boundaries

Read Matthew 8:1–17

Jesus stretched out his hand and touched [the leper], saying, 'I do choose. Be made clean!'

(verse 3a)

Most of us in the UK would have heard of the expression 'messy church' as a new way to engage with children in worship. I have often wondered how the imagery of 'messy' may serve to challenge tendencies of wishing to neatly 'stitch up' our understanding of everything about God with neatly crafted rules. This portion of scripture underscores the messiness of life (as seen and experienced by those in stories) which is not beyond the gaze of the Divine. Jesus refuses to keep himself removed from those who are declared unclean by well-thought theology and rituals. Perhaps the questions we should ask ourselves are: who are the people within our gaze? Who are those outside of our concern?

When he touched the leper, Jesus clearly and intentionally messed up the purity rules. This is a significant part of our calling to walk the way of Jesus. This is a different way of doing messy church: a way that reaches out across boundaries and includes unexpected people in the circle of God's healing love.

In Matthew, there are often two ways juxtaposed: narrow–wide; hard–easy; life–death; few–many; true–false; outside–inside; good–rotten/evil. The choice, though, may be larger and more complex than Matthew's choice. As Jesus' actions suggest in today's reading, sometimes rules are there to be broken, in the name of a God of liberation and love.

† Generous, Compassionate and Loving God, fill us with the music of your grace, shape us to your open-ended will and grant us the confidence and peace of your unbounded Spirit.

For further thought

Reflect on the place of healing in our life together. What 'miracles' have you seen in your own life or in the lives of those close to you? Consider where healing is needed and where your congregation is participating in such healing.

Saturday 20 June
Crossing over – following Jesus

Read Matthew 8:18–22

Now when Jesus saw great crowds around him, he gave orders to go over to the other side.

(verse 18)

I think it was the Swiss theologian Karl Barth who suggested that to understand scriptures (if we can fully do so), we must become much more than spectators. My way of responding to this challenge is to read scriptures with much imagination. So, for instance, when I come across texts that suggest or describe Jesus and/or his friend engaged in 'crossing over' from one place to another, I would always reread the whole account to check for any 'play' or connection with something larger than what may meet the eyes, ears, mind or heart. If there is a metaphor or expression that hints at the radical nature of Jesus' call, it is this idea of having to 'cross over'. For the habit of crossing over hints at adventure and risking into that which may draw us out of our comfort or fear zones. Jesus invites us to 'cross over' to the other side: to spaces where we can throw ourselves into the arms of grace.

I am known to easily get lost, even in a supermarket. Whatever part of the brain needs to work for reading maps, I think mine is largely underdeveloped. So, on family walks in forested and mountainous areas in France when maps fail and my family's good sense of direction leads us along often narrow trails, I have learnt to trust my wife and two sons, though I complain most of the way to the destination.

Discipleship requires imaginative faith, trust and commitment. Following Jesus is an invitation to an adventurous, unsettled and engaged sort of life – even for those of us who struggle with maps. When we cross over with Jesus, he is our guide and our goal, if we are up for the adventure.

† God-the-risk-taker, as your Spirit gives life to each breath we inhale, draw us closer to your adventurous way, release us from the safety of the borders we have drawn around our faith, and teach us that 'dying' is the most important act of living.

For further thought

The life of a disciple is not easy: it's uphill all the way. What are you doing with your life? What is the quality of my personal commitment to the Jesus way of full life for all?

The Gospel of Matthew (2) – 2 The storm and the sword

Notes by **Tim Yau**

Tim is a pioneer missioner for the Anglican Diocese of Norwich. His role is to establish a worshipping community in Round House Park, a new housing development in Cringleford, and to encourage missional practice across the region: not trying to get people to go to church, but to take the church to the people. To his children's delight, he is a *Star Wars* geek and still dreams of becoming a superhero. Tim has used the NIVUK for these notes.

Sunday 21 June
Faith and fear

Read Matthew 8:23 – 9:1

[Jesus] replied, 'You of little faith, why are you so afraid?'

(verse 26a)

It was supposed to be a dream holiday, two months exploring New Zealand. However, the screams, crashing bodies and the sheer volume of vomit pointed otherwise. The ferry had left the safe harbour of the capital Wellington in wild weather. It was exciting being buffeted by the wind and salt spray. However, once we hit the Cook Strait, it became a dangerous and fearful ordeal.

Thankfully, the ship made it through that storm unscathed, but at the time the sense of fear was very real. An unrelenting chaotic sea is something to be wary of: a reasonable fear. However, there are numerous unreasonable fears to contend with in this life, so many that sometimes we can feel lost and drowning in them. Unresolved fears can become a mind-storm and end up inhabiting and dominating our lives.

Here we see Jesus as master of the sea-storm and the mind-storm. The disciples feared the storm; the demonised men were in a storm of fear. Both sets were sinking and unable to rescue themselves. Jesus brings peace to external and internal storms. His presence conveys calm allowing us to see his true divinity, which in turn releases us into our true humanity. Have faith!

† Lord Jesus Christ, Son of God, have mercy. Help us to trust you in life's storms and have faith in you for our future. Amen

Monday 22 June
Faith and freedom

Read Matthew 9:2–13

'Which is easier: to say, "Your sins are forgiven," or to say, "Get up and walk"?'

(verse 5)

Santuari de Lluc is the spiritual heart of the island of Mallorca. The historic site nestles in an isolated valley of the Serra de Tramuntana and has been receiving pilgrims for nearly 500 years. People go to the monastery for varied reasons, but all have to travel from the relative ease of the flatlands to the twisting and arduous roads through steep mountain passes and lonely forests.

Facing the pilgrim's gate, looking down the shaded plaza towards the time-worn buildings surrounding the Basilica de la Mare de Deu, what struck me wasn't the scale, or the silence, but the simple cross overlooking it all, high on a hill silhouetted against the azure Mediterranean sky.

Indifferent locals, curious tourists and faithful pilgrims, whether they realised it or not, were on a spiritual journey. All roads led to the mountain cross. As I walked the way, I discovered the well-worn path needed serious attention. Rock falls and erosion made the going precarious. Some of my group gave up and turned back. It was easy to feel lost amongst the tree-shrouded trail, but when you looked up you got glimpses of the cross. Finally, I reached the summit. From the perspective of the cross, the walk looked uncomplicated and just a stone's throw away from the monastery.

Jesus called a paralysed man to walk from his life of incapacity; he called Matthew to walk from his life of sin. Jesus calls us to walk from whatever ensnares us, set free not to stumble on our own, but to walk to him. Will you walk to Jesus today?

† Lord Jesus Christ, Son of God, have mercy. Help us to follow your pilgrim way, to travel lightly through this world and to leave behind the things that prevent us from walking to you. Amen

For further thought

What is preventing you from walking to Jesus? Will you let him set you free? What might make you want to turn back?

Tuesday 23 June
Fervent faith

Read Matthew 9:14–26

Jesus turned and saw her. 'Take heart, daughter,' he said, 'your faith has healed you.'

(verse 22a)

My phone rang, the distant and unsteady voice of my wife echoed around my head: 'They're taking me in for emergency surgery.' My heart plummeted like falling masonry; she was bleeding and the baby inside her was dying. I felt the numbness of being apart from her and the powerlessness of being unable to help her. We were holidaying far from home, away from family and friends. Fear and desperation held my throat and gripped my guts, I held our toddler in my arms and all I could do was pray.

Where do you turn when you face personal tragedy? Thankfully, my wife survived the ordeal, but heartbreakingly we lost our unborn child, and with it the hopes and dreams that had grown around them. That initial despair grew into distraction, six years of tears and trying for a new baby. I was ready to give up – after all, I had a living wife and a growing boy to be thankful for – but she had faith. Faith in her body, faith in medical science, but most of all faith in God. She wasn't giving up. Today we have two boys and have grown in compassion for those with fertility issues.

Jesus always hears and responds to our prayerful desperation, although it may not be when, or in the way, we want. The synagogue ruler wanted his sick child well, the bleeding woman wanted a quiet healing. Neither got what they desired; they got much more. Jesus restores the dead girl's life and publicly restores the woman to the community. They had faith in Jesus; do you?

† Lord Jesus Christ, Son of God, have mercy. Hear our prayer, help us in our desperation, heal our infirmity, restore us to wholeness and give us the faith to be surprised by you. Amen

For further thought

What are you desperate for Jesus to do in your life and the lives of people around you? How will you bring this to him?

Wednesday 24 June
Faith and following

Read Matthew 10:1–15

Jesus called his twelve disciples to him and gave them authority ...

(verse 1a)

Lining up on a winter sports pitch the teacher started the football lesson. He blew his whistle to quieten down the rowdiest teens and pointed to the two most athletic boys. These would-be team captains then took it in turns to choose their players. Slowly the line-up was whittled away as each choice was deliberated over by the growing mob and new players joined their ranks. Finally, two of us remained and the earnest discussions turned into a bargaining process.

'We don't want them, they're useless!' one said.

'We'll swap the two of them for one of your good players,' came the swift reply.

The humiliation of being chosen last was bad enough, but being openly scrutinised, criticised and dismissed by my peers was worse.

Jesus called his disciples, but what were his selection criteria? Was it their spiritual aptitude, charismatic eloquence, formidable education, steely intelligence, religious vigour, theological nuance, exemplary character or mission experience? Outwardly, it was none of these things! The one thing they had in common was that when Jesus called, they followed. Faith and obedience. Jesus said 'come' and they came, he said 'go' and they went. Jesus saw past the external aspects of this ragtag bunch, he had faith in them, he believed they could do what he could do. So much so that when Peter and John were hauled in front of the Jewish ruling council for healing a lame man, the Sanhedrin were astonished by the courage of these 'unschooled, ordinary men' (Acts 4:13). Jesus believed in the disciples, and through their obedience God's kingdom came near.

† Lord Jesus Christ, Son of God, have mercy. Give us courage to be obedient when you call us to follow you, and faith to go when we don't see what you see. Amen

For further thought

When we respond to Jesus' call he equips us to go. What is stopping you going? How will he equip you to proclaim his message?

Thursday 25 June
Fight with faith

Read Matthew 10:16–33

'I am sending you out like sheep among wolves. Therefore be as shrewd as snakes and as innocent as doves.'

(verse 16)

We sheepishly entered the school gates. The school was like every other British comprehensive school: girls chatting in groups and boys kicking footballs around. The only differences were that there weren't any white faces to be seen and the majority of the girls wore *hijab* headscarves. I was a trainee youth worker attached to a local Pentecostal church and a team of us were being sent to the local predominantly migrant Bangladeshi Muslim secondary school to run a Christian Union. We were definitely in the minority; my team were mostly white English and middle-class and from outside of the region. We were conspicuous, nervous, underprepared and out of our depth, but we were honest, dedicated and a little bit stupid.

At first, the unruly kids got the better of us. They burst in, stormed out, spoke over us, denounced us, ridiculed us, and some of them made it their personal crusade to get us out of their school. It was hard and dispiriting work; why did we think we could do something Christian there? Nevertheless, we didn't give up, we didn't try to masquerade just as a youth drop-in, we were always upfront about our faith, and we prayed, and we loved them. Eventually, the atmosphere changed, the disruptive elements calmed down and our discussions and Bible studies became more fruitful.

Jesus sends us out knowing full well it won't be easy. We shouldn't be surprised about this; Jesus experienced it himself, why would we be exempt? So, let us not be scared off, but be genuine in our motives and clear about our call.

† Lord Jesus Christ, Son of God, have mercy. Protect us as you send us out, help us to not run from wolves but stand our ground. Give us the grace to be like you. Amen

For further thought

Who are the wolves that hunt you? Jesus said: 'love your enemies and pray for those who persecute you' (Matthew 5:44). Will you do this?

Friday 26 June
Faith and family

Read Matthew 10:34–42

'Do not suppose that I have come to bring peace to the earth. I did not come to bring peace, but a sword.'

(verse 34)

Today is my birthday. On special occasions, we're typically surrounded by family, friends and well-wishers making a special effort to show love, appreciation and solidarity. The thought that our nearest and dearest would ditch us for something or someone better would feel like a snub. We'd end up thinking 'what's wrong with me?' or 'what have I done to deserve this?' or, more probably, 'what's happened to them to make them be like this?' But what if we were in the middle of a national crisis, when our government was calling us to do our bit for the nation? Would we still feel snubbed knowing that there was something bigger calling our closest companions away?

Today there are some hard sayings from Jesus, but he knew what was coming for him and his disciples so there was a sense of urgency about his words. Therefore, the opening sentence should not be taken literally; Jesus was not advocating armed conflict. In fact, when a scuffle broke out between the temple guards and the disciples in the Garden of Gethsemane, Jesus told Peter, 'Put your sword back in its place, for all who draw the sword will die by the sword' (Matthew 26:52).

Jesus recognises that his message brings conflict; ultimately this might mean persecution and martyrdom, but most likely relational disharmony. God's command, 'Honour your father and your mother' (Exodus 20:12), is not being revoked but it is being challenged. Does our devotion to family outweigh our commitment to Jesus? Jesus' peace is less about happy families and more about reconciliation between humanity and God.

† Lord Jesus Christ, Son of God, have mercy. Forgive us when we're distracted from your mission; help us to follow you, even to the cross. Let our families experience your love for themselves. Amen

For further thought
Jesus calls us to take up our cross and follow him. What sacrifices will you make to do this whilst still honouring your relationships?

June

The Gospel of Matthew (2) – 2 The storm and the sword

Future faith

Read Matthew 11:1–19

'Are you the one who is to come, or should we expect someone else?'

(verse 3)

The security guard ran towards us, shouting, 'Get out of it you dumb kids, can't you read, "No trespassing!"?' We pedalled hard as our BMX bikes shot under the security barriers away from the Zoology faculty. I remember thinking to myself, 'What will the church council say, is this what they expect their youth worker to be doing?'

I lived in Cambridge, a historic jewel in Britain's academic crown, working with a church on the edge of the touristy city centre. The congregation mirrored the predominant culture of the city, middle class and well educated, with expectations that their kids would be the same. Taking over from a larger-than-life predecessor, I'd been tasked to run their in-house youth ministry, and within the well-established programme life ticked over.

I was content fulfilling my brief until I noticed the amount of local kids from the neighbourhood hanging out nearby on skateboards and BMXs. I invited them to our clubs and groups but they never came; their culture seemed so far removed from the church's culture, I realised they'd never come. Therefore, I bought myself a street bike and I started to hang out with them, they taught me to BMX, and eventually they asked me to ride with them.

To reach those who are far off entails breaking with expectations and doing surprising things. John the Baptist had certain hopes for the Messiah, but God had other plans. John was faithful in fulfilling his prophetic ministry, but Jesus was called to something different, not to continue where John left off, but do something unique.

† Lord Jesus Christ, Son of God, have mercy. Take us to new places, send us to new people, teach us to mission in new ways and surprise us with what you'll do through us. Amen

For further thought

When God opens a door for you, even if it is unexpected and out of your experience, will you have faith and walk through it?

20:20 vision

Notes by **Raj Patta**

Raj is an ordained minister in the Andhra Evangelical Lutheran Church in India, and recently completed his PhD at the University of Manchester. Working with the Stockport Methodist Circuit as a creative Bible study facilitator, Raj engages with communities to bring transformation. He is married to Shiny and has two sons, Jubi and Jai ho. He blogs at thepattas.blogspot.co.uk. Raj has used the NRSVA for these notes.

Sunday 28 June
God's sight and God's goodness

Read Genesis 1:1–5

And God saw that the light was good; and God separated the light from the darkness.

(verse 4)

The first two chapters of Genesis can be read as a poem about the beginning of creation, and provide a blueprint for the mission of God's wonderful handiwork. These stories have also been misused down the centuries as a tool of the powers-that-be: as *the* creation story, settling arguments over creation or evolution. In contrast, I discern three important things from this chapter. First, all that is good is seen by God; second, the sight of God looks for the good in all of creation; and, finally, God's sight and goodness are directly proportional to one another. In chapter 1 of Genesis, God saw several things that are good: light, land, sea, vegetation, wildlife and human beings. From the first light to the latest human beings, everything good came under God's sight. God's sight looked out only for goodness. Do you think the goodness of God *is* God's own commitment to seeking out the good in creation?

As we begin this week discerning our vision for 20:20, as faithful followers of God we are called to adjust our sight to be in line with God's sight, looking out for good among God's creation. This invites us to rectify our myopic vision: our judging others from our situation and criticising others based on our yardsticks.

† This week, keep a list of all the good things you see around you every day.

June

20:20 vision

Monday 29 June
Seeing with God

Read Psalm 11

The Lord is in his holy temple; the Lord's throne is in heaven. His eyes behold, his gaze examines humankind.

(verse 4)

The world's tallest statue has been unveiled in India, the statue of a freedom fighter called Sardar Patel (1875–1950). The statue is 182 metres tall and cost 30 billion Indian rupees, or about £330 million. This statue is called *Statue of Unity*, standing tall on the banks of the river Narmada, displacing several tribal groups from their native land. In my opinion, the real question is, why does a statue's height matter when poverty in India has been so dramatically on the rise?

The psalmist in Psalm 11 expresses the view that in God alone is his trust and refuge, not in any kings, statues and ideologies. Unlike the Statue of Unity, the God of this psalm truly sees and listens, especially to those like the tribal groups whose lands have been grabbed to build the statue. Psalm 11 suggests that nothing in this world and history goes unnoticed by God. God sees the slightest manoeuvre of injustice of our times, for God sees all.

As believers of such a God, the call for us as readers is to be watchful. The psalm calls us out of our insensitivity to injustice around us. The all-seeing God calls for faithful followers to never take their eyes off injustice and to strive for a just and peace-filled world today. It's time that the world listened to the cries of the tribal groups who have been displaced, and committed itself to work for justice.

† God who sees all, grant us a spirit to be watchful over the injustices around us. Forgive our short-sightedness and sharpen our vision. In Jesus' name. Amen

For further thought

Reflect on at least two concerns of justice, one nearer to your home context and the other in the global context.

Tuesday 30 June
Upside down God

Read Exodus 24:9–18

Now the appearance of the glory of the Lord was like a devouring fire on the top of the mountain in the sight of the people of Israel.

(verse 17)

When we talk about God, it is often about God's power over others. God is spoken as 'Almighty God', 'Our God is a great big God', 'Rich God', etc. These terms and titles project God as being in the categories of the privileged and powerful. In contrast to such theologies, God in Jesus grounds communities at the bottom of society, from below. Dalits, the so-called 'untouchables' in India, therefore understand God in the context of their 'outcastedness' as a 'Dalit God'. The language of God in Christ speaks to their experience of brokenness.

The text for today is a narrative of Moses, Aaron and other elders of the tribes meeting God on a mountain. Those on the mountaintop saw a God standing on 'something like a pavement of sapphire stone, like the very heaven for clearness' (verse 10). But for those below, the appearance of God was as a raging fire – like the pillar of fire that led the community through the wilderness. God appeared to them in the mundane, the ordinary and the everyday.

As we read this text today, we are called to envision a God from bottom-up, joining with the vulnerable communities who yearn for life. God in Jesus is an upside down God who identifies with the weak and the powerless. When we envision God from this perspective, we join with those at the bottom of society in their quest for justice, peace, equality and life. This text challenges us: will we work for God's liberation and transformation of our society today, in the ordinary and the everyday?

† God, you who have pitched your tent among us, help us to partake in your work of liberation and transformation today.

For further thought

What are the ordinary ways your community might speak of God and envision God?

The shock of God's vision

Read Habakkuk 1:1–14

Look at the nations, and see! Be astonished! Be astounded! For a work is being done in your days that you would not believe if you were told.

(verse 5)

This verse is part of God's answer to the complaint made by the prophet Habakkuk, whose name means 'embrace'. Habakkuk's faith in God challenged him to expose and speak out loud of the unjust systems and structures in his society ('destruction', 'violence' and 'strife'; verse 3) and to question God's silence in the face of growing evil during his time. Habakkuk embraces a deeper spirituality, for by his faith in God he could complain to God.

God takes serious note of Habakkuk's complaint; for God's ways are beyond human comprehension and sometimes are hard to believe. People who make complaints want to keep control of situations or take control into their own hands and look for answers the way they would want them. By making a complaint to God, Habakkuk probably thought that God might entrust the task of addressing their context to him, as he was a prophet available then. But God acted differently according to God's own way, preparing Habakkuk to brace for a shock and even one that would be hard to believe, for God roused the Babylonians.

How can we imagine a God who acts in God's own ways? For God's ways are mysterious. We may be inclined to try to solve all our problems by ourselves without being open to other perspectives and worldviews. We are called to embrace to stay open to God's mysterious ways, and to embrace humility. We might find that God is going to shock us, and we may even find it hard to believe that God can work in ways very different and subversive to our ways of doing. May God's wonder shock us and help us to be open.

† God of wonder, you are constantly bracing us for a shock by your mysterious ways. Teach us humility to be open to you and help us place all into your hands. Amen

For further thought

As you listen to the news today, in what surprising ways do you think God is working in our world?

Thursday 2 July
Seeing a new world

Read Acts 9:1–19

Saul asked, 'Who are you, Lord?' The reply came, 'I am Jesus, whom you are persecuting. But get up and enter the city, and you will be told what you are to do.'

(verses 5–6)

Saul, a strict follower of his religion, was on his way to Damascus to persecute the new followers of the Way. Dazed by a blinding flash of light, he fell to the ground and was left without sight for three days. 'Saul, Saul, why do you persecute me?' he heard a voice say (verse 4).

Lying ill in Damascus, perhaps Saul remembered his own religious texts. He may have have recalled when God appeared to Moses in a burning bush. Confronted by God, Moses asked for God's name (Exodus 3:13). In a similar way, realising that God is present, Saul asks, 'Who are you, Lord?' (Acts 9:5).

Speaking out of the burning bush, God replied to Moses, 'I am who I am' (Exodus 3:14). On the road to Damascus, God says to Saul, 'I am Jesus, the one you're hunting down. I want you to get up and enter the city. In the city you'll be told what to do next.' God here takes on the name of Jesus, whom the persecuted tiny minority have been following, putting into question Saul's religious fanaticism, his violent quest and his arrogance. Those three days without vision made Saul reflect, repent, confess and pray for a change in his life. He eventually got back his sight and served God humbly.

This text calls all its readers to examine how our public spheres have been taken over either by secularism or by fanaticism. The speech of God comes to each of us in different ways, and the challenge for us is to ask, whose voice is it? God knows our names – Moses, Samuel and Saul – but do we know God's name?

† God, forgive our spiritual blindness and our arrogance, and help us see truly.

For further thought

Think of the contexts where religious persecution is prevalent, and pray for people who have become victims of violence in the name of religion.

20:20 vision

July

Shining bright

For now we see in a mirror, dimly, but then we will see face to face. Now I know only in part; then I will know fully, even as I have been fully known.

(verse 12)

The Message's translation has a different version of these verses, comparing Paul's 'mirror' to a fog that we can't see through. Yet it won't be long until the mist lifts and the sun shines.

According to the UK's Highway Code, one must use headlights while driving when visibility is poor. Do you think negotiating a road in different conditions is similar to our spiritual journey? Writing to the church at Corinth, Paul explains the importance of love; perhaps you could say that love helps in times of poor visibility in the journey of faith. Paul might say that we are to understand that the fog and mist won't last for long, for the weather will clear soon. In times of poor visibility, we are called to turn on the headlights of love, so that we can continue the journey of faith. For Paul, God in Jesus is love personified; love shining brightly. When the God of love shines as the sun on our lives, then we know who that God of love is, and God knows who we are.

Yet our world today is stuck with poor weather due to human sin: especially our ecological imbalance. As we meditate on this text today, let us repent of our lifestyles that threaten creation. The God of love calls us to be enlightened by the Sun of Righteousness and to be a spark and a flame to love our creation and our neighbour. It's time to turn on our headlights of love and keep showing the way to a bright future for the coming generations.

† God, the Sun of Righteousness, who in Jesus became the embodiment of love and truth, shine on us so that we can see and generate love for you and for our creation. Amen

For further thought

How can your actions today help 'clear the air' around you?

20:20 vision

July

Beholding the dream

Read 1 Timothy 6:11–21

But as for you, man of God, shun all this; pursue righteousness, godliness, faith, love, endurance, gentleness.

(verse 11)

Anders Lustgarten's recent play *If You Don't Let Us Dream, We Won't Let You Sleep* is a provocative, political reading of the state today and an attack on financial capitalism. Writing to young Timothy, Paul encourages him to dream of an eternal life to dwell in the light of God's presence. In other words, dreams are not what we see in our sleep, but are rather what keep us from sleep, the sleep of complacency and sin. Paul was trying to capture that essence of living a dream in the light of God, which forms a template for exemplary Christian living. Paul mentions at least thirteen verbs to Timothy to enable him to be a 'man of God'. These verbs are still important for our spiritual vision today: run, pursue, run hard, seize, keep, don't slack off, tell, tell them to go after God, do good, be rich in helping others, be extravagantly generous, guard and avoid.

Paul's exhortation to Timothy is still relevant. To be a follower of Christ in the twenty-first century is a call to flee from violence and greed and pursue a life of wonder, faith, love, steadiness and courtesy. It is a practical vocation, a paradigm for 20:20 vision for our Christian living: a dream for us for this year and the years to come. In The Message's translation, Paul concludes his letter by saying, 'Overwhelming grace keep you' (verse 21). By our own strength we might not achieve this dream, but by the overwhelming grace with us, we will be able to run and pursue it.

† God of dreams, help us to pursue the cause of your kingdom here on earth. May we see your kingdom come. Amen

For further thought

What are your dreams for a kingdom of God's rule? What can you do to make them a reality and to see them arise around you?

20:20 vision

July

Readings in Numbers – 1 Travelling through the wilderness

Notes by **Mark Scarlata**

Mark is the lecturer in Old Testament and biblical theology at St Mellitus College, London. He was a congregational pastor in the US before moving to the UK, where he is an Anglican priest at St Edward, King and Martyr, Cambridge. He has published widely on the Old Testament, including *"Am I My Brother's Keeper?" Christian Citizenship in a Globalized Society* (Wipf and Stock 2013), *The Abiding Presence* (SMC Press 2018) and *Sabbath Rest* (SCM Press 2019). Mark has used the NRSVA for these notes.

Sunday 5 July
A travelling God

Read Numbers 4:4–16

When Aaron and his sons have finished covering the sanctuary and all the furnishings of the sanctuary, as the camp sets out, after that the Kohathites shall come to carry these, but they must not touch the holy things, or they will die.

(verse 15)

Packing up the car for a summer holiday can often be a tremendous ordeal. Even packing our own suitcases for a long trip can be challenging. We stuff in all our things just waiting to get to our destination where we can hopefully unpack and relax.

For the Israelites in the wilderness it was a different matter. Not only did they have to pack their own tents, but they had to carry the tent of God's dwelling. In Exodus, the details for the construction of the tabernacle are given in meticulous detail. The Holy God of Israel is coming to dwell in the midst of his people and the house (tent) where he will live must be completely holy. The tabernacle is the visible sign of God's presence and his covenant faithfulness to his people.

The Israelites were on a journey from death in Egypt to life in the Promised Land. Yet in between they had to travel through the wilderness, a place of testing and trust. All the while, God promised to travel with them and to abide in their midst. Packing up the tabernacle was a reminder of God's holiness, his presence and his desire to be in the heart of his people.

† God who dwelled in the heart of Israel and now who dwells in our hearts through the Holy Spirit, open our eyes to your presence with us this day.

Monday 6 July
The priestly blessing

> **Read Numbers 6:22–27**
>
> *The Lord bless you and keep you; the Lord make his face to shine upon you, and be gracious to you; the Lord lift up his countenance upon you, and give you peace.*
>
> (verses 24–26)

Some of the earliest evidence of the Old Testament text comes from a site called 'Ketef Hinnom' near Jerusalem. Archaeologists discovered two small silver scrolls that were inscribed with an ancient Hebrew script dating back to the sixth century BCE. Each of them included a version of what is known as the Priestly Blessing. These are the words God commands Aaron and the priests to proclaim over the people so that his name might always rest upon them. These silver scrolls, housed inside small amulets, were likely worn by the Israelites as a reminder of God's blessing each day.

The words are a reminder of relationship. God pours out blessing on us and watches over us. His face is directed towards ours and the brilliance of his holiness washes over us. He is gracious to us and gives us peace. When the priest spoke these words and when the Israelites wore this blessing each day, they were reminded of a God who is near and a God who desires to bless.

The act of blessing is somewhat foreign to our modern secular culture. Why would you bless someone without expecting something in return? The beauty of blessing is that it is a gift of grace. This is how God gives to us and this is how he wants us to bless the world. The letter to the Hebrews tells us that Jesus is the ascended great high priest. He now speaks these words over us so that his name might be upon us so that we might bring his blessing and peace.

† May the Lord who blesses us, Father, Son and Holy Spirit, make his face to shine upon us so that we might share his blessing with others.

For further thought

Write down a verse from scripture and keep it with you so that you might be reminded of God's blessing and pass it on to others.

Tuesday 7 July
Keeping the Passover

Read Numbers 9:1–14

The Lord spoke to Moses in the wilderness of Sinai, in the first month of the second year after they had come out of the land of Egypt, saying: Let the Israelites keep the passover at its appointed time.

(verses 1–2)

The Passover was the most significant Jewish festival that marked the final defeat of Pharaoh and God's deliverance of his people from slavery in Egypt. It was to be celebrated each year, but not simply as a memorial. The rabbis spoke of how at every Passover the people were to celebrate as if they were the generation of slaves who were about to be freed. This living memory becomes the central hope for God's salvation coming to his people once again.

For the Christian, the event of Passover takes on new meaning in the death and resurrection of Christ. He is the Passover lamb who gave his life as a sacrifice for our sin. But we must also remember that the sign of Passover is a sign of victory and God's sovereignty over the powers of evil and the forces in the world that oppose his reign. Jesus chose this meal to reveal what he was about to do not only as an atoning sacrifice, but also to demonstrate God's sovereignty and his final act of victory over sin and death.

When we celebrate Holy Communion we recall the whole story of God's salvation from liberation in Egypt to our own liberation through the cross. As we partake, we remember what Christ has done for us and we are reminded that he sends us out to bring his liberation, freedom and hope to the world.

† Jesus, the lamb of God who takes away the sin of the world, we thank you for liberating us from death. May we bring that liberation to the world.

For further thought

How might we become God's agents of freedom and liberation? How might we help others experience that freedom?

Wednesday 8 July
The cloud of fire

Read Numbers 9:15–23

On the day the tabernacle was set up, the cloud covered the tabernacle, the tent of the covenant; and from evening until morning it was over the tabernacle, having the appearance of fire.

(verse 15)

The cloud of glory over the tabernacle was a sign of the Divine Presence that travelled with Israel as they wandered throughout the wilderness. Not only did God rescue them from death and slavery, but he also promised that he would dwell at the heart of their community. That glory is described as cloud and fire that rested on the tabernacle where God dwelt.

The images of cloud and fire call to mind the mystery of who God is and how he can be represented in the physical world. Clouds obscure our view and fire is something that is both beautiful and terrifying at the same time. The biblical authors knew that no one could fully describe the presence of God, but the most critical thing was that his Divine Presence remained with them as they journeyed to the Promised Land.

The Divine Presence of the tabernacle will ultimately become the glory of God that dwells in the Incarnate Jesus Christ. John writes that Jesus 'tabernacled' among us (John 1:14), alluding to the images seen in Numbers. The God who came to dwell in the midst of people in the Old Testament came again in the Son to dwell with us and live with us in the flesh. After Christ ascended he left us the gift of his presence in the Holy Spirit that he might dwell with us for eternity.

† God of Glory, you dwelled in the tabernacle and were revealed through the Son. Dwell in us now through the Holy Spirit.

For further thought
Today we might pray that we experience afresh the Holy Spirit in our lives.

Thursday 9 July
The silver trumpet call

Read Numbers 10:1–10

The sons of Aaron, the priests, shall blow the trumpets; this shall be a perpetual institution for you throughout your generations.

(verse 8)

If you've ever heard the first call, or 'Reveille', played on the bugle early in the morning you'll have a good idea of why silver trumpets were prescribed for sending out alarms to the Israelites. They are loud! And this was the point. The clarion call would wake anyone from their slumber and alert them to the danger ahead.

Many churches throughout the world have bells that ring out. They might do so hourly or to announce the time of worship. Sometimes they ring for weddings or funerals, but whenever they are rung, they send out a reminder to the surrounding community that the church is still standing, that God is still present in the world and that he is here to protect and guide his people.

Oftentimes we need the sound of trumpets or bells to wake us up from our spiritual slumber. We can plod along with our reading and prayers without recognising that the powerful presence of God is with us and ready to guide us at all times. Maybe that trumpet call is an unexpected person we encounter or a situation that God leads us to. Whatever it might be, may we listen to the sound of his trumpet call announcing that the presence of salvation in Christ is with us and in the world.

† Lord, let your trumpets resound in the heavens and may we hear them on earth to know that you are always with us.

For further thought

Look out for opportunities today to remind others of God's presence with us in Christ.

Friday 10 July
Manna in the wilderness

Read Numbers 11:4–9

The people went around and gathered it, ground it in mills or beat it in mortars, then boiled it in pots and made cakes of it; and the taste of it was like the taste of cakes baked with oil.

(verse 8)

This is the second account of the manna in the wilderness. The first story comes in Exodus when the Israelites have left Egypt and entered into the desert. They complained that they had no food, but God provided the gift of bread each day that was like the bread of heaven. The sign was to demonstrate God's provision for his people, but the people also had to trust that God would continue to watch over them and give them their daily bread. This was especially true on the sixth day when they gathered twice the amount to prepare for their seventh day of sabbath rest.

In Numbers, the people are sick of God's bread. They have been in the wilderness for longer than expected and they long for days back in Egypt when they ate other things. The grass is always greener, as the saying goes, and at this moment Israel has completely forgotten their hopeless life as slaves under Pharaoh's brutal regime.

The manna, however, was God's ongoing gift that sustained his people till they reached the Promised Land. In John's Gospel, Jesus takes the image of manna and transforms our understanding of what it means to trust the Father and his gift of food for us: 'I am the bread of life. Whoever comes to me will never be hungry, and whoever believes in me will never be thirsty' (John 6:35). Jesus offers us the bread of life for our journey through the wilderness. He promises to be our physical and spiritual bread, to nourish us and sustain us. This is the true manna that comes down from heaven.

† Lord, feed us with the bread of life through your Son, Jesus Christ. And may we offer that bread to others as we journey through this world.

For further thought

Think of a way that you might offer the bread of life to others today. It could be feeding someone, comforting someone or sharing the gospel with them.

Saturday 11 July
The seventy elders

Read Numbers 11:10–17, 24–30

'I will come down and talk with you there; and I will take some of the spirit that is on you and put it on them; and they shall bear the burden of the people along with you so that you will not bear it all by yourself.'

(verse 17)

Moses had a hard life in the wilderness. He was trying to do as God commanded but the people kept complaining at every step and Moses had finally had enough. He was fed up with their lack of faith, but he was also fed up with doing everything himself! He is like the person who always tidies up after church, helps make the coffee, sets up for worship, washes the cups, puts away the dishes, and the list goes on. It can get tiring. Finally Moses turns to God and says, 'These are your people, you take care of them!'

Instead of relieving Moses of his calling, God raises up others to help him and ease the burden. In this instance, it's the seventy elders. God places his Spirit on them and they prophesy, though we're told they did not do so again. In this brief moment we're given a glimpse of a God who does not want his servants to carry the burden of ministry alone. Just as Moses needed help throughout his life, so too do we need the help of others in the Body of Christ to sustain the ministry God has given us.

At the end of the story it appears that God's Spirit spilled out a bit too much. Eldad and Medad, who weren't at the tent, also shared in Moses' ministry by prophesying in the camp. When Moses finds out, he says not to stop them, but he hopes that ALL people would share in God's Spirit. This simple expression of faith points to the future when God would pour out his Holy Spirit on all people at Pentecost.

† Lord, may your Holy Spirit rest on us so that we may do the ministry that you have called us to with the help of those around us.

For further thought

How might you include or inspire others to share in the ministry that God has placed on your heart?

Readings in Numbers – 2 Testing times

Notes by **Carla A. Grosch-Miller**

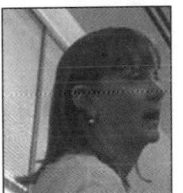

For Carla's biography, see p. 111. Carla has used the NRSVA for these notes.

Sunday 12 July
The cost of freedom

Read Numbers 11:18–23, 31–34

'For you have wailed in the hearing of the Lord, saying, "If only we had meat to eat! Surely it was better for us in Egypt."'

(verse 18b)

This week we read from Numbers chapters 11–25, a dramatic portrayal of a people who began bitterly complaining as soon as they set off from Egypt on their march from slavery to freedom. The stories, paralleled in the Book of Exodus, show both the people and God in a more unflattering light than Exodus: the crowd is unrelentingly whiny, God is angry and malevolent in response. It is helpful to remember that the Book of Numbers was put together after the exile, possibly soon after the return to a devastated Jerusalem. Folks were wrestling with why the temple and city were destroyed. They concluded that it was a punishment from a very angry God.

Another way to understand these stories is to consider the journey from slavery to freedom as one that necessarily has particular challenges, including the temptation to look back longingly for the certainties of slavery, how to find sustenance in an unknown wilderness, and leadership tests. The message that the biblical writers and editors of Numbers wanted to convey is of the necessity to trust God throughout all the vicissitudes of the journey. That message is as fresh today as it was 2,500 years ago.

† God of an unknown future, when I am tempted to look back on my shackles with fondness, remind me that freedom and grace are ahead.

Monday 13 July
The right use of power

Read Numbers 12:1–15

And they said, 'Has the Lord spoken only through Moses? Has he not spoken through us also?'

(verse 2)

Yes, God had spoken through Aaron and Miriam too, but undermining gossip and criticism of Moses' marital choice were not what was on God's mind. This little story is a reminder to humility for leaders and discernment to followers. Being chosen to lead does not give one carte blanche to pontificate on any old topic and especially not to disrespect one's colleagues. And not every word that comes out of the mouths of leaders is good and godly. Here Moses is held up as humility itself, despite his unique 'mouth-to-mouth' (literally, in the Hebrew; 'face-to-face' in the NRSVA) relationship with the Creator of All. Responding to Aaron and Miriam's impertinent chinwag, God clarified the chain of command: 1. God, and then 2. Moses.

Disappointingly, only Miriam is punished for the indiscretion. Stricken with white scales, she is cast from the camp for seven days. Aaron gets off scot-free, possibly because his priestly status would be threatened were he to become so blemished, possibly because women always get the blame. Protecting a powerful man's reputation is not just a contemporary phenomenon. *Plus ça change, plus c'est la même chose.*

Despite contextual discomfort (the Ancient Near East *was* highly patriarchal), we hear the message. On the journey from slavery to freedom, leaders may be tempted to overreach and followers may be duped into believing overconfident leaders. Both leaders and followers have an obligation to kindness and to wise discernment. No one is without power or responsibility.

† God of the freedom way, guard my lips from poisoned speech and sharpen my hearing to catch words of truth, that I may use my power rightly.

For further thought

Grandiosity may stem from insecurity. When you are tempted to undermine or disparage another, what fear is at work in you?

Tuesday 14 July
Count the cost

Read Numbers 13:1–3, 17–29

The Lord said to Moses, 'Send men to spy out the land of Canaan, which I am giving to the Israelites.'

(verses 1–2a)

It's good to get the lie of the land before proceeding forward. I once went on a ramble with a group, the leader of which assumed that the trail would be as it was the year before. Ha! After hours of thrashing through overgrown brambles, getting lost twice and trying to keep our cool on a hot day, we made it to our final destination. The leader was mortified and apologetic. We tried to make him feel better. All said though, it is best to do a 'reccy' (British for reconnaissance) before undertaking a walk in the wilderness.

Moses tells the scouts to assess the condition and fruitfulness of the land as well as whether it is occupied and fortified. He is doing what Jesus acknowledged we all should do: count the cost before committing (Luke 14:28).

Freedom costs. As binding as slavery is, it has its certainties: where the next meal is coming from, one's status, one's friends, how to behave to survive. All that is wiped away on the journey to freedom. The first step is a step into the unknown. New ways will need to be learned; meals may have to be skipped. Whilst the horizon widens, one's focus is often just on the next step. To know this beforehand helps the wayfaring.

The scouts brought back a cluster of grapes so large that it had to be carried in a frame by two people and reported that the people and fortifications were strong. Great is the fruit of freedom, and great are the challenges.

† God of the journey, prepare me for the realities ahead as I relinquish slavery. Clear my vision. Enable me to count the cost and commit to the freedom way.

For further thought

We do not give something up until we want something else more deeply. What freedom do you desire? What slavery stands in the way?

Vote your hope

Read Numbers 13:30 – 14:10a

Then the men who had gone up with [Caleb] said, 'We are not able to go up against this people, for they are stronger than we are.' So they brought to the Israelites an unfavourable report of the land that they had spied out, saying, '... All the people that we saw in it are of great size.'

(verses 31–32a and c)

There will always be naysayers who stoke fear and catastrophise. Enemies become giants as fear spreads; people abandon hope as they are foisted back on their survival instincts by powerful emotions. Reason and values-based thinking go out the window. This is brain physiology, pure and simple. In the face of threat, the limbic system hijacks the more recently evolved cerebral cortex, cutting off the possibility of using the brains God gave us to sort out complex problems.

The task of the leadership is to be the prefrontal cortex for the whole group, bringing reason and religion on board the ship before it sails. Moses and Aaron try this, and the crowd threatens to pelt them with stones.

It's always been this way. When we embark on a new and risky project, especially one that requires or demands CHANGE, we can count on resistance. It would be naïve not to.

Thought and commitment, reason and hope are key. In the summer of 2018, I heard the civil rights leader Jesse Jackson speak at Chautauqua, New York, USA. He commented on how some leaders stoke fear to achieve their political ends. He charged the crowd: *Vote your hope, not your fear*.

† God of the caged and the free, make my thirst for freedom strong and my courage to rattle the cage even stronger. Give me what I need to vote hope rather than fear. Amen

For further thought

Courage is being afraid of something and doing it anyway. What helps you to manage your fear and do what you need or want to do?

Thursday 16 July
One generation dies

Readings in Numbers – 2 Testing times

Read Numbers 14:10b–24

Then the Lord said, 'I do forgive, just as you have asked; nevertheless – as I live, and as all the earth shall be filled with the glory of the Lord – none of the people who ... have tested me these ten times and have not obeyed my voice, shall see the land that I swore to give to their ancestors.'

(verses 20–22a, 22c–23a)

Here's where it all goes wrong. Numbers chapters 11–25 tell the story of the wilderness wandering through the lens of believing that God is capable of destroying everything in rage at human foibles. After all, the postexilic writers had seen and suffered the fall of Jerusalem and being carried off to Babylon. Looking backward at their origin stories, they read the freed slaves' pleas for food and fears as rebellion. They conceived the divine response as devastating: the first generation to leave slavery will die in the wilderness at God's hand (God marches them into battle to be slain); it is their children who will enter the Promised Land.

God is a nasty figure in this story. And the people's fear-filled 'rebellion' is blamed as the cause of a generation dying before reaching the goal.

But is it not true that generations die and new ones arise with new ideas and possibilities? Sometimes that is the only way progress is made.

Numbers' telling of wilderness wandering is a dangerous story. Its portrayal of a wrathful, nasty God and a fearful people has been used to justify hate-filled judgement and violence by Christian people. Be careful how you tell it. Better, I believe, to draw the God of love and mercy we see in Jesus.

† God merciful and mighty, when I am tempted to believe that rage and judgement pave the way to peace, temper me and bid me to remember mercy and speak the truth in love.

For further thought

Rage, like fire, can burn for good or ill. How do you harness your rage in order to choose a constructive response to unjust situations?

Friday 17 July
By whose power?

> ### Read Numbers 20:1–13
> Moses and Aaron gathered the assembly together before the rock, and he said to them, 'Listen, you rebels, shall we bring water for you out of this rock?' Then Moses lifted up his hand and struck the rock twice with his staff.
>
> (verses 10–11a)

And now for the explanation of why Moses didn't make it to the Promised Land, instead dying on the top of Mount Pisgah within sight of it (Deuteronomy 34). In this version of the story (different from Exodus 17), God takes offence apparently because Moses struck the rock twice rather than ordering the rock to produce water, without attributing the miracle to God's 'sanctity'.

Oddly, the first generation having been slaughtered, it turns out that the second generation is just as whiny – but Moses and Aaron get the punishment. Someone has got to survive.

Setting aside the churlish characterisation of God, there is a point to be made. Namely, that leaders chosen by God need to remember from whence their power comes. Work enough miracles with a rod (parting the Red Sea, getting water from a rock) and one might get the idea that one is really special. Add to that the (occasional) adulation of the crowd and one might feel really very special.

People's expectations of their ministers and leaders can be unrealistic, elevating their divinity whilst ignoring their humanity. Worse yet, ministers and leaders carry their own set of unrealistic expectations. They are not called to be Jesus, but to point to Jesus. The finger pointing to the moon is not the moon. More realistic expectations on both sides increase the health and effectiveness of both pastor and people. Both are counselled to look to the Source, acknowledging where the power really lies.

† One True God, when I am elevated in my own mind or the minds of others, remind me that I am dust, beloved dust, but dust nonetheless. Help my life to point to you.

For further thought

Right self-esteem is to recognise both one's gifts and one's limitations, and to know oneself beloved of God. Do you have the balance right?

Saturday 18 July
Facing up

Read Numbers 21:4–9

And the Lord said to Moses, 'Make a poisonous serpent, and set it on a pole; and everyone who is bitten shall look at it and live.'

(verse 8)

The people are still whining; they get on God's last nerve. In a moment of now-characteristic nastiness, God sends fiery snakes to bite and kill them. Moses the middleman again intercedes and God instructs the construction of a bronze serpent (a play on words as the Hebrew words for both are similar). Anyone bitten who looks on it will be healed.

The ritual described here is similar to an ancient Near Eastern healing ritual known as sympathetic magic, an idea not unlike the hangover cure of a little more alcohol the morning after a big bender.

Could it be that this kind of healing ritual derives from the fact that there is no way through pain and difficulty except to go through it? Healing comes after the problem and the pain have been faced head-on, acknowledged and worked with. Staring at the bronze serpent is a facing up to the bad behaviour and lack of trust that sparked the snakebite in the first place.

Later, the bronze serpent made a home in the Jerusalem temple until King Hezekiah destroyed it when people started worshipping it (2 Kings 18:4). There is a lesson: facing into one's pain is different from worshipping it and having it become one's full identity. Victims become survivors who draw wisdom and strength through having faced up to the pain.

Even later, the writer of the Gospel of John compared the raised serpent to beholding the crucified Christ (3:14). The suffering of Jesus gives us courage to honestly face into our own suffering and grow through it.

† God of healing, when I am caught up in victimhood, give me clarity of sight and courage to face into the pain and traverse it, to come out the other side wiser and stronger.

For further thought

Every one of us carries some brokenness. Where is yours? Mercy invites you to welcome and work with it.

Readings in Numbers – 2 Testing times

July

Readings in Numbers –
3 Balaam and his ass

Notes by **Viv Randles**

Viv is a United Reformed Church minister based in southwest London. She has an MA in Old Testament studies from the University of Gloucestershire and dreams of one day completing a PhD on an Old Testament/Hebrew Bible topic. Her twin delights are seeing people light up with excitement as they discover the relevance of the Old Testament to Christian life today and fostering cats for a local animal rescue. Viv has used the NRSVA for these notes.

Sunday 19 July
Don't panic!

Read Numbers 22:1–14

Moab was in great dread of the people, because they were so numerous; Moab was overcome with fear of the people of Israel.

(verse 3)

The people of Israel have come to the end of their wanderings; the Promised Land is a step away, across the Jordan. Unfortunately, the leaders of Moab and Midian fear they may suffer the same fate as Og and Sihon. It is hardly surprising that the people of Moab were filled with dread at the sight of Israel's tents stretching into the distance. The New King James translation even describes them as 'sick with dread'.

Anyone who has suffered anxiety – stage fright, exam nerves, an anxiety disorder – can sympathise with Moab's fear. Balak, king of the Moabites, runs around in a panic, like a cartoon character, telling everyone his fears. Surely, this alien nation will overwhelm Moab, displacing its people and taking their land and resources.

Fear of strangers, especially in large numbers, can still make us 'sick with dread'. Huge numbers of refugees, fleeing war and poverty, have prompted whole societies to become 'sick' in response to what they see as a threat. Countries that once described themselves as Christian refuse hospitality and close their borders, afraid to feed the hungry and welcome the stranger as Jesus taught (Matthew 25:35).

† Am I afraid to love those who are different? How can God's love help me overcome my fear and open my heart to the stranger?

Oh, but, please ...

Read Numbers 22:15–30

'I will surely do you great honour, and whatever you say to me I will do.'

(verse 17a)

We are not good at receiving answers we do not want to hear. Balak certainly did not want to hear Balaam's refusal to come and curse Israel. Instead, he 'heard' an invitation to barter over the price of the seer's services: by no means an unusual next step in that time and place. Balaam, however, meant what he said, and none of Balak's promises of wealth could lead him to do what God forbade.

That Balaam tells these messengers to stay the night, while he listens for any further instructions from Yahweh, is taken by many commentators to imply that he secretly hopes God will let him go to Moab after all. But such a reading is harsh and judgemental; perhaps it is what the reader may have done in Balaam's place? Although Balaam may not be spoken of too kindly elsewhere in the Bible, here in these chapters his openness and obedience to God are complete and pure. It is, on this occasion as before, God who approaches Balaam, and it is God who instructs him to go with the visitors, even though he is not to do what Balak has asked.

Our refusal to accept God's 'no' to our prayers, hopes and dreams is part of our shared human weakness. Especially when those aims are good in themselves – a family, a qualification, a job – it seems unfair that we should be denied these things. But God sees more clearly than we can, and it is God's vision for us that holds our best and highest good.

† Loving God, when I stop my ears from hearing your call and close my eyes to the future you have planned for me, be patient with me and show me your way. Amen

For further thought

What might your life look like if you held less tightly to your own plans and sought God's way instead?

Tuesday 21 July
Prayer is not like a vending machine

Read Numbers 22:31–41

Balaam said to Balak, 'I have come to you now, but do I have power to say just anything? The word God puts in my mouth, that is what I must say.'

(verse 38)

On the way to Moab, God's displeasure is vividly demonstrated, as the angel of the Lord bars the way three times. Now, it is not Balaam alone who realises the foolishness of the task before him. Even the humble donkey has the wit to discern God's intention, turning away, or stopping entirely, whenever the path is blocked. In the same way that Balaam told Balak he could not go against God's wishes, the donkey shows that she too obeys God, even when expressly urged to do otherwise.

Meanwhile, Balak thinks he has achieved his hoped-for bargain with Balaam; that his offer of generous payment has persuaded the prophet to help him after all. Balaam, however, reminds the king once more that he can only say or do what God commands, no matter how great a sum is promised in reward. But Balak continues blithely on, sacrificing animals (presumably to his own Moabite god) and inviting his guests to join the party.

It is all too tempting for many of us to try to bargain with God. We may not fool ourselves into thinking we can offer God 'payment', but promises that we will go to church more often, spend more time reading the Bible, give to charity and other similar acts can be nothing more than an attempt to induce God to do what we want. But God does not work by human rules and God's blessings cannot be bought in cash or in kind.

† God of all mystery, when you are with me, let me rejoice; when you are hidden, help me trust.

For further thought
If we try to win God's favour by our actions, we throw back in God's face the gift of salvation by grace.

Doing it God's way

Read Numbers 23:1–12

'How can I curse whom God has not cursed? How can I denounce those whom the Lord has not denounced?'

(verse 8)

Picture the scene: the king and his companions waiting eagerly to hear Balaam's instructions on how to approach the God of the Israelites to win a curse, and not a blessing, on God's people. All eyes were on the seer now; rested and refreshed after his journey, surely the famous prophet was about to speak a powerful word on their behalf.

Again, an offering is made – the sacrifice of sheep and oxen – a sort of smoothing of the way between human beings and the divine. Balak would have expected this, or something like it, as perfectly normal, and Balaam probably thought little of it. Sacrifice or no sacrifice, God would do as God chose. And so it is.

We can only imagine Balak's horror and disbelief at what he hears when Balaam speaks his first prophecy over the Israelites. This was worse, far worse, than Balaam's earlier refusal to come at all to Balak's aid. In the ancient Near East, a word spoken was understood as highly effective, having its own power, and impossible to take back or cancel.

In our age, and certainly in many industrialised societies, our lives are full to overflowing with words. Many are superficial, temporary or simple custom: advertisements promise happiness if we buy their products, and who really expects a genuine answer to a polite, 'How do you do?' But we still make promises, sign contracts and take vows for the things that truly matter to us. We would be wise always to check that the things to which we commit ourselves are really what God wants.

† God of the Word, mark my words today, that I might speak wisely, kindly and boldly.

For further thought

What words, promises or agreements do you rely on in your daily living? Give thanks for the words that sustain you as you follow Jesus.

Thursday 23 July
The faithful fulfiller of promises

Read Numbers 23:13–30

'God is not a human being, that he should lie, or a mortal, that he should change his mind. Has he promised, and will he not do it? Has he spoken, and will he not fulfil it?'

(verse 19)

By this time, Balak is becoming anxious. Perhaps he wondered if Balaam might not be as powerful a diviner as his reputation had suggested. So he tries another approach, presenting Balaam with a limited view of Israel's camp; it might be possible to curse Israel in stages (tribe by tribe?). The sight of Israel's tents, rank on rank, almost as far as the eye could see, must have been very impressive and not a little unnerving.

We are not told what Balaam thought of this plan, or whether he was offended by the king's failure to recognise his authority and status as one who was on first-name terms with God. (Whenever Balaam refers to God as 'the Lord' in chapter 22, he is actually using the name Yahweh, revealed to Moses at the burning bush in Exodus 3:14.) Whatever he may really think, Balaam goes along with Balak's new idea. They repeat the sacrifices, and Balaam goes aside to wait for God to give him the message he is to say.

On hearing Balaam bless Israel again, Balak begins to panic again, presumably starting to feel helpless and vulnerable again, just as had been the case before he sent his first messengers to ask for help. Balaam, it seems, is of no use to Balak, as all he does is repeat God's blessings on, and promises to, God's people. How strange that although the Israelites had frequently questioned God's good intentions towards them while they were in the wilderness, this non-Israelite was utterly certain that God would keep his promises.

† Faithful God, when I struggle to trust you, thank you for keeping faith with me. Help me have faith in you. Amen

For further thought

In the ancient world, the changing of the seasons was seen as a way God kept his promises and sustained the cosmos.

Friday 24 July
The attentive pray-er

> **Read Numbers 24:1–14**
>
> *'The oracle of Balaam son of Beor, the oracle of the man whose eye is clear, the oracle of one who hears the words of God, who sees the vision of the Almighty, who falls down, but with eyes uncovered …'*
>
> (verses 3b–4)

Do you remember the cartoon character Yosemite Sam? He was forever hunting Bugs Bunny, and whenever the rabbit escaped, Sam would throw his hat on the ground and jump up and down on it in rage and frustration. By the time Balak has heard Balaam bless Israel a third time, the description of the king clapping his hands in anger and cancelling his offer to reward Balaam reminds me irresistibly of Sam. Balak has not received the curse for which he had asked and so he throws a tantrum like a disappointed, angry child.

Of course, Balak should not have been surprised by Balaam's words. He had been told, more than once, that Balaam could speak only what God gave him. We are back to that human problem of finding it difficult to hear, really hear, an answer other than the one we want.

Balaam begins his third speech with a description of the pray-er who understands that prayer is not about us telling God what to do. Instead, prayer is a matter of us being open to God – with open ears, open eyes and open hearts. Being open to God's will and work in and through us can be risky. It may require us to open our hearts to other people, whom we may not like or not think are worthy of blessing. It is then that our prayer can be most effective, because now it changes us. In this way, we are transformed, slowly but surely, and conformed to the image of Christ.

† Think of someone – an individual or a group – whom you don't like or who frightens you. Ask God to bless them. Be sure to pray *for* them, not *about* them.

For further thought

When was the last time that you felt changed by prayer, either alone or with others?

Saturday 25 July
Fulfillment is not a one-time-only thing

Read Numbers 24:15–25

'I see him, but not now; I behold him, but not near – a star shall come out of Jacob, and a sceptre shall rise out of Israel; it shall crush the borderlands of Moab, and the territory of all the Shethites.'

(verse 17)

Balaam's fourth oracle can leave us with mixed feelings. It is tempting to latch on to the vision in verse 17 and carefully ignore the threats of violence that follow. Let us not fall into the trap of cherry-picking the verses we like best, as though the text in which they are set somehow no longer matters.

The writers and editors of these chapters saw here the promise of Israel's divinely appointed king, who would conquer the nations whose lands bordered Israel. The star from Judah was, for the first readers of this book, King David, Israel's best king, the one most devoted to, and beloved by, Yahweh. Even admitting that David was every bit as human, weak and sinful as the rest of us, at his best he remains the ideal of ancient Near Eastern kingship (see Psalm 72 for more detail). His reign was a time of prosperity for the peoples of Israel and Judah, if less so for their neighbours.

Early in the life of the church, Christians read this passage as a prophecy of the birth of Christ; Jesus came from the tribe of Judah, being a descendant of David. If we hold Jesus to be the ideal king, we see a very different style of rulership: one of justice and peace achieved through forgiveness, instead of military might. When Christians today challenge governments to work for true peace and the good of all, we are as threatening to them as Balaam's words and David's actions were to the powerful of their own times and places.

† God of truth and justice, help me to follow Jesus fearlessly, and to pray always for your people for whom to speak in Christ's name is to risk all for his sake. Amen

For further thought

What do you think about this prophecy? What other passages in scripture would you want to bring into dialogue with it?

Running the race: the Bible at the Olympics – 1 Renewed in spirit

Notes by **Delroy Hall**

Delroy is a bishop in the Church of God of Prophecy, UK, and has been a pastor for nearly thirty years. A new area of ministry for Delroy is being appointed club chaplain for Sheffield United Football Club. Delroy is grateful for the gift of life and is still committed to the life of the mind and keeping fit. He has more than twnty-five years' experience as a trained counsellor. Delroy has used the NIVUK for these notes.

Sunday 26 July
Answering as one

Read Exodus 19:1–9

The people all responded together, 'We will do everything the Lord has said.'

(verse 8a)

The people answer as one. What a great starting position. When it occurs, what a blessing.

I can only imagine the excitement of the Israelites, having entered into a new land after escaping their captors. Deliverance brings forth euphoria and the people promise to do everything the Lord has said. Their new-found freedom is palpable; who would not feel free after escaping and being carried to a new land by God himself? There is no other response than to worship the Lord as an act of obedience.

It is said, especially to women, that 'the way to a man's heart is through his stomach,' meaning that cooking is an excellent way to win a man's affections. Obedience is the way to God's heart and to seek his divine favour. There is possibly a word of caution, though. With all good intention, it is not always good to make serious decisions when we are excited. As a counsellor I have often said to clients, 'Do not make important decisions when you are in the valley or on top of the mountain.'

The Summer Olympics, which just began in Tokyo, also exemplify such ideals of togetherness and obedience. What can we learn from reading the Bible alongside the games this week?

† Father and friend, let me be careful in making commitments for a closer walk with you when I am feeling all excited after all you have done for me.

Monday 27 July
Not too hard for you

Read Deuteronomy 30:11–20

No, the word is very near you; it is in your mouth and in your heart so that you may obey it.

(verse 14)

Reading this scripture, one gets the idea that God was into quantum physics even before human beings thought of it. Simply put, everything is connected. Everything.

God makes it clear our actions determine everything, but hold on a minute, there is something else. It is not our actions only, but what we have lodged in our hearts matters too. There is no escape. The importance of the intents of our hearts was not only conveyed by Jesus in the Sermon on the Mount, but even during the time of sacrificing animals. God has always been concerned about the intents and purposes of the human heart.

God cannot emphasise enough the consequences of blessings and life if we are obedient; and if we are disobedient, the consequences of pain and death are evident. Having life does not mean that we will physically live longer. No, it conveys the idea of enjoying the blessings and joys of life representing God's prosperity. How that happens, who knows, but it does. Similarly, death does not mean that we will literally die, but that life in all its expressions will be difficult.

In our personal lives, the same principles apply. I love this saying: 'Methods are many, principles are few, methods always change, principles never do.' The words of love, safety and protection uttered by God centuries ago to his people are still relevant today for us in the modern twenty-first-century age of Twitter, Instagram and all other human inventions. It is not too hard for us either.

† Lord, you expected your people centuries ago to be obedient to you. Today, you are no less demanding. Help us, as your people, to be obedient and show the world the blessings of your favour.

For further thought

What different life lessons do you see in the summer games? How might these carry over into ordinary life?

Fresh From the Word 2021

It may seem early, but *Fresh From the Word 2021* is now available to order.

Order now:

- direct from IBRA
- from your local IBRA rep
- in all good Christian bookshops
- from Amazon and other online retailers

To order direct from IBRA

- website: shop.christianeducation.org.uk
- email: ibra.sales@christianeducation.org.uk
- call: 0121 458 3313
- post: using the order form at the back of this book

£9.99 plus postage and packaging.

Fresh From the Word is available for Kindle, and in ePub format from online retailers such as Amazon.

Become an IBRA rep

Do you order multiple copies of *Fresh From the Word* for yourself and your friends or people in your congregation or Bible study group?

When you order three or more copies direct from IBRA you will receive a 10% discount on your order of *Fresh From the Word*. You will also receive a free promotional pack each year to help you share IBRA more easily with family, friends and others at your church.

Would you consider leaving a legacy to IBRA?

What's valuable about a gift in your will to IBRA's International Fund is that every penny goes directly towards enabling hundreds of thousands of people around the world to access the living Word of God.

IBRA has a rich history going back over 138 years. It was the vision of Charles Waters to enable people in Britain and overseas to benefit from the Word of God through the experiences and insights of biblical scholars and teachers across the world. The vision was to build up people's lives in their homes and situations wherever they were. His legacy lives on today in you, as a reader, and the IBRA team.

Our work at IBRA is financed by the sales of the books, but from its very start in 1882, 100% of donations to the IBRA international fund go to benefit our local and international readers. To continue this important work, would you consider leaving a legacy in your will?

Find out more

Leaving a gift in your will to a Christian charity is a way of ensuring that this work continues for years to come: to help future generations and reach out to them with hope and the life-changing Word of God – people we may never meet but who are all our brothers and sisters in Christ.

Through such a gift you will help continue the strong and lasting legacy of IBRA for generations to come!

To find out more please contact our Finance Manager on 0121 458 3313, email ibra@christianeducation.org.uk or write to International Bible Reading Association, 5–6 Imperial Court, 12 Sovereign Road, Birmingham, B30 3FH.

• To read more about the history of IBRA go to p. 28.

• To find out more about the work of the IBRA International Fund go to p. 370.

Tuesday 28 July
A new Spirit

Read Ezekiel 36:22–32

And I will put my Spirit in you and move you to follow my decrees and be careful to keep my laws.

(verse 27)

I love the Bible, especially the Old Testament. The powerful use of words and vivid imagery applied by the authors catapults us into another world and helps us to understand God in a deep and dynamic way. Today's scripture is such an example.

Reflecting on this scene lets us know the condition of God's people they had got themselves into, but God in his mercy confronted them about their wrongdoings and said what he would do to restore them. He would cleanse them, give them a new heart, relocate them to where they were meant to be and he would grant them a different desire that focused on him. God's work of restoration was complete.

What a wonderful scripture to learn from if you have tried to do your own thing and now have found yourself in a place similar to that of the children of Israel. You have found another god, worshipped something other than the true and living God. You are now walking a different path with a different destination and your life is pretty impoverished at the moment even though you may appear to have much.

God, because of his love for you, will clean you up. He will put you on another path with a new and bright destination. He will put a new spirit in your heart and will ensure your life will be filled with his blessings by replacing the drudgery you have grown accustomed to. The starting point for this new life begins with a personal acknowledgement of your wrongdoing and a willingness to let God lead your life.

† Saviour, I have sinned. Forgive me for how I have lived without you. Today, clean me, fill me, give me a new heart and spirit so that I willingly follow you wherever you lead me.

For further thought
How might the Olympics exemplify a spirit that inspires others?

Wednesday 29 July
Running the way of the Commandments

Read Psalm 119:25–32

Cause me to understand the way of your precepts, that I may meditate on your wonderful deeds.

(verse 27)

Looking at this short section of scripture I am tempted to spend time analysing each word, but alas, space and time do not permit.

It is a beautiful section of Psalms, but the whole psalm is a classic. Each verse gives honour and attention to God's word. Here, the writer recognises his present state in life and he calls on God to fix him. It does not appear that he is admitting to any sin, but there is an impassioned plea to the God of heaven as he surrenders his soul in obedience. Listen to some of the words of the psalmist as he surrenders in love to his eternal Father: 'Keep me from deceitful ways,' 'I have chosen the way of faithfulness,' 'I hold fast to your statutes,' 'I run in the path of your commands' (verses 29–32). These are such wonderful words of self-abandonment.

There is an important lesson we can learn from the psalmist. In life, many of us only consider changing our lives when we hit a crisis, whether by illness, a death in the family, redundancy or a breakdown of family relationships. The writer makes it clear. You do not have to wait to be pushed into a closer walk with God due to crushing life events. No, and a million times no. We can make the decision to follow and surrender to God when things are going well. Out of simple gratitude we can give our all to him, not because of what he has done for us, but because we recognise who he is.

† Dear Lord, let me learn from the psalmist; let me love you more not because of a crisis, but simply because of who you are.

For further thought

What can you learn from the discipline of the athletes you see on the news today?

Thursday 30 July
Jesus tempted

Read Mark 1:9–15

And a voice came from heaven: 'You are my Son, whom I love; with you I am well pleased.'

(verse 11)

I have always been fascinated by this verse of scripture. There is a word of commendation from God about his Son. One of the searching questions that could be asked is, what did Jesus do to warrant such an expression? It is strange when one considers living in the West. In particular, we are judged on the type of work we do and people give us an unspoken value judgement. Dependent on the job we do, it can elicit further conversation or end one there and then. Here though, we see something completely different. Jesus was given such a title not because he had done anything, but simply because God loved him. The question for me is, have I ever made a value judgement about someone based on their job, ethnicity, class, gender, disability or anything that marks them out as different from me? I wonder if I have. Yes, I am sure I have.

I recall some time ago a friend of mine who was about to give an important lecture at a prestigious teaching institution. She, being a senior official, introduced her partner to one of her colleagues. What happened next shocked her. For the whole evening her colleague turned his back on her partner. It was deliberate. Her partner was a black man and what her colleague failed to understand was that her partner, too, was an academic.

Jesus was tempted, and daily we are tempted to treat others who do not look like us as somehow less than ourselves. In this daily race of life we face daily tests on how we treat people. How did you do today?

† Majestic Lord, you loved Jesus when he had accomplished nothing. Give us grace, and help us to love others not based on their achievements, but because of who they are. What a challenge you have left us.

For further thought

Where has racism been manifest at the Olympics over the years? Where have the games risen above racism?

Friday 31 July
Paul's race

Read 2 Timothy 4:1–8

Now there is in store for me the crown of righteousness, which the Lord, the righteous Judge, will award to me on that day – and not only to me, but also to all who have longed for his appearing.

(verse 8)

Races have huge meaning for me. When I was twenty years old I was a 400-metre hurdler and was number two in Great Britain. Forty years on, I am unable to run the race with such vigour, strength and ability. I have changed. One thing I noticed was that in all the races I competed in there was only one person who got the gold medal. It was the winner, who never shared it with anyone else. When they stood on the podium they stood alone, proud and feeling elated. The standing area on the podium was not for the crowd, but for one person only.

In the race of the Lord, it is markedly different. Paul makes it clear. He speaks about the race of faith, but in this endeavour there is something that Paul stresses. He admonishes Timothy to do all he can to make full proof of his ministry. Like in the work of an athlete, what we often miss is the amount of training that needs to take place before the day of the race.

Here, Paul tells of two non-negotiable things that must take place before being granted the crown of righteousness. First, there is work we must do consistently and with commitment to our highest ability because we are serving the Master of the universe. Second, provided we have done our part we are all winners and we will all stand on the podium, in the number one slot, to receive our crown of righteousness. What a day that will be.

† Father, as believers, we are in the race of faith. Let us be true to our calling that we may receive a crown of righteousness.

For further thought

What race lies before you today, this year or in the years ahead?

Saturday 1 August
Run the race set before us

Read Hebrews 12:1–13

Therefore, strengthen your feeble arms and weak knees.

(verse 12)

Today might be a day you feel low, perplexed and discouraged. While we are in this life we will have those days, and sometimes we will have them occurring too often. I have my bad patches too.

My wife says that when she was praying for a husband she asked the Lord for someone who would bounce back quickly from life's difficulties. That prayer seems to have been answered.

As a pastor, I have had my fair share of difficulties. If I am going to be real and honest I have had low periods, and I daresay had I visited my doctor at the time I would have been clinically diagnosed with depression. Fortunately, as a trained psychotherapist, I knew the signs and symptoms and I knew what to do.

Not only did I have low periods, I had times of great fear when I was attempting to lead the church on a new journey and I was unsure of the way ahead. When my hands were low and my knees were knocking together I had to hold them up, and I did.

Sometimes we think all we need to do is pray and the Lord will always come to our rescue. Really? Not always. Look at the scripture closely. We are to 'lift up' hands which hang low. There are times when it is nothing more than sheer grit and determination that gets us through. At other times, we need the help of others. Whether with our own strength, the help of others or God, we must run the race that is set before us.

† Holy Father, knowing you are looking after us and you are continually strengthening us, I ask in those difficult times we will draw on the deposit of your grace to help us through trying times.

For further thought

Sometimes, running the race merely means putting one foot in front of the other.

Running the race: the Bible at the Olympics – 2 The nations as one

Notes by **Liz Clutterbuck**

Liz is a priest in the Church of England and leads a church in North London. She combines parish ministry with research, exploring how church impact and growth can be better measured. She is part of Matryoshka Haus, a missional community that intentionally works to build community in London. Liz is passionate about social media, film, baking and travel, and loves it when she can combine as many of her passions as possible! Liz has used the NRSVA for these notes.

Sunday 2 August
Be still and know

Read Psalm 46

God is in the midst of the city; it shall not be moved; God will help it when the morning dawns. The nations are in an uproar, the kingdoms totter; he utters his voice, the earth melts.

(verses 5–6)

Time and again humanity has lived through periods of almost unbearable tumult. War, violence and despotic regimes litter our history and shape our nations. By their very nature, these events are full of noise. As a young child, I remember hearing the beginnings of the first Gulf War on BBC radio, the quiet night broken by the shrieks of scud missiles. I was haunted by the sound of the air raid sirens used during the Blitz of the Second World War, heard on documentaries and TV dramas. The noise of uproar and of kingdoms tottering. Although the Olympics typically portray international harmony, they, too, have been the scene of violence, protest and discord.

Yet, in the midst of tumult, God is present. In the moment of silence, in the snatched breath, God speaks.

Many of us will never have lived in a war zone or through prolonged periods of violence, but we may well have experienced the tumult of how life is lived in the twenty-first century amongst divided nations. We often have little control over the political and social events that shape our lives. It can be easy to get caught up in the world around us and forget to stop and be still: to be still and know that God is with us.

† Lord, you are our refuge and our strength. Help us to find your stillness in the midst of tumult and to know that you are with us.

Monday 3 August
Wisdom to the nations

Read Deuteronomy 4:1–8

For what other great nation has a god so near to it as the Lord our God is whenever we call to him? And what other great nation has statutes and ordinances as just as this entire law that I am setting before you today?

(verses 7–8)

At the end of every Olympic Games, one nation tops the medals table. In recent summer games, the top three has included the USA, China, Russia or Great Britain.

Are they the greatest Olympic nations? Perhaps, but how is 'great' measured?

They are large nations, who fund sport and highly regard the kudos of success at an event like the Olympics. The USA is always going to do better at the Olympics than a tiny nation like the Pacific Island of Nauru; they have vastly different population sizes (Nauru has the smallest population of all Olympic nations) and amounts of money to spend on sport.

The people of Israel were a great nation because of the blessings bestowed upon them as God's chosen people. No other nation at that time was as close to the Lord God as they were. No other nation was led to a land promised to them by God. And when God was made man in Christ, the gift of greatness was extended to all.

Our triune God is a great God, but his gifts are no longer restricted to one chosen people; they are for all who turn to him and accept him. There is no table reserved for the 'greatest' amongst Christ's followers, thank goodness! There is simply an opportunity given to all who accept God's call to be the best they can be with all that God has given them.

† Father God, we thank you that you have chosen us as your beloved children. Help us to avoid competing with one another and to know that we are enough in your eyes.

For further thought

Are you competitive? Make some space to consider where competition may be unhelpful in your life and relationships with others.

Tuesday 4 August
Uniting in a joyful noise

Read Psalm 100

Make a joyful noise to the Lord, all the earth. Worship the Lord with gladness; come into his presence with singing.

(verses 1–2)

One of my favourite parts of the Olympics is the opening ceremony, particularly the parade of nations right before the Olympic flame is lit. Growing up, the reason I loved watching it was that it gave me a chance to cheer for the nation in which I was born: the tiny Pacific island kingdom of Tonga. As Tonga falls quite a way down the alphabet, I would have to watch a lot of countries march into the stadium before they arrived.

These days I still sit and wait to cheer for Tonga, but I also love observing the joy with which these teams arrive. Most of the athletes will not win a medal, but they are there to celebrate this great act of international unity. Many carry cameras and are as keen to capture the excitement around them as we at home are to watch it unfold on our screens.

This joy and unity is such a contrast with what we see so often in our world: turning away refugees at border crossings; years of violence over contested land; hate speech directed against those who are 'different'; and separation instead of unity.

At the 2016 games in Rio, this unity was embodied in the 'Refugee Olympic Team', in which refugee athletes from nations including Syria and South Sudan were invited to compete together, as a response to the global refugee crisis. The Olympics might appear on the surface as nation against nation, but at its heart is a message of unity and joy in the participation in this great event.

† Lord, thank you for your many blessings upon my life. Help me show more joy in the gifts that you have given me, so that they might enthuse and encourage those around me.

For further thought

Investigate what provision there is locally for you to support refugees, whether it's hands-on help or initiatives to raise funding.

Wednesday 5 August
Neither shall they learn war any more

Read Isaiah 2:1–4

They shall beat their swords into ploughshares, and their spears into pruning-hooks; nation shall not lift up sword against nation, neither shall they learn war any more.

(verse 4b–e)

The Olympics of 1948 took place in a still war-damaged London. There had not been a games since 1936 because while the world was at war, a show of athletic international unity was impossible. Many might have questioned whether, after years of international conflict, the Olympics could continue. Was sport a frivolous distraction from the need to rebuild nations and rehouse refugees? Would competition between countries reinforce the conflict that the world was trying to put behind them?

The divisions of war continued in one regard – the Axis powers were not invited to send athletes. But in other ways, the games were a sign of progress towards unity, as fifty-nine nations competed for sporting glory alongside each other. The London Olympics also featured their own version of beating swords into ploughshares, with RAF camps turned into accommodation for athletes.

Although there have been times in the Olympics' history (particularly during the Cold War) when competition has echoed international conflicts, there have been many instances of sport embodying something of peace between nations. A notable example of this took place at the recent Pyeongchang Winter Olympics in South Korea, where not only did athletes from North and South Korea parade together, they fielded a joint women's hockey team.

Humanity has not yet stopped learning about war, but every so often there is a glimpse of hope that reconciliation is possible and that weapons of destruction will be transformed into tools for good. May these signs encourage us to walk in God's ways of peace and love.

† Father God, may our nations learn your ways of peace, not war. We ask that through the power of your Spirit, the machinery of war would be turned into ploughshares and used for the good of humanity.

For further thought

Do you think that sport can help overcome the effects of war?

Thursday 6 August
Observing their deeds

Read Psalm 33

The Lord looks down from heaven; he sees all humankind. From where he sits enthroned he watches all the inhabitants of the earth – he who fashions the hearts of them all, and observes all their deeds.

(verses 13–15)

Whenever there's a big event, a phrase commentators will often use is 'the eyes of the world are watching …' It might be a space shuttle launch, a royal wedding or a world record in the 100 metres, but the sentiment is the same: this occasion is so momentous that it's grabbed the attention of people across our planet. We are united in our watching, our waiting, for this special moment.

While it's quite an exaggeration to suggest that the whole world tunes in to watch the Olympics, it is certainly true that it is an event that regularly draws in hundreds of millions of viewers from all over the globe.

Psalm 33 encourages us to turn this idea around. Instead of the eyes of the world watching, it is our Creator God watching all of humanity. The psalmist reminds us that God has fashioned our hearts and observes all our deeds. We cannot possibly escape God's watch or God's love.

World events encourage us to believe that humanity is in control, that we can dictate the events that receive global attention. However this psalm prompts us to remember that it is not in our power, it is in God's. Rather than looking to the world to be our saviour, our eyes need to turn their gaze upon the God of love.

† 'Let your steadfast love, O Lord, be upon us, even as we hope in you' (verse 22). Lord, protect us from the distractions of this world and encourage our eyes to remain fixed upon you.

For further thought

Where or what is distracting you from God's gaze? Before spending some time in silent meditation, write down your distractions to free yourself from them.

Friday 7 August
Deities of gold, silver and stone

Read Acts 17:16–31

'For "In him we live and move and have our being"; as even some of your own poets have said, "For we too are his offspring." Since we are God's offspring, we ought not to think that the deity is like gold, or silver, or stone ...'

(verses 28–29)

Paul's missionary journey has taken him to Athens, the home of the Olympics and where the first modern Olympic Games were held in 1896. Several centuries before Paul's arrival it was the destination of Pheidippides, who ran 25 miles from Marathon to Athens to announce the defeat of the Persians.

In between Pheidippides' marathon and the arrival of Paul, the Parthenon was built upon the Acropolis. Dedicated to the city's patron, Athena, it is almost certainly one of the 'shrines made by human hands' (verse 24) that Paul mentions in this passage. Nearly 2,000 years later, the first marathon of the modern Olympiad ran past this temple; as did the 2004 marathon. Many things in Athens have changed since Paul's time, but this temple remains.

Paul was incensed by these temples and the Greeks' worship of the deities celebrated within. How had they still not realised that they were God's children and did not need these human constructions?

Idol worship continues today. Love, money and power are still put on a pedestal. As is winning, especially a medal of gold, silver or bronze. The Olympics began in a place where emulating gods was the ambition, but today's games tries hard to celebrate being united in a love of sport and human endeavour.

† Creator God, we thank you that we are your offspring. Help us to celebrate all the gifts you have given us and to focus upon you instead of on human idols.

For further thought

What is at risk of becoming an idol in your life? Take some time to think and pray, before working out a plan to put God first instead.

Saturday 8 August
For the healing of the nations

Read Revelation 22:1–7

On either side of the river is the tree of life with its twelve kinds of fruit, producing its fruit each month; and the leaves of the tree are for the healing of the nations. Nothing accursed will be found there any more.

(verses 2b–3a)

Has there ever been a point in history when the healing of the nations has felt possible? Revelation presents a vision of God's kingdom that feels a very long way off.

Earlier this week, I mentioned the joy of the parade of nations in the Olympic opening ceremony. This moment also highlights signs of healing within or between nations. Throughout the years, new nations have been represented at the games: early on, as a result of decolonisation and a focus upon national self-determination. Towards the end of the last century, new nations emerged as the USSR broke up and conflict shaped the countries that once made up Yugoslavia: for example, the 1996 games welcomed eleven formerly Soviet states.

For these nations, carrying their flag into an international arena, watched by people all over the world, is a tremendous moment of pride. They are there, alongside other nations, having fought for independence, representation and autonomy. It can also be a moment of hope for the rest of the world. In 1992, South Africa was permitted to compete at the Olympics for the first time since 1960, having voted to abolish apartheid. Many around the world had hoped for an end to this regime for decades, and it had seemed out of reach. The presence of the team in 1992 and its arrival under its new flag in 1996 demonstrated the healing that was taking place in that nation.

The healing of the nations is only fully possible in God's kingdom, but we must look out for and encourage the first shoots of healing when they appear around us.

† Lord, we pray for the healing of the nations. For your kingdom to show itself on earth in all its glory, redeeming human failure. May we hold onto your hope when our world feels broken.

For further thought

Read or watch today's news and look for a situation in which nations need prayers for healing.

The Bible at the beach – 1 Resting

Notes by **Catherine Williams**

 Catherine is an Anglican priest who until recently worked for the Ministry Division of the Archbishops' Council in the Church of England. She continues to work in vocational discernment and combines this with spiritual direction, retreat leading and writing. Catherine lives in Tewkesbury, England. She is married to Paul, also a priest, and they have two adult children. In her spare time Catherine enjoys singing, theatre, cinema and poetry. She is also passionate about butterfly conservation. Catherine has used the NRSVA for these notes.

Sunday 9 August
Rest awhile

Read Mark 6:30–32

'Come away to a deserted place all by yourselves and rest a while.'

(verse 31b)

This week we will explore the importance of rest in the Christian life, together with the confidence and trust we have through knowing that God is constant in his care for creation: providing for and protecting his creatures, ourselves included. In today's passage, the disciples have returned from exciting and challenging mission work and are eager to tell Jesus all about it. Jesus encourages them to go to a quiet place in order to rest and recover. They've been so busy they haven't been eating properly. Jesus recognises and cares for their physical and psychological needs. He knows that in the excitement and demands of mission and ministry regular rest, meals and appropriate self-care can get forgotten. These ordinary staples of human existence are essential if followers of Jesus are to flourish and stay the distance. Unfortunately, this time Jesus and the disciples don't manage the rest they require: a great crowd is awaiting them on the far side of the lake, prompting some questions for us about the importance of boundaries! However, the principle of resting and recharging once a task is completed remains a good one – modelled by God – as we'll explore further this week.

† Lord, may I be open this week to hear and respond to your call to rest a while.

Contented

> **Read Psalm 131**
>
> *But I have calmed and quieted my soul, like a weaned child with its mother.*
>
> (verse 2a)

My children are adults, but I remember well those years when they were toddlers. Some days they were like whirlwinds, dashing about, eager to try new things, open to fresh ideas and asking question after question. 'Why?' and 'How?' were favourite words. When they were exhausted they would snuggle up on my lap, resting contentedly, completely relaxed, knowing themselves to be totally secure. This is the image the psalmist gives us in today's passage. Weaned children are learning to be independent and they no longer have to rely on others for their every need. They are able to go off exploring, knowing that their significant others will be there for them when they return, and will help and hold them if things seem scary or too big to handle.

When our hope is fixed firmly on God we can rest secure, knowing that nothing that happens to us can separate us from the love of God shown in Jesus Christ. We can relax and let God be God: we are safe. This is a psalm of confidence and trust in which the psalmist knows his place in God's economy and is calm and content in God's presence. He shows appropriate humility and hasn't over-stretched himself. Do you trust that God is there for you, come what may? Are you quiet and contented deep down in your soul? Cultivating interior contentment and a quiet heart enables us to let go of status, prestige and power, and trust that God knows all that we need and can be trusted to provide it.

† Thank you, God, that you give me freedom to question and explore my faith. Help me to trust, whatever happens, that I will always be secure in your love.

For further thought

This a very short psalm; try to learn it by heart, to encourage inner peace and contentment.

Tuesday 11 August
Don't worry!

Read Luke 12:24–31

'Do not keep worrying.'

(verse 29b)

Relax! Jesus urges us to let go of anxiety. Pointing to the natural world – birds and wildflowers – he indicates God's care for creation, hardwired into our world. Jesus calls out our unhealthy worrying. His teaching goes to the very heart of what it means to be human: to be made in the image of God. God's provision for his beloved people knows no bounds; he loves us so much that he sacrificed himself for us in Jesus; he gave everything for us. Therefore we really don't need to worry about what we are wearing or eating, or about what will happen from day to day. God is in control and if we allow him into the driving seat of our lives we will be astounded by the generosity of his provision.

In parts of our world, many have far more than they need or could ever use, much of it stashed away in cupboards, drawers and boxes, rather like the bigger and bigger barns mentioned earlier in Luke 12. In other regions people are starving, homeless, barely scraping out an existence; the imbalance is scandalous. Jesus urges us to seek God's kingdom first before anything else. When we do this then we see with God's eyes, our priorities shift and we realise that our preoccupation with acquiring and hoarding things is misplaced. When we recognise that everything comes from God then we are compelled to ensure a fairer distribution of the world's resources. We don't need to be frightened, God is longing to give us the kingdom; what more do we need?!

† Help me to stop worrying about my daily needs. Thank you for your love, care and provision for us all. Thank you too for the lessons we can learn from your beautiful creation.

For further thought

Give away or share something today with someone who needs it more than you do.

Wednesday 12 August
Distracted

Read Luke 10:38–42

Mary ... sat at the Lord's feet and listened to what he was saying.

(verse 39)

What distracts you from spending time with Jesus? What things take your attention away from following the Lord and growing in your discipleship? In today's passage we meet two women, Martha and Mary, who react very differently when Jesus comes to call. Mary stops her activity to sit and listen to Jesus. Martha is busy with many tasks, working harder and harder. Jesus is concerned for Martha, not because she is working hard at serving but because she has become too anxious and distracted to spend time with him. Perhaps envious of her sister, Martha finds fault with Mary publicly and asks Jesus to intervene on her behalf, rather than giving the honoured guest, whom she has welcomed into her home, her gracious attention.

Mary, says Jesus, 'has chosen the better part' (verse 42). Jesus invites all of us who are busy and distracted to sit and rest in his presence – and in so doing to know ourselves loved and valued for who we are, rather than what we do. Sitting at the feet of Jesus and learning from him strengthens us and builds and renews our faith; it is never wasted time. Mary, as she sits at the feet of her rabbi Jesus, is doing more than just listening. Her presence in that place, as a woman, breaks cultural norms and crosses societal boundaries: Jesus encourages her to be there, applauding her choice. Our time spent sitting at the feet of Jesus is a bold and courageous statement to a world obsessed with action, productivity and acquisition. Let's do more of it!

† Lord, forgive me when I am anxious and distracted by life's demands. Help me to see that time spent with you is the best choice.

For further thought

What are your greatest distractions? Take time today to sit still and listen to the Lord, giving him your full attention.

Divine rest

> ### Read Genesis 2:1–3
> *God rested on the seventh day from all the work that he had done.*
>
> (verse 2b)

In the opening chapters of Genesis we hear the story of God creating the cosmos, bringing order out of chaos, dividing up time and breathing life into his extraordinary creation. On the seventh day God rests, not because he is tired and needs a break, but because the work of creation is complete: he has finished creating. On the seventh day God delights in his creation and blesses and makes holy the day on which rest begins. The ability to enter into God's gift of rest is for everyone and everything; it has universal significance and worth. By creating a 'sabbath' – or set-aside time for rest – God is ensuring that for regular periods of time activity ceases, and creation can delight and find satisfaction in its Creator, knowing itself blessed as it enters into holy time.

In many places the idea of a regular and set time of rest has been eroded. Many people work almost continuously and feel guilty if they are seen to be doing 'nothing'. When one task is finished, it's not unusual to move straight onto the next, believing that constant productivity is the way to fulfilment and success. However, modern research has shown that the fewer hours people work and the more time off they have, the more productive and creative they become. Rest is the secret to human flourishing and we ignore it at our peril. Receive with joy and gratitude the gift of regular rest that God has given you and know yourself blessed.

† Lord God, thank you for your holy gift of rest. Help me to ensure that this gift is received and honoured by everyone I work alongside.

For further thought

Spend some time delighting in God's amazing creation. What can you learn about the rhythm of rest from the created order?

The Bible at the beach – 1 Resting

August

Friday 14 August
Provision and protection

Read Psalm 23

He makes me lie down in green pastures; he leads me beside still waters; he restores my soul.

(verses 2–3a)

Psalm 23: a favourite for many people; a special passage that is regularly chosen for life's memorable moments, especially weddings and funerals. It is unique amongst the psalms for being solely a testimony of the psalmist's intimate relationship with God. It speaks simply and beautifully of God's love, care and provision for each of us through the ups and downs of life and of our own desire to be with God throughout our lives, day by day. As such it has been a comfort and act of commitment for millions of people down the centuries.

Gloucestershire, where I live, is a very green and well-watered county. We have more than our fair share of meadows and rivers, which we sometimes take for granted. It's easy to forget that the psalmist David would have shepherded his flock in very dry and dusty terrain. Finding small patches of grass, and pools for the flock to graze and refresh themselves, would have been challenging for the shepherd. Knowing the right paths to avoid danger would have been life-saving for the sheep. The psalm's analogy reminds us that we should take advantage of the *green pastures* and *still waters* that come our way. In these oases God provides opportunities for rest, refreshment and restoration. Our bodies and souls are nourished and kept safe by God's provision of rest and security. More than that, God promises abundant life and a place at his table for eternity, where we will be *anointed* – treated as royalty.

† Lord, thank you for your unending provision and protection. Help me to recognise and appreciate the green pastures and still waters that you provide for rest and renewal.

For further thought

If you are very familiar with this psalm, read it in a different translation. What strikes you?

Saturday 15 August
Bow down and worship

Read Psalm 95:1–6

For the Lord is a great God, and a great King above all gods.

(verse 3)

As we end this week we take a moment to celebrate the glory and goodness of God before turning our attention to next week's theme: *At the beach.* Psalm 95 is a mighty hymn of praise in which the psalmist encourages us to worship God with our whole being. We are to use our voices to sing and shout praises, and the rest of our bodies to kneel before God, bowing down to worship him. We are reminded that God is a great king, vastly superior to all other gods. God is the Creator who encompasses his whole creation: the heights and depths, the dry lands and the seas.

Throughout this week we have explored the One who has created us, provides for us and protects us – who urges us to forget our worries and trust in his love and care for all his creation. We have been encouraged to follow God's example and to rest when our work is complete – allowing for regular time to stop, rest, delight in life and enter into God's blessing – knowing that there is nothing that can separate us from God's love shown in Jesus Christ, at whose feet we are encouraged to sit – learning about life from the master.

Psalm 95 reminds us that the sea belongs to God because he made it. Next week we will be reading and exploring a number of biblical stories set on or beside the sea. Water is a potent symbol of chaos and order, washing and cleansing, death and rebirth. In preparation give thanks for your baptism as you worship God this weekend.

† Lord, thank you for your word to me this week. Help me to both worship and rest in you with my whole being.

For further thought
Resolve to set aside a regular time each day, week, month and year to rest and delight in God.

The Bible at the beach – 1 Resting

August

The Bible at the beach – 2 At the beach

Notes by **John Birch**

Based in South Wales, John is a Methodist preacher who writes prayers, worship resources and Bible studies for faithandworship. com. He is constantly amazed at where these resources are being used and how God has blessed lives through them. Some of the prayers have been adapted for use within choral and contemporary worship settings. John has several published books, including *The Act of Prayer*, and in his spare time plays guitar, sings, and enjoys gardening and exploring the beautiful Welsh coastline. John has used the NIVUK for these notes.

Sunday 16 August
Where it began

Read Luke 5:1–11

When Simon Peter saw this, he fell at Jesus' knees and said, 'Go away from me, Lord; I am a sinful man!' For he and all his companions were astonished at the catch of fish they had taken, and so were James and John, the sons of Zebedee, Simon's partners. Then Jesus said to Simon, 'Don't be afraid; from now on you will fish for people.'

(verses 8–10)

Fishing is a bit of a mystery to me. I love walking along the beach as the tide is coming in, marvelling at seabirds hovering over the water before diving down and emerging a few seconds later, fish in beak. That's real skill!

What I can't do is look out over the vast area of sea in front of me and work out the best time or place to set up a fishing rod and line, or sail a boat, to stand the best chance of catching anything. That takes knowledge, skill and experience.

Simon Peter was an experienced fisherman; it was the family business. He was also intrigued by Jesus and the crowds that gathered around him, so was happy to lend his boat as a floating pulpit. What he wasn't expecting was to be paid in fish!

What Jesus saw within Simon Peter was the potential to be an evangelist, missionary and leader who would be greatly used by God. Like the fish hidden in the water, that couldn't be seen just by looking at the man. What Simon Peter glimpsed within Jesus convinced him that here was someone he wanted to follow for the rest of his life.

† Take that which I have, gifts, skills and talents, and use them in your service, to your glory. Amen

Monday 17 August
By the sea, calling Levi

Read Mark 2:13–14

Once again Jesus went out beside the lake. A large crowd came to him, and he began to teach them. As he walked along, he saw Levi son of Alphaeus sitting at the tax collector's booth. 'Follow me,' Jesus told him, and Levi got up and followed him.

(verses 13–14)

Jesus' staff recruitment programme can seem a little haphazard. The beach was busy and here's the crowd again, eager to catch his every word. Jesus obliged, but he was also looking through the crowd with an eye to the future. There may well have been potentially wealthy donors, local community leaders, wise and ethically sound people among the crowd, but Jesus only sees a hated tax collector, Levi, and knows instantly this is the one he wants for the job.

Apply for employment these days and you'll be faced by profiling and assessment tests, a reflection of the difficulty of seeing beneath the skin to the heart of a person. The same is true outside of work. Is the person on the phone who's telling me the virus on my computer needs removing telling the truth or not? Does the cheerful market trader selling genuine designer goods at knock-down prices have a face I can trust or not?

It also works the other way around. We listen to the words of Jesus as that crowd did and hear the challenge within but, knowing what we do, feel that God could never be interested in us. Tax collectors were known to line their own pockets from the taxes they received, but Jesus saw through the greedy eyes to a future Levi who would be hungry for truth, not profit. Jesus challenges us in our own relationships to see the potential within, and want the best for, all people.

† Within the bustle of this day help me to look at others as you might do, not to criticise but to see the best within them. Amen

For further thought
Always be willing to encourage those on the edges of your fellowship, that they might blossom and become the people God wants them to be.

Tuesday 18 August
A crowded beach

Read Mark 3:7–11

Because of the crowd he told his disciples to have a small boat ready for him, to keep the people from crowding him. For he had healed many, so that those with diseases were pushing forward to touch him.

(verses 9–10)

I get stressed in big towns and crowded streets, but if it's a favourite band or an inspiring speaker, you can put me in the middle of thousands and I'm happy. Every morning at a recent conference I heard inspiring words from the main speaker, followed by an extended time of prayer for healing. At the end of the week he must have been truly exhausted but still had to fly straight back to the US and his own church to continue the work there.

I'd have been with the crowd on the shore of Lake Galilee, pressing forward to hear what this charismatic teacher called Jesus had to say, keen to see miracles I'd heard about. But Jesus needed a break. It had been such a hectic time teaching, healing, combatting opposition and training up his disciples. With so little time to himself Jesus was tired, needing space, time for spiritual refreshment. But the crowds were thirsty for more, hence the boat.

Taking time out is important not just for those on the front line of mission. Within our daily lives it is so easy to become tired and lose focus on our calling, which is to be lights in this world. And if the lights go dim, who will see them?

Jesus retreated to the mountains to find rest and refreshment. I walk on the empty beaches nearby. Where do you go?

† May my enthusiasm for following and wanting to know more about Jesus never falter through the highs and lows of my daily life. Amen

For further thought

Think about places known to you where you can find time and space to simply be alone, and open to hear God's gentle whisper.

Wednesday 19 August
Beach mission

The Bible at the beach – 2 At the beach

> **Read Mark 4:1–9**
>
> *Again Jesus began to teach by the lake. The crowd that gathered round him was so large that he got into a boat and sat in it out on the lake, while all the people were along the shore at the water's edge. He taught them many things by parables …*
>
> (verses 1–2a)

When one of the founders of Methodism, John Wesley, was first asked to join his friend George Whitefield preaching in the open air to thousands of miners, Wesley's response was, 'I love a commodious room, a soft cushion, a handsome pulpit!' But he gave in and the results convinced him to leave the comfort of his cushion and take to the road!

Jesus had been teaching in the synagogue, but now needed to step outside and do things differently. There was a whole world needing to hear his message. The religious leaders might have thought it was all a bit of a stunt but soon saw the necessity as a crowd of people followed Jesus down to the shore of Lake Galilee, which is like a natural amphitheatre.

Jesus taught in parables, stories grounded in this world but with a spiritual meaning. This was not a typical synagogue congregation and Jesus needed to hold their attention. So, what better than to talk about farmers on those nearby hills, sowing seed in sometimes variable soil? A parable gets the brain cells buzzing if the truth within is to be found. Jesus encourages us in our thinking and understanding, and those parables are still part of our own journeys of discovery as we seek the truth and follow him in our everyday lives.

† Be a constant presence on my journey of faith and encourage me in the sowing of seeds in this, your beautiful garden. Amen

For further thought

Walk around a garden, your own if you have one or maybe a local park, and look at it afresh in the light of the parable of the sower.

Read Mark 4:35–40

A furious squall came up, and the waves broke over the boat, so that it was nearly swamped. Jesus was in the stern, sleeping on a cushion. The disciples woke him and said to him, 'Teacher, don't you care if we drown?'

(verses 37–38)

A few years ago, we were taken sailing by a friend on a large lake. It was all very picturesque and reassuringly calm as we started off, as neither of us had sailed before. However, as we got into deeper water the wind picked up, funnelled down the valley that fed the lake, and the water became choppy and less comfortable for such a novice crew!

I'd like to say that we battled through massive waves and feared for our lives, but that would be quite untrue. But I can now see how that might happen where the geography of an area influences wind speed, as it does on Lake Galilee, and the fishermen among the disciples would know how dangerous such a wind could be.

We can look at this story and see simply a miracle where a storm is stilled, which is a wonderful thing and worthy of retelling. But there's also merit in seeing it in a more symbolic sense. In the presence of Jesus, the disciples found calm and peace within the storm, just as we had confidence in our friend's ability to bring us safely back to dry land.

And that is a universal truth Christians have experienced throughout the ages: when we are fearful, doubt our abilities or worry about the future, Jesus does bring peace and calm in the storms of life. It's realising he is there with us in the boat that makes the difference.

† Thank you, Lord Jesus, that you are there in the storm to calm both wind and waves, bringing peace where there was fear and anxiety. Amen

For further thought

Have the storms and gales that you have experienced in life equipped you to help others through similar situations? Is there a way of offering this by way of service in your church or community?

236

Friday 21 August
From out of the storm

Read Job 38:1–11

Then the Lord spoke to Job out of the storm. He said: 'Who is this that obscures my plans with words without knowledge?'

(verses 1–2)

Most of us feel sorry for Job when we read his story. Maybe we can empathise with his suffering as a God-fearing man finding himself in such a miserable state, made worse by three so-called friends (known as Job's comforters) and their less-than-helpful advice. Words can be dangerous at times, sharp stones causing someone to stumble into even deeper water. Sometimes it is better to stay silent than simply offer platitudes.

Job finds himself in the perfect storm. His faith may be bruised but he still hangs on. Then he hears the voice of God, and the words are perhaps not what Job might expect, as they don't focus on the despair and anxiety that he's feeling. God paints a poetic picture of creation and asks Job if he can even begin to understand its intricacies and beauty, from the raging of the seas to the wonders of the night sky. Job begins to realise he may have spoken out of turn, got angry with God in his despair without understanding the bigger picture of God's love for all his creation. He is reassured that God has his best interests at heart.

Walking along the local beach when it's all but empty is how I find it easier to put life's frustrations into context. The daily rhythm of the tides is still a mystery to me, but they happen as regularly as when Job was around. I, too, can trust God to take care of me.

| Creator God, give me fresh eyes to see your glory reflected within the beauty and mystery of the universe in which I live. Amen

For further thought

Job at times was both angry and frustrated at God. Does his story show us that sometimes it's better to let all this emotion out?

Saturday 22 August
Breakfast on the beach

Read John 21:15–19

When they had finished eating, Jesus said to Simon Peter, 'Simon son of John, do you love me more than these?'

(verse 15a)

I have friends who enjoy wild camping along the coast of Wales. They'll sleep out on the beach, and as the sun rises, get a fire going and cook breakfast. They love the tranquillity of the experience and their togetherness with nature. The disciples were probably thinking about food when they were failing to catch anything at sea, when the newly resurrected Jesus tells them to cast their nets on the other side of the boat and bring some of their catch for him to cook as breakfast on the beach!

And it's while sharing food together that Jesus asks Peter the question, not once but three times. Was he now prepared to make the decision to give up everything and commit his life to spreading the good news, and take on the role of shepherd, caring for the flock?

Maybe it was also a gentle reminder of Peter's previous assertion that although others might desert Jesus, he would not. And then his courage failed him three times after Jesus was arrested. A chance then for Peter to accept forgiveness and move on.

It seems fitting that Peter's journey with Jesus, which began on this very beach, and after such a roller coaster of experiences, should now continue as he makes the final decision to swap fishing nets for a cross and continue the work to which Jesus had called him.

† Thank you, gracious God, that you accept me as I am and enable me to become the person you want me to be. Amen

For further thought

Have you in the past put off doing something you felt God was maybe calling you to do or get involved with, and is now the time to put that right?

The Bible at the beach – 2 At the beach

August

Romans 9–16 – 1 God's faithfulness

Notes by **Revd Dr Sham P. Thomas**

For Sham's bio, see p. 12. Sham has used the NRSVA for these notes.

Sunday 23 August
Choice of Israel

Read Romans 9:1–5

They are Israelites, and to them belong the adoption, the glory, the covenants, the giving of the law, the worship, and the promises; to them belong the patriarchs, and for them, according to the flesh, comes the Messiah, who is over all, God blessed for ever. Amen.

(verses 4–5)

There was an interesting investigative news report on how the jackpot lottery winners have fared later in their lives. Many of them received huge public attention at the time of their winning, as they were financially poor and the lottery was assumed to set them on a pedestal as it paved their way from rags to riches. However, the report revealed that many of them had ended up in debt and poverty. One of the issues raised in the report was the possibility of free gifts or sudden riches being unappreciated, and winners taken advantage of.

The choice of Israel as God's own people draws a parallel to a jackpot. Unlike a lottery, they did not even have to invest anything to qualify for the privileges God had bestowed on them. How did they respond to these privileges? This is the question Paul raises in this dense epistle and it raises questions for all those of us who receive God's gracious gifts in life. While revealing his agony over the ironic and tragic failure of the chosen ones in living up to their expectation, Paul describes shades of God's faithfulness. It is to this that we turn our attention this week.

† Lord, we have a legacy to be your children. May we never be complacent and may we aspire to rise to your expectation. Amen

God's faithfulness

Read Romans 9:6–18

So it depends not on human will or exertion, but on God who shows mercy ... So then he has mercy on whomsoever he chooses, and he hardens the heart of whomsoever he chooses.

(verses 16 and 18)

'Faithfulness! Is not that everything?' This is a commercial advert, popularised by one of the gold merchants in recent times in India vouching for the reliability and quality of his products. Attributes like faithfulness suit God more than a gold shop, though. No wonder, one recurring theme running through the Bible is God's faithfulness.

Paul raises three questions with regard to God's faithfulness in connection with the choice of Israel. First, if all are God's creation, what is the reason for God conferring special privilege to some and thereby implicitly disregarding others? Rather than looking for a politically correct answer to this disturbing proposition, Paul contends that it's God's will and pleasure alone to decide on how God should be faithful and to whom. God's authority and sovereignty are beyond human control and God does not need to justify any of God's actions or be apologetic about it. Second, what would happen if those who were favoured had failed God in return? Can God be bound by the negative response of the chosen ones? Will God fail in proceeding with the prescribed plan? Paul answers 'No' to these questions. God cannot be threatened, blackmailed or failed by the rebellion of the few. Third, should God remain faithful to those who have failed him? Will God show any faithfulness to them again? Paul says an emphatic 'Yes'. God can only be faithful, and his faithfulness endures forever. We can only be grateful for this unmerited gift of grace.

† Faithful God, instil faithfulness and forgive our faithlessness. Amen

For further thought

How is this principle of faithfulness applicable in our everyday relations?

The new people of God

Read Romans 9:19–33

What then are we to say? Gentiles, who did not strive for righteousness, have attained it, that is, righteousness through faith; but Israel, who did strive for the righteousness that is based on the law, did not succeed in fulfilling that law.

(verses 30–31)

When Global Positioning Systems (GPS) were introduced and used in travel on the road, it was another technological wonder to marvel at. When a familiar or popular route becomes obsolete or blocked, the GPS reroutes the journey and ensures that the user is guided to the originally destined place. If a technological aid like GPS can help us complete the planned journey and help us tide over any unexpected hurdles on the way, how much more God can accomplish, who is beyond any GPS. Just because a particular route God had chosen to achieve his goal has become redundant, the project is not abandoned *in toto*. God will accomplish the task with a new route and plan.

Paul explains that the failure of Israel to fulfil God's plan of blessing led God to choose another group as the new people of God. It is neither God's revenge on Israel nor an admission of God's failure in choosing a worthy agent in the first place. Rather, God cannot retreat on the proposed plan.

The constitution of the new people of God is also a warning that God cannot be bound by anyone as if they are indispensable. This holds true for the church today. The church is called to be God's agents and channel of divine blessings. However, the church cannot monopolise God or have the exclusive claim on God. While rejoicing at the grace of being chosen to be the children of God, we need to remind ourselves that God is not dependent on us. God can make even the stones 'shout out' (Luke 19:40) and God does not place all his eggs in one basket!

† Sovereign God, give us the humility to acknowledge your sovereignty and may we be privileged to be part of the new people of God. Amen

For further thought

How do we understand the statement that God can choose to be kind to some and hard on someone else?

Romans 9–16 – 1 God's faithfulness

August

The new righteousness

Read Romans 10:1–13

For there is no distinction between Jew and Greek; the same Lord is Lord of all and is generous to all who call on him. For, 'Everyone who calls on the name of the Lord shall be saved.'

(verses 12–13)

A top political leader in my country was once assessed by another leader as being the 'right man in the wrong party'! It was to suggest that while he had all the credentials and values to be a noble leader, the ideology of the party to which he committed his life was questionable.

Paul makes a similar diagnosis with regard to the failure of Israel in responding faithfully to the faithfulness of God. Paul suggests two sides of this failure. First, Israel was passionate about God but had gone about it in the wrong way. It happened in them following the letter of the Torah without grasping its major purpose of pointing to Jesus the Christ. It was like focusing on details while sidelining the larger picture. Second, they failed to appreciate salvation as God's gift and tried to earn it through their works. Receiving a gift, especially from God, is not self-demeaning.

The prognosis Paul offers is to acknowledge, accept and proclaim Jesus the Christ, in whom, Paul suggests, a new movement and a new righteousness were conceived in the world. Paul elaborates three major features of this new offer. First, rather than God choosing any particular people, it is the people's choice of Jesus as lord that constitutes them as the people of God. Second, all exclusive claims and any possible human divides like race and region are fractured and erased in bringing an inclusive movement in Christ. Third, this entire new initiative reveals the depth of God's mercy once more as Jesus is the chosen one of God. Those who acclaim Jesus will be honoured by God who sent him.

† Lord God, enable us to embrace the inclusiveness of the new righteousness in Jesus Christ, our Lord. Amen

For further thought

How do we relate with people of other regions and races even within our faith tradition?

Thursday 27 August
No excuse

Read Romans 10:14–21

But how are they to call on one in whom they have not believed? And how are they to believe in one of whom they have never heard? And how are they to hear without someone to proclaim him? And how are they to proclaim him unless they are sent?

(verses 14–15a)

In my pastoral context, some parents shared their agony in parenting, especially with regard to the studies of their children. In desperation they would say, 'We have walked the extra mile and stretched to ensure they had the comforts and not to bother about anything, be it food, clothing, money and the like. They only need to study well. But why don't they do it?'

Like a pained parent, Paul laments the rebellion of Israel despite God's best and gracious efforts. God had chosen them in the first place and sent prophets to guide them. It would have been an appropriate and grateful response if they had heeded God's Word. On the contrary they refused to abide by God's will without citing any reasons. This was not only disrespectful but callous on their part and hence it was unpardonable. Accepting or rejecting the gospel for the right reason is what is expected from each one of us.

However, a person's refusal of the gospel cannot be an excuse for God's messengers to become silent or to excuse themselves from the duty of sharing the good news of God. It is only by sharing the message that an opportunity is opened up and space created for diverse audiences to hear and decide on the gospel. For this reason, all who belong to God are to proclaim the gospel without being judgemental on its acceptance or rejection. The call for the believer is to be faithful rather than successful in being a messenger of the Word.

† God of the Word, may we not refrain from our mandate of receiving you and may we share your good news without fear or favour. Amen

For further thought
What are the challenges in sharing the gospel in your culture and particular local space?

The remnant

Romans 9–16 – 1 God's faithfulness

August

Read Romans 11:1–12

So too at the present time there is a remnant, chosen by grace. But if it is by grace, it is no longer on the basis of works, otherwise grace would no longer be grace.

(verses 5–6)

I recall the story of a scientist who worked for many months to make a new apparatus and asked his young assistant to carry it upstairs for further experimentation. While carrying, it fell from his hand and broke. The scientist worked again for months to make another apparatus and, to the surprise of many, asked the same assistant to carry it upstairs. It was indeed a risk that the scientist took to give another chance to the failed man!

We have already noted that God will fulfil his plan irrespective of the hurdles like the rebellion of the chosen agents. For this, the sovereign God will entrust another group replacing the ones who rebelled. But will God give another chance to those who failed? The answer is an affirmative yes, as it is not in the nature of God to match the outright rejection and condemnation meted out to him. Since God's choice is independent of the merit of the chosen ones, their demerits too do not dissuade God from offering another chance. This is indeed the epitome of the enduring faithfulness of God.

Paul advances the concept of remnant to prove his point. They are the minority who strive to remain faithful to their calling even while the majority choose to turn in rebellion. This remnant is a sign that God will never be left without partners and hence is a sapling of hope. On the other hand, it is also a sign that God can work with the little that is available. This in turn would empower the remnant to remain on course.

† Thank you, Lord, for your gracious endurance even while we prove to be difficult to deal with.

For further thought

How would you respond to the statement, 'there is a church within the church, and outside the church'?

Saturday 29 August
The olive trees

Read Romans 11:13–24

They were broken off because of their unbelief, but you stand only through faith. So do not become proud, but stand in awe. For if God did not spare the natural branches, perhaps he will not spare you.

(verses 20b–21)

This week, we have been following Paul's propositions exhibiting God's faithfulness and God's choice of Israel as the chosen people. When they failed in accepting Jesus the Christ, whom God had sent as the fulfilment of their expectation, they lost their privileged status in the eyes of God. At the same time, those who were outside this privileged group came to accept Jesus Christ and became the new people of God. How should this new group position themselves in conjunction with the people of Israel and how should they understand themselves in relation to God?

The church, the new people of God, comprised mainly of gentiles, cannot make any exclusive claims for themselves. Apart from Jesus being a Jew, the new believers in Christ came to hear about Jesus through the pioneering work of many missionaries including Paul, a Jew. God had never imagined a church as an exclusively non-Jewish community. The new people of God were also advised to eschew all traits of arrogance about their election. Paul suggests two reasons for this stand using the familiar imagery of a gardener undertaking grafting. Firstly, their election, as in the case of Israel in the first place, was purely an act of God's grace as they, like Israel, did not have any claims or merit for such a privileged position. Secondly, if Israel had been rejected for their rebellion, God will not shy away from doing the same with the Gentiles under similar circumstances. The way to experience the sustained faithfulness of God is to break the cycle of arrogance and be faithful in being humble servants of the sovereign and gracious God.

† Faithful God, help us imbibe that your grace is meant to evoke awe, not arrogance, in our life. Amen

For further thought

How can we avoid exclusivism and arrogance about our relationship with God?

Romans 9–16 – 1 God's faithfulness

August

Romans 9–16 – 2 Different gifts

Notes by **Yvonne Dawkins**

 Yvonne is an adult educator who has lived and worked in the Caribbean, the US, the UK and Singapore. She has worked in theological education, mission and social outreach and international mission. As a commissioned worker for the United Church in Jamaica and the Cayman Islands, she provided administrative leadership for the church's various mission, outreach and community development projects for eleven years. She is now academic dean of undergraduate studies at the University of the Commonwealth Caribbean in Kingston, Jamaica. She is married with one son. Yvonne has used the NIVUK for these notes.

Sunday 30 August
The ways of God

Read Romans 11:25–36

Oh, the depth of the riches of the wisdom and knowledge of God! How unsearchable his judgments, and his paths beyond tracing out! 'Who has known the mind of the Lord? Or who has been his counsellor?'

(verses 33–34)

One of the challenges of being a Christian is that Christian values run counter to the values of the world. The perspectives that are rewarded in the world are different from the perspectives of God's word. God's way may seem unusual by the world's standards.

Visitors to a new country are likely to notice that greetings differ in different places. When I travel from home in the UK to home in the Caribbean, I remind myself that a verbal greeting is required every time I enter a room. 'Good morning' is repeated several times throughout the day. My son once asked me why in the Caribbean people continue to say 'good morning' when it was no longer morning, while in the UK a nod is sufficient. I explained that it was part of the culture and we should learn the culture of any place we visit.

Similarly, we should strive to understand the mind of God. God's way may seem counter-intuitive so it may not come naturally. We must read God's word, study, reflect and choose to follow its counsel. As we learn about God we understand the wisdom of God's way.

† God of wisdom and knowledge, as we learn more about you, may we understand your ways and walk in them.

Monday 31 August
Different gifts

> **Read Romans 12:1–8**
>
> *So in Christ we, though many, form one body, and each member belongs to all the others. We have different gifts, according to the grace given to each of us.*
>
> (verses 5–6a)

How often we compare ourselves with others! Perhaps we wish we had the talents and skills that we admire in others or we allow ourselves to feel a little superior because some things come easier to us: speaking in public, making friends, finding our way in a new city. Yet different gifts should not lead to gloating or jealousy. In wisdom, God has made us different.

To be different means to be not alike in nature, form or quality. Many countries celebrate diversity, and we Jamaicans are proud of ours. We celebrate our different ethnic groups, while affirming our common goals.

Yet although in many parts of the world we have this ideal of respecting diversity, we are sometimes uncomfortable with living with those who are 'different'. In Romans 12:1–8 we are reminded that God's way is different from the ways of the world. God's way celebrates difference. In our personal lives, being open to those who are different challenges us to consider new perspectives and to question old assumptions. In our relationships with others, appreciating the gift of diversity allows us to have a more complete experience of community and being 'one body'.

Appreciating the gift of difference requires some grace on our part. It will mean stepping back from our comfortable but arrogantly held views about people who do not look like, sound like or think like us. Yet we cannot be the whole church without the gifts and presence of each other. It is God's way.

† Father God, forgive us for excluding others whom we do not understand; teach us how to truly love each other, making space for those who are different. Challenge us to be respectful and affirming of those who do not see life the way we do, celebrating each other and so finding our way to a complete community. In Jesus' name. Amen

For further thought

What differences can you note among the people with whom you have interacted today? How are these differences challenges, and how might they be opportunities?

Never flag

> **Read Romans 12:9–13**
>
> *Love must be sincere. Hate what is evil; cling to what is good.*
>
> (verse 9)

Social media has changed modern communication. Language and everyday speech include new words and old words with changed meanings. 'Friend', 'unfriend', 'emoticons', 'hashtag', 'LOL' … the list goes on.

On social media, communication is more personal, yet more public. Audiences are larger, yet more intimate details are shared. Communication style is more informal and more succinct. Emotions are expressed more blithely, showing casual indifference. Communicating in this way may impact our views of love and relationships. Are we trivialising these sentiments, reducing them to icons that we simply click on?

In Romans 12:9–13, Paul gives us a formula for love: clinging to good, being devoted to each other. For Paul, love is about honour, zeal, service, hope, patience, faithfulness and hospitality. These are *doing* words! The meaning is clear when God challenges us to love one another. In 1 John 4:7–8 we are reminded that this type of love only comes from those who are 'born of God and know God'. Love cannot be reduced to an image on a virtual platform. Every time we insert an emoticon or click the 'like' button we should ask ourselves what we really mean to say!

Love is action! Today, you may initiate or respond to a conversation, or observe a social media exchange. As a disciple of Christ, are these idle or insincere conversations? Do your words cause pain and injury? Is your communication disingenuous, pretentious and shallow? Do you mean the words when you click 'like' or 'love'? Is your meaning the same as God's meaning?

Remember: 'Love must be sincere' (Romans 12:9). This is God's way.

† May we reflect the beauty of Christ in everything we do by living the love of Christ every way we can.

For further thought

Write your own list of action words for love and how to live in community.

Wednesday 2 September
Never avenge

Read Romans 12:14–21

Do not repay anyone evil for evil. Be careful to do what is right in the eyes of everyone. If it is possible, as far as it depends on you, live at peace with everyone.

(verses 17–18)

Restorative justice seems to be a counter-intuitive concept. To focus on the rehabilitation of the offender and not his punishment seems to empathise with the suffering of the offender rather than that of the victim. Restorative justice requires parties who have a stake in a particular offence to come together to identify meaningful ways of dealing with the consequences of the offence. The focus is not on assigning punishment for a crime but rather on restoring relationships in a community, or addressing some long-standing inequalities that may have contributed to the committing of the offence in the first place.

In January 2018 the Jamaican Government launched a state of public emergency in parts of Jamaica to crack down on an increase in crime. Later that year, the United Church in Jamaica and the Cayman Islands launched a National Peace Initiative focused on promoting peace and building good relationships in community. This initiative includes both victims and perpetrators and explores ways of addressing conflict and pain that have long-term benefits. It gets to the source of the offence, rehabilitating the offender as well as giving voice and appropriate power to the victim.

Today's reading encourages us to find ways of addressing conflict that are not focused on revenge and retaliation but on the hard work of building relationship and refusing to harbour bitterness. It is difficult and counter-intuitive. Yet it is God's way. Yet this is impossible without the grace of God because it runs counter to our human instinct to exact revenge when we have been wronged. Let us pray for that grace every day.

† Lord, by your grace heal our pain. By your grace show us how to forgive. By your grace strengthen us to overcome evil with good. In Jesus' name we pray. Amen

For further thought

Restorative justice is often an option supported by local police. Is it available in your community, and how has it been used recently?

Romans 9–16 – 2 Different gifts

September

Thursday 3 September
God and the civil authorities

Read Romans 13:1–7

Give to everyone what you owe them: if you owe taxes, pay taxes; if revenue, then revenue; if respect, then respect; if honour, then honour.

(verse 7)

Paying what is due may not be difficult to accept as a principle, but in reality we may find it hard to relate it to all aspects of our lives. One such debt is the debt of loyalty and civic duty to our country. Jamaica's national pledge is an oath taken by the citizens of the country that is repeated at national events. It is a promise and a prayer. Are we living as good citizens in God's world? Even where governments are corrupt and civil authority is not trustworthy, it is God's way that we should pay our debts to community.

Think of your own country. Are there ways in which you feel convicted to pay what you owe to your community as one who is called by God? And yet, the passage set for today can be interpreted to say that a government is always right. What do you think Paul's response would be to governments that claim too much power and oppress their citizens? What other scriptures speak to those situations?

† God our creator who has put us in community, you have challenged us to pay our debts of loyalty by promoting, justice unity and peace. Lead us to follow your way. In Jesus' name. Amen

For further thought

Consider how you can be a more active citizen in your community.

Friday 4 September
Love and the law

Read Romans 13:8–14

The commandments … are summed up in this one command: 'Love your neighbour as yourself.' Love does no harm to a neighbour. Therefore love is the fulfilment of the law.

(verses 9a and 9c–10)

When we are returning home after a trip we may use a map to find directions or use our memory to find our way home. A map gives us a guide; alternatively, since we have travelled the way before, we could rely on memory. In Romans 13, Paul describes the law as a script to be followed in order to be reconciled with God. For many generations, God's people relied on the law and attempted to follow the commandments. The law provided a map that would lead them to a relationship with God. Paul writes that as of Jesus' coming, love supersedes the law. Love leads us home to God since we can be led by our experience of understanding who God is. We do what we should because we know what God requires and our hearts desire to please our God.

My Jamaican grandmother would often use many old phrases to reinforce the things she said. One of her favourites was 'Who feels it knows it.' She would often use this phrase when my mother disciplined us, and we complained to Grandma. I think she meant it literally, that when we felt the consequences of our actions we were likely to remember that discipline and avoid repeating our mistakes.

This passage in Romans reminds us that love is not only a matter of knowledge but a matter of experience. We have to feel it to know it. Love leads us to learn more about the God with whom we have relationship; love challenges us to respond with a desire to do what would please God.

† Gracious God, let me live out of your love; and open my life to love others. Amen

For further thought

If I say I love God, I should learn of God. When I learn of God, I understand God. When I have experienced God's way I will know how to walk in it.

Romans 9–16 – 2 Different gifts

September

251

Saturday 5 September
Don't judge

Read Romans 14:1–12

You, then, why do you judge your brother or sister'? Or why do you treat them with contempt? For we will all stand before God's judgment seat. It is written: '"As surely as I live," says the Lord, "every knee will bow before me; every tongue will acknowledge God."' So then, each of us will give an account of ourselves to God.

(verses 10–12)

The tendency to expect everyone else to do things the way we do things is very human. We may assume that our way of thinking and doing is so logical that it should be the norm. In the context of the church community this may lead to separation between believers due to conflict over belief and practices that are different.

This passage today makes the point that in the case of issues that are not core to the teachings of Christ, there are three reasons why we should not judge other Christians. God has already accepted those we don't agree with (verses 1–4); each must be fully convicted in his own mind how to honour God (verses 5–6); Christ died for all and it is God who has the authority to judge, not us (verses 7–10).

The Jamaica Council of Churches (JCC) includes this statement in its Mission and Vision statement: to encourage 'the visible unity of the Church in Jamaica, the Caribbean and the Global Community in the execution of the ministry and mission of Jesus Christ.'[9] Jamaica has many, many different churches, yet the JCC's statement acknowledges that 'visible' Christian unity is necessary and commits its members to work towards that goal.

Do we sometimes lose sight of our purpose in the world as we give in to the temptation to quibble about disagreements instead of living in ways that tell others that we know how to be 'one in the spirit'?

† Oh God, you are one God. Forgive us for every divisive conversation, every futile argument regarding differences in the body of Christ. Make us ambassadors of Christian unity, who show honour and respect for other Christians, despite our differences.

For further thought

How is your local church making visible the one, united body of Christ?

9 Jamaica Council of Churches (n.d.), 'Mission / Vision' (jamaicacouncilofchurches.yolasite.com/vision-mission.php, last accessed 30 April 2019).

Romans 9–16 – 3 Welcome one another

Notes by **Clare Nonhebel**

Clare is a published author of thirteen fiction and non-fiction books including an e-book co-written with a death row prisoner. She is currently working on *Flourish!*, a book about grace and mental health based on the gardening project she volunteers at in Dorset, UK. To find out more, visit clarenonhebel.com. Clare has used the NIVUK for these notes.

Sunday 6 September
Don't trip one another up

Read Romans 14:13–23

Therefore let us stop passing judgment on one another. Instead, make up your mind not to put any stumbling-block or obstacle in the way of a brother or sister.

(verse 13)

This passage shows a shrewd understanding of the obstacle that Christians can be to each other in the practice of their faith – particularly by rating some as more Christian than others!

Paul calls us to respect the different ways that individual believers follow their conscience, and not to belittle one another's fears. Perfect love casts out fear. If some believers are beset by insecurities, their fellow believers need to love them more perfectly.

I knew a young woman who cleaned her small home every day – all day. Exhausted, she wept, 'I can't live in this filthy place!' A kind counsellor explained that the place was clean but her view of herself was tainted, ever since being raped by someone she trusted. But as well as providing counselling, the counsellor also helped her to move to a new 'clean' home for a visible fresh start.

Passing judgement is equally damaging when it labels a person unclean (an inferior, second-rate Christian) or when it ranks them as clean (beyond reproach) and fails to deal with the stumbling-block they may be to others, by insensitive behaviour or an overbearing attitude. Both verdicts are unhelpfully judgemental.

† Father of the whole Christian family, help us to be respectful of one another's priorities and gentle with one another's fears.

Monday 7 September
Accept one another

> **Read Romans 15:1–13**
>
> *Accept one another, then, just as Christ accepted you, in order to bring praise to God.*
>
> (verse 7)

I've recently been involved in an oral history project, interviewing people from a Christian community who created the foundations for a successful project for disabled people.

Listening to the accounts of life in a close-knit live-in community has been challenging: how on earth did all these strangers, different personalities from varied walks of life, find a way to live together – and then to welcome in so many people whose lives were in chaos, to help them find healing and peace?

Love of neighbour is an attractive concept, till the concept becomes the reality of everyday annoyances: someone sprays food while they eat or borrows the car and brings it back with an empty tank; someone uses the communal fund to buy food that no one else likes; one needs to talk while another needs peace …!

As one member commented: 'I thought I was a loving person till living with people made me realise how many barriers I put up. There was a rule that if we couldn't resolve a conflict quickly, we'd call in a third person to mediate.'

Accepting and welcoming everyone God sends is never going to be easy. Some Christians fear that disagreements are a bad witness to non-believers, so gloss over conflicts that need to be addressed. Many people leave church – some never to attend a church again – not because of theological differences but because they feel belittled or bullied.

Facing the challenges of love and the pain of differences needs courage – and sometimes a gifted mediator!

† Father, help us to be real when we struggle to love our neighbour. You didn't tell us to make light of our difficulties but to bring our burdens to you to make them light.

For further thought

Can some secular guidance on group dynamics, mediating conflict or clear communication be useful to churches? Or do we reject them because they're 'not Christian'?

Tuesday 8 September
Welcoming outsiders (genuinely!)

Read Romans 15:14–22

As it is written, 'Those who were not told about him will see, and those who have not heard will understand.'

(verse 21)

Reading this passage, it seems that Paul may have faced some criticism from believers for being 'a minister of Christ Jesus to the Gentiles' rather than making his fellow Jews his priority.

It's human nature to enjoy belonging to a friendly and welcoming group – and then to become less welcoming to new people who want to join, or to insist they fit in with the old-timers' ways.

St Benedict reversed this, ruling that every newcomer to the Benedictine order should be expected and allowed to change it, for everyone's benefit.

Nowadays, when 'Gentile' non-churchgoers come to church or get to know Christians for the first time, they face an unfamiliar culture. What do certain words and phrases mean? Why does no one applaud the singers? Why does everyone keep standing up and sitting down?

Established Christians can benefit from newcomers' reactions and insights and, above all, the freshness of the gospel to those hearing it for the first time. Through them, we are reminded of how powerful and intimate the love of Jesus is and what a difference it can make – and has made – to our lives.

Paul's focus on the gentiles was not a rejection of the existing believers: it ensured that the whole Church gained from the newcomers' fresh perspective and understanding, so the gospel and worship of God would never become an over-familiar routine.

† Lord, help us to listen to and learn from new believers, not just teach them or 'correct' their impressions of our church culture.

For further thought

How understanding am I of another Christian's sense of mission, when it makes them less available to me and to my own projects and priorities?

Romans 9–16 – 3 Welcome one another

September

Wednesday 9 September
An uphill struggle

Read Romans 15:23–33

I urge you, brothers and sisters, by our Lord Jesus Christ and by the love of the Spirit, to join me in my struggle by praying to God for me.

(verse 30)

When Paul calls his life a struggle, he's not exaggerating. His letters, as well as the book of Acts, describe hazards such as shipwrecks, illness and snake bites and frequent vengeful attacks on his reputation and his life, including from people who considered themselves followers of Christ.

It's clear that the people who really knew and loved him saw him as a role model and a hero, but it's easy to forget that heroes get tired and anxious and desperate and need the prayers of other strugglers.

Being told to love our neighbour as ourselves is a balancing act: we must pray for each other, including for those who, like Paul, seem way ahead of us – more heroic, more spiritual, closer to God.

And we must pray for ourselves; if not, our prayer for others has no reality. People who say, 'Oh, I never pray for myself!' are not relying on God in the everyday struggle. We have nothing to offer others unless we first receive from God.

In this passage, Paul reminds us of the need to receive and to give. The gentiles receive the spiritual free gift of being called by God, along with his chosen people, the Jews. And they in turn are asked to give material help to Jewish communities poorer than themselves. Paul gives all he has to all the churches he visits, and receives the joy of their hospitality and love.

It's the balance of giving and receiving, praying and struggling and rejoicing, that draws so many different communities into one church, the body of Christ.

† Father God, make us generous in asking for blessings for each other, and humble in asking for help for ourselves.

For further thought

Am I more willing to share with and to give to certain people in need, than I am with others?

Thursday 10 September
Dear each and everyone

Read Romans 16:1–16, 21–23

Greet Philologus, Julia, Nereus and his sister, and Olympas and all the Lord's people who are with them.

(verse 15)

I tend to skim over lists of names in the Bible, especially the hard-to-pronounce ones.

But this passage shows that Paul really held people in his heart while he was working and travelling and teaching and being imprisoned and beaten. He prayed for individuals he knew and remembered for different reasons.

Some of those mentioned are relatives of his; others are fellow workers, helpers and missionaries, and their household members.

As well as greeting people by name, Paul mentions the people with him: his fellow worker; the scribe who wrote the letter for him; the man whose house he was staying in; even the city's director of public works.

Did Paul like all these people, I wonder? I hope not. I hope he accepted them just because they were the people God put in his path: the welcomers and the initially half-hearted or suspicious; the relatives he hadn't chosen; the people he had to rely on for material needs or safety, as a stranger in a new place.

It's daunting to come across someone we don't naturally warm to. Our liking for people has nothing to do with their virtues: our friends may be full of faults, while someone with admirable qualities we may really dislike. But thankfully God doesn't ask us to have warm fuzzy feelings towards all the people he sends. He asks us to love them as ourselves – flawed people whom we don't always like.

I hope that's why Paul wrote. To Julia, Philologus, Nereus and his sister, and all the others. And us.

† Father of your whole human family, help us to pray from the heart for each person you bring to mind now, especially for X and Y whom I struggle to like.

For further thought

If I can't love someone as my dearest friend, can I love them as a thorn in the flesh, sent to humble my pride?

Romans 9–16 – 3 Welcome one another

September

Friday 11 September
Don't be duped

Read Romans 16:17–20

I rejoice because of you; but I want you to be wise about what is good, and innocent about what is evil.

(verse 19b)

It's not a virtue to be naïve. Jesus told us to be pure as doves but as shrewd as serpents. There are, sadly, people – even apparently good, holy people – who take advantage of gullible souls.

We want to love God's people, so we try to see goodness in everyone. But to accept every person uncritically, on their own terms, is not loving them in reality.

Jesus welcomed everyone the Father sent to him but he didn't trust everyone, because he saw into their hearts (John 2:24–25).

Among survivors of childhood abuse, Christians commonly ask, 'How do I honour my father and mother, as the Commandments say – when my mother or father abused me (and maybe others as well)?'

We can honour each person's reality as a person created by God, whom Jesus loved enough to die for. It doesn't demand that a son or daughter honour some fantasy version of a loving parent or allow that person to take control of their life or to harm others.

An autistic man told me that a neighbour asked if he would be his friend and if he would trust him. When he said yes, the neighbour asked for his bank card and security PIN number. He told him, because he wanted a friend and because he had been told it was wrong to tell lies.

God asks us to be like children in trusting him, our Father, but to be adult in identifying people who are in reality serving the one Jesus called 'the father of lies'.

† Father, help us to forgive the sinner, having acknowledged the harm that sin does, and to know when to walk away from evil.

For further thought

We are called to be Christians – not easy prey for people with no intention of doing good.

Saturday 12 September
The one and only

Read Romans 16:25–27

Now to him who is able to establish you ... to the only wise God be glory for ever through Jesus Christ! Amen.

(verses 25a, 27)

The whole of the gospel and all the prophetic history leading up to it give the same message: only God is good.

Because worship is about acknowledging worth, we have to be really careful we're not worshipping someone or something by giving it more than its genuine worth. To worship money is false, because money has no lasting worth: it can't save the owner from spiritual deadness. To worship a nation or political group is false worship, because any human group contains both good and evil, and we can't embrace both.

Loyalty to country or family can become a kind of religious fervour, but we need discernment. For instance, America claims to have the greatest justice system in the world, while still subjecting damaged people to agonising executions. In Britain, some public figures have been honoured with titles bestowed by the Queen, then later revealed as frauds or criminals. We may love our country but not worship it, blind to its faults.

Psalm 116:10–11 says, 'I trusted in the Lord when I said, "I am greatly afflicted"; in my alarm I said, "Everyone is a liar."'

Thank God, we are only asked to worship and trust God. Only God is entirely good.

To the only wise God be glory for ever through Jesus Christ. Yes, that's it.

† Abba, Father of all, take your great power and reign over all earthly authorities, nations and cultures, till all take their rightfully humble place: on their knees worshipping you.

For further thought
Are some of my allegiances, loyalties or patriotism distracting me from worshipping God above all?

Romans 9–16 – 3 Welcome one another

September

Fake news and the Good News
– 1 Fake news

Notes by **Deseta Davis**

Deseta is assistant pastor of a Pentecostal Church. Her main vocation is as a prison chaplain, helping to bring hope to those who are incarcerated. With an MA in theological studies, she previously worked as a tutor in black theology, bringing the study of theology to a range of people who had not previously considered it. Deseta is married to Charles, and they have two grown-up children and a granddaughter. Deseta has used the NIVUK for these notes.

Sunday 13 September
True or false?

Read Deuteronomy 18:18–22

You may say to yourselves, 'How can we know when a message has not been spoken by the Lord?' If what a prophet proclaims in the name of the Lord does not take place or come true, that is a message the Lord has not spoken.

(verses 21–22a)

This week we are concentrating on news or what is commonly known today as 'fake news'. We will be looking at prophets, mainly false prophets, and the consequences of making false prophecies both to the prophets themselves and to the people to whom they prophesy.

The influence of media in the twenty-first century is undeniable. Many of the population's beliefs today are powered by it. A lot of what was deemed as false or unacceptable ten years ago has now become the norm which has mainly been one of the great effects of the media. I wonder if the media could be seen as a modern-day prophet, whether true or false.

Today, we prefer to have prophecies of hope, peace and comfort and in many of the texts this week that is how the false prophets prophesied. However in this text God tells of the consequences of false prophecy: it would end in the death of the prophet.

The question as to how we differentiate between true and fake news is as pertinent today as it was in the day of the prophets. It is difficult to answer but according to this text, if it does not come true, then it is fake!

† Ask God to help you differentiate between true and fake news in today's media.

Leading with integrity

Read 1 Kings 13:11–24

The old prophet answered, 'I too am a prophet, as you are. And an angel said to me by the word of the Lord: "Bring him back with you to your house so that he may eat bread and drink water."' (But he was lying to him.)

(verse 18)

This text always amazes me. The young prophet from Judah speaks the truth to Jeroboam the king. He speaks truth to power about what will happen in the future, even giving a sign. The young prophet was obedient, doing all he was told by God. The old prophet then brings fake news and lies to the young prophet. The prophet believes him and dies because of his disobedience.

I am quite amazed that the young prophet suffers such a consequence of fake news. He trusts the old prophet (maybe too quickly), does not check out where the news has come from and eventually succumbs to the consequences.

Maybe this could teach us a lesson that believing fake news can bring consequences and maybe just as many consequences to the hearer as to the author.

The sad thing here is that the older prophet showed no real integrity. Leaders should lead ethically. It is important not to say things just to get a reaction or to drive through personal agendas. This demonstrates a lack of integrity.

This text shows us that anyone can be authors of or followers of fake news. Leaders need to be aware of the influence they hold over their followers. It is the function of a leader to constantly and consistently give out news, whether through preaching, teaching or just in the capacity of leading. A leader with integrity will speak what they believe God is saying with a true and open heart that will lead the people into doing what is right.

† Ask God to reveal any areas in your life that may lack integrity.

For further thought

How can you address the areas that have been revealed?

Fake news and the Good News – 1 Fake news

September

Standing out from the crowd

Read 1 Kings 22:4–28, 34–35

The messenger who had gone to summon Micaiah said to him, 'Look, the other prophets without exception are predicting success for the king. Let your word agree with theirs, and speak favourably.' But Micaiah said, 'As surely as the Lord lives, I can tell him only what the Lord tells me.'

(verses 13–14)

Lies can be easy to believe, especially when one sounds good or like something that you want to happen or really want to believe will happen. Ahab was desperate to believe he would live, trying to make out that Micaiah was the false prophet. Yet he had his doubts, so much so that he took off his kingly garments and went into battle hoping the enemy would not know he was the king. All to prove Micaiah was wrong.

Micaiah stood out from the crowd to speak truth to power. He could have cowered, fallen in line with what everyone was saying and prophesied the falsehoods that everyone wanted him to, but he could not condescend to this. He knew what the consequences of standing up for the truth would be, but he continued to stand his ground.

The many falsehoods going around today sometimes discourage us from speaking truth to power. It pushes us into following the crowd and keeping our heads down to keep us out of trouble. I wonder if we should be like Jeremiah who said, 'his word is in my heart like a fire, a fire shut up in my bones. I am weary of holding it in; indeed, I cannot' (Jeremiah 20:9). Maybe this should be our stance. God has called us to speak truth to power and even if it is not what the powerful want to hear, we need to suffer the consequences and speak much-needed truth in this time of fake news.

† Courageous God, who supports us in our time of need, give us the courage to stand up and speak the truth to power even though we may know the consequences of our actions.

For further thought

Is there an area that needs your prophetic voice? Seek this out and find the courage to speak.

Wednesday 16 September
The truth makes you free

Read Jeremiah 23:16–32

This is what the Lord Almighty says: 'Do not listen to what the prophets are prophesying to you; they fill you with false hopes. They speak visions from their own minds, not from the mouth of the Lord.'

(verse 16)

Once I watched a TV programme called *Click* which gives news and recent developments in the world of computer technology. On this edition, it showed the heads of famous politicians superimposed on other figures and the politicians' 'heads' were speaking things that seemed to really come from them. The broadcaster said that soon it will be impossible to distinguish between the generated and the real.

A lot of people's news today comes from social media. This form of media has become a game-changing phenomenon within communications. It is easier for groups to organise movements and make their voice heard, whether for good or for ill.

People are more prone to listen to and believe social media than the 'normal' news, as it has become the main source of their social arena and, therefore, their main access to news. This is true even though a lot of it may be fake, and deliberately so.

In today's text, the prophets plan the lies and tell them for their own gain. They invent what they say for their own agendas. They use the name of God to give authority to their own ideas. The inhabitants of Jerusalem were fed by these false prophets with the vain hopes of being able to drive out the Babylonians and shake off their yoke entirely, making them free for the future.

As much as we would all want to hear the good prophecies, lies keep people bound to falsehoods. It would be far better to know the truth and work within its parameters for, as Jesus said in John 8:32, 'the truth will set you free.'

† Loving God, in this world of fake news, help us to find the truth that sets us free.

For further thought
Can you check your resources (library, internet) to find out what could be classed as one of the biggest fake news stories of our time?

Fake news and the Good News – 1 Fake news

September

Voices, voices, voices

> **Read Jeremiah 28**
>
> *'From early times the prophets who preceded you and me have prophesied war, disaster and plague against many countries and great kingdoms. But the prophet who prophesies peace will be recognised as one truly sent by the Lord only if his prediction comes true.'*
>
> (verses 8–9)

There are many voices vying for our attention today. Whom do we listen to? Hananiah was another voice prophesying falsely which again the people listened to, desperately wanting hope and comfort. In an age where there is no shortage of voices to hear, we need the discernment of God so as not to be fooled by deception.

In the prison where I work as chaplain, I visit many men who are mentally unstable. They continuously hear voices. These voices sometimes tell them to do very bad things, some of which have brought them in contact with the criminal justice system and eventually into prison. Those who are well mentally cannot understand how these men hear and listen to these voices. The fortunate ones either lose the voices (maybe through medication) or learn to live with them. The others tend to live a life of torment, seeking ways to diminish the voices or doing what the voices tell them.

It is difficult to know which voice to follow or believe at times. How do we tell truth from fake? Were the people to believe Jeremiah or Hananiah?

In biblical days there were two criteria for discerning truth: the prophet would not teach error or lead people astray (from God), or prophetic predictions of the future would come true.

Not only was Hananiah leading the people astray, his predictions did not come true. As said in Sunday's text, it can be difficult to assess today's news: what is true or what is fake. But with a little more research and help from God, we could become more aware of which voice to follow.

† Ask God to help you to listen to the voice of truth from the many voices that are vying for your attention.

For further thought

What are the criteria you would use for separating true and false news?

Friday 18 September
The gospel is not for sale

Read Micah 3:5–12

This is what the Lord says: 'As for the prophets who lead my people astray, they proclaim "peace" if they have something to eat, but prepare to wage war against anyone who refuses to feed them … Her leaders judge for a bribe, her priests teach for a price, and her prophets tell fortunes for money.'

(verses 5 and 11a)

Micah championed the cause of the underprivileged. He spoke out against injustice and greed. Micah's words are particularly aimed at leaders treating the poor unjustly. Prophets should have the poor at heart, yet in this text the poor are being even more marginalised by the fake news these prophets peddle.

A few years ago, I worked temporarily for a Christian TV station. I was struck by one person in particular who vowed to give her whole month's wages to one of the campaigns that was running. Although this could be seen as sacrificial giving, I was very uncomfortable as she was saying that she did not have the money but would give it so God would bless her. I decided to leave the job after this as I did not feel God's will was for the poor to give everything they had to those richer than themselves or to get a 'greater' blessing. These campaigns, I believe, disproportionately affect the poor. Indeed, some people preach that if you don't have enough to live on, it's because you are not giving enough or your faith is weak. The sad thing about it is that some of these leaders are living a great, rich life whilst their givers cannot find the next meal.

As in the days of the prophets, some preachers today seem to preach for a cost. They will not preach unless the people pay to enter a meeting or give money for a blessing. However Jesus said, 'Freely you have received; freely give.' The Gospel is NOT for sale!

† Gracious God, I pray for the people in poverty. As you freely gave your life for us, may we freely give our lives for them.

For further thought

What can you do to help those who are living in poverty in your area? Can a free event be arranged to help them?

Tricks of the trade

Read Acts 13:1–12

They met a Jewish sorcerer and false prophet named Bar-Jesus, who was an attendant of the proconsul … The proconsul, an intelligent man, sent for Barnabas and Saul because he wanted to hear the word of God. But Elymas the sorcerer (for that is what his name means) opposed them.

(verses 6–8)

The false prophet, Bar-Jesus, deceives through tricks and magic. He becomes an adviser to the proconsul (which is worrying, to say the least). Although he prophesies lies and tricks which people believe, in today's text he is directly seeking to turn aside the proconsul from believing the truth. It was more than likely a ploy to keep his influence over the proconsul.

The same could be said today. Some advisers to governments and leaders give advice according to their own agenda. They are fearful of losing power and, therefore, advise accordingly. Sometimes through manipulation of numbers, policies and laws the people are 'tricked' into believing the fakery. These are done many times to prevent people from believing and accepting the truth.

Paul would not accept this and condemned Bar-Jesus to blindness. Fake news can bring blindness and darkness over a nation. Many nations of the world are not getting truth in their news or are very controlled as to what they can listen to. The governments in these countries want the population to hear and believe as true what is put out, which is not always truth. However although those in the West believe in 'freedom of the press', this also opens up the way to fake news and does not guarantee truth.

Fake news is very topical today and generally comes through abuse of power. This week we have seen how fake news can affect both the author and the listener. How we discern between true and fake news is an important aspect in life but how we deal with it is even more important.

† Pray for your government, asking God to help them to be open and truthful.

For further thought

Could you put on an evangelising event using a magician to show the difference between truth and fake?

Fake news and the Good News – 2 Good news

Notes by **Dafne Plou**

Dafne is a journalist and social communicator who works on technology for development in an international organisation. Her work includes travelling to other Latin American countries to lead workshops and seminars and speak in conferences. At her local church in Buenos Aires' suburbs, she works to build community and fellowship through the liturgy. She is a women's rights activist and participates in the women's movement in her country. Dafne has used the NRSVA for these notes.

Sunday 20 September
Why take the risky way?

Read Luke 4:14–21

Then Jesus, filled with the power of the Spirit, returned to Galilee, and a report about him spread through all the surrounding country. He began to teach in their synagogues and was praised by everyone.

(verses 14–15)

Jesus had come home and was becoming quite famous. Reports spread and the first-century equivalent of journalists, TV and radio presenters, and social networks were abuzz with him. Would they comment on his teachings, would they talk about his looks, his charm, the strength of his dissertation? Was he getting more fans, people willing to follow him and overflow the synagogues where he taught?

Surely a tricky situation for someone who had received a messianic call. No doubt, Jesus remembered the temptations he had confronted not long before. Fame, power, privilege, recognition. So there he was that sabbath day with the scroll of the prophet Isaiah in his hands, choosing a reading … and he didn't do it randomly. He decided to reveal his mission that day. Nazareth had seen him growing up, and now it was time to disclose his commitment.

And Jesus chose to proclaim risky news. Headlines would have highlighted Jesus promising 'good news to the poor'; 'release to captives'; 'sight to the blind'; 'freedom for the oppressed'; 'a year of the Lord's favour'. His preaching undoubtfully showed a clear bias for the marginalised, the needy, the unwanted and their need for justice, rights, inclusion. Would his fans still follow him? They would have to choose and commit themselves, too.

† Jesus, keep calling us. May the Holy Spirit encourage us to follow your way and keep to your commitments. Amen

Hard to believe

> **Read Luke 24:13–27**
>
> *Some women of our group ... were at the tomb early this morning ... they had indeed seen a vision of angels who said that he was alive. Some of those who were with us went to the tomb and found it just as the women had said ...*
>
> (verses 22–24)

Hard to believe ... For these disciples, it was hard to believe Jesus had died and, with him, all their dreams of his messianic kingdom. Even having listened to the women's and their own friends' testimony, Cleopas and his colleague had decided in such a short time to leave Jerusalem and go back home, feeling sad and defeated. Were their enthusiasm, experiences and beliefs so easily subdued?

In despair, these disciples decided to go back to their place, though I sense that a small spark of hope remained, still hidden in their hearts. Otherwise, why would they listen to this stranger talking about Moses, the prophets and interpreting the scriptures? Perhaps he could chip away at despair and disclose good news ... Why might Jesus have appeared in this way? As a good shepherd, he didn't want his own to go astray. As a patient and loving redeemer, he was there at the door, knocking and waiting for the flame to glow.

During dictatorship, church leaders working for human rights and against oppression always repeat, 'We must stand by hope, against all despair.' As they walked to Emmaus, Jesus and his disciples stood by hope. Despair did not win. Amazing good news!

† Jesus, our good shepherd, you always lead us with hope to a new world of trust and justice. Be with us today and always. Amen

For further thought

On the internet, search for artwork featuring the disciples on their way to Emmaus. Reflect on their new encounter with Jesus.

Tuesday 22 September
A witness in spirit and truth

Read John 4:21–29, 39–42

The woman said to him, 'I know that Messiah is coming' (who is called Christ). 'When he comes, he will proclaim all things to us.'

(verse 25)

The Samaritan woman was not just an ordinary woman taking care of her daily routine. She listened to this foreign rabbi, she reflected on his words and also questioned him and gave her reasons for disagreeing. But her trust in him and respect for him grew as the conversation flowed and deepened. She even confessed her troubled life and was anxious to try this living water the rabbi was offering her. She was thirsty for a new life that would allow her to go back to her village with a renewed spirit, free from past mistakes and ready to live in truth. The grace of redemption was present at the well.

As the dialogue with the Samaritan woman grew in meaning and relevance, Jesus too disclosed his true nature and power. His call to worship God in spirit and in truth included perceiving God's presence and responding with drastic changes in one's way of life.

When the Samaritan woman came back to Jesus, leading her neighbours and encouraging them to listen to whom she believed was the promised Messiah, she was already growing in the good news and paving the way for more to come. Her life had turned upside down. She felt she was trusted and regarded with esteem. People in the village had believed in her words and had followed her to find out more about what this visitor had to reveal to them. She had become a fervent disciple and was bringing others to an encounter with God's grace.

† God, may your grace be with us and lead us to carry good news to those who feel trapped and need freedom in spirit and in truth. Amen

For further thought

How can your church community share the good news with those who feel marginalised because they have 'broken the rules'?

Good news of grace

> ### Read 1 Corinthians 15:1–11
> *... if you hold firmly to the message that I proclaimed to you – unless you have come to believe in vain.*
>
> (verse 2b)

When political refugees started to flow into Argentina in the early seventies, not everybody embraced them in solidarity. People from Chile, Uruguay and Brazil came to the country running from the horrors of persecution, imprisonment and torture. Were all Christian churches ready to receive them? Not all members agreed to, nor did local and national governments and civic groups. How could the faithful 'hold firmly to the message' (verse 2) and to the certainty that they were called to serve those suffering for political reasons?

When his parish was bombed by paramilitary action groups that represented those who wanted to do away with political refugees in their city and country, Bishop Pagura (in the city of Mendoza, Argentina) did not leave his pulpit. He stood firm and when political persecution broke out in his own country, his courage inspired him to write a song to uphold faith in a new era to come. He chose a tango, a traditional popular rhythm in Argentina, to affirm hope in resurrection and in God's lasting love to bring his children to liberation from cold nights, tough hearts and devastated souls.

Would a song affirming faith be enough? Bible experts tell us that in today's reading Paul uses in fact a confession of faith by Christian communities in Corinth. 'Hold firmly to the message,' they affirm. Let us proclaim that Jesus' grace towards all of us, that we express in deeds, statements and songs, has not been in vain.

† Jesus, talk to me this morning with music and songs. Help me to fill my spirit with psalms and melodies. Amen

For further thought
Who are the Christian witnesses who have challenged and nourished your community or country?

Thursday 24 September
One man for the people

Read John 11:49–52

'You do not understand that it is better for you to have one man die for the people than to have the whole nation destroyed.'

(verse 50)

'I am here standing for life,
I am here standing for those who were killed,
I am here standing for those who are in danger.'

Women human rights defenders who work to end gender violence introduce themselves with these sharp words in every street demonstration. It is moving to hear dozens of women saying this 'lay litany' in one voice. In so doing, they denounce the growing murder rate among women and call on society and state to put an end to this crisis.

When Jesus declared he was the resurrection and the life (John 11:25), he was affirming his support to survivors, his protection to those in danger and his struggle for the full life for his people. But did he need to die and sacrifice himself to save his nation from destruction and bring back those who had been dispersed, as Caiaphas prophesied?

It is difficult to understand. But as I listen to the litany of the women's rights defenders in the protest marches, I am certain that Jesus is with them, paying attention to their words, nourishing their activism, standing by them as they seek justice and equality in this world. And this is indeed the good news of Jesus' resurrection from the cross: the assurance that the resurrected Christ has the power to bring together those who are dispersed, be they atheists, agnostics, non-believers, Christians, or people of other faiths and religions, and move them to acts of fairness that put an end to wrongness, inequity and sorrow.

† Help us, dear God, to support and care for those who struggle for a just world. Amen

For further thought

Where do you see the power of the resurrected Christ around you in the struggles your society is facing?

Fake news and the Good News – 2 Good news

September

Get up and stand on your feet!

Fake news and the Good News – 2 Good news

September

Read Acts 26:1–20

'Get up and stand on your feet; for I have appeared to you for this purpose, to appoint you to serve and testify to the things in which you have seen me and to those in which I will appear to you.'

(verse 16)

When I was a child, I enjoyed going with my father to the prayer services that took place every Thursday at the mission chapel, in the port area of Buenos Aires. But it wasn't the prayers that attracted me or the other children that attended these services. Prayers at that time were long and wordy, full of rhetoric. It was the testifying, just before the prayers, which truly fascinated me. We sat in awe listening to all those men and women telling the congregation about their past lives, full of hazards, wrongdoings, lies, deceits, struggles with alcohol, even prison, and their encounter with the love of Jesus that changed them forever.

Paul's testifying before King Agrippa was not different. He, too, described changing his life forever after the vision on the way to Damascus. There he heard the call, 'Get up and stand on your feet' (verse 16) and he accepted the challenge of becoming a witness of God's power and grace. The early church so cherished Paul's testifying that we can almost feel it has been transcribed word by word, for the nourishment and blessing of the new believers, their communities and those to come.

Men and women who testified at the mission chapel repeated Paul's words: 'Someone told me to get up and stand on my feet.' Was it a preacher? Other faithful people? People who at some point cared for them? By the grace of God, the stories of their new lives nurtured others and helped them to grow. They, too, were able to witness the wonders of Jesus' love to those at the borders, like the marginalised in the port area.

† Keep us aware, dear Jesus, and ready to tell others about your gospel of care, justice and love for those who seem to be invisible or unwanted in our selfish world. Amen

For further thought

How many times is Paul's conversion told in the New Testament? How does his experience still challenge us today?

Saved by the good news

Read Romans 10:1–15

*And how are they to proclaim him unless they are sent? As it is written,
'How beautiful are the feet of those who bring good news!'*

(verse 15)

New religious trends nowadays emphasise individual well-being.
They stress that being fine with ourselves and the creation around
us is the right thing to achieve. There's also a kind of Christian
preaching that points to individual peace and comfort in the
relation with God. No challenges, no commitments; just sitting in
an auditorium or in front of the TV listening to a religious service
will do. Getting involved in a community seems not to make sense
any more. Who is willing to be sent? Who is ready to put his or her
feet at the service of the gospel?

When Paul recalls Isaiah's image from Isaiah 52:7, he's telling us
that being a Christian means moving on to announce, to share,
to advocate and to show others by action and deeds that Jesus is
with us, resurrected, strong and victorious. This is the reason why
our feet, our wheelchairs, our crutches, whatever we use to move
on, are beautiful, a beauty beyond fashion and stereotypes. And
there is much to announce, because there's need for justice and
non-discrimination, and Jesus shows the way with generosity and
the assurance of his redeeming love.

Let's get up, let's leave our comfortable seats and get on! The
word is with us, on our lips and in our hearts! And we cannot keep
it to ourselves, but must proclaim it with enthusiasm as we go in
life.

† Be our light, Jesus, to illuminate our way and make our feet go happily faster as
we share with others your eternal love. Amen

For further thought

How does your church 'beautifully' proclaim God's good news?
How could it do so even more?

The Gospel of Matthew (3) – 1 Resting with Jesus

Notes by **Erice Fairbrother**

Erice is a Benedictine Solitary, an Associate of the Order of the Holy Cross in New Zealand, and a spiritual companion for those seeking to live a contemplative life. As Chaplain to the Associates of the Order, she is often travelling: mentoring, teaching, leading retreats and quiet days. Erice is a published writer, poet and a retired Anglican priest who supports herself through working as a publisher. Regular skype chats with her four grandchildren are her constant source of delight. Erice has used the NRSVA for these notes.

Sunday 27 September
An invitation

> **Read Matthew 11:25–30**
> *'Come to me, all you that are weary and are carrying heavy burdens, and I will give you rest ... For my yoke is easy, and my burden is light.'*
>
> (verses 28 and 30)

'Take time out' – this common expression reminds us that it is good to get some rest – and there are many pathways for us to do just that. Reading, hiking, painting or relaxing with friends are just some examples among many. They provide moments of respite from the heavy life experiences we carry; moments for renewal of body, mind and soul. It is indeed good to be reminded to take time out and get some rest.

'Come to me' – Jesus invites us to rest too. However this rest is not so much about *time out* as *time in* – an invitation to 'opt in' to a relationship with him where we will find a rest that is more than momentary respite and care. This is lasting rest, experienced as a 'yoke' of companionship with God, a companionship that brings relief from carrying life's burdens alone. In the readings this week we meet Jesus living in the heart of human society, yet still having the capacity to listen and reach out. We meet him modelling the life of companionship with God; how wearing that divine 'yoke' can sustain us as we deal with all the things the world in turn deals to us.

† God, source of all peace, give me grace to say 'yes' to your invitation to rest in you.

Monday 28 September
No time like the present

Read Matthew 12:1–14

'I desire mercy and not sacrifice.'

(verse 7b)

Growing up in 1950s New Zealand, it was not uncommon to hear adults say, 'there's no time like the present' – don't do it later, do it – and do it now! Jesus might be saying the same thing to his critics who challenged him for letting his disciples be fed and for not hesitating to heal on the sabbath. The laws in his contemporary context regulated such matters – regulations by which Jesus, in making basic human rights the greater priority, opened up a larger social question: whom do laws serve? Who benefits socially, on the one hand, and who are excluded from social advantage because of them, on the other? It's a continuing debate for us too.

There are many instances in society and in faith communities where we come across these tensions; where responding with mercy conflicts with accepted, legislated community values. As Missioner in a poor suburb in the early 2000s I was under pressure from social agencies to resist giving families food parcels at the time they needed them, creating tensions between ensuring children in those families were fed when they were hungry, and policies dictating how often they could be helped.

Jesus doesn't avoid the debate; by making acts of mercy a priority he showed what argument could not: that neither hunger nor healthcare can be put off until later. Similarly, working to ensure a context of social justice long term can't be put off either. One can't be sacrificed for the other. Both are acts of mercy, both require our attention and for both there is 'no time like the present'.

† God of mercy, give me compassion to stand with those whose need is great, and the courage to advocate for change that will make a difference.

For further thought

What social issues concern you at this time, what conflicting priorities are at stake? Are there insights from today's reading that can be applied to the situation?

The Gospel of Matthew (3) – 1 Resting with Jesus

September

The importance of signage

Read Matthew 12:38–50

Then some of the scribes and Pharisees said to him, 'Teacher, we wish to see a sign from you.'

(verse 38)

We all need signs. They send us in the right direction, they help us when we find ourselves in unknown territory, they encourage us to keep going, they reassure us we're not going to get lost. People around Jesus asked for a sign. They wanted to test him as to whether his teaching was going in the right direction. Jesus declined. Instead, he made the claim that he himself was the sign they needed, inviting them to decide for themselves based on what they see as well as hear. He refers them to Jonah (a reluctant sign if there ever was one!), whose preaching to the people of Nineveh caused them to change direction and turn their lives towards God.

Throughout history many have been recognised as signs for the world: prophets who have caused great shifts in direction through courageous teaching and example. Martin Luther King (USA), Gandhi (India), Te Whiti O Rongomau (NZ) and Nelson Mandela (SA) are representative of all who have stood against the tide of opinion, pointing us in the direction of peace, reconciliation and justice for a better world. That they were true signs was demonstrated in the shifts for good that their leadership caused. It's the challenge Jesus issues to his hearers. The truth of his teaching is shown by the changes of direction that are made as a result of his words. Today's reading challenges us too: to be signs of hope in our time and communities. We don't have to be world leaders, just God's people living what we believe, showing there is another way.

† O God, help me to be a sign of your goodness by being the person you have created me to be: at home, at work and alongside my friends in my community.

For further thought

What does being a sign mean for you? Share your reflections with a friend; what are the challenges, what are the joys?

Wednesday 30 September
Sowing is a seasonal thing!

Read Matthew 13:1–9, 18–23

'But as for what was sown on good soil, this is the one who hears the word and understands it, who indeed bears fruit and yields, in one case a hundredfold, in another sixty, and in another thirty.'

(verse 23)

In 1888 Vincent van Gogh painted this parable, depicting a very nineteenth-century sower at work in his field. Painted now in 2020 it would look very different, perhaps with images of automated farm equipment and machinery, or a farm manager painted with iPad in hand! In whatever way we might visualise it, the parable's understanding of the ground which receives the seed still holds true: that the soil of our lives should be prepared and receptive for God's sustainable harvest to grow within us. However, such receptivity can't be assumed; at different seasons of our lives, readiness to receive has varied according to situations we've found ourselves in and the challenges we've faced.

Some years ago, as a vicar in a university city, I often heard concerns from students who, having been brought up in the faith, were struggling to keep it alive in a university context; they were wrestling with challenges to former understandings of life-giving behaviour, struggling to find a spiritual compass that would hold true in contexts of philosophical and theological debate. They were discovering that the soil we begin with has to be worked over at each stage of our lives. For many, well-known spiritual practices such as regular daily prayer or mentoring by a spiritual companion have proven to be great ways of renewing that soil. As I reflect on this parable at this time of writing, I'm thankful that sowing is a seasonal thing; whatever the season, the sower it seems never fails to be there, sowing God's good news of unconditional love, creating new opportunities for growth.

† Creator God, keep me ever thankful for your faithfulness throughout all the seasons of my life, and grant that I may continue to grow and bear fruit in your world.

For further thought

Take some time to reflect on past seasons of your life. Recall times of receptivity to God and what that has meant in your ongoing journey in the faith.

Thursday 1 October
Something has to be done!

Read Matthew 13:24–30, 36–43

*'The slaves said to him, "Then do you want us to go and gather them?"
But he replied, "No; for in gathering the weeds you would uproot
the wheat along with them. Let both of them grow together until the
harvest; and at harvest time I will tell the reapers."'*

(verses 28b–30a)

Weeds, it has been said, are flowers that never made it onto the list of acceptable plants. However there are acceptable plants which, when transplanted from their natural habitats, become dangerous weeds in their new environments. Someone in today's parable, it seems, has been doing some transplanting; we can imagine the frustration of the field-workers! Something must be done!

In New Zealand there has been similar frustration toward colonists for the same thing. Plants brought from the northern hemisphere have developed into threats to our own native flora and fauna. Something has to be done! We have learned that it takes care to remove transplanted flora without damaging native growth among which they have become established. The work of conservationists exemplifies that necessary protection and care, as does bio-security screening at airports, which works to stop any unwelcome threat at our borders.

Care is needed when impulses to judge, to decide what is acceptable or not in our lives, our churches and society, confront us. Often our 'judgement calls' are transplanted, inherited attitudes from other people, other times and contexts, so that it becomes important to scrutinise them, deciding what to keep in order to nurture good growth in the world we are in now. There are many examples of communities who, having experienced violence and injustice, have gathered together, set aside differences and worked to build communities where compassion could replace violence as normative. Perhaps this is God's true harvest-time: the time when unconscious bias and prejudice are set aside for love of neighbour, and the establishing of God's commonwealth of peace on earth for everyone.

† God of all truth, free me from old learnings and attitudes and help me to see my
neighbour and all of your creation as you see them.

For further thought

Reflect on your own story. What things were important to you once but no longer have the same meaning? How hard has it been to let them go?

Friday 2 October
Seeing God in the familiar

Read Matthew 13:44–58

'Prophets are not without honour except in their own country and in their own house.'

(verse 57b)

In my church in New Zealand we have, over the years, elected three women bishops, none of whom were born and raised here, reminding us as today's reading does that it is hard to recognise what we seek in those closest to us. Jesus makes the wry comment that prophets/leaders are valued anywhere except close to home; it is no less true in the stories of women's leadership in our church. An inability to see past the familiar in our own contexts and communities can blind us to the treasure that is God already at work beside us. During a teacher training day at a local school, teachers were asked to write down the names of every child in their class. At first pens moved rapidly as names came readily to mind, then they slowed as some names and faces were not so easily recalled: a research-based exercise demonstrating that even the best of teachers can overlook quieter, familiar pupils and so miss hidden talents and potentially future top-achievers.

These parables are a reminder to pay attention so that we don't overlook where God actually is. We all want and pray for a peaceful world, yet it is an irony that in our yearning we can miss where peacemakers are quietly at work: facilitators of restorative justice meetings, doctors we know working with Doctors without Borders, Riding for the Disabled and other local charities. We're familiar with many of them; what if we were to them as gospel pearls, nets full of God's goodness, revealing where God's realm is being realised right where we are?

† God of all creation and all people, keep me open to seeing where your Spirit may be at work. Show me how I might share in that work.

For further thought

Is it possible to see God's work being done by others who are not part of your faith community?

The Gospel of Matthew (3) – 1 Resting with Jesus

October

God's rest – a lived reality

Read Matthew 14:1–12

The king was grieved, yet out of regard for his oaths and for the guests, he commanded it to be given; he sent and had John beheaded in the prison.

(verses 9–10)

This week we have met Jesus as he has been challenged for his care of the hungry, had his teaching rejected and his healing ministry questioned; what kind of rest is this? Perhaps it is more of a spiritual resilience that upholds us no matter what we might face, a depth of trust that allows us to grieve, rage or react however we might need to when life's pain becomes too much. I wonder if that was what sustained Jesus and his friends as they received news of John's gruesome death and quietly buried him. As a child at Sunday school, shielded from any expression of feelings, this was for me just a story, distant, not very real.

Later, however, it did become very real. I remember when, on receiving an email asking me to pray for a family of faith whose son had died in a similar way, I began to understand how real that ancient story actually was. There was no comfort of time or distance now, no escaping the impact of it; only tears and candlelight could articulate my prayers in the face of it. It was a reminder to me that there is neither distance nor time – not even faith – that can shield us from the depths of human suffering, nor from the reality that words won't always be able to express the impact we experience. Perhaps this is the time when faith has to become lived prayer, visible and real, embodying God's hope in a commitment to actively live in love with our neighbours no matter the cost.

† Increase my trust, O God, so that I might learn to love my neighbour as you have loved me and not be afraid.

For further thought

We are used to using words to say what we believe. Can we trust that others might actually be able to see what we believe?

The Gospel of Matthew (3) – 2 You are the Messiah

Notes by **Pete Wheeler**

Pete leads St Peter's, an Anglican Church plant on a deprived 1960s estate in Aylesbury, UK. Having spent the previous twenty years working composing, producing and licensing music for film and TV, he trained at St Mellitus Theological College, London. He is married to, and leads church with, Ali, a graphic designer. They have two teenagers. As well as music, Pete's creative downtime involves golf and lapsang souchong. Pete has used the NIVUK for these notes.

Sunday 4 October
You do it!

Read Matthew 14:13–21

As evening approached, the disciples came to him and said, 'This is a remote place, and it's already getting late. Send the crowds away, so that they can go to the villages and buy themselves some food.' Jesus replied, 'They do not need to go away. You give them something to eat.'

(verses 15–16)

Have you ever heard a story of a life being saved, and called it a miracle? That's what I think this week's readings in Matthew are all about: seeing the miraculous saving work of a Messiah.

Jesus, saddened by the death of his cousin John, wants to withdraw to a quiet, remote place, but the people, hungry to be fed by the Messiah's teaching, follow him.

What Jesus does next is astonishing. Despite tiredness and sadness, Jesus draws on the one thing that can give him the impetus and strength to minister in such times … compassion (verse 14). Compassion is a compelling and deep desire to draw closer, to meet the needs of, provide for and feed God's people. Compassion is the motion of your heart prompting you to act. Compassion is enabling.

Imagine their surprise as the disciples turn to Jesus expecting him to act immediately in great power, and instead he looks at them and simply says, 'You do it.' And they do. The Messiah gives thanks and passes the food to the disciples (verse 19). Who performs the miracle?

Meet the Messiah who comes to save and feed his people … through ordinary folks like you and me.

† Lord Jesus, help me to listen to my own heart and allow it to be broken for the things that break yours. Give me a compassion that is compelling, that I may do your will.

Monday 5 October
The Messiah calls ... Come!

Read Matthew 14:22–36

'Lord, if it's you,' Peter replied, 'tell me to come to you on the water.'
'Come,' he said.

Then Peter got down out of the boat, walked on the water and came towards Jesus ...

Then those who were in the boat worshipped him, saying, 'Truly you are the Son of God.'

(verses 28–29, 33)

The Messiah is empowering! Earlier, on a remote hillside, Jesus turned to his hungry disciples and said, 'You do it.' And they did. Now, walking towards them on distant waters, Jesus beckons Peter – 'Come!' And Peter does. The Messiah is calling.

The Messiah is calling! Jesus' invitation to 'Come!' compels Peter to get out of the boat and Jesus welcomes Peter's desire to reach him. He draws Peter, you and me into the moment. Sometimes my fear influences how I welcome and invite others into my life. I fear rejection. I forget that the Messiah is here.

The Messiah is here! It has been said that both fear and faith have something in common: they both believe in something that hasn't happened yet. Fear then, is just faith that is placed in the wrong outcome. Peter's faith wanders momentarily to an outcome based on fear: that he will sink and drown. Sometimes my fear of failure influences my decision making. I forget that the Messiah is Saviour.

The Messiah is Saviour! Immediately, Jesus reaches out to Peter in his moment of need (verse 31). Matthew wants his Jewish readers to realise that the God of Israel is here to stay. He has not forgotten them or you. His promises are always faithful, for the Messiah is worthy.

The Messiah is worthy! What follows is an outpouring of open and uninhibited worship: not only a reaction to what they have seen Jesus do, but, more importantly, a revelatory recognition of who he is. 'Truly,' they confess, 'you are the son of God' (verse 33).

† Messiah, Saviour, help me to remember that your Holy Spirit is ever present. I will not be afraid, for you are with me. Teach me then to turn fear into faithful action.

For further thought

Again, Jesus withdraws to pray (verse 23). We are building a picture of how the Messiah prioritises his time, and prayer and reflection seem to be high on the list!

Tuesday 6 October
Peter, you and me

Read Matthew 15:1–20

Jesus called the crowd to him and said, 'Listen and understand. What goes into someone's mouth does not defile them, but what comes out of their mouth, that is what defiles them.'

(verses 10–11)

In 1845–49 a great potato famine devastated the country of Ireland. Year after year the potato crop was pulled from the ground looking healthy. Yet when they were cut into, every single potato was found to be rotten from the inside out, affected by a terrible blight.

On the outside, it is easy to keep up appearances, and even easier to believe that 'doing good' can somehow bring us back into relationship with God. Yet works, customs, traditions and even Torah law cannot release us. Only the work of a Messiah can set us free. Jesus points out to the Pharisees that what goes *in* to a person's mouth is, therefore, of little consequence compared to what comes out of it! And what comes out is determined by the shape and posture of our hearts.

Despite this teaching, Peter struggles to remember all this (see Galatians 2:11–14). A children's song I wrote, 'Peter, You & Me', tells the story of his journey in recognising Jesus as Messiah. Here's a verse and chorus:

Jesus called the crowd and said, 'Now listen, understand. It's not the things he eats which brings a sin into a man. It's what you think and say and do, which shows what's in your heart.' And Peter knew this was his chance to make a brand-new start. And just like Peter I keep learning that his love for me is true. He'll always be my friend for life no matter what I do And though I may feel ordinary, To him I'm not just anybody. He came to set us free; Peter, you and me.

† Jesus, you have done it all. You are the Messiah. Let the shape of my heart reflect your great love for me in everything I say and do.

For further thought

'And just like Peter I keep learning ...' Are you committed to lifelong learning like Peter? How might you renew your heart and mind today? Perhaps start reading a new book?

The Gospel of Matthew (3) – 2 You are the Messiah

October

Wednesday 7 October
Faith and reason

Read Matthew 15:21–28

Then Jesus said to her, 'Woman, you have great faith! Your request is granted.' And her daughter was healed at that moment.

(verse 28)

I have heard and read many differing interpretations of this passage, probably because it's not that easy to understand the context and mannerism in which Jesus is speaking. Today, I just want to draw two simple things out of this passage.

Firstly, it's this woman's simple faith in the Messiah's redeeming power that is the motivation for her to go deeper. Jesus says her faith is 'great', yet she may have known very little about Jesus. What matters is that she believes in *who* he is. Perhaps the quantity of your faith matters less than *whom* you choose to put it in?

Sometimes when I ask people if they might get involved in a ministry, or gather friends to read the Bible together, I get a reply along the lines of, 'I don't really know enough to do that!' Or, 'If I can just get myself into a good place, then my faith will follow!' Well, if you are waiting until you know enough, or have enough faith, you will never put yourself fully into God's hands! God desires that we come to him in weakness and in humility, not in strength and pride.

Secondly, like this Canaanite woman, it's reasonable to reason with God (verse 27). Abraham even debates with God on behalf of Sodom (Genesis 18:22–33). Jacob, Moses, Jonah, David, Job, Nehemiah … the list goes on. Reasoning with God can be part of our faith journey. Even in our fragility, God is pleased that we come to him, to wrestle and reason. He is strong enough to cope, and lovingly patient with us.

† Messiah, you are enough for me in every way. Teach me to trust you so that I live life taking risks, however large or small, for you.

For further thought

What's preventing you from pressing forward? Do you need all the answers, or just a simple faith? Do you need to be in a good place, or just a place where God is?

Thursday 8 October
A question of identity

Read Matthew 16:13–20

'But what about you?' he asked. 'Who do you say I am?'
Simon Peter answered, 'You are the Messiah, the Son of the living God.'

(verses 15–16)

At a music industry conference, having misread a name badge, I realised my colleague and I had mistakenly met and struck up conversation with the wrong person. I remember the confused look on my colleague's face as I subtly (and cowardly!) stepped a pace backwards out of that conversation, leaving him to discover the identity error for himself, much to our later amusement.

Right in the centre of Matthew's Gospel, a critical question of identity is asked of Peter by Jesus himself. What will Peter say? Will he get it right?

Unfortunately, in the fourth century, Bishop Theodore of Mopsuestia got it rather wrong, suggesting that Jesus was not that different from us, other than that God was particularly close to him. Theo's claim would mean that Jesus was little more than a jolly nice role model for doing good. But how would that save us? This is not the gospel!

This same question of Jesus' identity is recurrent throughout Matthew's account: at Jesus' baptism ('This is my Son', Matthew 3:17); Caiaphas' questions ('Tell us if you are the Messiah', Matthew 26:63); the disciples in the boat ('Truly you are the Son of God', Matthew 14:33); the Roman soldier at the cross ('Surely he was the Son of God!', Matthew 27:54).

Peter's confession, that Jesus is the Messiah, the God-Man, doesn't just announce Jesus' arrival, but heralds the coming kingdom of God! In this kingdom, evil is driven out, the sick are healed, the lowly are lifted, the hungry are fed and the dead are raised to life! Jesus is Lord! Hope is here.

This is the gospel!

† Lord, I'm sorry for all that I've done. I'm a sinner saved by your love. You, Lord, are the Messiah, the Son of the living God. Build your kingdom here, I pray.

For further thought

Today, find and have a listen to the song 'Everyday' by Tom Smith. I can imagine Peter singing this song, confessing Jesus as Saviour and Healer.

The Gospel of Matthew (3) – 2 You are the Messiah

October

Friday 9 October
The descent

Read Matthew 17:1–13

But Jesus came and touched them. 'Get up,' he said. 'Don't be afraid.' When they looked up, they saw no one except Jesus.

(verses 7–8)

In 1982, an American man, Larry Walters, attached some helium balloons to a garden chair and took off into the air, only to discover he couldn't get down as he'd hoped. Passing passenger aircraft spotted him as he drifted into federal airspace at 16,000 feet. He eventually came down, unharmed, but landed on power cables, causing a blackout for miles around.

Like Larry's ambition to stay in the air, Peter tries to preserve and memorialise this glorious moment of ascent by building a tent on the mountain. But the 'gravity' and reality of the Messiah's plan is one of descent: to 'tabernacle' among us, revealing his radiant glory (John 1:14). Indeed, mountains in scripture always demonstrate a downward, descending movement of God's grace and activity, flowing down the slopes and outward into all creation. Later, Peter recognises this moment as a call for Jesus' followers to be a prophetic voice in this world (2 Peter 1).

So, when you encounter God on the mountain there is only one way to go: back down and out into the world, reflecting his glory as you go. It's a scary prospect to descend. We fear a power blackout.

So where are your eyes focused? In the valley of the shadow, what distracts you? Perhaps you begin to compare yourself to others? Perhaps past memories hold you back? If you're in the valley and need a fresh revelation of the Messiah, then lift your head, look back up the mountain and focus your eyes solely upon Jesus (Hebrews 12:2).

He is worthy. He is sufficient. His grace is enough.

† Messiah, help me to keep my eyes fixed on your radiant glory. Walk with me today in the valley, by the power and presence of your Holy Spirit.

For further thought

Need encouragement? Read 2 Peter 1 to hear Peter remember this mountain moment and use it to encourage others in their discipleship journey.

Saturday 10 October
The freedom of the kingdom

> **Read Matthew 17:22–27**
>
> *'What do you think, Simon?' he asked. 'From whom do the kings of the earth collect duty and taxes – from their own children or from others?'*
>
> *'From others,' Peter answered.*
>
> *'Then the children are exempt,' Jesus said to him.*
>
> (verses 25b–26)

To the twenty-first-century world, most people's definition of freedom is being able to do *whatever* you like, *whenever* you like, with, or to, *whomever* you like. Sometimes there is a hurriedly added caveat: 'as long as you're not hurting anyone!', they try to explain.

However, this kind of freedom does hurt. It's the freedom of the addict to be bound by their addiction; the freedom to be greedy and self-obsessed; and it prompts us to view our neighbour's freedoms as a limitation on our individual freedom – all of which is actually no freedom at all.

God's freedom is something different. It is the freedom to live in God's kingdom, under the reign of the king, loving and serving others within its loving bounds. Much like a proper football match needs two goals, a referee, pitch markings and rules that each team are happy to play within. Without them, no one enjoys it.

In this exchange, the Messiah tells Peter that there will be no 'tax' for the inhabitants of God's coming kingdom (verse 26). After all, why should God's children pay tax for worshipping in the temple of their Father? Nevertheless, Jesus also gives Peter a way to witness the Messiah in the prevailing culture: it is Jesus' provision that will pay the tax, and by paying it with Peter, he also demonstrates a kingdom kinship. They are sons together.

Sometimes, changing how the world works isn't an immediate option for us. We must witness Christ's freedom to our culture, modelling it through loving and serving others.

† Messiah, thank you for the true freedom of living in your kingdom. Teach me to rely on your provision and to be patient with others as I seek to make you known.

For further thought

How might you apply some of these freedom principles to living an ecologically sustainable lifestyle? The freedom to care for creation is an essential part of kingdom living.

The Gospel of Matthew (3) – 3 The greatest commandment

Notes by **Edel McClean**

 Edel is a Roman Catholic laywoman currently employed as a learning and development officer within the Methodist Church. She is a spiritual director, supervisor, facilitator and coach. She grew up in Northern Ireland and now lives in Bury, England. She is passionate about Ignatian discernment and integrating a lived awareness of God into all that we do. Edel has used the NRSVA for these notes.

Sunday 11 October
Wedding invitations

Read Matthew 22:1–14

'Go therefore into the main streets, and invite everyone you find to the wedding banquet.'

(verse 9)

This is a tough passage with which to begin the week. This parable has been used to justify terrible things, by people who think themselves placed to decide who's 'in' and who's 'out', forgetting that it's the host, not the guests, who decides who's dressed for the party.

It seems extraordinary that anyone would so determinedly resist attending a wedding or murder the hapless deliverer of the invitation. Nor is the king a model of generosity; when 'the wedding is ready' (verse 8), he steps aside and dispatches his troops to destroy those murderers and burn their cities (inhabited by the innocent as well as the guilty). Then he sends out his slaves to muster whoever can be found (watching cities drenched in blood going up in flames might provide motivation). Finally sitting down to the feast, the king spots someone wearing the wrong clothes, and when he proves speechless, he is pitched out into the outer darkness.

Those final lines, for me, are where the hope lies. For we know another man who stood silent before his accuser and who was nailed hand and foot, outside the gates of the city, where there was weeping and gnashing of teeth.

† Jesus, friend and brother, help me to seek and to find you, even when everything seems bleak.

Monday 12 October
Love the Lord your God

Read Matthew 22:15–22, 34–40

'You shall love the Lord your God with all your heart, and with all your soul, and with all your mind.'

(verse 37)

You might notice the difference between the version of this commandment found in Deuteronomy and the one found here. Matthew's comes via a translation of Hebrew into Greek into English, so that Deuteronomy's 'strength' becomes Matthew's 'mind'. It's interesting to wonder why we've travelled from 'strength' to 'mind', different traditions having different understandings of the elements of the human person.

Whatever elements you believe make up the human person, this commandment says all are capable of loving God. Our heart can beat lovingly, our soul can contemplate lovingly, our mind can enquire lovingly, our strength can labour lovingly. What the commandment is attempting to encompass is that we are to love God with *everything*.

Our love of God is to encompass the whole of our lives. It is to influence how we engage with our emotions, how we understand ourselves, how we pray, how we think, where and why we labour. Like a sponge underwater, our whole being is to be saturated, filled up to the brim, dripping with the love of God.

I've had the privilege of meeting a few people who really do seem to live this way. They have a kindness, a wisdom, a balance, a no-nonsense gentleness, a deep trust in God. Just being in their company is to catch some of the overflowing of their love for God. Just being in their company is to feel both loved and challenged to have the courage to offer God the whole of myself in love.

† Jesus, friend and brother, help me to open up the whole of my heart, soul, strength and mind, to live in love of you.

For further thought

In what part of yourself – heart, soul, strength or mind – do you find it hardest to live lovingly? How might God want you to respond?

The Gospel of Matthew (3) – 3 The greatest commandment

October

Tuesday 13 October
Warning against hypocrisy

Read Matthew 23:1–12

'They do all their deeds to be seen by others ...'

(verse 5a)

Today's passage, at its core, is a call to humility. Humility is, unfortunately, a slippery virtue. 'Humblebragging' and 'virtue signalling' are common critiques on social media and they seem to capture exactly what Jesus is criticising here. When Jesus says that the scribes and Pharisees 'do all their deeds to be seen by others' (verse 5), he could easily be commenting on a selfie-obsessed society.

The question is of inner intention: whether we choose to do something because it is the right thing to do, or because it will make us look good. It's not always easy to untangle even our own motivations. It's natural enough to want the respect, approval and love of our colleagues, members of our congregation, family or friends. Often (but not always) the admiration of people who love us will be won by doing the right thing. What's harder is to ask if we want the respect, approval and love of God just as much, even though the rewards seem less tangible?

Sometimes discernment means taking decisions which will change how people think of you, such as the choice between spending more time with an elderly parent or attending the church house group, between giving yourself rest or serving on a church committee. It helps to ask God how God looks at the options, to check which might give God greatest pleasure. Then, whether others notice or approve or not, you can pay attention to your most important audience and live your decision with confidence.

† Jesus, friend and brother, help me to pay attention to how you want me to live in this world with you.

For further thought

Where do you notice the desire to act in ways that will win the approval of others? Can you ask God how to respond to those desires?

Wednesday 14 October
Faithful endurance

Read Matthew 24:1–14

'... the love of many will grow cold. But anyone who endures to the end will be saved.'

(verses 12b–13)

It is hard to live through what is happening in our world. In the West there is a coarsening of public discourse, a rise of populism. On top of that we face global warming and the havoc being wreaked by our addiction to plastic. Two thousand years on from Christ's words in our reading today, the world has not lost its brutality.

I'm attracted to the idea of 'enduring to the end' in verse 13. Christians often emphasise the importance of celebration, rejoicing, thankfulness. Endurance is not a word in vogue, and yet I talk to faithful Christians who find their church attendance a practice in endurance rather than enthusiasm. I talk to faithful Christians who campaign and volunteer and advocate and yet feel that things keep getting worse. I talk to charity workers who leap into action after natural disasters when within days public attention is diverted to some new disaster.

Unglamorous endurance is the ability to keep believing that God is at work, to keep putting one foot in front of another even though a gale is blowing in your face, to keep your love glowing even when it feels 99 per cent impossible. Such people will be saved, and what's more, such people will save us, for they are our ambassadors of hope.

† Jesus, friend and brother, help us to endure lovingly, in the face of the darkness in our world.

For further thought

Where do life, work and ministry feel like endurance for you? How does Jesus respond to your endurance?

The Gospel of Matthew (3) – 3 The greatest commandment

October

Thursday 15 October
Keep awake

Read Matthew 24:33–44

'Keep awake therefore, for you do not know on what day your Lord is coming.'

(verse 42)

My earliest memory of this passage is from seeing it painted on the gable ends of Gospel Halls in towns and cities across Northern Ireland, presumably as a command to get your house in order given the unpredictability of the time of either your own death or the Second Coming. For a child it was a terrifying image. In reality it is more likely that Matthew's intention was to refer to the crisis coming to Jerusalem and the surrounding lands in the war between Judea and Rome. People assumed that life would continue as it had always been when suddenly the city was riven with violence. The passage is rightly terrifying, but for the unpredictability of life as much as of death.

It adds perspective when we watch the news. The immigrants pouring out of impoverished countries where they can imagine no future, the people caught in the crossfire of civil wars, the parents desperately trying to keep their children safe in war zones – these people are not different from us. They are in every way as deserving as us, as good, as kind. They have the same hopes, the same fears, they care for their family and friends just as we do.

In the midst of this unpredictability we cannot assume that the perils of life will never come to our door, but in the terrifying moment, the Son of Man also comes. This is not warning but reassurance. Whether we are the one taken or the one left behind, Jesus will be by our side.

† Jesus, friend and brother, in the insecurities of life help us to trust that our security is in you.

For further thought

What feelings are evoked by the prospect of the Son of Man coming to you? How might Jesus want to reassure you?

Waiting with expectant attentiveness

Read Matthew 25:1–13

'Keep awake therefore, for you know neither the day nor the hour.'

(verse 13)

While it's tempting to interpret this parable as advice about storing up good works or faith, or hope, that doesn't really fit with Matthew, nor with the audience to whom Jesus was talking. This is Jesus pointing to his own Messianic identity: 'I am the Bridegroom.' Have his people held themselves in preparedness, are they awake to see the coming of their Messiah, or have they fallen asleep, off guard and unprepared? Are they awake enough to see what's right in front of their eyes, or have they stopped paying attention, stopped waiting, stopped expecting God to get involved in their lives, so that they aren't prepared when he comes? Some of them, obviously, were awake. Many, roused from drowsiness by Jesus' words and deeds, got to their feet and followed. Others continued to drowse on, not seeing who it was who had come to them.

So are we prepared? 'Stay awake, because you do not know either the day or the hour.' Chances are that Jesus isn't talking about final judgement, this is not about what we've stored up to produce as evidence of our goodness at some future date. This is more about whether we live in expectation. Whether we expect him to be involved here and now. Are our eyes open? Are we willing to be surprised? Are we willing to see him come in his own time and in his own way? Because he will surely come to us – one way or another – but not necessarily as we expect.

† Jesus, friend and brother, help us to keep our eyes and ears open to the ways in which you seek to come to us today.

For further thought

How might living with a sense of active expectation of Jesus coming to us change our experience of our day-to-day lives?

The Gospel of Matthew (3) – 3 The greatest commandment

October

Saturday 17 October
Sheep and goats

Read Matthew 25:31–46

'Lord, when was it that we saw you hungry and gave you food, or thirsty and gave you something to drink?'

(verse 37b)

Jesus is all over the place in today's passage. He is the one telling the story. He is the one sitting on the throne. He is also in the hungry, the thirsty, the strangers, the naked, the sick, the prisoners. His words point towards his refusal to be confined and contained. This account is intended, at least in part, as a comfort for Matthew's persecuted early Christian community, and continues to serve as a comfort to persecuted Christians, with the assurance that Jesus sees and cares about their suffering.

I also find myself wondering if some sheep are a little goat-like and some goats a little sheepish? Even people who care for people in need 90 per cent of the time, will walk by 10 per cent of the time. Even people who 90 per cent of the time are utterly selfish, 10 per cent of the time will greet those in need with kindness. In that case, it would seem, the goat herd might be significantly diminished.

It's also true that, choosing to be in the latter group, choosing to turn a blind eye to the suffering of others, is likely in the end to inflict suffering on ourselves. As James Baldwin wrote, 'it is a terrible, an inexorable law that one cannot deny the humanity of another without diminishing one's own.'[10]

The other insight that strikes me is that Jesus recognises his flock as those who choose to visit the sick and the imprisoned. And so it seems unlikely that Jesus would have the will to imprison people in eternal agony, without also desiring to go to meet them there.

† Jesus, friend and brother, help me to be a carrier of your generosity and kindness to those whom I meet today.

For further thought

Think of one or two people whom you strongly dislike. Can you see anything 'sheepish' in them?

---

10 Baldwin, J. (1991), *Nobody Knows My Name* (London: Penguin), p. 71.

1 The beginning – the heavens declare

Notes by **Heather Prince** and **Andrew Kruger**

 Heather and Andrew were raised in South Africa, and married there in 2013. Andrew is ordained as an Anglican priest and has a master's in theology from the University of Kwa-Zulu Natal. He served on the secretariat of the Anglican Church of Southern Africa's Prayer Book Revision project and is an avid scholar of the liturgy. Heather and Andrew live in New Jersey, USA, where Andrew serves as priest-in-charge at Trinity Episcopal Church in Cranford. Heather is a graduate student in astrophysics at Princeton University and a qualified yoga teacher. They have used the NRSVA for these notes.

Sunday 18 October
Worship on Mars

Read Genesis 1:14–19

And God said, 'Let there be lights in the dome of the sky to separate the day from the night; and let them be for signs and for seasons and for days and years.'

(verse 14)

This week, marking a Mars rover mission proposed by NASA for this year, we consider the Bible's perspective on stars, the universe and earth's place in it all.

While the possibility of a human colony on Mars is still the stuff of science fiction, the thought of how Christians might worship on the red planet is an interesting proposition. Our worship on earth has been shaped, informed and enriched by seasons and years. Easter Day, for example, is always held on the first Sunday after the vernal equinox. In the northern hemisphere this coincides wonderfully with spring 'announcing' Jesus' resurrection.

Those who worship in the southern hemisphere are required to think more creatively about how to celebrate Easter in autumn. There are ways of thinking about resurrection life that are in step with autumn. For example, Easter comes on the heels of rains and harvests that make life possible for people through the winter.

What would the rhythm of worship look like on Mars? It takes Mars approximately twice as long to orbit the sun compared to earth. Would a church on Mars celebrate Easter 'twice a year' at the same times that the feast is kept on earth? Summer and winter on Mars are both more extreme and longer in duration; how might these 'super seasons' shape and inform worship on Mars?

† Source of life, you have established the seasons and the years; help us to worship you in tune with the rhythms of the earth. Amen

The mystery of suffering

> **Read Job 38:31–38**
> *'Can you bind the chains of the Pleiades, or loose the cords of Orion? Can you lead forth the Mazzaroth in their season, or can you guide the Bear with its children? Do you know the ordinances of the heavens? Can you establish their rule on the earth?'*
>
> (verses 31 and 33)

The book of Job is a fascinating text that explores, among other things, the problem of pain and suffering in the human experience. Chapter 1 of the book asserts that Job is a righteous man whom Satan is allowed to afflict. Therefore the narrative begins by subverting the popularly held notion that righteous living leads to health, whereas sinful conduct results in suffering.

Job's three friends, together with a fourth speaker, Elihu, offer their poetic theories as to why Job is suffering so much. For the first time, at chapter 38, the voice of God is introduced to the dialogue. God's speech compares Job's limited knowledge to God's infinite awareness, understanding and insight. In particular God's speech highlights Job's ignorance of meteorological phenomena and constellations.

The Gaia spacecraft studies the Milky Way by mapping out the positions and motions of a billion stars, and will release this data in 2021. To do this it observes the stars from space using efficient CCD (charge-coupled device) cameras. The many years put into planning and executing this state-of-the-art mission allow astronomers to study the Milky Way with unprecedented accuracy, but the billion stars mapped by Gaia still constitute only one per cent of the estimated 100 billion stars in our galaxy.

Despite remarkable technological advances, our knowledge of the stars and of suffering remain limited. When confronted with those who are suffering, our silent supportive presence is always valued far more than any of our best rationalisations or platitudes.

† Omniscient and faithful God, help us to trust in your love and wisdom when the trials of this life bring us to our wits' end. Amen

For further thought

Looking at the stars one night this week, consider both how much we know about the universe, and how much more there is to know.

Tuesday 20 October
The universe is even bigger than you think

Read Psalm 8

*O Lord, our Sovereign, how majestic is your name in all the earth! …
When I look at your heavens, the work of your fingers, the moon and
the stars that you have established; what are human beings that you are
mindful of them, mortals that you care for them?*

(verses 1a and 3–4)

It is hard to conceive of just how huge the universe is. One of the
longest flights in the world is around 9,000 miles (or 14,500 km)
from Auckland to Doha. It takes about eighteen hours on a Boeing
777 flying at an average speed of 500 miles per hour. Light travels
more than a million times faster than a plane, so light would take
one-twentieth of a second to travel this distance.

The journey between the earth and the sun takes light just over
eight minutes. Completing the same journey at 500 mph would
take you about twenty years at the speed of a Boeing 777. By
comparison, light would take a long 100,000 years to cross the
Milky Way galaxy, and 110 million years to travel across the local
supercluster, which contains many clusters of galaxies including
the Milky Way. There are an estimated *ten million* superclusters of
galaxies in the observable universe.

God's loving attention encompasses the vastness of the entire
universe, yet God still cares intimately for every creature on earth.
When Psalm 8 was composed, people could only see the nearest
and brightest stars in our galaxy, which nevertheless inspired such
awe in the psalmist. How much more amazed should we be, now
that we are more aware of the majestic mysteries of creation!

† O Lord, the heavens proclaim your majesty and declare your splendour; fill us with
wonder as we contemplate the vast expanse of interstellar space. Amen

For further thought
How does the vastness of the universe affect your perception of
God?

1 The beginning – the heavens declare

October

Wednesday 21 October
The limitation of language

> **Read Psalm 19:1–6**
>
> *The heavens are telling the glory of God; and the firmament proclaims his handiwork ... There is no speech, nor are there words; their voice is not heard; yet their voice goes out through all the earth, and their words to the end of the world.*
>
> (verses 1 and 3–4)

The first part of Psalm 19 (verses 1–6) articulates how God is made known to humanity through the natural world. Later, in verses 7–10, the psalmist goes on to show that God is revealed through the law or the revelation of scripture. These 'natural' and 'ethical' sections are linked. The sun is to the natural world what the scriptures are for the person seeking understanding. As the sun warms the earth, so the scriptures give light to human reason. However, the eloquence of the heavens and the scriptures will always be limited by human words.

No speech can adequately describe the nature of reality. This is illustrated by the concept of wave-particle duality in quantum mechanics: electrons and light cannot be described as purely particles or waves, but behave like one or the other depending on the situation. An electron is sometimes well-described by the scientific concept of a particle and sometimes behaves like the scientific concept of a wave, but ultimately it can't be fully described by either.

Similarly, we can describe God using many different metaphors – a rock of refuge, a mother hen, a sacrificial lamb – but God's true nature can never be fully captured in human concepts and language. The Heisenberg uncertainty principle of quantum mechanics acknowledges a fundamental limit to how much we can know about reality; it states that you can either make a very good measurement of where a particle is or how fast it is going, but you can't measure them both precisely at the same time. Both science and religion leave space for mystery.

† Almighty God, you revealed yourself to Elijah in the sound of sheer silence; grant to us both the desire to know you more deeply, and the serenity to accept your mystery. Amen

For further thought

Take a moment to leave space for mystery today.

Thursday 22 October
Easter and the Big Bang

Read Psalm 33:6–9

By the word of the Lord the heavens were made, and all their host by the breath of his mouth … Let all the earth fear the Lord; let all the inhabitants of the world stand in awe of him.

(verses 6 and 8)

Psalm 33 references the first creation story of Genesis which tells of how God spoke creation into existence. The first words of God in Genesis are, 'Let there be light!' (1:3). It is a happy coincidence that these poetic words echo scientific reality.

The early universe was dominated by intense, hot light. As the universe expanded and cooled, the light elements (hydrogen, helium and lithium) were formed. The hydrogen present in the water molecules in our bodies was created during the first few minutes after the Big Bang. Later on, once the universe had cooled even further, stars formed and fused together the heavier elements in their cores, including carbon, which is vital for forming organic compounds. These stars exploded in violent supernovae which spread the heavy elements through the interstellar medium, and some of the carbon and oxygen ended up in humans, in the food we eat and in the water we drink.

Rowan Williams, the former Archbishop of Canterbury, writes, 'When we celebrate Easter, we are really standing in the middle of a second "Big Bang", a tumultuous surge of divine energy as fiery and intense as the very beginning of the universe.'[11] The resurrection of Jesus Christ is nothing less than a new Creation that makes abundant life available to us. May each of us stand in awe of this reality at work in us, through us and among us.

† God of radiant light; set us ablaze with the power of your love and propel us into the world to live and proclaim the gospel of the living Lord. Amen

For further thought

What images would you use to describe God's energy of life in the resurrection?

1 The beginning – the heavens declare

October

---

11 Williams, R. (2010), *Tokens of Trust* (Westminster: John Knox Press), p. 95.

Friday 23 October
There is no Planet B

Read Psalm 115:14–18

The heavens are the Lord's heavens, but the earth he has given to human beings.

(verse 16)

The possibility of the earth being destroyed and humanity being forced to colonise another planet has certainly captured the imagination of Hollywood in recent years. The 2014 film *Interstellar* starring Matthew McConaughey and Anne Hathaway comes to mind. Set in a dystopian future where humanity is struggling to survive, the film follows a group of astronauts who travel through a wormhole in search of a new home for humanity. Hollywood films aside, escape from the earth for sanctuary on some distant habitable planet is highly unlikely.

None of the planets or moons in our solar system are habitable for humans without extreme terraforming. Even sending microscopic probes to the nearest star is a wildly ambitious undertaking with many unsolved problems. The Breakthrough Starshot project aims to send tiny 'nanocraft' to our neighbouring star system, Alpha Centauri, by using lasers to push on lightsails attached to the nanocraft, accelerating them to a significant fraction of the speed of light. Such a journey would take over twenty years, and this technology wouldn't be scalable to allow humans to travel in the same way.

In short, there is no Planet B for us to escape to. Christians may be tempted to take solace in the popular understanding of 'going to heaven' as a way of escaping earth. But God's new creation has begun already, on this earth, with the resurrection of Jesus Christ. Our participation in that new creation necessarily includes taking care of the planet which God has given us.

† Generous God, you have placed the earth in our care; quicken our conscience, that we might be good stewards of your new creation. Amen

For further thought

How can science and religion work together for the good of the planet? What can your church community do?

A priest and an astrophysicist

Read 1 Chronicles 16:23–34

Ascribe to the Lord the glory due his name; bring an offering, and come before him. Worship the Lord in holy splendour; tremble before him, all the earth. The world is firmly established; it shall never be moved.

(verses 29–30)

The past week's reflections have been written by a married couple: Andrew, an episcopal priest; and Heather, an astrophysicist. We routinely encounter people who are surprised that a theologian and a scientist can get on well enough to want to share life and a home together. While it's true that we often respond to the scriptures differently, those responses tend to enrich rather than divide us.

Heather's first reaction to reading about a 'world firmly established and immovable' was to baulk at the scientific inaccuracy. The earth is hurtling through space, orbiting around the sun at 30 km per second, and the sun itself is orbiting around the centre of the galaxy at 200 km per second. Our galaxy is moving towards the nearby Andromeda Galaxy, with which it will collide in a few billion years, but not before our sun heats up enough to cause a runaway greenhouse effect making the earth uninhabitable. I think that God is even more worthy of worship for creating and sustaining life on this fragile, tiny planet in this huge, complex universe than if God had created a stable, simple environment on an unmoving planet for us to live in.

Andrew's first reaction to this text was excitement at finding what is essentially a poem embedded in a history book (1 Chronicles). The poem is in the shape of a psalm and includes parts of Psalm 105, Psalm 96 and Psalm 106. Here is an example of how our ancestors wrote liturgy by adapting, combining and revising existent holy texts for their time and circumstances. Enriching an ancient psalm with imagery from contemporary astrophysics seems like a worthwhile endeavour.

† O God, you created a complex and risky world; inspire our imagination that we may worship you in ways that are both ancient and new. Amen

For further thought

In Ancient Israel, the earth was thought to be a flat disc fixed on the waters, supported by mountains. How might our present understanding change how we think of God?

1 The beginning – the heavens declare

October

The heavens declare – 2 The ending

Notes by **Alesana Fosi Pala'amo**

Alesana is head of the practical theology department at Malua Theological College in Samoa. Ordained as a minister of the Congregational Christian Church Samoa, his research interests include Christian ministry, youth and social ministries, Pacific research methodologies, theology and pastoral counselling. Alesana received his PhD at Massey University New Zealand, with his research on pastoral counselling practices of Samoans. Alesana and wife Lemau have three sons, Norman, Alex and Jayden. Alesana has used the NRSVA for these notes.

Sunday 25 October
Wisdom as the foundation

Read Proverbs 3:19–26

The Lord by wisdom founded the earth; by understanding he established the heavens ...

(verse 19)

Brainwave Trust Aotearoa highlights the early years of a child's development as fundamental to shaping the child's later adolescent and adult years (www.brainwave.org.nz). These 'early years' often range from birth to around three years old. Brain development for the child in the early years captures various experiences that become the foundation for learning in later years. The child's motor skills, speech recognition and use, and social understandings of various contexts are also developed in the early years of the child. Interventions that I often use when counselling parental issues mostly involve exploring the foundational early years of any children involved.

Today's reading shares the importance of having a solid foundation. Wisdom is the foundation of God's created world. God in his wisdom knew what was good for the created world and designed all created beings accordingly. When creation faulted, God knew in his wisdom how to correct the fallen world. Jesus Christ was sent to atone the sins of creation, through his death and resurrection to life. Jesus Christ, the incarnation of God's Wisdom, is the foundation of our entry into God's everlasting kingdom through our faith and acceptance of Christ as Lord.

† Lord God, grant us your wisdom that reminds us to have Jesus Christ as the foundation of our lives.

Remember your roots

> **Read Isaiah 51:13–16**
>
> *You have forgotten the Lord, your Maker, who stretched out the heavens and laid the foundations of the earth.*
>
> (verse 13a)

Forgetfulness is a human condition that most people experience. Take, for example, forgetting where you left the house keys, or the name of a colleague you associated with a decade ago; these situations happen from time to time. Yet with effort and patience in trying to recall names, places and events, remembering a person's name, for example, slowly comes back. Remembering therefore requires effort and deliberate action to evade forgetfulness.

Remembering your roots is a call not to forget one's family and the communities in which one was raised. It means not getting caught up in who we have become, by being overly consumed by any successes and prosperity in the present, yet forgetting the simple and humble beginnings where it all started. Remembering your roots is a call not to forget God's hand in creation, where he has made us the way he intended. It is no accident, our heritage we were born from, our skin tone, nationality, culture and the language that we speak; these are all part of God's grand design in creation. Our part is to accept how God has created us and never to forget all God has done for us.

The prophet Isaiah reminds us how the people of Judah, during the Babylonian captivity, forgot how God restores His people and brings them comfort and salvation. Remembering God takes effort and deliberate actions, such as taking an active role in church practices, and a solid personal prayer life with regular reflections upon the Bible. Such practices ground us in not forgetting that God provides for, comforts and blesses us each and every day.

† God our comforter and provider, help us to always remember that you have made us exactly how we are supposed to be. May we never forget your love and concern in our lives always. Amen

For further thought

Consider and pray for three people that have made some of the greatest impacts on your life today. If you are able, make contact and thank them.

The heavens declare – 2 The ending

October

Tuesday 27 October
Praise the Lord through our actions and words

> **Read Psalm 148**
>
> *He has raised up a horn for his people, praise for all his faithful, for the people of Israel who are close to him. Praise the Lord!*
>
> (verse 14)

Samoa is rapidly changing in many ways. Even praising the Lord has been influenced by changes in Samoa today. Influences including technological advancements, global media, pursuing education and economic stability, migration abroad and returning to Samoa, these have all given rise to a concept I call 'a changing Samoan self'. Such a concept aligns with Western individualistic ideals, ideals that at times clash with a collective and communal focus Samoans are used to. A changing Samoan self has impacted the Samoan way of life, including the lived experiences of its traditions and culture known as *fa'asamoa*.

In the past, sunset marked a time for households to gather together for family evening devotions. It was quiet time for families to worship and praise the Lord. This practice has slowly diminished in its importance, overlooked for extended working hours, school commitments, and using the extra hour from daylight savings for outdoor chores and recreational activities such as touch rugby or volleyball. Praising the Lord through family evening devotions has become not as important for some Samoan families, in line with a changing Samoan self.

Psalm 148 reminds us that all things created in the heavens above and the earth below, must praise the Lord. Everyone, from the kings of the earth to the old and the young, must praise the Lord. For God is Lord of all creation, who has redeemed His people through the salvation Jesus provided with His life, death and resurrection to eternal life. Regardless of changes in the world that we live in, we must remain faithful in praising the Lord through our actions and our words.

† Help us, God, to remain faithful to you by exalting your name through our voices, and praising you, Lord, through our actions. Amen

For further thought

Who is lord? The striving for monetary success, fame and status, or our Lord God Creator of all things great and small? Praise the Lord!

Wednesday 28 October
Timeless

Read Psalm 102:25–27

They will perish, but you endure; they will all wear out like a garment. You change them like clothing, and they pass away.

(verse 26)

On a recent trip to Rome with my wife for the International Association for Counselling (IAC) Conference, we managed to visit the Vatican City and some of the many important sites. We both observed that several of the pagan and Christian statues featured men who were mostly naked with the exception of a few fig tree leaves covering up their midsections. Later we learned from a friend in Rome, well-versed in Roman art and architecture, that the sculptors and artists often depicted their subjects completely unclothed to remove clues that could date their artwork. In other words, presenting the statues in such a way ensured that they become timeless, to remain valid and interesting from the first century CE up until now.

The psalmist in today's reading writes about the timeless nature of God. The author of Psalm 102 is considered to be either King David, Daniel or Nehemiah. Whoever the author may be, the psalmist is one who is under great stress and afflictions. Yet comfort can be found in God, who created all things and remains eternal with years that do not end. God cannot and should not be limited to any time frame. God is infinite and beyond all creation for God is timeless. Likewise, God's love has no limits. God sacrificed his only Son for the sins of the created world. Jesus was not confined to death nor the tomb, and rose victoriously so that all who believe in him can also live eternally, in the kingdom that God has prepared beyond this lifetime.

† Our Infinite God, help us to remember that you supersede all things and remain eternal beyond time. All things are possible through you, our Lord. Amen

For further thought

Try to think outside of the box today. Possibilities are limitless; we ourselves construct and constrict our own limits.

The heavens declare – 2 The ending

October

The patience of a thousand years in a day

Read 2 Peter 3:8–13

But do not ignore this one fact, beloved, that with the Lord one day is like a thousand years, and a thousand years are like one day.

(verse 8)

Initially growing up in the Congregational Christian Church (CCCS/ EFKS) at Vailoa Faleata, Samoa, then at Bankstown EFKS in Sydney, I sometimes wondered what it would be like to become a *faifeau* (minister). As a pastor's kid, there was the expectation by family members and others that one of us would also follow our parents and become faifeau and *faletua* (a minister's wife).

When I passed the entrance exam to Malua Theological College in Samoa to train for four years as a minister, I asked my father for advice about becoming a theological student. I was told to be patient and endure all things. Further, my father challenged me that if I ever felt that I could not cope any more with the pressures of my studies in Samoa, and wanted to quit and return to Sydney, that was precisely the moment that I needed to be patient and endure all things.

God shows us how to be patient, since 1,000 years is like one day to God. The passage from the apostle Peter's second letter teaches about how God stands above time. God waits patiently for his created beings to come right, repent and return to Him in faith by living according to God's will and purpose. God is a patient God, whereas human beings often become impatient when trying to meet their material and worldly needs. This letter teaches us to be aware of false teachings about God, repent of our worldly ways and return to Him before the day of God, when our Lord returns to judge all of God's creation.

† Lord, forgive us for sometimes keeping you waiting upon us. Your patience contrasts with our impatience when we only pursue our worldly and material desires. Help us to trust you and return to you, amene.

For further thought

Are we too busy with our daily lives to remember God? We must slow down, look up from our devices and see God's love that surrounds us.

Friday 30 October
Out with the old, in with the new

Read Revelation 21:22–27

And the city has no need of sun or moon to shine on it, for the glory of God is its light, and its lamp is the Lamb.

(verse 23)

'All things new': this is one way to understand today's reading. White Sunday in Samoa is one day of the year where the children in the parishes enjoy all things new. Celebrated on the second Sunday each October, White Sunday has the worship services led by the young children and the youth. Biblical narratives and the Gospel message are retold through plays, creative dance and singing songs. Contemporary messages about Christian living are also told. Parents buy brand-new white clothes for their children to wear especially for White Sunday. Following the evening service, a *to'ona'i* (feast) is held for the Sunday school, where children also wear brand-new casual wear for their special day.

Today's reading is part of a series of visions the apostle John saw in the first century, while exiled to the Greek island of Patmos. This particular vision describes the coming of a new city, a new Jerusalem for God's faithful people. Its city gates remain open to all who have become renewed. It has no need for a temple like the old Jerusalem, since God and the lamb both dwell in the new city. The glory of God and the lamb are its light that keep the city lit. There is no dark and there is no night. The nations that occupy the city are made up of those who have become new, with no unclean traces of their former lives that remain. Entry into this new Jerusalem is through faith in God, having been cleansed by the blood of the lamb sacrificed for all.

† Lord, thank you for the new Jerusalem that awaits all your faithful ones beyond this life. Help us to uphold lives worthy of your glory in the world in which we live, amene.

For further thought

Do we often romanticise about our past lives and limit any personal growth? Let us embrace our lives today, with a view towards tomorrow.

The heavens declare – 2 The ending

October

The wrath of the lamb

> **Read Revelation 6:12–17**
>
> *... calling to the mountains and rocks, 'Fall on us and hide us from the face of the one seated on the throne and from the wrath of the Lamb; for the great day of their wrath has come, and who is able to stand?'*
>
> (verses 16–17)

As a youngster growing up in Taumarunui, New Zealand, we had a young baby lamb named Willie as one of our family pets. We cared for Willie in his cubbyhole in the laundry of our house. Our family took turns in feeding Willie, using warmed-up milk in a glass Lee bottle fitted with a baby's plastic teat. Willie was a social animal, always liked playing with us, and followed us wherever we led him in our backyard that opened out onto open fields and farmland. Willie became part of our family and often joined us indoors in front of the fireplace during the winter months. Sometimes Willie even followed us siblings into the church for Sunday worship to the surprise of our parents.

The lamb mentioned in today's reading is different to the lamb I shared my upbringing with. Christ is the Sacrificial lamb of God. The vision that the apostle John witnessed is about the sixth of seven seals that he saw. God who is seated on the throne and Christ the Sacrificial lamb of God will pass judgement upon the world at the end of days. Yet there is good news. All who have been smeared with the blood of the Sacrificial lamb of God, simply, all who have accepted Christ as Lord, will be spared from the wrath of the lamb. Just as the firstborn sons of the ancient Israelites were spared from death when their doorposts were smeared with the blood of a young lamb, so too will all who have accepted Christ be saved at the end of days.

† God of Grace, thank you for the salvation we have been gifted through Jesus Christ. May we rejoice in your grace through our faith in Christ, rather than face the wrath of the Lamb. Amen

For further thought

Which would you prefer to be on the receiving end of: the wrath of the lamb, or being saved by the blood of Christ?

The Bible on the world stage

Notes by **Helen Van Koevering**

After living in southern Africa for most of her adult life, Helen, raised in England, moved to the USA in 2015. Helen is rector of St Raphael's Episcopal Church in the Diocese of Lexington, Kentucky, where her husband serves as bishop. She previously served as a parish priest and as director of ministry for the rapidly growing Anglican Diocese of Niassa in northern Mozambique. She is discovering new perspectives for life-giving faithfulness in her new context. Helen has used the NIVUK for these notes.

Sunday 1 November (All Saints' Day)
Suffering and hope: Desmond Tutu (1931–)

Read Romans 5:1–11

... we also glory in our sufferings, because we know that suffering produces perseverance; perseverance, character; and character, hope ... You see, at just the right time, when we were still powerless, Christ died for the ungodly.

(verses 3–4, 6)

This week we read the Bible through the eyes of faithful men and women who made a difference on the world stage. We begin on All Saints' Day, when Christians around the world give thanks for pioneers in the faith from whom we can learn.

Archbishop Emeritus Desmond Tutu is revered for his leadership and witness during the anti-apartheid struggle in South Africa through the 1970s and 1980s. He received a Nobel Peace Prize in 1984, and chaired the Truth and Reconciliation Commission in South Africa after his retirement as Archbishop of the Anglican Church of Southern Africa. Tutu has always been an advocate of Black and African theology. It is appropriate that he is remembered on All Saints' Day, as he saw continuity between African traditional belief and life around him. He led his nation through the darkest hours of the anti-apartheid struggle: an example of the hope of reconciliation and power of forgiveness, an advocate for his people and a voice for the voiceless. However, Tutu's leadership on the world stage is defined by his prayerful spirituality, his love of others and a fun-loving sense of humour that have won over a polarised people and church both locally and globally.

† God, may we also learn to live out the power of forgiveness for reconciliation, and know the joy of witness to Your love. Amen

Living out justice: Dorothy Day (1897–1980)

Read Psalm 9

The wicked go down to the realm of the dead, all the nations that forget God. But God will never forget the needy; the hope of the afflicted will never perish.

(verses 17–18)

Dorothy Day, born in Brooklyn, New York, became interested in radical social causes as a way to help workers and the poorest when a student in Chicago. In 1916, she returned to work in New York City as a journalist on socialist newspapers, participated in protest movements and struggled through a turbulent private life. Her Catholic faith began to take form after the birth of Tamar, her daughter, in 1926. It was whilst covering the 1932 Hunger March in Washington, D.C. for some Catholic magazines that she understood how society could serve the poor and the unemployed. Together, Day and Peter Maurin founded the *Catholic Worker* newspaper, spawning a movement of houses of hospitality and farming communes replicated throughout the United States and other countries.

At the *Catholic Worker*, Dorothy Day lived a life faithful to the injunctions of the gospel. Often the newspaper quoted G.K. Chesterton's famous observation that Christianity hadn't really failed – it had never really been tried. Day's life was spent trying. Her passion was for those on the forgotten margins, and her pilgrimage ended at Maryhouse in New York City, where she died among the poor.

Psalm 9 and its partner, Psalm 10, form one of the Psalter's most forceful statements on behalf of the poor. The stark realities of oppression and injustice are not ignored in this psalm. God in these verses is a 'refuge for the oppressed' (verse 9) and the psalm promises that 'God will never forget the needy' (verse 18). Dorothy Day lived these verses out in her own day, in her own way.

† Lord, the demands of the gospel are not easy, but they are real. Help us to be open to the call of the gospel in our own lives and for those around us. Amen

For further thought

What action could I take for those around me to know the gospel? Who are the needy and afflicted around me?

The day of the Lord: Martin Luther King Jr (1929–68)

Read Amos 5:18–24

'Woe to you who long for the day of the Lord! Why do you long for the day of the Lord? That day will be darkness, not light … But let justice roll on like a river, righteousness like a never-failing stream!'

(verses 18 and 24)

Martin Luther King alluded to this verse, a key text for the 1960s American Civil Rights Movement, on two famous occasions in his life. In his most famous speech, 'I have a dream', delivered to 250,000 gathered at the Lincoln Memorial during the march on Washington, D.C. in 1963, he quoted this verses. And he quoted it in his famous 'Letter from Birmingham Jail', written in the margins of a newspaper later that year. King took the radical call of the Hebrew prophets to social change, encouraging and defending the strategy of non-violent resistance to racism and unjust laws as creating 'constructive tension' towards that end. As a Baptist minister, King responded to criticisms that social change should be fought solely in the courts and not the streets with persuasive sermons. As an activist challenging entrenched social injustice, he argued on legal, political and historical grounds. King aligned himself with what he called the extremism of Jesus rather than the lukewarm 'do-nothingness' of the complacent church. The question, he wrote, was not whether to be extremists, but rather whether to be extremists for hate or for love. Love enabled action in the face of injustice and provocation, the experience of suffering and the need for courage for the oppressed to demand freedom.

Martin Luther King, assassinated in Memphis, Tennessee, at age thirty-nine, has been remembered annually with a federal holiday on 15 January in the USA. His legacy is non-violent protest to racial injustice around the world, for, as he said, where there is injustice anywhere, there is injustice everywhere.

† Lord, thank you for those who have spoken out for radical faith and courage in the face of injustice. May we also know the enabling power of the Holy Spirit to speak for freedom and justice today. Amen

For further thought

What are the global injustices which stir you to join in seeking change through generous engagement and prayerful action?

Reimagining our future: Abraham Joshua Heschel (1907–72)

Read Psalm 119:33–40

Teach me, Lord, the way of your decrees, that I may follow it to the end. Give me understanding, so that I may keep your law and obey it with all my heart. Direct me in the path of your commands, for there I find delight.

(verses 33–35)

Abraham Joshua Heschel was a Polish-born American rabbi and a leading Jewish theologian and philosopher of the twentieth century. In the Second World War, he had been arrested by the German Gestapo and deported to Poland. He lost his sisters and his mother to Nazi bombing and concentration camps, and never returned to Germany, Austria or Poland for the awful memories held there. Yet he believed the teachings of the Hebrew prophets were a clarion call to social action in the USA. He worked for African-American civil rights, marching alongside Martin Luther King in Selma, later writing that, 'when I marched in Selma, I felt my feet were praying.' He protested against US action in the Vietnam War. His theological works argued that religious experience is a human yearning for spirituality and love, a fundamentally human impulse that meant no religious community could claim to be holding the religious truth. For Heschel, the Hebrew prophets were characterised by their experience of God turning towards humanity, taking on human feelings as 'divine pathos' for the voiceless, poor and oppressed that was the ongoing living out of God's rage in the words of the prophets.

His desire for God, and for God's commandments, is captured by the remarkable Psalm 119. The longest psalm in the Psalter, Psalm 119 rhapsodises not just about the goodness of God's teaching, but also about the joy it brings. Following God's teaching, in the vision of this psalm, is not dull drudgery, but delight. There is perhaps no more fitting epitaph for the life and witness of Heschel, who delighted in God's commandments even as he fought racism.

† Lord, let us not forget the heartbreak and rage of God of which the prophets remind us, and never forget our call to hear and act in solidarity with the poorest. Amen

For further thought

Who has modelled the Christian prophetic life to you?

Thursday 5 November
The life of freedom: William Wilberforce (1759–1833)

Read Galatians 5:1, 13–25

It is for freedom that Christ has set us free. Stand firm, then, and do not let yourselves be burdened again by a yoke of slavery ... Since we live by the Spirit, let us keep in step with the Spirit.

(verses 1 and 25)

William Wilberforce was raised in an evangelical merchant family and a friend of evangelicals like John Newton, the former slave trader who penned the hymn 'Amazing Grace'. Wilberforce came to faith at the age of twelve and lived out the Christian gospel as a wealthy Cambridge-educated politician from 1885. He is most remembered for his devotion to the abolition of slavery and to philanthropic causes.

Despite immense opposition, illness and threats to his life, he introduced the Abolition Bill almost annually in the 1790s, whilst also supporting numerous evangelical or philanthropic societies through his circle of friends and the Christian 'Clapham Sect'. These societies included the Church Missionary Society in India and Africa, the British and Foreign Bible Society, the School Society, the Sunday School Society and the Society for Bettering the Condition of the Poor, focused on relieving the suffering of the manufacturing poor, reform in hospital care, asylums, infirmaries, refugees and penitentiaries. The Commons finally voted to abolish the slave trade in 1807 and Wilberforce continued to lobby other governments to end the institution of slavery. Just three days before his death in 1833, he heard that the House of Commons had passed a law emancipating all slaves in the British Empire.

For Wilberforce, keeping 'in step with the Spirit' made him a lifelong, tireless, compassionate public servant with gifts of leadership, persistence and persuasion, whose partnerships for change serve as a model for Christians working together to bring freedom and social justice to the world.

† Lord, may we surround ourselves with models of faithful change-makers, and know the hope, compassion and peace we need to be the change we want to see in the world. Amen

For further thought
How are you, your church and your community being the change you want to see in this world?

The Bible on the world stage

November

Seeing Jesus in the vulnerable: Mother Teresa (1910–97)

Read Proverbs 31:17–21

She sets about her work vigorously; her arms are strong for her tasks. She sees that her trading is profitable, and her lamp does not go out at night ... She opens her arms to the poor and extends her hands to the needy.

(verses 17–18 and 20)

Mother Teresa was born Agnes Bojaxhiu, taking the name of Teresa after St Thérèse of Lisieux when she became a nun. Born in Macedonia to parents of Albanian descent, she taught in India for seventeen years before she experienced her 'call within a call' to the slums of Calcutta. She was canonised in 2016, becoming Saint Teresa of Calcutta, 'saint of the gutters', a lifelong missionary to the poorest. Her model of holiness showed divine mercy to all, defended the God-given dignity of human life, spoke truth about the crime of poverty to the powerful and encouraged the practice of compassion.

Mother Teresa's humility, empathy and commitment, combined with her incredible managerial and organisational skills, changed lives. Within two years of arriving in Calcutta's slums in 1948, she had established a school, a home for the dying destitute and won canonical recognition for her Catholic congregation, the Missionaries of Charity. During the next two decades, she established a leper colony, an orphanage, a nursing home, a family clinic and a string of mobile health clinics. In 1971, Mother Teresa opened her first American-based house of charity in New York City (opening another later for those infected by HIV/AIDS), and in 1982 she went to Lebanon to aid children in Christian East Beirut and Muslim West Beirut. In 1979, she received the Nobel Peace Prize for her humanitarian work for the suffering, unwanted and unloved, which, by her death, included 4,000 Missionaries of Charity, thousands more lay volunteers, and 610 foundations in 123 countries. Perhaps more than any other person in the twentieth century, she exemplified the so-called 'capable woman' in Proverbs 31: a model of perseverance, common sense, hard work and faith.

† Father of all, may we too use our skills for the common good to your glory. Amen

For further thought

Consider your skills and abilities as God-given and for God's glory in God's world. Does that change anything for you?

The love of a martyr: Oscar Romero (1917–80)

Read Isaiah 40:1–11

A voice says, 'Cry out.' And I said, 'What shall I cry?' 'All people are like grass, and all their faithfulness is like the flowers of the field. The grass withers and the flowers fall, because the breath of the Lord blows on them. Surely the people are grass. The grass withers and the flowers fall, but the word of our God endures for ever.'

(verses 6–8)

After just three years as Archbishop of El Salvador, Oscar Romero was assassinated at the altar in 1980 for his commitment to justice for the poor at a time of civil war and persecution. Romero's story is the story of a Eucharistic church for all, reaching out to those at the margins of society. He exemplified a prophetic church challenging systems of oppression and exploitation, and an evangelising church that practises what it preaches. Romero was to call this living with the poor the 'violence of love'.

Romero believed the incarnation of Jesus meant that the life, death and resurrection of Jesus are a present reality, active in each generation of the church. As the good shepherd lays down his life for his flock, so Romero died with and for the 'church of the poor', having discovered that it is in the experience of the laity that church doctrine is to be founded. He became one crying out as a voice of the voiceless, like the voice in Isaiah 40. He found strength in retelling the stories of the hundreds who were arrested, tortured and disappeared in the tensions in El Salvador at the time: a servant leader in the reality of El Salvador's challenging wealthy minority and army. Romero calls us all to conversion to solidarity with others around the world. Through his own death, even, Romero showed that flowers might fall, but the Word of God endures forever, even in the face of oppressive regimes.

† Eternal and companioning God, we thank you for life through Jesus Christ. May we continually be aware of the life we share with the poorest of this world. Amen

For further thought

What does the 'church of the poor' mean to you? What might it mean to those in another context? Where is God in your awareness of the life of the poorest?

The Bible on the world stage

November

Jeremiah – 1 A call to pluck up and to break down

Notes by **Stephen Willey**

Stephen is a Methodist minister who has been involved in mission to the economic world through industrial chaplaincies and work against human trafficking. With four churches in Birmingham, England, three in deprived areas, Stephen is committed to seeing people's potential fulfilled. He is especially concerned for the young and vulnerable. Stephen has used the NRSVA for these notes.

Sunday 8 November
Jeremiah's call

Read Jeremiah 1:1–10

'Before I formed you in the womb I knew you, and before you were born I consecrated you; I appointed you a prophet to the nations.' Then I said, 'Ah, Lord God! Truly I do not know how to speak, for I am only a boy.'

(verses 5–6)

When the devastating truth about the precarious state of the nation must be told to Judah's king and its 'princes, priests and people', God chooses to speak through the lips of a young person. Jeremiah is afraid because he is 'only a boy' (verse 6), but God tells Jeremiah that he is valued, deeply known and loved. God reassures him that those who do not want to hear his message will be unable to overthrow him.

In recent years it has become clear that children have sometimes spoken the truth about leaders within the church and been disbelieved. Several years ago, when we started openly talking about safeguarding young people, a colleague was painfully reminded of a young person many years previously who had come to him and told him that his father (a church leader) had been abusing him. The minister was astonished at such a story; 'This can't be true,' he thought, and he didn't believe the boy.

Fear that their testimony would be doubted, ridiculed or disrespected has prevented vulnerable people speaking up about the truth in the past. God encourages Jeremiah, showing him, and us, how to speak up.

† Risen Jesus, you welcomed little children. Hear our prayer for children and vulnerable people and help us to listen to their voices.

Monday 9 November
Seeing well

Read Jeremiah 1:11–19

*The word of the Lord came to me, saying, 'Jeremiah, what do you see?'
And I said, 'I see a branch of an almond tree.' Then the Lord said to me,
'You have seen well.'*

(verses 11–12a)

Cycling through a local park, I came across a collection of photographs of a young man alongside many cards, flowers, candles and balloons. When I got to church, just a stone's throw away, I was told that the man had been killed in a knife attack. A similar attack had happened a few months previously, with another local person killed.

In the area where this violence happened, there seems to be a kind of resigned acceptance that this is how it is and will always be. In the same area there are also signs of an insidious violence linked to xenophobia: the rise of groups which condemn people who are perceived as not being like 'us' and are not able to defend themselves.

By using generalisations, or tolerating violence in our communities, it might be possible that we are lulled into a damaging perception of what is ordinary. If hatred is seen as normal or even, in a way, acceptable, our community and our church might be sleepwalking into an acceptance of violence, as if there is no other way.

The leaders of Judah have fallen into a trap at the time of Jeremiah. They can't see the wood for the trees! In contrast, Jeremiah stands alone, with only God to support him. Jeremiah sees, with the clear eyes of a young man, the branch of an almond tree and, later in this passage, an ordinary boiling pot. These commonplace things make an impression on Jeremiah as he takes God's perspective, revealing threats to the nation and a challenge to the people.

† Living God, you made this beautiful world and us in your own image. Never let us accept violence as normal or allow ourselves to consent to fear, indifference or hatred.

For further thought

Look at recent news articles concerning your neighbourhood. What unacceptable things in your community are treated as normal?

Jeremiah – 1 A call to pluck up and to break down

November

Tuesday 10 November
False gods fail to satisfy

> **Read Jeremiah 2:1–13**
>
> *Be appalled, O heavens, at this, be shocked, be utterly desolate, says the Lord, for my people have committed two evils: they have forsaken me, the fountain of living water, and dug out cisterns for themselves, cracked cisterns that can hold no water.*
>
> (verses 12–13)

The young man who came to our coffee bar was shaking and distressed. 'I need money for my mother's funeral,' he said to me. I replied, 'We can do a funeral for you for free if you have no money.' I invited him to return the next day with the details. He never came. I am sure that he was deeply distressed and had a strong feeling of loss but it became clear that he was first and foremost focused on obtaining the drugs which he was dependent on, not on the loss of a parent.

It has been said that addicts attempt to get satisfaction by repeating over and over again behaviours that aren't working, actions that will always fail to fulfil. Perhaps most typical is the gambler who tries to reproduce the excitement of making the bet, or makes another futile attempt to regain lost money.

God reminds the people of Judah how things once were, when their ancestors were faithful and followed God's commands. Now the people have turned towards worthless things. It is as if they have developed an addiction to false gods who promise water but have nothing real to offer. The people repeat rituals towards these make-believe gods, rituals that cannot satisfy. They worship fake gods that can never deliver. Jeremiah tries to convince his listeners of their false-god addiction which is putting the nation at risk. His people continue to forsake God, repeating behaviours which cannot bring comfort or relief. Ultimately, these behaviours lead to disaster.

† God of love, support those who this day are attempting to free themselves from addictions. Especially we pray for any family members, friends or neighbours who are struggling to be free.

For further thought

What are the false gods that people around me are devoted to? How can our hearts find rest in the God of truth and love?

Wednesday 11 November
Shaking in anguish

Read Jeremiah 4:19–31

My anguish, my anguish! I writhe in pain! Oh, the walls of my heart! My heart is beating wildly; I cannot keep silent; for I hear the sound of the trumpet, the alarm of war. Disaster overtakes disaster, the whole land is laid waste.

(verses 19–20a)

I remember the first time I read in public: I had practised Psalm 8 until it was word perfect. However, even though I had a Bible in front of me, my heart was thumping, knees trembling as I stood high up in the pulpit and looked out at the people. My voice shook as I started to speak the beautiful words, 'O Lord, our Lord, how great Thy name throughout the earth.'

Jeremiah's words were not comforting words; they were words about destruction. When Jeremiah spoke, it was not just him shaking, but the whole world seemed to be shaking uncontrollably (verse 24). As the walls of their city are assailed and war appears to be about to overwhelm the people, as Jeremiah himself writhes in pain and sorrow, the people are trying to put on a face, by enlarging their eyes with paint and wearing the jewellery of a false religion. The people are pretending that things are not so bad when their nation is 'gasping for breath' (verse 31). Jeremiah's reaction, in contrast, is a real response to a terrifying reality. He is overwhelmed with fear and sorrow, he is fainting and weak, but he doesn't try to 'dress things up' to make them seem more palatable. Jeremiah speaks vividly and honestly about the horrors that he is seeing.

† Holy Spirit, breath of life, your fire wells up within us. Breathe in us when the world is shaken, comfort us when all seems to be lost, yet do not withhold your truth from us.

For further thought

What shakes your world? Where do you speak vividly and honestly about what you see?

Jeremiah – 1 A call to pluck up and to break down

November

No shame, no peace!

Read Jeremiah 6:13–26

... everyone is greedy for unjust gain; and from prophet to priest, everyone deals falsely. They have treated the wound of my people carelessly, saying, 'Peace, peace', when there is no peace. They acted shamefully, they committed abomination; yet they were not ashamed, they did not know how to blush.

(verses 13b–15a)

A few years ago, a prominent British politician unashamedly said 'greed is good'[12] and in the same speech mocked those whom he perceived to have certain disadvantages. Powerful leaders today and in Jeremiah's time may claim that they are speaking boldly or clearly. They may suggest new ways to see things or say that they, alone, can find the solutions to the issues facing people and the nation, but often they disappoint.

We may be discouraged when the promises of politicians fail to be fulfilled or perhaps, as we get older, we become jaded and our increasing cynicism makes us distrust all politicians. Jeremiah, a young person, sees that things could have been different for his nation. He knows that only God's way leads to peace and justice. In Jeremiah's time it seemed like everyone was trying to pacify God whilst not paying heed to God. Human beings were behaving as if they had the wit to somehow pacify the Creator of the universe!

Jeremiah shows that we cannot pacify God by hollow ritual or religiosity. When the whole nation is overwhelmed by corruption and it seems that none of the leaders can be trusted, Jeremiah remains firm. His small voice, which will reverberate through the centuries, tells the truth and resists the pressure to conform. Jeremiah can only give people a message which talks of God's desire for righteousness and justice. Failure to follow God's way will lead to sorrow and mourning.

† God our Creator, your promises do not fail us nor does your love abandon us. Help us to take our responsibilities seriously as we participate in the life of our nation and our world.

For further thought

What do we see that wakes us up to reality? Do we see things we are afraid to speak about?

12 Nicholas Watt, 'Boris Johnson invokes Thatcher spirit with greed is good speech', (*The Guardian*, November 27 2013).

Friday 13 November
That I might weep

Read Jeremiah 8:22–9:11

O that my head were a spring of water, and my eyes a fountain of tears, so that I might weep day and night for the slain of my poor people! O that I had in the desert a traveller's lodging place, that I might leave my people ...

(verses 1–2a)

When Jesus wept over Jerusalem (Luke 19:41), he was deeply sad at the failure of the people to recognise the things that make for peace. Over the centuries, prophets expressed profound sorrow when they saw the failures of their nation. Jeremiah, deeply emotionally tied to his people, feels torn; he longs to be apart from his people for they have forsaken God, but, although he distrusts them, he also loves his people. He loves them, and the thought of their destruction is terrible to him. In this he is unlike Jonah who is angry to see disaster averted by God's compassion towards Nineveh (Jonah 4:1–2).

Global climate change is referred to by some as 'slow violence', a gradual destruction of environments and livelihoods especially affecting the world's poorest people. Although a disaster for some, climate change is possible for others to ignore. Its creeping violence requires millions of people in wealthy countries to come together to make a commitment to live more simply, in ways that are sustainable for the whole planet. The number of times Jeremiah speaks to a people who do not heed him has echoes of those who speak about climate change and the potential catastrophic warming of the planet. It might be tempting to run away or, alternatively, to condemn those around us who are not taking the risks seriously, but like Jeremiah we need to keep speaking, stay in touch with our emotions, and remember that those in denial about this violence and the potential consequences are our people too.

† Jesus our light in the gloom, you have known our sorrows as well as the joy of resurrection. Release in us the tears that lead to you, the water of life.

For further thought

Am I like Jonah, wanting God to punish others? How can I remember that all God's children are worth protecting?

Heal me, O Lord

Read Jeremiah 17:5–18

O hope of Israel, O Lord! All who forsake you shall be put to shame ... for they have forsaken the fountain of living water, the Lord. Heal me, O Lord, and I shall be healed; save me, and I shall be saved; for you are my praise.

(verses 13a and 13c–14)

The young woman, Malala Yousafzai, who bravely fought for her right to education, is an example to many of us in Birmingham, England. She came to our city for healing after being shot in the head at the age of fifteen and she continued her education here. When she became the youngest person to receive the Nobel Peace Prize, it was wonderful to see the international community supporting her.

Standing on the stage addressing the world's leaders, she reminded me of the young man whom we have journeyed with this week: Jeremiah, the boy called by God to speak out. Jeremiah who, with fear and trembling, though he was very young, kept speaking out. Jeremiah who spoke God's truth which was hard to hear.

Yet in this passage we can see, in a somewhat older Jeremiah, a niggling doubt alongside his faithfulness. 'I have been faithful,' he says. 'Be faithful to me, God.' In this terrible time of fear and violence Jeremiah seems to have doubts about his relationship with God. However he courageously carries on saying the things which most of his countryfolk do not want to hear.

Jeremiah continues to inspire us today. People who are willing, at great personal cost, to speak the truth about their contexts bravely and with conviction help us to see clearly. Jeremiah brought a fresh perspective to his world, discovering in ordinary things deep truths, wonderful and terrible, about our daily lives.

† Spirit of God, through grace you breathe our lives back into life. Lead us again to living springs; refresh and encourage us even when our road is treacherous.

For further thought

Where do we need healing today? How can we talk about it? Do we want to talk about it?

Jeremiah – 2 Jeremiah's tribulations

Notes by **Bola Iduoze**

Bola is a qualified accountant with more than twenty years' experience. She has a passion for coaching and mentoring and jointly manages a mentoring platform with her husband Eddie (mentoringplatform.com). Bola assists her husband in pastoring at Gateway Chapel in Kent, UK, and is a published writer and speaker. Bola and Eddie have two children. Bola has used the NIVUK for these notes.

Sunday 15 November
Made perfect by our Maker

Read Jeremiah 18:1–11

But the pot he was shaping from the clay was marred in his hands; so the potter formed it into another pot, shaping it as seemed best to him. Then the word of the Lord came to me. He said, 'Can I not do with you, Israel, as this potter does?'

(verses 4–6a)

When I was a young child in Nigeria, making clothes was a tradition during celebratory seasons. A tailor would come to our home and get us measured. We would pick a design but my Mum would have a design in mind for each child and, irrespective of our plan, she always insisted that she knew the right design appropriate for us. The tailor would then design the material as Mum said.

I once asked the tailor why she kept sewing according to Mum's pattern and not ours. The tailor said, 'Your mum had something in mind when she bought the material, so I bought just enough for that style.' Irrespective of our preferences, the person who provided the material had her wishes fulfilled. When the tailor finished her work, we almost always liked the design Mum picked because it came out perfect.

God is the designer of our lives and uses different things to show us the plan for us. The potter has something in mind, so he will shape accordingly. Ultimately, the design comes out good, just as the potter planned from the start. God is a great designer and his designs for our lives are perfect, so we should submit to him and his plans because he will make it as seems good to him.

† Lord, give me the grace to submit to your plans for my life as you make me fit for your purposes.

I cannot stop speaking the Word

Read Jeremiah 20:7–18

But if I say, 'I will not mention his word or speak any more in his name,' his word is in my heart like a fire, a fire shut up in my bones. I am weary of holding it in; indeed, I cannot.

(verse 9)

I was privileged to know a man who was persecuted as a young believer when he converted from Islam to Christianity. Not only was he converted, but he had a very strong sense of ministry and truly believed he was saved and called to propagate the gospel.

His father was a very rich Muslim leader and felt having a Christian son would be a problem and embarrassment to him. So he informed the young man to make a choice between receiving continued sponsorship from him and being disowned for preaching Christ. The gentleman went to pray and had to get back to his dad to tell him that preaching Christ for him was not an option. God's Word in the heart of this gentleman was like fire, shut up in his bones and it could not be held in. He could not disown Christ in favour of his family inheritance.

Things were very bad for this man initially, but eventually God took care of him and he's a successful pastor today. He was also able to introduce Christ to all his siblings and his mum.

God's Word cannot be contained. Irrespective of the hardships around us, we can hold onto the Word and speak God's Word until the Word helps us overcome our limiting or challenging environment.

Jeremiah had it tough, but he still couldn't stop sharing God's Word.

† Lord, let my mouth declare your Word without restriction, whatever comes in my way.

For further thought

Think today of those who are oppressed on account of their religion.

Tuesday 17 November
When worshippers do not want the truth

Read Jeremiah 26:1–15

'This is what the Lord says: Stand in the courtyard of the Lord's house and speak to all the people of the towns of Judah who come to worship in the house of the Lord. Tell them everything I command you; do not omit a word.'

(verse 2)

We expect to come to church to hear God's Words, but it's interesting to note that not every worshipper wants to hear the truth of the Word. God sent Jeremiah as a preacher to preach the whole of his message. God's intention was to give his people an opportunity to repent; however, that did not happen. The people rebelled against the messenger and were about to kill him for preaching what he did.

In my young adult years, I was in a little church in Ibadan, Nigeria, where our new pastor was addressing a particular issue that was of concern to a couple of members. These individuals were long-standing members of the church and one of them was an officer in the church. The men were polygamous: they each had multiple wives. They had reported the new pastor to the local board because he preached the message that God's design for a home was for men to have only one wife. Some of the board members wanted the pastor to apologise; however, he insisted that he didn't preach anything personal but scriptural.

Jeremiah's people, too, rebelled against the message he preached, even though Jeremiah was speaking directly as directed by God. We may not always want to hear that Word. Sometimes it is difficult and challenges us. We may even reject it; that is sad, but will not change God's Word.

† Lord, help me not to be stuck in my ways but to be open to correction from your Word.

For further thought

Can you think of a time in your life when difficult advice from a friend or a mentor was exactly what you needed to hear?

God raised intercessors

Read Jeremiah 26:16–24

Then the officials and all the people said to the priests and the prophets, 'This man should not be sentenced to death! He has spoken to us in the name of the Lord our God.'

(verse 16)

Jeremiah had the task of preaching a hard message to a congregation that was interested in neither hearing that nor changing. Listening and responding to God made Jeremiah build more enemies amongst the people he was sent to. This is a tough place to be as a messenger: Jeremiah had to deliver a message that was not accepted and even become a person who was not accepted.

After delivering the hard message, the people started to make a plea to send Jeremiah into jail while some even wanted him dead. That wasn't the first time there would be oppositions against God's servant. That same situation had happened to Uriah the son of Shemaiah from Kiriath Jearim who prophesied against the city (verses 20–23). He was hated and became a fugitive. He was eventually captured and killed.

God, however, intervened in the case of Jeremiah and he had an intercessor who pleaded for him. God spared him because Ahikam son of Shaphan supported Jeremiah. Just when he needed deliverance, God raised a man who provided the right support for Jeremiah and Jeremiah escaped death by the mob.

God is still in the business of delivering his people. Every time God gives us a commission, he also sets men and women in place to support and assist us.

† God, help me to trust in you even when it looks like I am surrounded by enemies and have no way of escape.

For further thought

When was the last time you felt someone's support in a challenging time? When was the last time you stood up for someone else?

God is in charge of our leadership

Read Jeremiah 27:1–15

'Tell this to your masters: with my great power and outstretched arm I made the earth and its people and the animals that are on it, and I give it to anyone I please. Now I will give all your countries into the hands of my servant Nebuchadnezzar king of Babylon ...'

(verses 4b–6a)

In many developing countries, elections are fraught with injustice and corruption. I remember being part of a few elections in Nigeria. Generally speaking, Nigeria is divided into the Southern and the Northern part. For a long time, the ruling parties and persons have been from the Northern part of the country and this usually makes the Southerners feel neglected and underprivileged. This is simply because there is a belief that the ruling power will take care of the North and everyone else will be neglected.

Nigeria's political situation is even more interesting because a lot of the Southerners are Christians, whereas the Northerners are generally Muslims. I can relate to the complaint of the Israelites who may not have found Jeremiah's message of submitting to Babylon attractive.

It is, however, important to note that God has an agenda for the world which he created. He was going to allow his people to go into captivity for a period of time and there was nothing anyone could do about it, but to submit to God's plan and programme.

God has a programme for our land; we need to pray and co-operate with him and the leaders he has put over us for a period and a purpose. In doing this, we will see his plans established and his will accomplished in our lives and land.

† Lord, we pray for your plans and purpose to be fulfilled in our lands. Help us to co-operate with you and establish your agenda in our land.

For further thought

In what circumstances are we to challenge God's plans, like Abraham did in Genesis 18:22–33?

Jeremiah – 2 Jeremiah's tribulations

November

Did God really say ...?

> **Read Jeremiah 28**
>
> *Then the prophet Jeremiah said to Hananiah the prophet, 'Listen, Hananiah! The Lord has not sent you, yet you have persuaded this nation to trust in lies. Therefore this is what the Lord says: "I am about to remove you from the face of the earth. This very year you are going to die, because you have preached rebellion against the Lord."'*
>
> (verses 15–16)

Prophecies are very attractive to people. Many want to know what their future holds and so some unscrupulous prophets develop their ministries to say what people want to hear. Amazingly, God is equally interested in showing us our future if we will be diligent enough to search for it, hear it and change our lives accordingly.

When I was younger, we used to have some people called prophets who went from place to place declaring things they saw. They did this for financial gain, and some bigger ones even got airtime on the state radio and TV stations to prophesy about different things, from who would become the next president to the date they believed Jesus was coming. Sadly, over time, these prophecies were not proven to be true. That led to many people thinking *all* prophecies are lies. Surely not all prophecies are lies, but there are some prophets who prophesy not in order to declare God's mind, but for financial gains or to please their audience.

Hananiah was one of such false prophets. He felt Jeremiah was a hardliner and decided to prophesy an end to the captivity of God's people. God got upset with his false declaration and he was punished for it with death.

Every time God speaks to his people through his prophetic word, the evidence is that God's word comes to pass.

† Lord, grant me the grace to read and listen to the truth of your word today.

For further thought
Where might you hear God speaking today?

Saturday 21 November
God has a good plan

Read Jeremiah 29:1–14

'For I know the plans I have for you,' declares the Lord, 'plans to prosper you and not to harm you, plans to give you hope and a future. Then you will call on me and come and pray to me, and I will listen to you.'

(verses 11–12)

God's people were in exile, yet God sent them a word of comfort and hope. God gave the assurance of growth, settlement, development and increase to his people in exile. The disposition of someone in exile would typically be that of an unsettled person ready to move back to their own place of promise. But God instructed his people to settle down and increase.

God assured his people that he had a plan for them and that plan is relevant to us today. My husband, Eddie, and I moved to Cyprus under God's instruction in 1994 and worked as farmhands for a while. It was a very uncomfortable place to be, but we heard God clearly. All the time, I was unsettled and wanted to move back to the UK, but God told Eddie that we should settle down in Cyprus. We did and met some amazing people whom we were able to help spiritually, emotionally and even financially over the period. By the time God wanted us to move into the next phase of his plan for us, we were richer in relationships with him and the people around us.

Our sojourn in Cyprus and the lessons we learnt there, though tough, are a big part of our message and ministry today. God had a plan. We should endeavour to submit to the plans he has for us; they are plans for our future.

† Father, help me recognise the plan you have for me, so that I will follow in line with the path that you have prepared for me.

For further thought
What do you do when you feel God's plan is hidden?

Jeremiah – 2 Jeremiah's tribulations

November

Jeremiah – 3 Glimmers of hope

Notes by **Nathan Eddy**

Nathan is editor of *Fresh From the Word* and an enthusiastic reader of the Bible. Nathan is also an amateur singer, poet and cyclist, and a lover of old maps, bookstores, coffee shops and getting lost in cities and forests. He is passionate about Jewish–Christian dialogue, about ancient and modern Hebrew, and about getting ordinary Christians reading the Bible every day, beginning with himself. He has lived in Manchester and Norwich, UK, and now lives in London with his family. Nathan has used the NRSVA for these notes.

Sunday 22 November
Beginning again

Read Jeremiah 30:1–11

But as for you, have no fear, my servant Jacob, says the Lord, and do not be dismayed, O Israel … Jacob shall return and have quiet and ease, and no one shall make him afraid.

(verse 10)

Jeremiah is a difficult book to read. It comes from a different world, and it is not always clear how it is organised. But it is also difficult because of the subject matter. Trauma, exile, pain and terror are things we want to avoid, not consider head-on. Yet Jeremiah won't let us evade these issues.

Chapters 30–31 are sometimes called the 'book of consolation' (Jeremiah is asked by God to write a 'book' or scroll in verse 2 of today's reading). These chapters are a respite in the story of a people which has 'heard a cry of panic, of terror, and no peace' (verse 5). Against all the odds, here God reveals that he will not make an end of his people (verse 11). Although the Book of Jeremiah continues for another twenty-two chapters, these chapters of exquisite comfort are a fitting place to end our IBRA reflections on Jeremiah this year.

These verses are not mere optimism in the midst of a crisis. They are words of profound hope. They reveal the mystery of God: a God of mercy and forgiveness who unfolds new beginnings in the midst of dead ends.

Sometimes, when life is at its bleakest, God finds a new way through. Will Israel trust and follow? Will you?

† God of consolation, comfort all who mourn today and give them surprising hope.

God the healer

Read Jeremiah 30:12–22

For I will restore health to you, and your wounds I will heal, says the Lord.

(verse 17a)

Refugees have been filling TV screens in recent years, whether at the US/Mexico border, the borders of Europe or at African borders like the one between Uganda and South Sudan. Yet for those of us lucky enough to have a roof over our heads and a stable society around us, it is hard to understand the upheaval and trauma of exile. The Babylonian army's sieges of Jerusalem in 597 and 587 BCE remain foreign experiences indeed, for many.

In today's reading, Jeremiah gives a poignant and painful insight into the experience: cries of panic and terror (verse 5); incurable hurt and pain (verse 12); the devastating experience of feeling forgotten, humiliated and hard-done-by (verses 13–14).

In Jeremiah's blunt assessment, the national disaster of exile was due to Israel's sin (verse 14). But other assessments are possible – and Jeremiah's God in these verses emerges not as a punisher, but a healer: 'I will restore health to you' (verse 17). Restoration is a new act of God, a physical gaining of strength and health. Pain is overcome by God's powers of life, and the city will again be secure, a place of thanksgiving (verses 18–22) with a just leader.

As I first read Jeremiah's words, I felt their foreignness to my own situation. But as I ponder them, I am aware how fragile my life is, and how fragile are the bonds that unite communities and societies. I can begin to sense some of the terror at life's uncertainties, and I can feel the pulse of God's promise, too.

† God of the outcast, gather us in, and gather all of us in, that all might find life.

For further thought
Look up pictures on the internet of Bidi Bidi in Uganda, the world's largest refugee camp, and consider the ingenuity, joys and struggles of the residents there.

Jeremiah – 3 Glimmers of hope

November

Tuesday 24 November
An everlasting love

Read Jeremiah 31:1–14

I have loved you with an everlasting love; therefore I have continued my faithfulness to you.

(verse 3b)

Today's reading begins three days on the remarkable Jeremiah 31. We saw yesterday how God's restoration works for the whole city and the whole people. Today we see that, ironically, the weakest in society – the pregnant, the old, the blind and the lame – will be led back by God and will form the cornerstone of the new city (verse 8). The city that seemed destined to slip from history at the 'strong hands' of the Babylonians (verse 11) will now take up tambourines, and dance (verse 4). The very people who suffered so grievously will rejoice and form a new community of justice and safety. The new community will be richly provided for in language similar to Psalm 23; the community will be shepherded, watered and fed.

Reading about the restored city, safe for all (verses 8–9), I think of the homeless in London, where I live. In 2017 almost 600 homeless people died on the streets, more than one every day. On Boxing Day, my church hosts a turkey dinner for the homeless prepared by a local hotel. The sound of laughter rings out the whole day. A local hairdresser sets up shop and cuts as many heads of hair for free as he can. The problems of homelessness are complex and won't be fixed by a free meal. But for one day, at least, we are one city, one people, rejoicing and sharing. On that day, the most vulnerable take the lead and show me true joy.

† God, never let my comfort blind me to the suffering of others, but use me to bring your comfort to others, so bring me true joy.

For further thought

According to this passage in Jeremiah, what would be a biblical vision for society's responsibility for the most vulnerable?

Jeremiah – 3 Glimmers of hope

November

Rachel's tears

Read Jeremiah 31:15–30

Rachel is weeping for her children; she refuses to be comforted for her children, because they are no more.

(verse 15b)

And Rachel wept.

Rachel, of course, had lived hundreds of years before this. She was the beloved of Jacob unable to bear children, until she bore Joseph (Genesis 30:23–24). She died giving birth to her second son, Benjamin (Genesis 35:19). Here, she weeps for her precious children who lost their lives at the hands of the invaders. But God offers an astounding promise: she must dry her tears, because her children shall return (verse 17). God still 'remembers' the people ('Ephraim') and is 'deeply moved' by their plight (verse 20).

As Christians reading Jeremiah, we might want to comfort Rachel (this passage is quoted in Matthew 2:18). After all, God promises a new future to Rachel and the Christian Bible ends with victory, not death. But for the sake of all who grieve the loss of children, I think it is important to let Rachel weep, and to have the courage to hear her pain. In a moving reflection on this passage, the Jewish philosopher Emil Fackenheim suggests that Rachel is still weeping; now, over her children lost in the Holocaust, or Shoah. Though healing might come, though other children might be born, life cannot remain the same (Fackenheim's article, 'New Hearts and the Old Covenant', is collected in *The Divine Helmsman* edited by Crenshaw and Sandmel, 1980).

Fackenheim concludes his essay with a powerful story. A Hasidic Jew from Warsaw survived the war and made his way to Israel, where he adopted many children orphaned by war, becoming the grandfather to many. The lives of those lost can never be replaced, and we must never forget them. But life also goes on in ways beyond our imagining.

† God of Rachel, our hearts are broken for your lost children in every age. Gather again the threads of life and stitch us into a people of wholeness and peace.

For further thought

How have people you know overcome tragedy and loss? If appropriate, gently begin a conversation with someone about their journey through grief.

A new covenant

> **Read Jeremiah 31:31–40**
>
> *I will put my law within them, and I will write it on their hearts; and I will be their God, and they shall be my people.*
>
> (verse 33b)

A new covenant, written on the heart: this is God's promise to Jeremiah. And God's teaching or instruction will be placed 'within' the people (verse 33). In the Bible, the word 'heart' can also mean 'mind', and these two images of heart and of what is 'within' people speak of a new creation. Knowing God's teaching will be second nature; instruction will no longer be necessary (verse 34). Wonderfully, the Aramaic translates 'within' as 'gut'. In this renewed humanity, following your 'gut' will also be following God's will.

For Jeremiah, the cycles of nature themselves are a sign of God's faithfulness. The 'fixed order' of the sun, moon and stars, the turn of the seasons, is a sign of God's commitment to Israel (verses 35–36). For an agrarian society like Israel, the turn of the growing seasons is crucial for survival. Here, the natural cycle is a sign not only of God's control, but also of God's personal devotion to his people. What a remarkable deity emerges in these few verses. 'The Lord of hosts is his name' (verse 35)!

These verses, among the most familiar in Jeremiah, are read in Lent in the Christian lectionary. They evoke the radical newness of the covenant God makes in Jesus. But let's not strip these verses of their power within Jeremiah's vision itself. Already in Jeremiah the new covenant can be understood on its own terms, as a wholly unmerited, wholly new action of the God of Israel. It might be found in the 'Old Testament', but Jeremiah's vision is startlingly new indeed.

† God of all newness, set your law deep within me and write it on my heart of stone, that I might live in you and you in me.

For further thought

Jeremiah lived in an age long before human beings were able to bring about global climate change. What might he have to say about it, do you think?

Friday 27 November
Money where your mouth is

At the height of the Babylonian siege of Jerusalem, the word of the Lord comes to Jeremiah: although prospects are dire, Jeremiah must buy land and commit to the future of his people. The passage tells us that Jeremiah pays seventeen shekels of silver for a field, signs and seals the deed and has it witnessed, and instructs his scribe to bury it in an earthenware jar for safekeeping. Perhaps the climax comes in verse 15: 'Houses and fields and vineyards shall again be bought in this land.'

I am struck by Jeremiah's commitment to his community. He does not merely offer words, but puts his money where his mouth is. He invests in the future and puts his own well-being on the line. It is interesting to me that the promise of the Lord in verse 15 regarding houses, fields and vineyards comes *after* Jeremiah's action. Jeremiah's action itself seems to enable the astonishing new future. Despite all the evidence to the contrary – despite the blackened trees surrounding the city, despite the starvation, despite the rubble – life will win out. Life will go on, and go on abundantly.

I am reminded of an experience of disaster faced by my home town in rural Vermont, USA, while I was in high school. In the space of two years, two large fires devastated my town's high street (Main Street, in American parlance). One shopkeeper who lost his store could have walked away with a large insurance payout, and no one would have held it against him. Instead he chose to rebuild the shop. Without his courage and commitment, I wonder if the town would have recovered.

† God of life, bless my house, and bless the fields and vineyards that sustain me; and bless all who work in them.

For further thought

We have no other record of the earthenware jar in which Baruch sealed Jeremiah's deed of purchase (verse 14). Perhaps the Bible itself is this vessel.

Jeremiah – 3 Glimmers of hope

November

Hope from the ashes

> **Read Jeremiah 32:16–25, 42–44**
>
> *Yet you, O Lord God, have said to me, 'Buy the field for money and get witnesses' – though the city has been given into the hands of the Chaldeans.*
>
> (verse 25)

Jeremiah leads us in prayer in today's reading. This prayer shows signs that it might have been added by later editors; the words are similar in tone to certain psalms and to a passage in Nehemiah (9:6–38). Regardless, they sum up the radical hope that Jeremiah himself embodies. The prayer builds to its last verse, verse 25: in the midst of the siege, while the siege ramps are thrown up against the very city walls (verse 24), God asks Jeremiah to buy the field. The Babylonians will not have the last word; God will. There is life yet in the soil and in the people.

I feel challenged by these words. It is tempting to give up hope when times are difficult, particularly in the face of complex, nationally divisive issues like Brexit in the UK or Trump's presidency in the US. Jeremiah's example, however, is one of steadfast commitment and investment. Jeremiah was only one person, yet his action was significant. Houses were built again in Israel.

More than any other prophet, Jeremiah's message and his life were fully integrated. It is not possible to tease apart his word from his actions; indeed, the Word of God burned within his bones themselves (20:9). From a Christian perspective, Jeremiah serves as a paradigm of Jesus' suffering, but also of the radical newness that Jesus made possible through his preaching, his actions and his life itself. Jeremiah's example hangs in the air for us all: in times of crisis, will we commit our lives to our communities as he did?

† God of surprises, give me courage to live my life that I might show your values to those around me, no matter the odds or the cost.

For further thought

If you had to describe Jeremiah in ten words to a friend who had never read the Bible, what words would you choose?

Trumpet calls and whispers: encountering the holy in Advent – 1 Trumpet calls

Notes by **Catherine Williams**

For Catherine's bio, see p. 225. Catherine has used the NRSVA for these notes.

Sunday 29 November (Advent Sunday)
God's holy mountain

Read Exodus 19:10–25

As the blast of the trumpet grew louder and louder, Moses would speak and God would answer him in thunder.

(verse 19)

This week's readings feature biblical trumpet calls. We will be looking at how trumpets announce major events, sound battle cries, summon God's people to worship, warn of impending doom and herald Christ's Second Coming, Last Judgement and the full reign of God's kingdom. In today's reading the Lord tells Moses to consecrate the people as they approach God's holy mountain. The trumpet calls here direct the people and also indicate when Moses and God are in conversation. The heavenly trumpet blasts are frighteningly loud and God's presence is accompanied by the elements in full force: smoke, thunder and lightning. God's absolute and awesome power is revealed. Moses stands in an extraordinary place as the bridge between the people and God, communicating both ways and holding the boundaries so that the people are kept safe. It's good to be reminded of the absolute power of God, and of our need to respect and submit to it. But as we enter into Advent, we are also looking towards God coming to us in Jesus as vulnerable, human and entirely accessible. Coming to meet us where we are, so that in time we might ascend to be with the risen Christ in glory.

† Lord, may I hear your trumpet call to action, witness and worship this Advent.

Monday 30 November
Jubilee!

Read Leviticus 25:1–15

You shall have the trumpet sounded throughout all your land … It shall be a jubilee for you.

(verses 9 and 10)

Today's trumpet call, played on a ram's horn on the Day of Atonement, announces the beginning of a Jubilee Year for the Israelites. Every seventh year was set aside as a sabbath, which was a year of rest for the land when no crops were grown, the soil being allowed to remain fallow to encourage its restoration. After a run of seven sabbatical years, following the forty-ninth year, a Jubilee Year was declared: a 'super-sabbatical'. In this year not only the land would lie fallow, but all property would be returned to its original owners, all debts cancelled and slaves restored to their families. The Jubilee was a holy year, set apart to restore all to its original state – recognising that everything comes from Yahweh and belongs to him. It was a year dedicated to simple living and liberty.

When Jesus stands up to speak in the synagogue in Luke 4:18–21 he quotes from Isaiah 61, declaring that the Spirit of the Lord is upon him: 'to proclaim the year of the Lord's favour'. He is identifying his presence as part of God's Jubilee – the beginning of a time of eternal liberation and restoration for the entire cosmos, as the kingdom of God breaks in. What a different place our world might be if we continued the practice of Jubilee years: committing ourselves to rectify the huge imbalance between rich and poor. The presence of Jesus in our lives makes for a continual Jubilee that should encourage us to work for justice, mercy and peace for all. Whom or what could you liberate this Advent?

† Dear Lord, everything I have and all that I am belongs to you. May I be generous with your abundance and eager to work for justice, mercy and peace.

For further thought

Learn more about the global movement for debt justice, by exploring the work of a charity such as Jubilee Debt Campaign or Tearfund.

Tuesday 1 December
A faithful blast!

Read Joshua 6:1–7, 15–21

'Take up the ark of the covenant, and have seven priests carry seven trumpets of rams' horns in front of the ark of the Lord.'

(verse 6b)

As Joshua and the Israelites enter the Promised Land, their first obstacle is the large walled city of Jericho. God says that he has given the city over into their hands; all the Israelites need to do is follow God's instructions and they will be victorious. God's strategy, however, seems foolish! It involves marching around the city walls with warriors, priests and trumpets following the Ark of the Covenant for six days. On the seventh day they are to march around the walls seven times, with the priests blowing the trumpets. When a long trumpet blast is sounded everyone is to shout and the walls will collapse. The Israelites do exactly this, and the plan is successful. Only Rahab the prostitute, from amongst those in Jericho, is spared. She's an unlikely choice for elevation, but becomes key in the history of salvation as a direct antecedent of Jesus.

There are a number of elements to note here for our Christian discipleship. Firstly, the Israelites intentionally acknowledge that God is present and active, which is indicated by processing the Ark of the Covenant. Secondly, Joshua and the people are obedient to God's command despite it appearing ineffectual and a bit strange. The people have faith that God is in control and will keep his promises. More than that, God's choices are often surprising and unexpected. God is the champion of the little, the least and the outsider. We do well to remember that God's ways can be very different to our ways, but when we trust, are obedient and have faith, extraordinary things can happen!

† Lord, help me to trust in you and to believe that you are in control, even when I struggle to understand your ways.

For further thought

Which walls in your life, church or community would you like to see the Holy Spirit break down during this time of Advent?

Trumpet calls and whispers: encountering the holy in Advent – 1 Trumpet calls

Wednesday 2 December
Heed the warning

Read Joel 2:1–16

Blow the trumpet in Zion; sound the alarm on my holy mountain!

(verse 1a)

Trumpet calls in scripture are used in various ways. Yesterday the blast of the trumpet was a battle-cry. In today's passage it's used firstly as a warning and then as a summons to worship. Joel's first trumpet call declares that disaster is imminent. A plague of locusts is on the way and it's like an invading army. Joel describes the destruction in apocalyptic imagery: the Day of the Lord is coming. Crises in the Older Testament, both environmental and military, are often described prophetically as a foretaste of Judgement Day. The cosmos reacts, with earthquakes and darkness. Light and life are extinguished. However, all is not lost. Joel calls for repentance, believing that disaster can be averted if people turn back to God. The second trumpet call in this passage is a call to worship. Trumpets were blown at major religious festivals, such as the Festival of the New Moon (Psalm 81:3). For Joel, the trumpet call heralds a holy fast that will mark a turning again to the Lord, who will be gracious and merciful to his people because he is 'slow to anger, and abounding in steadfast love' (verse 13).

What crises are we facing at present? Do we need to sound a warning that will wake others up to imminent disaster? Are we in danger of walking into ecological, political or social catastrophe? As Christians let's take heed of Joel's second trumpet call this Advent and gather together to turn back to the Lord, as we prepare both to celebrate God with us in Jesus, and await with expectation his Second Coming.

† Lord God, help me to put you first in all things. Open my eyes to the crises that are emerging on our planet and give me courage to sound your warning.

For further thought

During this Advent season consider setting aside time to 'fast' on a regular basis. Use the time to turn to God in prayer.

Thursday 3 December
All rise!

Read 1 Corinthians 15:51–58

For the trumpet will sound, and the dead will be raised imperishable, and we will be changed.

(verse 52b)

My son is a professional actor and musician: he studied trumpet performance at a music conservatoire. Amongst the most glittering and famous pieces in the trumpet repertoire are the solo passages in Handel's aria *The Trumpet Shall Sound* from *Messiah*: it's always a great thrill to hear Harrison practising or performing it. The aria comes towards the end of a long oratorio and the trumpeter needs to stay mentally alert in order to play this virtuosic call to resurrection. Handel based the opening bars of the trumpet part on the fanfare that was sounded in English assize courts in the seventeenth century when the judge arrived and the clerk called, 'All rise.' Handel knew his audience would recognise this fanfare and make the connection with the Day of Judgement.

St Paul writes to the Christians at Corinth about the mystery of the Day of the Lord heralded by a trumpet call. The dead will be raised and in a split second all will be changed, both outwardly and inwardly. Our bodies will no longer be subject to death and decay, but will be part of God's new creation. In his resurrection Jesus Christ has won the victory over death and opened the way for all to be liberated into glory. Throughout creation God has been active in defeat of chaos and we await the day when all will be transformed and made new. This is our future hope but it also shapes our present living. Paul commands us to stand firm in our faith; nothing we do in the Lord will ever be wasted.

† Thank you, Lord, that you have opened for us the path to everlasting life. Help us to hold onto this future hope in such a way that it shapes our daily actions and decisions.

For further thought

Listen to Handel's aria: *The Trumpet Shall Sound.* Can you hear the hope, mystery and awe of the Day of the Lord?

Trumpet calls and whispers: encountering the holy in Advent – 1 Trumpet calls

December

341

With Christ and in Christ

Read 1 Thessalonians 4:13–18

For the Lord himself, with a cry of command, with the archangel's call and with the sound of God's trumpet, will descend from heaven, and the dead in Christ will rise first.

(verse 16)

In yesterday's passage the Corinthians were concerned about what would happen to the living on the Day of the Lord. In contrast the Thessalonians are concerned to hear from Paul about how those who have already died will fare at the Lord's return. Paul reassures them. They can be confident that those who have already died will rise first and come with Christ as he returns. All will meet together and be with Christ forever. This would have been comforting encouragement for the Christians at Thessalonica who were enduring persecution and martyrdom for their faith. Paul uses strong imagery taken from Old Testament apocalyptic literature – especially the book of Daniel – to describe the Second Coming of Christ, and it includes cries, calls and trumpets; it will be noisy! Some Christians take these descriptions of the 'Rapture' as literal, others see them as word-painting – imagining detail that none of us yet knows. The important point is that the Lord will return and we are to look forward to that day with anticipation. Advent encourages us to hold together God's incarnation in Jesus at Bethlehem, with the hope of Jesus' Second Coming.

Did you notice that Paul encourages the Thessalonians not to grieve for the dead as the pagans do? He is not saying that it's wrong to grieve; it's entirely natural and human to feel deep sadness at the death of loved ones. But our grieving is always in the context of Christian hope: the knowledge that one day we will be reunited with those who have entered before us fully into God's eternity.

† Lord Jesus, thank you for the resurrection. One day we will be united with you and with all those we love but see no longer. May we always hold onto this hope.

For further thought

Take time this Advent to comfort and encourage someone recently bereaved.

Saturday 5 December
The final trumpet

Read Revelation 11:15–19

Then the seventh angel blew his trumpet ...

(verse 15a)

Today's trumpet call comes from the book of Revelation and is the final trumpet call of all time. John's vision records a series of seven trumpet calls played by angels and heralding a sequence of apocalyptic events. In Greek *salpinx* indicates a straight narrow bronze tubular instrument, neither the silver priestly trumpets from the temple nor the *shofar* ram's horn. Each blast is a wake-up call, summoning people to repentance. The seventh and final call leads into loud voices announcing that 'the kingdom of the world has become the kingdom of our Lord' (verse 15). The longed-for future has arrived: God's work is accomplished and his universal reign is fully realised in Jesus Christ. Whilst the previous six trumpet calls announced various disasters, the final call initiates joy and worship, singing and praise. The cosmos responds to the presence of God with full force, similar to that recorded in the book of Exodus on Mount Sinai – at the beginning of this week.

Travelling through Advent we prepare ourselves to celebrate God coming to us as a vulnerable infant in Bethlehem. We remember God with us in time, born as one of us in a specific place, joining in with our humanity: Jesus – living and dying amongst us. But at Advent we also look forward to the time when the entire world will be given over to the Son, as prophesied in Psalm 2, and God will be king over all. This is not some distant dream but is realised daily as faithful Christians worship and witness to Jesus, bringing in God's kingdom moment by moment.

† Lord, may your Spirit blow through me like a trumpet, so that I may herald the coming of God in Jesus Christ.

For further thought

Do one thing today to advance the kingdom of God. Do another tomorrow, and the next day ...!

Trumpet calls and whispers: encountering the holy in Advent – 2 Whispers

Notes by **Paul Nicholson SJ**

Paul is a Roman Catholic priest belonging to the Society of Jesus, a religious order popularly known as the Jesuits. He currently works in London as socius (assistant) to the Jesuit Provincial. He edits *The Way*, a journal of Christian spirituality, and is author of *An Advent Pilgrimage* (2013) and *Pathways to God* (2017). Since his ordination he has worked principally in ministries of spirituality and of social justice, and was novice-master between 2008 and 2014. Paul has used the NRSVA for these notes.

Sunday 6 December (Second Sunday of Advent)
The Lord was not in the earthquake

Read 1 Kings 19:9–18

The Lord was not in the wind; and after the wind an earthquake, but the Lord was not in the earthquake; and after the earthquake a fire, but the Lord was not in the fire; and after the fire a sound of sheer silence.

(verses 11b–12)

The use of CGI (computer-generated imagery) in films and television has accustomed viewers to spectacular effects. Hurricanes, conflagrations, battles and earthquakes are all realistically summoned up at the touch of a button. It is easy to get caught up in these and the stories they illustrate. Returning to real life, when the movie ends, seems rather humdrum by comparison.

Elijah, on Mount Horeb, witnesses nature at its most dramatic. On another occasion, perhaps, these events themselves might have revealed God to him. The wind recalling God's power; the fire, God's majesty; the earthquake, God's strength. But in this story, that's not how it worked. Only the stillness, after all the drama, invited Elijah out of the cave to recognise and speak with God.

This week's readings explore what it means to discover God in quiet stillness. They offer an invitation to step aside, at least briefly, from the noisy busyness characteristic of many lives today. To switch off the computer, put down the phone, get away from the traffic. And to do this not simply as an escape, but expecting that by doing so we become more able to hear a God who sometimes speaks in whispers, easily drowned out.

† God asked Elijah: 'What are you doing here?' If God asks you that in this time of prayer, how will you answer?

Monday 7 December
Held in the arms of God

Read Psalm 131

But I have calmed and quieted my soul, like a weaned child with its mother.

(verse 2)

The 'mother and child', Mary holding her infant son, is a popular theme in Christian art. As a theme it allows for great variety. Jesus may be a slumbering baby or a boisterous toddler, Mary an elegant queen or a simple peasant-girl. Similarly, an artist can have different intentions, from impressing on the viewer the majesty of the incarnate God, to demonstrating the frail humanity of this God become man.

Some of these paintings have the effect of drawing whoever spends time with them more deeply into silence. A sleeping infant resting on the breast of a mother who looks down with a loving gaze is a powerful invitation to be still, if only so as not to wake the baby! This idea is taken one step further in Psalm 131. Here I am more than a passive onlooker, but am encouraged to identify myself with that baby, resting safely in its mother's embrace. This, says the psalmist, is what it is like to know myself held securely in God's arms.

Do you know from your own experience what that is like? You might remember a time of prayer when you could have made these words from the psalm your own. Or perhaps you recall holding a trusting child, or even being such a child yourself. The reason this is such a powerfully recurrent theme in art is that it is a strong yet common human experience. We can return repeatedly in memory to this kind of experience to deepen our relationship with, and appreciation of, the God who shows us a parent's love.

† Lord, let all that is within me grow still, so that I can know myself held in your loving arms.

For further thought
Today, can you find a Christmas card that you like, showing Mary with her baby son, to use as an image for reflection in a time of quiet?

Trumpet calls and whispers: encountering the holy in Advent – 2 Whispers

Weathering life's storms

> **Read Luke 8:22–25**
>
> *Jesus woke up and rebuked the wind and the raging waves; they ceased, and there was a calm. He said to them, 'Where is your faith?' They were afraid and amazed, and said to one another, 'Who then is this?'*
>
> (verses 24b–25a)

For Jews of Jesus' time, the sea was the great symbol of chaos. Indeed, one of the signs of God taking control in the 'new heaven and new earth' of the Book of Revelation is that there is no longer any sea, which island-dwellers might regret. To experience a sudden storm at sea, far from land in a small boat, is to know at first hand the effects of this chaos and the terror it can provoke. It's no wonder the panic-stricken disciples are anxious to rouse Jesus from his slumbers.

What follows is a powerful demonstration of the way God works. Jesus doesn't need to match the storm in its intensity, or wrestle with the forces threatening to overwhelm them. A simple word on his part brings calm, and in this calm the disciples come to a deeper knowledge of who he is. If this man can quell a tempest with a word, what does this say about him and about their relationship with him?

Gospel stories like this invite us to say, 'Yes, I've been there, I know what that's like.' You may never have been rescued from a small boat swamped by high waves. But you are likely to have had the experience of being almost overwhelmed at times, only to have been saved by God. A serious illness, the break-up of an important relationship, financial troubles or the death of a loved one: any of these storms can threaten to knock my life's journey off course. But where I am conscious of God's help, any of them can also deepen my faith.

† Lord of sea and sky, help me to know you in the calm that follows the storm, that I may trust you more fully when the winds threaten to blow me off course.

For further thought

Notice the weather where you are today. How might that help you picture something of your current or past relationship with God?

Trumpet calls and whispers: encountering the holy in Advent – 2 Whispers

December

Wednesday 9 December
Silence and speech

Read Ecclesiastes 3:1–8

For everything there is a season, and a time for every matter under heaven …

a time to tear, and a time to sew; a time to keep silence, and a time to speak.

(verses 1 and 7)

The kind of wisdom presented in the Book of Ecclesiastes is presented as advice from an experienced royal counsellor to those who would follow in his footsteps. Such a counsellor needs to be ready for anything: war or peace, triumph or disaster, the favour or disfavour of his patron. So he is anxious to impress upon those who would learn from him that all these things can be turned to advantage; that, in religious terms, God can be seen at work in all of them.

Of course, it's easier to recognise God at work in some experiences than in others. Creative sewing would seem to have more in common with a creator God than tearing the sewn cloth. And perhaps, in our own context, having your say and not letting anybody silence you is more easily thought to be a proper response to God than sitting meekly and quietly in a corner.

Deeper reflection, though, shows that both are important. Sometimes the best way to ward off an attack is not to argue back, but to hold your tongue. A day that is wholly without silence is likely to be an unreflective one, filled with doing but with little space to appreciate God's gifts. There is wisdom in knowing when to speak and when to remain silent, a wisdom that is the fruit of experience but is also itself something given by God. Perhaps the focus of my prayer today can be to pray for that wisdom.

† God, you were pleased when King Solomon prayed for wisdom above all. Grant me the wisdom to see today when to speak and when to keep silent, in your service.

For further thought

Consider all the 'times' mentioned in this reading: which come easily to you, and which do you find more challenging?

Trumpet calls and whispers: encountering the holy in Advent – 2 Whispers

December

Thursday 10 December
Silence as an aid to understanding

Read Nehemiah 8:1–12

So the Levites stilled all the people, saying, 'Be quiet, for this day is holy; do not be grieved.' And all the people went their way to eat and drink and to send portions and to make great rejoicing, because they had understood the words that were declared to them.

(verses 11–12)

How do you respond when you read the Bible, or hear it read, particularly on a day when a passage touches you deeply? Today's reading sketches three kinds of response, by people who have been greatly moved while listening to the rediscovered word of God.

First, they weep, an impulse we can still recognise when hearing news, good or bad, that affects us profoundly. Then they are encouraged to go and celebrate, as a way of expressing their gratitude to God for what they have heard, and making sure that everyone is included in the thanksgiving. With the weeping and the celebrating of a great crowd gathered in a town square, it is easy to imagine a scene of great commotion.

In the midst of all this uproar, there is encouragement to make room for a third response. 'Be quiet,' the Levites suggest. Quiet, so that there is time for the word that they have heard to sink deeper. Quiet, so that they do not simply hear and forget. Quiet, to allow what has been a general message proclaimed to a crowd the time to become a personal communication between God and each individual.

It is clear here that the weeping has its place, and so does the partying. Those are spontaneous responses, heartfelt and shared. To allow myself to be led in my prayer to an equally heartfelt silence, shared by God and myself and even, in common worship, with others, is an equally fitting response to God's word.

† Today let the focus of my prayer be wordless. I sit silently in response to the word that I have heard, letting God plant it more deeply in my heart.

For further thought

Seek out a quiet place sometime today and simply stay there for a few moments, savouring the silence.

Trumpet calls and whispers: encountering the holy in Advent – 2 Whispers

December

348

Friday 11 December
Who is the greatest?

Read 2 Corinthians 10:7–18

We do not dare to classify or compare ourselves with some of those who commend themselves. But when they measure themselves by one another ... they do not show good sense. We, however, will not boast beyond limits, but will keep within the field that God has assigned to us.

(verses 12–13a)

Michael Flanders and Donald Swann wrote and performed comic songs in the mid-twentieth century. The chorus of one of my favourites, 'A Song of Patriotic Prejudice' offers a satirical send-up of narrow, jingoistic English patriotism. It offers a roll-call of the other nations of the British Isles, then of Europe, and finally of the world, criticising their national characters when set against the supposedly incomparable virtues of my countrymen and women.

Paul has clearly encountered similar comparisons, although with more serious intent, among the people of Corinth. Nobody has embraced this novel Christian faith as fervently as they have, and even among themselves they jostle for first place. Paul responds with a twofold strategy. First, he points out that he himself has more right to be regarded as a 'top Christian' than they do; he has believed longer, worked harder, suffered more. Then, switching tack, he insists that anyway such comparisons are meaningless, and indeed betray a profound misunderstanding of discipleship.

In place of noisy boasting, he advises quiet restraint in our dealings with one another. This should be seen in context. Nowhere does Paul deny the gifts that he has been given by God, nor even the good use to which he has put them. If I can acknowledge the talents God has bestowed, and all that they have enabled me to achieve, I will be better able to continue to employ them fruitfully. But collaboration, not competition, is the key Christian witness. I leave the question of who is best to God, while I work quietly with others to spread God's word.

† Lord, I thank you for the gifts that you have given me. Help me to work with others to use them fruitfully in your service.

For further thought

What particular gifts has God given to your country or your church, to be used in the building up of the realm of God?

Trumpet calls and whispers: encountering the holy in Advent – 2 Whispers

December

Times when speech becomes impossible

Read 2 Corinthians 12:1–10

And I know that such a person – whether in the body or out of the body I do not know; God knows – was caught up into Paradise and heard things that are not to be told, that no mortal is permitted to repeat.

(verses 3–4)

The twentieth-century philosopher Ludwig Wittgenstein ended his *Tractatus Logico-Philosophicus*[13] with the enigmatic sentence: 'What we cannot speak about we must pass over in silence.' Some experiences are simply beyond words and so can never be fully described or shared. This is the kind of experience that Paul alludes to as he tries to explain his own position to the people of Corinth. It is not so much that he has been forbidden to speak of a type of prayer that is commonly called mystical. It is more that the intensity of what he felt fourteen years previously is still beyond his power to convey.

You may not think of yourself as someone whose prayer is like this, and you may well feel that the heights of mysticism are beyond you. Yet, those things that are deepest in your own life are probably not able to be put into words. Think of the love you have for those closest to you; or a cause that you are passionate about; or, indeed, the intricacies of your own relationship with God. You may pass on to others something of these, but you're eventually likely to feel that your attempts to do so have been inadequate.

We have looked this week at some of the different parts that silence has to play in a life of Christian discipleship. In what can be a busy, and noisy, run-up to Christmas, it can be difficult to find a quiet place and time to meet God. The invitation remains, though, for those who would want the power of Christ to dwell in them.

† Memorial events sometimes start or end with 'two minutes' silence'. Let your own prayer include such a timed silence today, simply resting in the awareness of God's presence.

For further thought

Recall a time this week when you have enjoyed a moment of silence. Write a little about this, or share the experience with another person.

13 Wittgenstein, L. (2001), *Tractatus Logico-Philosophicus* (Abingdon: Routledge Classics), p. 89.

Trumpet calls and whispers: encountering the holy in Advent – 3 Encountering the holy

Notes by **Ann Conway-Jones**

Ann is a biblical scholar, teacher and freelance writer. She holds honorary research fellowships at the University of Birmingham and The Queen's Foundation for Ecumenical Theological Education. She is fascinated by the different ways in which Jews and Christians have read the scriptures, and passionate about making academic scholarship accessible. She is Chair of Birmingham Council of Christians and Jews. Anne has used the NRSVA for these notes.

Sunday 13 December
Jacob's ladder

Read Genesis 28:10–22

Then Jacob woke from his sleep and said, 'Surely the Lord is in this place – and I did not know it!' And he was afraid, and said, 'How awesome is this place! This is none other than the house of God, and this is the gate of heaven.'

(verses 16–17)

This week we focus on a series of momentous encounters in which human beings glimpse something of the awesome nature of the divine. The veil between earth and heaven is briefly lifted. God is holy – wholly other, indescribable, and beyond all our categories; yet in these moments the transcendent becomes present. And lives are transformed.

We start with Jacob, the trickster, on the run from home, having stolen his brother Esau's birthright. He comes to an ordinary sort of place, and takes what looks like an ordinary stone to use as a pillow. But his dream is far from ordinary: he sees heavenly messengers, and receives a divine promise, a repeat of God's pact with his grandfather Abraham. Despite his estrangement from Esau, Jacob now has hope that he will return to his father's house in peace. Much is to happen before then – Jacob himself will be tricked by his uncle Laban – but the promise stays with him. He starts by consecrating the stone, to mark the place as a 'house of God' – *Beth-el* in Hebrew. It is to become a site of pilgrimage and worship, a permanent reminder of mystery beyond our comprehension.

† Ye holy angels bright, who wait at God's right hand, or through the realms of light fly at your Lord's command, assist our song, for else the theme too high doth seem for mortal tongue.

Moses enters the thick darkness

Read Exodus 20:18–21

Then the people stood at a distance, while Moses drew near to the thick darkness where God was.

(verse 21)

After the giving of the Ten Commandments, Moses climbs Mount Sinai again. He is alone as he draws near to the 'thick darkness' (verse 21). In the book of Exodus, God is often described in terms of 'glory' – an extremely bright light so dangerous that it needs to be surrounded by a protective cloud. The thick darkness is that cloud. It hides God from human view, because to know God fully is beyond what human beings can bear.

Gregory of Nyssa, who lived in the fourth century, used this story of Moses ascending into darkness to argue that it is impossible to grasp the essence of God. He wrote:

> *For in this is the true knowledge of what is sought, and in this is the seeing which consists in not seeing, that what is sought transcends all knowledge, cut off on all sides by incomprehensibility, as by a kind of darkness.*

(Life of Moses 2.163)

The closer we get to God, Gregory seems to say, the less we understand. His insight, and its relationship with Exodus 20:21, travelled down the centuries, eventually reaching the anonymous fourteenth-century English author of a book entitled *The Cloud of Unknowing*. In this manual of contemplative prayer, readers are warned that they will discover only darkness between themselves and God. But they are urged to reconcile themselves to waiting, and 'smite upon that thick cloud of unknowing with a sharp dart of longing love' (chapter 6).

† Immortal, invisible, God only wise; in light inaccessible hid from our eyes, Most blessèd, most glorious, the Ancient of Days; almighty, victorious, Thy great Name we praise.

For further thought

Have you ever felt in 'the cloud of unknowing'? As you journey in faith, do you come to know more or less?

Tuesday 15 December
The call of the seraphim

Read Isaiah 6:1–8

Then I heard the voice of the Lord saying, 'Whom shall I send, and who will go for us?' And I said, 'Here am I; send me!'

(verse 8)

Isaiah is in the Jerusalem temple when the scene in front of him morphs into something else. The earthly temple becomes a portal to the heavenly one. God towers far above him, with the hem of the divine robe enough to fill the building around him. And God is attended by heavenly beings, referred to as 'seraphim' – a word with connotations of fire and burning. The snakes that bit the Israelites in the wilderness (Numbers 21:4–9) were also designated seraphim. And the bronze serpent on a pole which healed them was said to have stood in the temple until Hezekiah removed it (2 Kings 18:4). Maybe this item of temple furniture triggers Isaiah's vision. He imagines bright fiery snake-like beings with wings as guardians of the divine throne. They cover their faces, because even they are not able to withstand a direct vision of God, and they call to each other with words we now know as the Sanctus. This clue as to the content of heavenly song has made its way into Christian Eucharistic liturgies, in order that we might join our worship and praise with that of angels, archangels and all the company of heaven.

Isaiah is terrified at the idea that he has seen God, ruler of the heavenly host and creator of the world. But one of the seraphim burns his mouth with a live coal and, like the Israelites in the wilderness, Isaiah is healed and forgiven. He has been made ready for his mission.

† At His feet the six-winged seraph, cherubim with sleepless eye; Veil their faces to the presence, as with ceaseless voice they cry: Alleluia, Alleluia, Alleluia, Lord Most High!

For further thought

How do you imagine angel-song?

Wednesday 16 December
A bright cloud from the north

Read Ezekiel 1:1–14

As I looked, a stormy wind came out of the north: a great cloud with brightness around it and fire flashing forth continually, and in the middle of the fire, something like gleaming amber. In the middle of it was something like four living creatures.

(verses 4–5a)

Ezekiel is in exile in Babylon. He was among the first wave of high-ranking Judean officials to be forcibly marched there in 597 BCE, ten years before Jerusalem was destroyed. Now he sits by the river Chebar (the 'ch' is pronounced like a 'k'), no doubt anxious and disconsolate. Then he experiences what is probably the most surreal vision in the Bible, later referred to as the chariot (*merkavah* in Hebrew) vision. Within a great storm cloud, fire flashing all around, Ezekiel makes out four 'living creatures'. Later in the book they are identified as cherubim (10:20). The vision seems to be drawing on ancient imagery for God, both flying on the wings of the wind (Psalm 18:9–12) and enthroned upon the cherubim (Psalm 99:1). These are not the sweet child-like cherubs of European art, but terrifying hybrid beings with four faces each. When Moses is given instructions for the tabernacle, God promises to meet with him from between the two cherubim on the Ark of the Covenant (Exodus 25:22). And there were cherubim guarding the ark in the holy of holies of the Jerusalem temple (1 Kings 8:6–7). So in this vision, it is as if the temple cherubim have come to life and carried their precious cargo – the glorious divine presence – away from Jerusalem. For the priest Ezekiel, this explains why the Babylonians were able to overrun the temple; God was no longer present there. But the appearance of the divine chariot-throne in this place of exile promises that all is not lost.

† O tell of His might, O sing of His grace, whose robe is the light, whose canopy space, His chariots of wrath the deep thunderclouds form, and dark is His path on the wings of the storm.

For further thought

What place do dreams and visions have in your experience of God?

Thursday 17 December
The likeness of a throne

Read Ezekiel 1:15–28

And above the dome over their heads there was something like a throne, in appearance like sapphire; and seated above the likeness of a throne was something that seemed like a human form.

(verse 26)

Ezekiel's vision, if anything, gets more bizarre. Now there are wheels within wheels, and rims full of eyes. Over the heads of the living creatures is a dome, a firmament, reminiscent of the dome separating the waters described in Genesis 1.6–7. Above the dome is a sapphire throne. 'Sapphire' here refers to lapis lazuli, a deep blue stone with golden flecks, suggestive of the night sky. God is seated on the throne, although not named as such until the end. Ezekiel describes God in anthropomorphic terms, as having a human form and 'what appeared like the loins' (verse 27). But note how many times he uses the words 'something like'. He makes it clear that nothing about God can be pinned down; what is being described is beyond description. There is a mysterious term *hashmal* in the Hebrew (verse 27), translated as 'amber' or 'electrum' or 'gleaming bronze', but no one really knows what it means. Ezekiel concludes by saying, 'This was the appearance of the likeness of the glory of the Lord' (verse 28) – he has only seen God at three removes.

Artists have tried to reproduce Ezekiel's vision (versions by Raphael and Rubens can easily be found online), but it resists all such attempts. God's transcendence is conveyed by the strangeness of the imagery. The God whose majesty fills heaven and earth here becomes present in one place. God is holy and unapproachable, but also free, mobile and eternally watchful – hence all the eyes on the rims of the wheels.

† With glorious clouds encompassed round, whom angels dimly see, Will the Unsearchable be found, or God appear to me?

For further thought

Are you ever frustrated by the inadequacy of words?

Friday 18 December
Worthy art thou

> **Read Revelation 4**
>
> *The twenty-four elders fall before the one who is seated on the throne and ... cast their crowns before the throne, singing, 'You are worthy, our Lord and God, to receive glory and honour and power, for you created all things, and by your will they existed and were created.'*
>
> (verses 10–11)

John, like Ezekiel, is in exile, stranded on the island of Patmos. Maybe he thinks of himself as a new Ezekiel, or a new Isaiah, because he picks up their imagery and weaves it into new configurations. A door opens into heaven and, taken up in the Spirit, he sees the divine throne. There are flashes of lightning and peals of thunder reminiscent of Ezekiel's vision. And the sea of glass, like crystal, echoes Ezekiel's dome 'shining like crystal' (1:22). The throne is static, however – there are no wheels; instead, it is the living creatures which are full of eyes. They each have six wings; here the influence is Isaiah's seraphim. And rather than having four faces each, they have become like the four animals referred to by Ezekiel. Later, the lion, ox, human being and eagle will be taken as symbolic of the four evangelists. So we see how the imagery travels down the generations, continually being reused and reworked.

The message of Revelation is that God is the ultimate reality behind all earthly appearances, and it is to God that all worship is due. As well as drawing on ancient Israelite imagery, it seems likely that this picture of the divine throne was designed to pit God against the Roman emperor, whose cult was sweeping the Mediterranean world. Revelation's readers are being asked to choose where their loyalty lies.

† Holy, holy, holy! All the saints adore thee, casting down their golden crowns around the glassy sea; cherubim and seraphim falling down before thee, who wert, and art, and evermore shalt be.

For further thought

What does the concept of 'heaven' mean to you? Where do your ultimate loyalties lie?

Saturday 19 December
The lamb who was slain

Read Revelation 5

Then I saw between the throne and the four living creatures and among the elders a Lamb standing as if it had been slaughtered, having seven horns and seven eyes, which are the seven spirits of God sent out into all the earth.

(verse 6)

As John's vision continues, he notices that the figure on the throne is holding a scroll, but it seems that no one is worthy to open it. Then he hears that the Lion of Judah has conquered. As well as a lion being an obvious symbol of power and victory, this is a reference to Jacob's dying words over his son Judah (Genesis 49:9–10), taken as messianic prophecy. There is a contrast, however, between what John hears and what he sees. For between the throne and the four living creatures is not a lion, but a slaughtered lamb. Whether this is to be thought of as the Passover lamb, sacrificial lambs in general or the lamb of Isaiah 53:7 is not clear. But hopes for the messianic conquest are being placed with the crucified Christ. Those around the throne sing a new song, in which the lamb is worshipped on an equal footing with 'the one seated on the throne' (verse 1).

William Blake painted a watercolour of this scene in Revelation 4–5, entitled *The Four and Twenty Elders Casting their Crowns before the Divine Throne* (it can be found through www.tate.org.uk). Looked at carefully, most of Revelation's dramatic visual imagery can be identified. The hardest thing to spot amid the splendour is the lamb – it is a pale, very dead-looking, passive creature at the foot of the throne, surrounded by what looks like the prongs of a crown. Blake has captured the Christian proclamation that victory is achieved through weakness and vulnerability.

† As with joyful steps they sped to that lowly manger bed; There to bend the knee before him whom heaven and earth adore; So may we with willing feet ever seek Thy mercy seat.

For further thought

When and where might God's presence become real to you this Christmas?

The Word became flesh: Christmas with John – 1 In the beginning was the Word

Notes by **Kate Hughes**

Kate worked for the Church in Southern Africa for fourteen years. Since her return to the UK she has worked as a freelance book editor, initially specialising in theology but more recently widening her work (and mind) to include books on gardening, dog training, climate change, sociology and gender studies. She lives on a small council estate in Coventry with Ruby, her Cavalier King Charles Spaniel, and preaches regularly at her local Anglican church. Kate has used the NRSVA for these notes.

Sunday 20 December
God's love revealed

Read 1 John 4:7–19

God's love was revealed among us in this way: God sent his only Son into the world so that we might live through him.

(verse 9)

Christmas is the time when we think not of what we can give to God, but of what God has given to us. And it is John, in his Gospel and his letters, who writes most movingly of what that means for us: that we can love because God loves us first. We can love God because he has already revealed himself to us as someone who is loveable. He is not a distant, unknowable, inexplicable deity. He has translated himself into a form, a language, that we can understand because the one thing all humans know about is what it is like to be human.

Yet at the same time this human being, this baby born in Bethlehem, remains God. How the man Jesus behaves is how God behaves. And because we know that God loves us, we can have the confidence to love others, to 'love one another as I have loved you' (John 15:12). In the eleven days between now and the end of the year, we shall be exploring John's take on the difference that God's love can make in our lives.

† Help us, O God, to find in John's writings a new assurance of your love for us.

Monday 21 December
Light and darkness

Read John 1:1–9

The light shines in the darkness, and the darkness did not overcome it.

(verse 5)

When I lived in Africa, I found it very disconcerting to have Christmas in the middle of summer. Coming from the northern hemisphere, Christmas was a time for lights at the darkest time of the year: candles around the house and strings of lights on the Christmas tree and in the window that looked out onto the road. Nobody knows exactly when Jesus was born; 25 December is an arbitrary date chosen by people living in the northern hemisphere. But wherever we are living, the effect of light in darkness remains one of the greatest themes in John's Gospel.

There is so much darkness in the world: the darkness of mental illness, especially depression; the darkness of fear; the darkness of cruelty – for both those who receive it and those who give it; the darkness of hopelessness. The list is endless. But in all these situations God's light is there, it shines on in spite of the darkness, it can give people hope and guide them through the darkness. 'The darkness is not dark to you; the night is as bright as the day, for darkness is as light to you' (Psalm 139:12). In prayer and in practical support, God can use us to keep his light shining in the darkness that can never destroy it.

† Lord, show us how we can help, by our prayer, words and actions, to keep your light shining in the darkness.

For further thought

Think of one area of darkness in the world. How could you work with God to keep the light shining there?

The Word became flesh: Christmas with John – 1 In the beginning was the Word

Tuesday 22 December
Making God known

Read John 1:10–18

No one has ever seen God. It is God the only Son, who is close to the Father's heart, who has made him known.

(verse 18)

For me, as for many people, the reading of the first chapter of St John's Gospel at the midnight service on Christmas Eve marks the true beginning of Christmas. Not the buying and wrapping of presents, the cooking, the decorating the Christmas tree, the visit to 'Santa' in the local store, the hanging up of stockings or putting out of shoes for St Nicholas. Christmas truly begins when we join with our Christian family to hear the words, 'And the Word became flesh and lived among us' (verse 14).

An alternative translation of verse 18 has 'It is the only Son' rather than 'It is God the only Son'. Personally I think this alternative is clearer, but both phrases clearly state the incredible truth that in Jesus, the man, the carpenter from Nazareth, we see what God is like. When God takes human form and lives and teaches and dies, he is simply being himself. We can look at Jesus and know God. We can read the accounts of his life in the Gospels and know that this is how God acts and speaks and thinks. And if we are part of a local Christian congregation, we represent Christ's presence in the world, and we in our turn have to make God known through his only Son.

† Father, help us to know your Son so that we may know you more clearly.

For further thought

What does Jesus tell you about God?

Wednesday 23 December
Believing Jesus

Read John 2:13–22

After he was raised from the dead, his disciples remembered that he had said this; and they believed the scripture and the word that Jesus had spoken.

(verse 22)

The temple in Jerusalem was the centre of the Jewish religion. It was the place where prayer was offered daily to God, where people went on pilgrimage at the great festivals, where people sorted out their relationship with God through offering sacrifice in repentance or thanksgiving. The local synagogue was the place for weekly prayer and teaching; only in the temple could the essential sacrifices be offered. Over the years, supporting businesses had grown up providing the animals needed for sacrifice, and coins to pay for them that did not show the image of a heathen god. All this brought noise and the busyness of a marketplace to the temple and destroyed the atmosphere of prayer that should have been there.

Pictures of today's incident often show Jesus as angry, lashing out with his rope. But perhaps, like some of the earlier prophets, he was primarily acting out a truth. The old system of sacrifice had outlived its usefulness. People no longer needed to offer sacrifice in order to relate to God. Jesus himself was the way to God. Believing what Jesus said, believing what Jesus did, seeing his death and resurrection as the final sacrifice that replaced the old system, so that there was no longer any need for a temple building and a system of repeated sacrifices – that is what his actions in the temple represent.

† Thank you, Lord, that through the one final sacrifice of your Son we can always come to you.

For further thought

In what way do the life and death of Jesus make temple sacrifices unnecessary?

Let God grow in you

Read John 3:27–36

'He must increase, but I must decrease.'

(verse 30)

Living in the wasteland on the edge of towns, dressed in animal skins, living on honey and locusts, and doing some hellfire preaching – John the Baptist always seems a bit weird to our modern understanding. But he wouldn't have seemed weird to the people of his own day. John was very much in the tradition of the older Jewish prophets. He was fulfilling the role foreseen by Isaiah, preparing the way for the Lord.

But John knew clearly that he was just the messenger, the herald proclaiming the coming of the king. According to John's Gospel (1:31) he had no idea who was coming after him; it must have been a surprise, perhaps even a shock, to discover that the one he was proclaiming was his cousin Jesus from Nazareth, the stay-at-home carpenter. Yet John immediately starts to give way to Jesus, allowing his own disciples to follow him. As Jesus begins his ministry and takes centre stage, John accepts that his role will soon be over – and he can rejoice that he has done what God sent him to do (verse 29).

We share John's work of preparing people to follow Jesus. But once the other person meets Jesus, we need to step back, to decrease in order that God can take over and increase. While remaining available to help and encourage, we need to leave God to do his work and lead the other person in a way that may be very different from ours. We are the messengers; the baby in the manger is the message, the Word of God.

† Help us to prepare the way for people to meet you, Lord, but then to have the grace to leave them with you.

For further thought

In what ways do you need to decrease so that God can increase in your life?

Friday 25 December (Christmas Day)
The light has come into the world

Read John 3:16–21

'Indeed, God did not send the Son into the world to condemn the world, but in order that the world might be saved through him.'

(verse 17)

The writer of Genesis 6:13 ('God said to Noah, "I have determined to make an end of all flesh …"') portrays God as losing patience with humankind. Men (and women) have just become too disobedient and violent; everything about them is corrupt, so God washes his hands of them and sends a flood to get rid of them all (except righteous Noah and his family, of course). The reality is that God tries endlessly to help his people behave properly. But overall they just don't get the message. So he comes himself in the person of his Son.

But God does not come as the wrathful judge of Genesis. Jesus shows us, by his life, death and resurrection, what God is really like: the relationship he wants with human beings; the lengths to which he will go to help people achieve this. Jesus does not spend all his time pouring out judgements on people, condemning their sin and failure. Jesus is simply there. He is light, shining in a world that has gone dark. His light makes us look at ourselves, to judge ourselves, to turn away from the darkness and discover the joy of living in the light of God's presence.

Christmas Day offers us the opportunity to again let the light into our lives, to accept the pain of seeing ourselves clearly, but also to rediscover the self we are meant to be, living in the light that Jesus brings to us simply by being himself: the Son of the God who comes to save us, not to wash his hands of us.

† O holy child of Bethlehem, Jesus the Son of God, be born in us today, so that we may always walk in your light.

For further thought
What does living in the light mean for you?

Saturday 26 December
Passed from death to life

Read John 5:19–27

'Very truly, I tell you, anyone who hears my word and believes him who sent me has eternal life, and does not come under judgement, but has passed from death to life.'

(verse 24)

Several years ago I read Bill Bryson's book, *A Short History of Nearly Everything*. I found it fascinating, especially the part about the stars, the sky and the weather. But throughout the book there was a hole. A God-shaped hole. Bryson repeatedly said how incredible the universe was, but he couldn't say how it started. If there was a Big Bang, who created the elements that went bang? Going back as far as science can at the moment, Bryson met a blank. If we believe in the one who sent Jesus into the world, we meet God, even though how God created the world still remains a great mystery.

It is God who makes sense of our existence. It is God who knows the person he has created, however much it gets distorted by sin. It is God who is there to help us to overcome everything that prevents us becoming the person we were created to be. To help us become fully human. Jesus shows us what it is like to be a human being according to God's pattern. We can become loving as he was loving. We can share the world's suffering as he shared it. We can have eternal life as Jesus has it. We just have to trust him, trust God, to be speaking the truth, and as Jesus said elsewhere in John's Gospel, 'you will know the truth, and the truth will make you free' (8:32).

† Jesus, I believe that in you is life and the life is the light of all people. Thank you that I can share that life.

For further thought

What does passing from death to life mean for you?

The Word became flesh: Christmas with John – 2 God's greatest gift

Notes by **Kate Hughes**

 For Kate's biography, see p. 358. Kate has used the NRSVA for these notes.

Sunday 27 December
Knowing

Read John 10:11–18

'I am the good shepherd. I know my own and my own know me.'

(verse 14)

The picture of the leaders of Israel as shepherds is a common one in the Old Testament. God is also seen as the shepherd of his people Israel. The word 'shepherd' conveys an image of care, nurture, commitment. But, as the Old Testament prophets frequently point out, Israel is plagued by bad leaders, negligent shepherds who ignore and mislead their flock.

But Jesus is a good shepherd, the very best kind of shepherd. He cares for his sheep, he notices when one goes astray and looks for it, he is ready to die in defence of his flock. Above all, he *knows* his sheep. He knows how each of them looks, he knows their characters and odd behaviour, he knows which one is likely to stray, he knows where the best grass can be found, he knows when there is likely to be danger from a wolf.

And his sheep know him as well. They know that he is a good shepherd, that he will care for them and defend them from danger, they know that he will lead them in the right way to safe pasture with good grass. This is a wonderful picture of what our relationship with Jesus can be. We all belong to his flock unless we deliberately walk away, but many people don't know this or know God. And if we know the shepherd, we can trust him to care for us, to be involved in our life, to lead us in the right way. What a gift!

† The Lord is my shepherd, I shall not want, and surely goodness and mercy shall follow me all the days of my life.

Monday 28 December
Saving not judging

Read John 12:44–50
'I came not to judge the world, but to save the world.'

(verse 47b)

When I lived in Johannesburg in the 1980s, my walk to work at a Theological Education by Extension college took me past the Fort Prison. This prison for people on remand, not yet tried or sentenced, was notorious for the mistreatment of prisoners. The staff seemed to be very careless about where they left wet bars of soap, so that a surprising number of prisoners slipped on them at the top of stone staircases and fell to their death. Some members of staff at the Fort were simply wicked, and many people judged them. But as I walked past, I asked God to bless them.

If this seems strange, blessing other people isn't simply a cosy way of making them feel better and having nice things happen to them. Asking God to bless someone is more like aiming one of those swords that you see in science fiction films – swords that send out a beam of light that penetrates the other person. To bless someone is to direct a beam at them through which God's light and power can pass into them. Instead of judging others, which is only too easy, blessing them can help God to work his work of salvation, to save even the wicked from their wrongdoing. God blessing people can change them, change their situations for good. Use the positive power of blessing on those who particularly seem to need it, work with God to save the world and don't waste energy on judging people.

† O God, may the power of your blessing change and save us all.

For further thought
Think of someone who needs God's blessing. Ask God to bless them, and hold them in your prayer as God brings his light to them.

Tuesday 29 December
Way, truth, life

Read John 14:1–7

Jesus said to him, 'I am the way, and the truth, and the life. No one comes to the Father except through me. If you know me, you will know my Father also.'

(verses 6–7a)

As we get to know Jesus, we realise that we are on a journey. Jesus shows us the way to grow into a right relationship with God, yet he doesn't just show us the right road; he is himself the road. It is by taking Jesus into ourselves that we learn to think with his mind, act as he acted, love as he loved. Jesus shows us the truth about God; he is God's truth in human form. And he enables us to truly live: he 'came that they may have life, and have it abundantly' (John 10:10).

Jesus shows us the Father: 'Whoever has seen me has seen the Father' (John 14:9). When we read about Jesus healing, teaching, loving, forgiving, judging, suffering and defeating death and sin, and believe that he lives the truth, we can know that that is how the Father also acts. Jesus shows us the Father, and only through him can we truly discover how much the Father loves us. This is the USP, the Unique Selling Point, of Christianity. Through Jesus we are enabled to know God not as a demanding God to be kept on our side with sacrifices – though he will make demands on us. Through Jesus we get to know God not as a distant deity who set the world going and then withdrew to leave human beings to make a mess of it. Through Jesus we can know that the God we follow and worship is a perfect Father who loves each one of us totally.

† 'Love so amazing, so divine, demands my soul, my life, my all.' Amen

For further thought

What does it mean to have God as our perfect loving Father?

Conquerors of the world

> **Read 1 John 5:1–5**
>
> *Who is it that conquers the world but the one who believes that Jesus is the Son of God?*
>
> (verse 5)

The world can be a very frightening place. Terrible things happen to people. They are haunted by what they have seen and experienced. In human terms they can seem to lose everything: home, livelihood, family, country. Or they have to endure ill-health that robs them of all normal life. And all of us encounter the simpler forms of human wickedness and are called upon to respond with love, courage and obedience.

We have already thought over the past few days about God being with us as light in the darkness. But he isn't there just to help us through. With God's help we can be not only survivors but conquerors. How do we know this? Because Jesus, the love of God in human form, confronted everything that human beings could do to him and yet never stopped loving them and forgiving them. He conquered by never swerving in his love and obedience to his Father, in offering back to the Father the task that he had been sent to do: to break sin's power over human beings. To transform death itself.

We can conquer all that the world and human wickedness can inflict on us because Jesus shows us, to paraphrase Romans 8:39, that there is nothing in all creation that will ever be able to separate us from the love of God that he showed. If we have faith that what God did in Jesus he can also do in us through his Spirit, then nothing will be able to shake our love and obedience.

† God, thank you that with your help I can not only face the wickedness I meet in the world and in myself, but conquer it by faith in you.

For further thought

What will it mean in your own life to conquer the world with love and obedience?

Thursday 31 December
Walking in the light

Read John 8:12

'I am the light of the world. Whoever follows me will never walk in darkness but will have the light of life.'

(verse 12b)

When I sit down for a meal, I light a candle (any excuse – I love candles!) and say a short prayer asking God to lighten our darkness and save us from all the perils and dangers that can happen to us when we are in the night of temptation, failure, suffering, mental illness, wickedness. Darkness affects us all and it can be a time of danger. A time of temptation to doubt God, to lose faith, to give up the struggle or to get stuck in our wickedness.

The original of my prayer comes from the office of Compline (available on www.churchofengland.org), the last service said by monks and nuns before they go to bed. I have altered 'dangers of *this* night', the night about to come, to 'the dangers of *the* night' to make my prayer wider. If we can follow Christ, we are walking in the light; the night may seem very dark and overwhelming, but we are in fact moving through it or learning to rest quietly within it, knowing that Christ the light of the world is there with us.

Whatever your darkness may be, whatever the darkness of those we pray for, step into the new year holding on to God, to Jesus the light of the world, and you will have the light of life. My other 'candle prayer' is a thanksgiving: 'Thank you, Lord, that the light shines in all our darkness, and the darkness can never overcome it.'

† Lighten our darkness, Lord, we pray, and in your great mercy defend us from all perils and dangers of [the] night.

For further thought

Who especially needs light in their darkness and protection in the night? A friend with depression, the leaders in a civil war, someone struggling with doubt?

The Word became flesh: Christmas with John – 2 God's greatest gift

December

IBRA International Fund: would you help us?

Will you work with us and help us to enable Christians from different parts of the world to grow in knowledge and appreciation of the Word of God by making a donation of £5, £10, £25 or even £50? 100% of your donation will be used to support people overseas.

How your donations make a difference:

£5.00 buys 2 copies of *Fresh From the Word* in Ghana
£10.00 prints 11 copies for India
£25.00 sends 10 books and 100 daily readings lists to Cameroon
£50.00 could fund the sending of 1,000 IBRA reading lists to a country that does not currently receive IBRA materials Our partners are based in ten countries, but the benefit flows over borders to at least thirty-two countries all over the world.

Partners work tirelessly to organise the translation, printing and distribution of IBRA Bible study notes and lists into many different languages, from Ewe, Yoruba and Twi to Portuguese, Samoan and Telugu!

Did you know that we print and sell 7,000 copies of *Fresh From the Word* here in the UK, but our overseas partners produce another 45,000 copies in English and local languages? With the reading list also being translated and distributed, IBRA is reaching 657,632 Christians around the world.

Faithfully following the same principles developed in 1882, we still guarantee that 100% of your donations to the International Fund go to support our international brothers and sisters in Christ.

If you would like to make a donation, please use the envelope inserted in this book to send a cheque to **International Bible Reading Association**, *5–6 Imperial Court, 12 Sovereign Road, Birmingham, B30 3FH* or go online to **shop.christianeducation. org.uk** and click the '**Donate**' button at the top of the page.

Global community

Our overseas distribution and international partners enable IBRA readings to be enjoyed all over the world from Spain to Samoa, New Zealand to Cameroon. Each day when you read your copy of *Fresh From the Word* you are joining a global community of people who are also reading the same passages. Here is how our readings impact people across the globe:

Ghana

Gladys reads *Fresh From the Word* with her devotional group in Ghana every Monday, Wednesday and Friday. She says that the book has been a source of motivation and encouragement for their members, and shared the following about her own experience:

66 *Personally, this book has been my source of inspiration during the darkest time of my life. I can emphatically say that it is by the grace of God and the continuous encouragement I get from reading the book that has kept me alive till today.* 99

India

The Fellowship of Professional Workers in India value the global community of IBRA readers:

66 *The uniqueness of the Bible reading is that the entire readership is focusing on a common theme for each day which is an expression of oneness of the faithful, irrespective of countries and cultures.* 99

Cameroon

Reverend Doctor Peter Evande of the Redemptive Baptist Church in Cameroon has distributed IBRA daily readings for ten years, and says:

66 *The use of writers from different cultural backgrounds makes IBRA notes richer than others. That aspect also attracts people from different backgrounds to love them. The structure and seasons of the Christian year help many people.* 99

United Kingdom

Sue, from the UK, has read IBRA notes for twenty-two years:

66 *I have had many days where it feels as though the notes have been written just for me. I like the short reading for each day as this can easily fit into a daily routine and be kept up with. I also really like reading the views of the writers from overseas for an international view.* 99

Where people are following IBRA daily readings

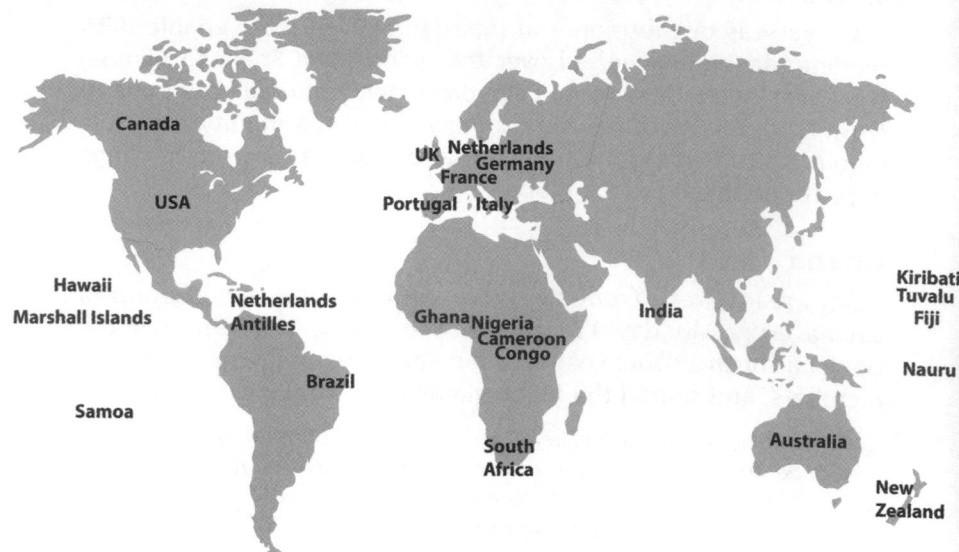

We love to hear our readers' favourite places to read and reflect on our daily readings. Get in touch and tell us where YOU'RE reading – perhaps you too have a favourite, or an unusual or exciting place to enjoy your Bible reading. Email ibra@christianeducation.org.uk

66 *My favourite place is my home in Nottingham, but over the past 25+ years, the IBRA daily notes have travelled with me to Nevis in the Caribbean, Australia, Malawi and India as well as many locations in the UK!* 99

66 *Luxembourg – sat with a coffee outside my caravan.* 99

66 *When I wake up – in bed with a cup of tea!* 99

66 *A small hut in Tonga – the very first thing in the morning.* 99

66 *In my sitting room by the side of my wife (so I can share).* 99

To find out more visit: www.ibraglobal.org

International Bible Reading Association partners and distributors

A worldwide service of Christian Education at work in five continents

HEADQUARTERS
IBRA
5–6 Imperial Court
12 Sovereign Road
Birmingham
B30 3FH
United Kingdom
www.ibraglobal.org
ibra@christianeducation.org.uk

SAMOA
Congregational Christian Church in Samoa
CCCS
PO Box 468
Tamaligi
Apia
isalevao@cccs.org.ws / lina@cccs.org.ws

Congregational Christian Church in Tokelau
c/o EFKT
Atafu
Tokelau Island
hepuutu@gmail.com

Congregational Christian Church in American Samoa
P.O. BOX 1537
1 Kanana Fou Street
Pago Pago, AS 96799
cccas@efkas.org

FIJI
Methodist Bookstore
11 Stewart Street
PO Box 354
Suva
mbookstorefiji@yahoo.com

GHANA
Asempa Publishers
Christian Council of Ghana
PO Box GP 919
Accra
gm@asempapublishers.com

NIGERIA
IBRA Nigeria
David Hinderer House
Cathedral Church of St David
Kudeti
PMB 5298 Dugbe
Ibadan
Oyo State

SOUTH AFRICA
Faith for Daily Living Foundation
PO Box 3737
Durban 4000
ffdl@saol.com

IBRA South Africa
The Rectory
Christchurch
c/o Constantia Main and Parish Roads
Constantia 7806
Western Cape
South Africa
Terry@cchconst.org.za

DEMOCRATIC REPUBLIC OF THE CONGO
Baptist Community of the Congo River
8 Avenue Kalemie
Kinshasa Gombe
B.P. 205 & 397
Kinshasa 1
ecc_cbfc@yahoo.fr

CAMEROON
Redemptive Baptist Church
PO Box 65
Limbe
Fako Division
South West Region
evande777@yahoo.com

INDIA
All India Sunday School Association
NCCI Campus
Civil Lines
Nagpur
440001
Maharashtra
sundayschoolindia@yahoo.co.in

Fellowship of Professional Workers
Samanvay
Deepthi Chambers, Opp. Nin.
Tarnaka
Vijayapuri
Hyderabad 500 017
Telangana
fellowship2w@gmail.com

REPUBLIC OF KIRIBATI
Levett Print of the Kiribati Uniting Church
PO Box 8
Bairiki, Antebuka
Tarawa
Republic of Kiribati

IBRA scheme of readings 2021

Join us again next year when we shall be exploring the following themes:

Against the grain: looking again at familiar stories

Epiphany: a light to the nations
The mystery revealed

Gospel of Matthew

Dealing with disappointment

Song of Solomon

1 and 2 Peter

The responsibilities we share
Fresh start
Living planet
Building a community
Life in community

The Passion with Matthew
Stories and questions
The holy city

Easter: with the rising of the sun
Break of day
Rising early

1 and 2 Thessalonians

On the road
First steps
Walking with Jesus
The journey of faith

Fire in the Bible
God and fire
The power of fire

20:20 vision

Readings in Numbers

Running the race: the Bible at the Olympics
Renewed in Spirit
The nations as one

The Bible at the beach
Resting
At the beach

Romans 9–16

Fake news and the good news

The heavens declare

The Bible on the world stage

Jeremiah

Trumpet calls and whispers: encountering the Holy in Advent
Trumpet calls
Whispers
Encountering the holy

The Word became flesh: Christmas with John
In the beginning was the Word
God's greatest gift

Fresh From the Word 2021
Order and donation form

International Bible Reading Association

	Quantity	Price	Total
AA180101 *Fresh From the Word 2021*		£9.99	
10% discount if ordering 3 or more copies			
UK P&P			
Up to 2 copies		£3.95	
3–8 copies		£5.95	
9–11 copies		£8.95	
12 or more copies		Free	
Western Europe P&P			
1–3 copies		£7.95 per copy	
If ordering 3 or more copies please contact us for revised postage			
Rest of the world P&P			
1–3 copies		£8.95 per copy	
If ordering 3 or more copies please contact us for revised postage			
Donation Yes, I would like to make a donation to IBRA's International Fund to help support our global community of readers.			

£5.00 ☐   £10.00 ☐   £25.00 ☐   £50.00 ☐   Other ☐

TOTAL FOR BOOKS, P&P AND DONATION

Title: _____   First name: _____   Last name: _____

Address: _____

_____

Postcode: _____   Tel.: _____ _____

Email: _____

Your order will be dispatched when all books are available. Payments in pounds sterling, please. We do not accept American Express or Maestro International. HOW WE USE INFORMATION ABOUT YOU AND RECIPIENTS OF YOUR INFORMATION: We will use your information in performance of your contract with us and the provision of our services to you including our legitimate interests. For further details please view our full privacy policy and your rights at www.ibraglobal.org/privacy

CARDHOLDER NAME: _____

CARD NUMBER: ☐☐☐☐ ☐☐☐☐ ☐☐☐☐ ☐☐☐☐

START DATE: ☐☐ ☐☐   **EXPIRY DATE:** ☐☐ ☐☐

SECURITY NUMBER (LAST THREE DIGITS ON BACK): ☐☐☐

SIGNATURE: _____

Please fill in your details on the reverse

Ebook and Kindle versions are available from Amazon and other online retailers.

Gift Aid declaration *giftaid it*

If you wish to Gift Aid your donation please tick the box below.

I am a UK taxpayer and would like IBRA to reclaim the Gift Aid on my donation, increasing my donation by 25p for every £1 I give.

☐ I want IBRA to claim tax back on this gift and any future gifts until I notify you otherwise. I am a UK taxpayer and understand that if I pay less Income Tax and/or Capital Gains Tax than the amount of Gift Aid claimed on all my donations in that tax year it is my responsibility to pay any difference.

Signature: _____ Date: _____

Thank you so much for your generous donation; it will make a real difference and change lives around the world.

Please fill in your address and payment details on the reverse of this page and send back to IBRA.

☐ **I have made a donation**

☐ **I have Gift Aided my donation**

☐ **I would like to know more about leaving a legacy to IBRA**

☐ **I would like to become an IBRA rep**

☐ **I enclose a cheque (made payable to IBRA)**

☐ **Please charge my MASTERCARD/VISA**

Card details will be destroyed after payment has been taken.

Please return this form to:

**IBRA
5–6 Imperial Court
12 Sovereign Road
Birmingham
B30 3FH**

You can also order through your local IBRA rep or from:

• website: shop.christianeducation.org.uk
• email: ibra.sales@christianeducation.org.uk
• call: 0121 458 3313

IBRA
International Bible Reading Association

Registered Charity number: 1086990